A Memoir

OF THE

REV. JOHN KEBLE, M.A.

LATE VICAR OF HURSLEY.

VOLUMES

I & II

AMS PRESS
NEW YORK

𝔄 𝔐𝔢𝔪𝔬𝔦𝔯

OF THE

REV. JOHN KEBLE, M.A.

LATE VICAR OF HURSLEY.

BY THE RIGHT HON.

SIR J. T. COLERIDGE, D.C.L.

"Te mihi junxerunt nivei sine crimine mores,
 Simplicitasque sagax, ingenuusque pudor ;
Et bene nota fides, et candor frontis honestæ,
 Et studia a studiis non aliena meis."
Joannes Secundus.

VOL. I.

𝔖𝔢𝔠𝔬𝔫𝔡 𝔈𝔡𝔦𝔱𝔦𝔬𝔫,
With Corrections and Additions.

OXFORD and LONDON:

JAMES PARKER AND CO.

1869.

Library of Congress Cataloging in Publication Data

Coleridge, John Taylor, Sir, 1790-1876.
    A memoir of the Rev. John Keble, M.A., late
Vicar of Hursley.

    Reprint of the 2nd ed. published in 1869 by
J. Parker, Oxford.
    1. Keble, John, 1792-1866. 2. Church of England—
Clergy—Biography. 3. Clergy—England—Biography.
I. Title.
BX5199.K3C7   1977   821'.7 [B]   75-30019
ISBN 0-404-14024-6

Reprinted from an original in the collections
of the University of Chicago Library

From the edition of 1869, Oxford and London
First AMS edition published in 1977
Manufactured in the United States of America

AMS PRESS INC.
NEW YORK, N.Y.

TO

SIR WILLIAM HEATHCOTE, BART.

————◆————

MY DEAR HEATHCOTE,

IN placing your name at the head of this Memoir, I fulfil a plain and pleasant duty. I dedicate it to a favourite pupil of JOHN KEBLE; who became his fast friend; and was his only patron.

I wish I could feel secure that the Memoir does no injustice to his memory. Such as it is I present it to you, as flowing at least from a grateful heart. To him I owe more than I can well express; and among the greater of those many obligations I count it not the least, that for so many years I have been able to call myself your affectionate and faithful friend,

J. T. COLERIDGE.

HEATH'S COURT,
Dec. 26, 1868.

PREFACE

TO THE SECOND EDITION.

———◆———

SOON after the death of John Keble, a letter was written to his nearest and dearest surviving relative, by one who knew him as well as he loved him. I venture to print the following extract :—

"I suppose that no man has died in England within our memory who has been so dearly loved, and whose memory will be had in such tender reverence by so many good men. It will be long before many will cease to say to themselves when in doubt, 'What would Keble say to this?' or to remind themselves of his ways and sayings; and of Hursley as it was in his time; and of all that made his judgment a law, and his companionship delightful. However, I think it is not the companionship that comes most into the mind just now. What I think remarkable, was not how many people loved him, or how much they loved him, but that everybody seemed to love him with the very best kind of love of which they were capable.

"It was like loving goodness itself; you felt that what was good in him was applying itself directly and bringing into life all that was best in you. His ready, lively, transparent affection seemed as if it was the very spirit of love, opening out upon you, and calling for a return, such as you could give. At the same time its unsuspectingness was almost alarming. *You* were probably too near to him to know that singular mixture of triumph and shame which, I think, he caused to many of his friends, by the unreserved

affection which he poured out upon them, on the faith of
their possessing all the singleness and purity of heart which
he felt in himself.   But it was, I think, very common ; and
I believe that numbers of persons were continually urged
forwards by a kind of shame at feeling themselves so
much behind what he appeared to think of them.

"His influence for some time has been so silent, that
one hardly knows what his loss may be to the Church.
But it is impossible not to fear that many people will be
liable to do wild or angry things, when they are relieved
from that silent control which was exercised by the general
reverence which all men felt for him.   However, that is
in Higher Hands."

There is not a syllable of exaggeration in this
beautiful extract ; and it is owing to the general
feeling, so well described in it, that I find myself
called on to prepare a second edition of this book
very long before I had any expectation of such a
call being made on me ; and a sense of this has
naturally made me more anxious to correct some
inaccuracies which had crept into the former edition.
This I have endeavoured to do.

But beside inaccuracies as to facts, friends have
suggested in private, and critics through the press
have pointed out, what seem to them omissions, or
faults in the conception of the work as well as in
the execution.   In some respects it will be found,
I hope, that attention has been paid to such remarks ; and where it has not been, this must not
be attributed to want of respect, or consideration.
This indeed would have been unpardonable in me ;

for so far as I know, I have been treated even by
the most decided of my critics with a respect and
kindness which I wish I deserved, and for which
I feel sincerely grateful.   Sometimes, however, I
have not agreed with my advisers, sometimes I have
found myself unable to do what they desired.   There
are faults I suppose in every work, which are so
interwoven with the main web that they cannot be
removed without unravelling the whole piece.   I am
too old to recast the work ; and I desire it should
be borne in mind, that from the beginning I expressly limited myself to a certain part, and did not
undertake the whole of Keble's history.

I must now mention some new matter, which will
be found in this edition.   Since the issue of the
former, two parcels of letters have been found, the
one to Hurrell Froude, the other to his father,
the Archdeacon ; they were found singularly enough
with a small quantity of plate, and some personal
jewels of little value, in a house formerly the property of the latter, and for many years occupied by
his sister, which is now the property of Mr. William
Froude.   He was good enough to place them unreservedly in my hands ; and I have published a
few, which will be found in their proper places.   All
are written in the same spirit, and with the same
ability, which are characteristic of the letters I had
before printed ; and should it be thought right to
publish an independent selection of his letters, many
of them I hope will be found in it.

A more important addition will be found in the Appendix, which I have annexed to this volume. This mainly consists of papers from which I made extracts in my concluding chapter. I have thought it better now on many accounts to print them at length ; by so doing I am aware some repetition will appear, and it will be seen, I fear, not only that I was too sparing, but also that I was injudicious in my selection. By printing them as I now do, I shall give a more adequate view of the inward and domestic life of Keble, the want of which has justly been complained of ; and I can more conveniently place the purchasers of the first edition on a footing with those who may possess themselves of the second, as copies of this appendix will be printed separately for their convenience.

J. T. C.

HEATH'S COURT,
    April 24, 1869.

PREFACE

TO THE FIRST EDITION.

———◆———

SO much time has elapsed since it was understood that I had commenced the work which I now publish, and in itself it might seem to have required so little, that a few words of explanation may be proper; and but a few will be all that I can offer. When I undertook my task, some of my best friends doubted whether I had still strength of body or mind sufficient for it. Beginning it with perhaps too much eagerness and anxiety, it was not long before I was stopped by an illness, some effects of which have never wholly left me—one of them has been the inability, sometimes, to work at all—and always to do so for more than a short period of time from day to day.

This will be accepted, I hope, as an excuse for delay; what effects the same circumstance may have had on the book itself, it is useless for me to consider; no explanation will cure its faults, or supply its short-comings: though I hope it may help to acquit me of inconsiderateness in undertaking, and of carelessness in executing it.

I expressed very early, and I believe more than once, what I now desire very earnestly to repeat, my fear that in printing many of John Keble's letters to myself I might lie open to the imputation of bringing my own name too forward. I find now that in the beginning I had hardly realised the extent to which this would go; and yet, as I advanced, I knew not how to avoid it. I could not think it right to alter his expressions, perfectly sincere as I knew them to be, though certainly exaggerated. The truth is, he was so humble, and at the same time so loving to his friends, that it seemed as if in his mind all the weakness and imperfection were in himself, all the strength and goodness in them. His letters must be read with this thought in the mind of the reader.

It may be said that I might not only to some extent have escaped this difficulty, but added much to the interest of my Memoir, if I had made more use of his letters to other friends and less of those to myself. There is much truth in this remark, and I have done what I could to comply with it. But it is not every possessor of his letters to whom I could properly apply. Many of them were written to persons on their own troubles and difficulties, and such, though very interesting, the holders would be little likely to give me for publication, and certainly I could not ask them.

To some extent I trust this may be taken for an answer, without more specification ; but I must say a particular word as to one, perhaps his dearest and most honoured friend, who will be in every one's mind—Dr. Pusey.   I suppose he possesses large numbers of important and interesting letters.   He has always been so kind to me, that I should be ungrateful if I doubted his readiness to help me— indeed to volunteer his help, wherever he felt he could do so properly.   Yet it is obvious that from the very intimacy which subsisted between them, combined with the extreme delicacy of the subjects to which their correspondence must have principally related, his letters might be just such as he would think it improper as yet to make public.   I have therefore never applied to him ; and for reasons not exactly the same, but of the same kind, I have pursued the same course with Dr. Newman.

The work no doubt suffers in consequence.

Keble's Letters to Hurrell Froude would have been specially interesting ; writing to this pupil first and friend after, whom yet he always loved as a *younger* brother, he would have been presented in a new light.   Mr. W. Froude, Hurrell's representative, was ready to communicate the letters if they could be found, but the search for them has been unsuccessful.

The help which I have received has come from so
many persons, that I am compelled to ask the far
larger number to accept a general, but most hearty
expression of my gratitude. What has been done
for me by some has been acknowledged, or will
appear, in the work itself ; such for example as
Mr. Wilson. Beside much specific information, he
placed in my hands a great many letters of which
I have made free use.

But it would be wrong if I did not specify by
name three ladies, who may yet I fear think it an ill-
return for their kindness—Miss Baker, Miss Maria
Trench, and Mrs. Cooke Trench—to whom I must
add the Author of the " Daily Readings." I was
very desirous of giving an authentic account of
Keble in his office of Pastor of Hursley ; and if I
have succeeded in doing so, it is to be attributed *entirely* to the communications they were good enough
to make to me. I cannot thank them too warmly.

In such a work as Keble's Life it was impossible,
at least I have found it so, not to touch on many
matters once the subject of hot controversy. When
I began, I hoped I had laid down for myself a rule
by which I might escape the responsibilities of a
Church Historian. Perhaps I ought to have foreseen how impossible it would become in the progress
of the work strictly to observe that rule. I am

sensible that sometimes I have not; and in consequence I may possibly have given pain or offence
to excellent persons who now survive. I beg such
to believe that I regret this very much. I do not
know that I have anywhere questioned the motives
of those from whose judgments I have been compelled to differ; and if I impute error to others,
I am not so unwise as to suppose that I may not
have fallen into it myself.

J. T. C.

HEATH'S COURT,
    Dec. 24, 1868.

I OUGHT not to part from this work without one
word upon another and far greater, now in progress
at Oxford, designed in part for the same purpose;
I speak of Keble College. It is indeed a great conception and an almost unprecedented memorial; but
it is more than a mere memorial, (if it were not,
Keble would have shrunk from it,) it is an institution
dedicated to the academical education of numbers,
who without it may be unable to obtain that in-
estimable advantage. What is now being attempted
at Oxford in another way testifies to the need, and
I wish it every success; but I still venture to think

that the Collegiate system is essential to the completeness of an Oxford training.

Our undertaking, however, requires very much larger help than it has hitherto received, and I cannot but earnestly press this consideration on all who feel grateful to Keble, and would be glad to honour his memory; and also on all who desire to extend Oxford education not in a sectarian or illiberal, but truly Christian spirit, to a large class much desiring, much needing, and, without this help, quite unable to compass it.

CONTENTS.—VOL. I.

CHAPTER I.

PAGE

Introduction.—Birth.—Boyhood 1

CHAPTER II.

Undergraduateship.—Corpus Christi, 1806—1811 . . . 9

CHAPTER III.

John Miller.—George James Cornish.—Charles Dyson . . 22

CHAPTER IV.

Final Examination.—Election at Oriel.—University Prizes.—
Sidmouth.—Ordinations.—First Curacy 47

CHAPTER V.

Tutorship and Second Residence at Oriel.—Death of Mrs. Keble.
—1818—1823 70

CHAPTER VI.

Return to Fairford, 1823.—Southrop.—Pupils.—Hurrell Froude.—
"Christian Year" 108

CHAPTER VII.

Hursley Curacy.—Death of Mary Ann Keble.—Return to Fairford.—1825, 1826 130

CHAPTER VIII.

PAGE

Return to Fairford.—Publication of "Christian Year."—1826, 1827 146

CHAPTER IX.

Provostship of Oriel.—Edition of Hooker's Works.—India-House Examinations 175

CHAPTER X.

Paignton.—Poetry Professorship, and Lectures.—Assize Sermon, 1833.—The Tracts.—Death of Mr. Keble.—1835 . . . 205

CHAPTER XI.

Coln St. Aldwyn.—Engagement with Miss Clarke.—Acceptance of Hursley Vicarage.—Marriage, and Settlement at Hursley.—Visitation Sermon.—Hurrell Froude's "Remains."—A. Knox.—Version of Psalms.—Creweian Oration and Wordsworth.—1839 233

CHAPTER XII.

1840.—Library of the Fathers.—Charles Marriott.—Dr. Arnold.—Tract 90, and Subsequent Proceedings 260

MEMOIR

REV. JOHN KEBLE.

CHAPTER I.

INTRODUCTION.—BIRTH.—BOYHOOD.

IT is not without sincere misgivings that I commence this memoir. My sense of the difficulty
of writing it properly, as well as of the importance
that it should be written, if at all, fully, delicately,
faithfully, lovingly, has become more strong the
more I have had occasion to consider it with reference to myself. I will not affect to deny, that if
the duty had been cast on me some years earlier,
there were personal circumstances which, at least
in part, might have seemed to recommend me for
the performance of it—the most affectionate intimacy, and the closest communion of feelings and
opinions, the possession of an unbroken correspondence from the year 1811, and the kind confidence
with which the representatives of deceased friends
were ready to confide to me a large number of his
letters ; these were among those circumstances. But

I feel now that my great age, and impaired strength
of mind, as well as body, are more than equivalent
disadvantages ; indeed, a serious illness since I began to prepare for my work has added much weight
to this consideration.   Nor can I forget that the
very advantages I speak of have a tendency to mis-
lead me in the composition, and to disturb the proportions of my work, to make me dwell too much
at length on parts exceedingly interesting to myself, but which may seem of less importance to
those, a great proportion probably of my readers,
who may be specially desirous to know of the part
which John Keble took in the different measures
and movements of our times in Church matters,
and who will find themselves disappointed.   For
when I consented to the request made to me, I felt
that I was not in any way competent to write the
history of our Church for the last forty years, which
yet seemed a necessary part of any complete account of his work on earth.   In these very important
matters my narrative will be deficient, and many of
my readers will be disappointed.

Under all these circumstances, I cannot complain
if I am asked why I have undertaken to write at
all.   In answer, I will not dwell on reasons of minor
and in themselves perhaps insufficient importance.
The truth is, that I was requested by one to whom
at the time it was almost impossible for me to refuse any such thing ; and the performance of my

promise, in so far as I am able, appears to me now in the light of a sacred duty.

My readers, however, will gather from what I have said, that my work will not assume to be a complete biography; indeed, independently of the reasons which apply to myself personally, it seems to me that the time has hardly yet arrived when this could be done, at once so freely and so dispassionately as it ought to be, if done at all. Some one will be found, I have a good hope, in due time to accomplish this more important task; to whom what I am about to do may be of some service. The George Herbert of our days ought not in the end to be left without his own Isaac Walton.

I must still farther, however, and perhaps in justice to myself, warn my readers that they are about to enter on a most uneventful story; few persons have lived so long, and achieved so great a name, about whom there is so little of change or incident to record. His life was passed in his father's house, in his college rooms, in his curacies, or in his vicarage, in occasional Long-Vacation rambles, in visits to the sea-side for the alleviation of sickness. He earnestly avoided publicity; happily for himself ·perhaps, neither the Crown nor the Church thought him a fit subject for promotion, which I need not say he never solicited, and I believe would have declined. Those who desire to read an exciting story will do well to close this book at once; but there are still

some, I believe, who either out of personal regard
or grateful veneration may desire to know intimately his character, the manner of his passage
through life, and the performance of his duties ;
how he lived, and how he died. As well as I can,
I will try truly and simply to gratify the wishes of
such readers. My object will be to present a full
and faithful picture of his character ; faithful, I hope,
though drawn unquestionably in a reverent spirit,
and with a loving hand.

I will not detain my readers by any further preface, nor will I consume time by any account of
John Keble's family pedigree ; it was a matter in
which he took little interest. He never, that I remember, mentioned to me the name of any one of
his ancestors, except that of Joseph Keble, of whose
strange taste (as it seemed to him) he spoke slight-
ingly, in employing himself as a Law-reporter ; he
did not know at the time the importance of the
office, nor how much ability, industry, and learning,
a successful discharge of it implied. Joseph Keble
was a Reporter of the decisions of what is now styled
the Court of Queen's Bench from 1660 to 1678 ; he
did not, however, possess the qualifications of a good
one, and his volumes are of little authority. I never
heard Keble speak of Joseph's father, Richard, a lawyer of greater eminence. Mr. Foss, in his careful and

useful book, "The History of the Judges," records
of him, that the Parliament made him a Welch
Judge in 1647, a Serjeant in 1648, and one of the
Commissioners of the Great Seal after the King's
execution, together with Whitelocke and L'Isle. I
do not know the precise reasons, but it is perhaps
presumably not to his dishonour, that he found
favour neither with Cromwell nor Charles II. The
former displaced him in 1654, and the latter, upon
his Restoration, excepted him from the Act of In-
demnity ; perhaps he was one of the Regicide
Judges. Probably Keble knew nothing of these
circumstances, and if he had known them, his
passionate loyalty for the memory of Charles I.
would have prevented his dwelling on them with
much pleasure or interest.

John Keble was born on St. Mark's Day, 1792,
at Fairford in Gloucestershire. I saw it stated by
a correspondent of the "Guardian," that he had
represented himself on one occasion to have been
born in Hampshire, and I dare say he may have
expressed himself so as to be misunderstood in
that sense. Among the many letters, with the use
of which I have been favoured, I have found one
to George Cornish in which, dating from Hursley,
he speaks of a visit he had just paid with his ma-
ternal uncle to Ringwood, "to see his *mother's*
native place." The passage is characteristic, and
I will extract it ; the silence in it as to his own

place of birth would be almost conclusive if there were any real doubt about it :—

"As I hinted before, these are terrible times, and I have just been laying out oceans of money on a new brown jacket for my boy James, not to mention a journey which I took last Monday and Tuesday thro' Lyndhurst and Lymington to Ringwood, in order to see my Mother's native place ; to be sure it was at my Uncle's expense, but no matter for that. I am very glad I went ; altho' I could not have believed all memorials could have vanished in so short a time. Of the Parsonage where she lived, not one stone stands upon another, and there is but one person in the place who recollects her ; however, Uncle shewed me where she used to sit in Church, and that was well worth going for. Ringwood is a much nicer place than I had expected ; the meadows looked so beautifully green now all other grass is brown, and the alders, cattle, boats, and islets, were strewn about in various distances under a hot sun and thunder-cloud, making altogether a very pretty Flemish landscape. And Lyndhurst is the nicest place, in the middle of the Forest. I think Archery meetings there would be very nice things, but not half so nice as a meeting of you and me—which, that it may happen soon, and last long, is the sincere wish of your ever affectionate J. K., Junr."

The interest he thus took in Ringwood, and his own settlement in Hursley, might well make him call himself a Hampshire man, a phrase easily mis-understood, but there is no doubt that he was a Gloucestershire man by birth. He was the second

child and eldest son of the Rev. John Keble and
Sarah Maule, the daughter of the Incumbent of
Ringwood ; three sisters and one brother, now the
only survivor, completed the family circle. A few
words must be said of his father. He was, I should
suppose, a good scholar, and a man of considerable
ability, besides that he was a clergyman of exemplary piety. He alone educated the two brothers
up to their going to Oxford, and he had fitted both
to be not merely successful competitors for Scholarships at Corpus Christi College at unusually early
ages, but to enter on the studies of the University
with credit and advantage. John Keble always spoke
and wrote of him with singular love and veneration.
I think I scarcely ever received a letter dated from
Fairford during his lifetime, in which his health or
employments were not mentioned, or some remark
of his quoted ; and in several rather important incidents in the son's life a word, even a look, from the
father sufficed to determine his decision. It seemed
indeed at all times to be John Keble's main object
to consult his pleasure, and in the decline of his life
to give him help and comfort. He was the Vicar of
Coln St. Aldwin's, about three miles from Fairford ;
he resided at Fairford in a house which was his own
property. He lived to his ninetieth year, taking occasionally a part of the Sunday duty to within a very
few months of his death.

I have not been able to recover any noticeable

anecdotes of John Keble's boyhood. I certainly
heard when we were Undergraduates together, that
his father had never compelled him to study, and
that he was taught only when he liked to learn.
I have not been able on enquiry now to verify this
story, yet it was so much the common understanding with us in College, that I do not doubt it was
substantially true ; and however unwise as a general
rule, it may not have answered ill with such a boy.
Certain it is that his proficiency both in Latin and
Greek, and in Latin composition, at fifteen, would
have done credit to distinguished boys of the same
age at the best public school. One little circumstance I think worth recording before I pass from
his boyhood, because it seems to furnish proof that
even at that period he displayed to an attentive observer the same character for which he was so remarkable through life. One of his Godfathers was
Mr. Stafford Smith, the Rector of Fladbury. Between the two families there seems to have been
a good deal of intimacy, and he saw a good deal
of his godson ; he always designated him by the
title of John the Good.

CHAPTER II.

MR. KEBLE had himself been a Scholar and Fellow of Corpus Christi, and it was natural that he should desire to place his sons at the same college; I dare say, too, that the value of the scholarship, it's certainly leading to a fellowship, and the good preferment which the College offered, were not without their weight in determining his choice. Moreover, he seems to have maintained personal relations with the governing members of the house. Accordingly, he had trained John for the competition, and a vacancy occurring, he went with him to Oxford in December, 1806. I do not know what opponents John Keble had to encounter, except that he had one distinguished Etonian, but he was successful; and on the twelfth of that month was elected Scholar, wanting then more than four months of completing his fifteenth year.

It is a coincidence perhaps worth notice, that Edward Copleston, afterwards Provost of Oriel, and Bishop of Llandaff, was elected at about the same age a Scholar of the same College, having been educated also by his father, a country clergyman, and never sent to any school; like Keble also in this, that he entered Oxford at this early age, a youth

well advanced in scholarship, and in the practice of
easy and accurate composition ; like him, too, in due
time he was a distinguished Prize Man, and one of the
few who stand out among the Poetry Professors of the
University in remarkable and enduring distinction.

In a chapter which I was allowed to contribute
to the deservedly popular "Life of Dr. Arnold" by
the Dean of Westminster, I observed that Arnold's
character was affected not so much by the authorities of the College, as by its constitution and system, and by the residents whom it was his fortune
to associate with there ; and that I should hardly
do justice to my subject, unless I stated a few particulars, and what I was at liberty to mention as to
the latter. This applies with equal truth to Keble,
and I venture, therefore, to transfer to this place
what I then wrote, and the rather because the
Corpus of their day is now a thing of the past, not
remembered by many, and not unworthy of commemoration :—

"Corpus is a very small establishment : twenty Fellows
and twenty Scholars, with four Exhibitioners, form the foundation. No independent members were admitted except
Gentlemen Commoners, and they were limited to six. Of
the Scholars several were Bachelors, and the whole number
of Students actually under College tuition seldom exceeded
twenty. But the Scholarships, though not entirely open,
were yet enough so to admit of much competition : their
value, and still more the commendable strictness and impartiality with which the examinations were conducted,

(qualities at that time more rare in college elections than now,) insured a number of good candidates for each vacancy, and we boasted a more than proportionate share of successful competitors for University honours. It had been generally understood (I know not whether the statutes prescribe the practice) that in the examinations a large allowance was made for youth; certain it was that we had many very young candidates, and that of these many, remarkable for early proficiency, succeeded. We were then a small society, the members rather under the usual age, and with more than the ordinary proportion of ability and scholarship; our mode of tuition was in harmony with these circumstances: not by private lectures, but in classes of such a size as excited emulation, and made us careful in the exact and neat rendering of the original; yet not so numerous as to prevent individual attention on the Tutor's part, and familiar knowledge of each pupil's turn and talents. In addition to the books read in lecture, the Tutor at the beginning of the Term settled with each Student upon some book to be read by himself in private, and prepared for the public examination at the end of Term in Hall; and with this book something on paper, either an analysis of it, or remarks upon it, was expected to be produced, which ensured that the book should really have been read. It has often struck me since that the whole plan, which is now, I believe, in common use in the University, was well devised for the tuition of young men of our age. We were not entirely set free from the leading-strings of the School: accuracy was cared for: we were accustomed to *viva voce* rendering, and *vivâ voce* questions and answers in our lecture-room, before an audience of fellow-students, whom we sufficiently respected; at the same time, the additional reading trusted to ourselves alone,

prepared us for accurate private study, and for our final
exhibition in the Schools.

"One result of all these circumstances was, that we lived
on the most familiar terms with each other: we might be,
indeed we were, somewhat boyish in manner, and in the
liberties which we took with each other; but our interest
in literature, ancient and modern, and in all the stirring
matters of that stirring time was not boyish—we debated
the classic and romantic question, we discussed poetry and
history, logic and philosophy; or we fought over the Penin-
sular battles and the continental campaigns with the energy
of persons interested in them. Our habits were inexpensive and temperate; one break-up party was held in the
Junior Common-room at the end of each Term, in which we
indulged our genius more freely; and our merriment, to say
the truth, was somewhat exuberant and noisy; but the authorities wisely forebore too strict an enquiry into this.

"It was one of the happy peculiarities of Corpus that
the Bachelor Scholars were compelled to residence. This
regulation, seemingly inconvenient, but most wholesome
as I cannot but think for themselves, and now unwisely
relaxed, operated very beneficially on the Undergraduates;
with the best and the most advanced of these, they associated very usefully. I speak here with grateful and affectionate remembrance of the privileges which I enjoyed in
this way."

In this way, I may now add, that Keble formed
one of the closest and most valuable friendships of
his life.

Such was the body into which John Keble was
introduced in December, 1806, a mere lad, remarkably home-bred and home-keeping, who had seen

as little of "men and cities," I suppose, as a lad of
his age could well have seen ; yet ready at once to
take a forward place in the studies, and become
a well-accepted member in the society of the college. He was in truth still but a boy, with less of
confidence, and knowledge of the world, than would
be found commonly in boys of the upper part of
the fifth form in any of our Public Schools. Many
of his letters to his sisters and brother, written soon
after the commencement of his academic life, were
preserved, and have been entrusted to me ; they are
the simple outpourings of an affectionate, home-loving,
and clever boy, with a great deal moreover of that
joyous fun and humour, which he never lost entirely
even in the most anxious years of his life. I will
make but one extract from the very first ; it is curious that he should have commenced by a trouble
in being too late for chapel on his first Sunday
morning. His father, it seems, was an old friend of
Dr. Eveleigh, then the Provost of Oriel ; he had gone
up, as I have said, with his son to the election, and
the two were entertained at the Oriel Lodge. Writing
to his eldest sister, Elizabeth, he says :—

"I have scarcely begun studying yet this Term—however,
there is a lecture appointed for Friday in Mr. Darnell's
room—it will be however in a play of Euripides, which I
have before read. I tell you this for the edification of
Jones and Thomas—I hope they are both good children,
and behave well whilst I am gone.

"I had almost got into a scrape on Sunday morning, when we were all to be in Chapel. I slept at the Provost's that night, and got up in the morning with the intention of going to chapel—I had even gone to my room to wait for the time of going—yet after all I was too late. This was owing to my having mistaken the bell at Oriel, which goes rather later than Corpus, for the latter. I was quite frightened at first, when I found I was not in time : however, by my father's mediation, I was excused by the President for my absence."

Oxford, C.C.C., Jan. 20, 1807.

In November, 1807, I find him writing in Latin to his brother, who was then preparing to follow his steps, and contend for a coming vacancy ; he writes with apparent ease, and, so far as I can judge, correctly and elegantly ; and he had then nearly finished Æschylus in the Lecture-room. He was very fortunate in his Tutor, Mr. Darnell, the late Rector of Stanhope—a man of excellent taste and accurate scholarship, one of those ornaments of Oxford, whom Bishop Barrington in the wise exercise of his great patronage, and profiting by the knowledge of the University, which he had the means of acquiring from his residence at Mongewell, delighted to transplant into places of honour and profit in his own diocese of Durham. Darnell evidently understood and appreciated Keble, and cultivated his taste with care ; he lived to be proud of his pupil, and on some occasions in after-life, when it was sought to do him honour, testified to the high opinion which he entertained of him.

In the spring of 1808, John Keble was probably preparing to compete for the English Verse prize; the subject was "Mahomet," and he was not successful, the prize being awarded to Mr. Rolleston, who had also been successful in the preceding year. The rule had not then been made, which this circumstance caused to be laid down, that no once successful candidate should compete for the same prize a second time; Keble understood that had it then existed, the prize would have been awarded to him. Of this poem I find an extract in my " Silva," but I will not insert it here, for it would give a wrong impression of his general compositions of the same date; it was evidently written after the style of English prize poems of that day, brilliant and flowing, but with no great originality of thought.

He wrote for other prizes during his undergraduateship, but was never successful; it is evident from his letters to his father, who was in his entire confidence in these, as in all other matters, and to whom he seems to have submitted all he wrote for his criticism, that he was too much distracted by the labour necessary for preparing to try for the First Class both in Classics and Mathematics; but in nothing was the difference of age so likely to stand in his way as in these competitions. I had the good fortune once to be successful against him, but I was

two years his senior, and had had the advantage
of six years' training at Eton.

I was myself elected a Scholar in April, 1809.
I found Keble in his third year highly distinguished
in the senior classes of the college, both in Classics
and Mathematics. Darnell was no longer Tutor,
nor in residence, he had been succeeded by George
Leigh Cooke. It is no disparagement of this excellent man to say that he was not equal to his eminent predecessor in scholarship or taste ; but he was
inferior to no man in industry, or zeal, good common
sense, patience, and excellent temper, to all which
he joined a genuine sense of humour, and delightful
simplicity of manner. As my whole undergraduateship was passed under his tuition, and as I owed
much of whatever success I had to his care, I
should be ungrateful if I missed this opportunity of
expressing the gratitude which I feel towards him.
He has long passed out of this life, and, owing to
my election to a Fellowship at another college, and
my early departure from residence, our intercourse
was only occasional; but my friendly relations with
my old Tutor only ceased with his life. For what
remained of Keble's preparation for the Schools,
he and I were in the same class, and he found in
Cooke a most useful Tutor, sparing no pains in
completing the work which Darnell had more than
laid the foundation of.

I was soon upon terms of familiarity with Keble,

which rapidly ripened into friendship. We became correspondents in 1811. We lived on the same staircase, he in a garret over my rooms. I see now his seat by the fireside, and a cupboard conveniently near; into which it was said that in the early times, when he had hardly courage to resolve on trying for the First Class in both Schools, he would convey his *Principia* rather rudely and hastily, if an intruder broke in upon his study of them; which he pursued at that time, to use a slang term, " on the sly." Although I was so much inferior to him in many respects, and so much his junior in standing, yet I was his senior in age, and I came from intimate and improving intercourse at Eton with some of the ablest and most studious boys in the school, and I was able at least to appreciate his mind and acquirements. We saw a great deal of each other. This was a period when the Lake Poets, as they were called, and especially Wordsworth and my Uncle, had scarcely any place in the literature of the country, except as a mark for the satire of some real wits, and some mis-named critics of considerable repute. I possessed, the gift of my Uncle, the " Lyrical Ballads," and " Wordsworth's Poems," (these last in the first edition). It is among the pleasant recollections of my life, that I first made the great poet known to Keble. As might have been expected, he read him with avidity; the admiration for his poetry, which he conceived in youth, never waned in after life; indeed, when he

came to know the man it was augmented, I may rather say completed, by the respect and regard which
his character inspired.   It was hardly possible for
Keble to be a very enthusiastic admirer of any
poetry, unless he had at least conceived a good
opinion of the writer.   I may say, in passing, that
Wordsworth's admiration of the author of " The Christian Year," and the volume itself, was in after life very
warm ; there were few of the many tributes which
he received, which he set a greater value on, than
the mention made of him by Keble in the Theatre
at Oxford, when he received his honorary degree ;
and the dedication to him of the *Prælectiones.*

In 1810 and 1811 respectively, George J. Cornish
and Thomas Arnold were elected Scholars, the former
from Westminster, the latter from Winchester.   I
think neither of them could have been in the lecture-
room with Keble, but they became fully accepted
members of our society, and on intimate terms with
him.   Of the latter I surely need say nothing generally—nor will I repeat what I have said elsewhere
of the unhappy interruption of his intimate intercourse with Keble ; to both it was a bitter trial, and
I am sure that in neither did it extinguish the tenderest love for the other.   Both Cornish and Arnold
were great accessions to our society.   I must yet add
to this list the mention of six others, Noel Thomas
Ellison, afterwards Fellow and Tutor of Balliol, John
Tucker, T. Trevenen Penrose, John Bartholomew,
William Henry Turner, and Charles Dyson ; the first

of these was elected to a Durham Scholarship at the
same time at which I was elected, and the last two
I found in residence as Bachelors when I joined the
College ; of Cornish and Dyson it will be part of my
plan to say a few words more in detail. Tucker
and Turner, I am happy to say, survive. Of Ellison
I must say in passing, that joined to considerable
talents, he had an originality and earnest simplicity
of manner as well as warmth of heart, which made
him a most delightful companion and loved friend.
Balliol men will never forget that he was one of those
who, succeeding as Tutor to the late Master, carried
on the system which has raised that College· to its
present eminence, with a zeal, and genial heartiness, that could not but contribute largely to its
success. There is a sonnet among Keble's miscellaneous poems, written on a visit to him at Huntspill,
which at once testifies to Keble's love of him, and
paints with a single felicitous touch the winning
character· of the man.

Thus I have named a few of those who formed
our small circle, and looking back through the medium of affection and regret, seeing everything dis-
tance-mellowed and softened, perhaps glorified, I
may exaggerate our activity in the studies of the
place, the simplicity and ease of our social intercourse, the delights of our walks, and the intellectual interest of our earnest talks together. I may
exaggerate, but I do not invent ; and one proof

I think is this, that although many of us were soon scattered to fellowships in other Colleges, and took different courses in life, became immersed in other cares, and pursued different professions, in one thing we all agreed — our hearty love and preference for Corpus Christi, and the looking back with unmixed and undiminishing delight on the days we passed together within her walls.   Keble gave utterance to his feelings, when he quitted it, in the following lines, which can have no more appropriate place than here :—

> " How soft, how silent, has the stream of Time
> Borne me unheeding on, since first I dream'd
> Of Poetry and Glory in thy shade,
> Scene of my earliest harpings.   There, if oft,
> (As through thy courts I took my nightly round,
> Where thy embattled line of shadows hid
> The moon's white glimmerings) on my charmed ear,
> Have swelled of thy triumphant minstrelsy
> Some few faint notes : if one exulting chord
> Of my touched heart has thrill'd in unison,
> Shall I not cling unto thee ?   Shall I cast
> No strained glance on my adopted home
> Departing ?   Seat of calm delight, farewell !
> Home of my muse, and of my friends ! I ne'er
> Shall see thee, but with such a gush of soul
> As flows from him, who welcomes some dear face
> Lost in his childhood—yet not lost to me
> Art thou ; for still my heart exults to own thee,
> And memory still, and friendship make thee mine."

> *June* 27, 1811.

The insertion of these verses reminds me that I had brought from Eton the practice of the set to which I belonged, of keeping each a "Silva" (as we ventured to call it), into which we transcribed, among other and better but not more valued things, our own efforts in prose and verse. Keble and Arnold adopted it, and to this may be owing the preservation of a great many of their youthful poems. It may well be believed, that I turn over those yellow pages now and then with intense interest; and although, no doubt, I regard the compositions with too much partiality for a critic, yet I think I may safely say that they bear unanswerable testimony to the taste and scholarship, as well as the original ability, of some at least of the students of that day.

CHAPTER III.

IN placing these three names at the head of this
chapter, and devoting it to a short account of
them, I am not unmindful of Cowper's clever warning against framing records of " names of little
note ;" nor does it escape me that I may seem to
depart from my proper subject. But Keble's character through life was but a strict development of
his character in youth ; and his early friendships
were among the more powerful agents in its formation. His disposition was social, his affections very
warm, breaking through the restraint of his natural
shyness ; and although his purity of spirit secured
him from loving any one wholly unworthy of his
love, yet his humility was so great that he was apt
not merely to undervalue himself, but to overvalue
whatever there was of good or great in those whom
he loved. It may easily be understood, therefore,
how open he was to influences from his friendships,
and how enduring his friendships were.

I think it well on these grounds to select the three
of all whom I am at liberty to mention, whom he
seemed to me to love most dearly among his asso-

ciates while an Undergraduate, and who in different
ways and degrees most influenced his habitual way
of thinking and feeling in after life. They are the
three whose names I have prefixed to this chapter.

John Miller was not a Corpus man, but of Wor-
cester College, and in what way Keble first became
acquainted with him, I cannot now state. He had
passed his examination, and been placed in the
First Class in Classics a year before I came to Oxford, and I think I met him for the first time in
the year 1810 in the Theatre. He had gained the Bachelor's Prize then newly instituted by Lord Grenville
for Latin Prose, and I had been fortunate enough to
win the Undergraduate's for Latin Verse. Thenceforward through life he treated me with the greatest
kindness, and I could not but love and honour him
more and more the longer I knew him. But with
Keble his relations were more close, and from an
earlier period; as young men they had so much in
common, in their habits, and characters, and in their
simplicity of manner and original humour, that when
thrown together they could not well escape an intimate friendship; and as they walked on in the path
of that profession to which they were both devoted,
there was on almost all points such agreement as
to its obligations, and the manner of discharging
them, as well as to the various questions which
from time to time agitated Churchmen, that the
early friendship could not but endure and ripen into

the closest intimacy. Keble, indeed, was sure to regard Miller with reverence, and he always spoke
and wrote of him with that feeling on his mind ;
but this did not prevent them from genial merriment and familiarity when they met. Those were,
indeed, white days to Keble ; here and there through
his correspondence the visits of Miller to Fairford,
or their meetings elsewhere, are mentioned with real
delight. It is thus that he speaks of him in a
letter to Cornish, dated from Fairford, Sept. 22,
1818 :—

"We have got good Miller regularly settled, I do not
mean married, only fifteen miles from us, in one of the
prettiest little ravines in the chalk escarpment beyond
Highworth, nearly in a line from us ; and the church,
close to which stands his parsonage, is a pattern of neatness ; it has, moreover, one of the prettiest Saxon door-
ways I ever saw. Tom and I pilgrimed it over there the
other day, and found *Hooker* and his father and sister at
home, but thank God no Joan to mar the quietness of the
family party, which was just what you would expect. You
must come and see us and him. I assure you he enquired
after you very particularly. What a book his is, (he alludes to the Bampton Lectures) ; the more I go on pon-
dering it, the more light it seems to throw on every subject, and hardly any thing else that I take up that does
not put me in mind of it. If I must *jure* into any man's
verbs, I think on the whole it would be his."

Miller, like Keble, retired early from Oxford into

the country, and, except when he returned at intervals at the request of his College to assist for a time
in the tuition, he passed his days residing with his
father, or his brother and sister, devoted to the duties
of his profession, and always in rural parishes. He fell
asleep in 1858, after a short illness, in his seventy-first
year, and was laid by the side of his brother, in his
own quiet churchyard, lamented not least by those
among whom he had ministered for so many years ;
who, (as has been well said in a short memoir to
which I am much indebted,) however incompetent
to form a judgment of him in other respects, were
fully able to estimate his worth as a " Christian
minister, a neighbour, and a man." The " other respects" here mentioned refer to his published works ;
there were several of these, the most important the
Bampton Lectures for 1817, and a volume of Sermons published in 1830. The ordinary fate of published sermons is almost proverbial, and I fear these
have not escaped it ; but they are of remarkable
merit, and I am sure will richly repay the study of
any reader. Both have received testimonials as unsuspicious as they are valuable. In the " Life and Correspondence of Bishop Jebb" is a letter from him,
in which he first shortly expresses in the strongest
terms the general impression which the Lectures
had made on him, and then goes through a long
and minute examination of them, expressing differences of opinion as to several particulars, but de-

tracting nothing from his general admiration. Of the Sermons, Robert Southey writes :—

"These are, in the true sense of a word which has been most lamentably misapplied, Evangelical. I do not know any discourses-in which revealed truths and divine philosophy are brought home with such practical effect to all men. They have the rare merit of being at the same time thoroughly intelligible, thoroughly religious, thoroughly discreet[a]."

In another letter he says of them :—

"They are unlike any others which I have ever read. They are thoroughly Christian in their spirit, and philosophical, comprehensible by the plainest understanding, and as satisfactory to the judgment as they are to the feelings[b]."

These are testimonies to which of course I add nothing of my own ; but I will mention two other small but very interesting publications by him, "A Christian Guide for Plain People," published in 1820, and "Things after Death," of which the second edition was published in 1854. Of the former of these two, Keble says this in a letter to me of April, 1820 :—

"Have you read a little publication of Miller's which I sent to James Coleridge, and if you have, how do you like it ? Miller has been quite unwell since he wrote it, and we

* Southey's "Life and Correspondence," vol. vi. p. 90.   [b] Ibid.

began to be rather alarmed about him; chiefly, I believe, on the notion that he was too good to live; but I am thankful to say that he is now much better. Perhaps you do not know that he is in part returned to College, as he comes up for the last three weeks of every Term to Collectionize. And from this, and his being situated within fifteen miles of us in the country, I hope to see more and more of him; and if I am not very much the better for doing so, I know whose fault it must be. Lest you should think his style in this new book too obscure for the 'Plain People,' I must tell you that he made Moliere's experiment; for he gave the Sermons to his servant, quite a rustic lad, to read before he printed them, and the man said he understood them all except the fifth, which accordingly M. made plainer, till the youth professed himself satisfied with it. And his father, the Clerk of the Parish, had given the greatest proof of his understanding even of this the obscurest part, for he said to Miller, 'O yes, Sir, I see what you mean, you mean such and such people (naming them) by the one of your two classes, and such and such by the other.' Now, as it happened, the Sermons were written while M. was in Herefordshire, before ever he had set his eyes on the said people. I call this a very satisfactory experiment, quite as much so as most of Sir Humphrey Davy's; and it seems to establish, what I have long wished to believe, and am now almost convinced of, viz. that poor people, generally speaking, have much greater understanding of what we say to them, than most of us are apt to fancy; in short, that ignorance as well as infidelity comes more from the heart than from the head."

I think I shall be forgiven for adding what he

wrote on the same subject, about the same time, to Dyson, who was then an incumbent in Yorkshire :—

"I wish I could send you a little book which Miller has just published, called a Christian Guide for Plain (not ugly) People. It seems to me to be just what we want; but Parker apparently does not think well of its sale, as he has only printed 500 copies of it. The worst of it is, that people are determined beforehand to fancy every thing Miller writes so very hard to understand. Do you not think there is a great deal of laziness in that kind of objection, urged as we continually hear it against both Divinity and Poetry? Miller, however, has done more than most men to secure this book's being intelligible to those for whom it is written, for he made his servant read it, like Moliere rehearsing his plays to the old woman, and altered some places which he did not understand, but found him perfectly up to the general drift of it. I wonder whether people that write tracts for the poor generally take this method ; it seems mere common sense for them to do so, and yet one can hardly think they do. One thing is, the poor certainly understand the meaning of a sentence very often when they could not for their lives explain the single words of which it is made up ; and if I find it so in Gloucestershire, which is a mere Bœotia, much more, I ween, do you in Yorkshire, which is so famed for the shrewdness of its rustics."

This was the man between whom and Keble the closest communion of feelings and principles existed. They were strikingly alike in the warmth of their home affections, in their early and absolute renunciation of the honours of the world, in their devotion to their profession from the very beginning, and always in the most quiet and humble line in which its duties could be presented to them; alike, too, in this, that retired as were their lives, their interest was sensibly alive as to all the questions which from time to time arose and affected the Church; upon these they never failed to take counsel together, and they spared no pains to advance what they deemed her true interests.

I had known Cornish, who was born at Ottery St. Mary, June 7, 1794, from his childhood well; we separated as boys, he for Westminster, and I for Eton, and we met again upon his election as Scholar in 1810. He had grown to be a young man of very gentlemanly appearance, with somewhat of reserve, and what might almost be taken for haughtiness in his manner; this was in reality the result of great refinement of feeling and of shyness. No one, indeed, had less of haughtiness in his nature; he was very modest, of keen sensibilities, and accurate taste; and these rather than great vigour, or power of sustained application, were the characteristics of his intellect. He was pure-hearted as a child, and very affectionate; his seeming coldness soon yielded to the kindness of his reception amongst us; and his

geniality with a kind of Cervantic humour, which
he often displayed very amusingly, made him soon
a great favourite. He was just the person to attract
Keble's love; and I see in their correspondence to
the end of his life the tenderness in Keble and
somewhat of the manner of an elder brother towards him. This tenderness, in kind as well as in
degree, extended itself to the other members of
his family, and to his widow and children after his
death. He was placed in the First Class for Classics at the Michaelmas Examination for 1813, and
in due course became Fellow, and afterwards Tutor
of the College; but the University life was not to
his taste. He, too, had devoted himself to pastoral
duty, and having married early, he retired to the
curacy of Salcombe, near to Salcombe Hill, his
father's house; he dwelt after a time at Packcombe,
a sweet secluded cottage in the hills at a little distance. But he was not a man to be overlooked,
and at Michaelmas, 1828, he was collated by his old
master, Bishop Carey, to the united Vicarages of Ken-
wyn and Kea, a large and important Cure in Cornwall. Here he acquired high estimation in the diocese, and was clearly marked out for advancement;
but his health, never strong, and too severely tried
by losses of his children, and by family afflictions,
gave way, and he died in the prime of life, Sept.
10, 1849, dearly loved. highly honoured, and tenderly
lamented.

It was thus that Keble wrote respecting his illness and death to Dyson :—

"So I missed seeing him once more, and the last time was at our consecration. It is such a comfort to me to think of him here, with old Tom, Coleridge, and others. About him it seems purely selfish to grieve. Yet one does grieve very much; one feels that this world can never be the same without him; the things which he would have said, or thought, on different occasions, come so naturally into one's mind. . . . .

"What a time it seems since we have met, and how much I seem to have to say! but I don't like saying it now, because it is not all about him."

Then at the close of his note, he adds :—

"*Private.* My dear Dyson, do ask for me that I may meet *him* again. . . . Ever your most loving J. K."

The reader of "The Christian Year" must have been thankful to Keble for appending to the stanzas on the Twenty-first Sunday after Trinity the exquisite little poem to the Redbreast. It is by Cornish. He was one of the band of friends who were from time to time interchanging amongst each other their compositions. He continued to write, as occasions moved him, as long as he lived. Upon his death, at the request of his parishioners, a volume of his sermons was printed, and to this, by the desire of some of his friends, was appended a selection from these verses. I have often wished, and I still wish, that these last had been published in a separate small

volume. The sermons have much merit, and must
have been a valued and appropriate present to his
parishioners ; but, as commonly happens with sermons, their circulation was not large, and was limited,
I think, to a single edition.   Unfortunately they
buried the poems, which deserve another fate, unless I am deceived by my love for the author, and
my familiarity with some of the scenes and persons
alluded to in them.   I own I can never read several
of them without being much affected, and I do not
think I am in error when I say that they are so
tasteful and finished in composition, so imaginative,
so true, and so full of genuine tenderness, that they
would give pleasure to a larger circle if they were
more generally known.   I do not wholly despair that
this may yet be done ; and I could I believe add
some which might well have a place among them.
I will insert a specimen conceived in the same spirit
as the lines on the Redbreast.

Come to the Woods.

When the hour of meeting's nigh,
And thy heart is beating high,
  Come to the woods, the woods, lad.
And if the boughs are ringing,
With all their minstrels singing,
  Do thou, too, rejoice,
  And utter a voice
    More glad.

> Or if on Winter's tide
> Floats Autumn's wither'd pride,
>   Come to the woods, the woods, lad.
> Why should the bard be dumb ?
> 'Tis meet that thou shouldst come
>   Their Spring gifts to repay,
>   And make the pale day
>   Less sad.

The Poems already published are so little known, I fear, that I will venture to add one from them :—

Dreams.

> My dearest love, to whom I owe
>   That I am whatsoe'er I be ;
> Whose sun-lit eye, in hours of woe,
>   Has bid the darkest shadows flee ;
> Whose steady step the path pursued,
> That from afar thy wisdom viewed ;—
>
> If brightest promise disappear,
>   Joy after joy perchance decay,
> I still can dry the flowing tear,
>   All thankful for the joys that stay ;
> For Mercy and eternal Truth
> Surely have followed me from youth.
>
> Only, " my life's celestial sign,"
>   Thy presence must be with me still ;
> The rest I freely can resign,
>   Obedient to the Master's will.
> Not thee ! not thee ! my anguished heart,
> Not yet from thee has learnt to part.

D

And yet Life's fairest hours are fled,
　The latter sands too plainly run ;
And Time his early snow to shed
　Upon our brows has now begun ;
And swifter does the torrent flow,
Ere yet it seek the gulf below.

Hence, idle dreams ! the day is ours,
　And we will "work while it is day,"
And consecrating all our powers
　To God, and, living as we pray,
In calmness wait His power to prove,
Whose knowledge but subserves His love.

May, 1845.

I might have hesitated to reprint these stanzas, but
that since I commenced this little notice of the husband, the wife to whom they are addressed has been
called to her rest. I am at liberty now to say, that
there is not a syllable of exaggeration in this out-
pouring of love ; it is but justice to the wife from
the husband, who had tried and never found her
wanting. His was a nature which required support,
and, as I have said, he was severely tried ; beyond
his own immediate circle, he had painful sorrows;
within it he lost child after child ; and though he
bowed in Christian submission to the blows, his sensitive nature could not sustain them without injury.
In all these sorrows she was his earthly stay and
comfort. He died ; and what she had been to
him, she continued to be to her children, until her

strength failed under the severity, and the continuance of the calls made on it, and she departed in peace. She was, indeed, what in one of his poems he calls her, a noble woman.

I have felt it to be no departure from my main object to dwell for a little while on the memory of John Miller and George Cornish. In respect of Charles Dyson, I may say, with the strictest accuracy, that no memoir of Keble, however short, could be complete which omitted to give some idea of this dear friend. Perhaps no man of equal virtue, sweetness, cultivation, and ability, ever passed through life so little known beyond the circle of his own family and friends ; and yet I think no man was ever more loved and revered within that circle, or exercised a more powerful influence over the minds of those with whom he was intimate. Keble was among these ; the intimacy commenced, as I have said, at Corpus, and continued to the end of Dyson's life unbroken ; and I speak with substantial accuracy when I say that there was scarcely a step which he took, especially in matters connected with his profession, or the Church, to which he did not make Dyson first privy, ask his co-operation, if the thing admitted of it, and always seek, if he did not always follow, his advice. The extracts from the correspondence, which I shall have occasion to make, will shew this in numerous instances. It may suffice now to say, that it was Dyson very mainly who overcame his reluctance to publish "The Christian Year," and to whom, perhaps, above all his other friends, the world owes that great gift when it was first made.

Charles Dyson was the grandson of the Jeremiah Dyson of whom Johnson in his life of Akenside records, that the poet physician "would perhaps have been reduced to great exigencies, but that Mr. Dyson, with an ardour of friendship that has not many examples, allowed him three hundred pounds a-year;" munificence indeed, when the times and Mr. Dyson's own means are considered. Dyson once said to me, "My grandfather was satyrized by Horace Walpole, but he was a noble fellow; he would not sell the places at the table of the House of Commons, as his predecessors always did, but appointed Hatsell freely, losing £6,000 thereby, and Hatsell in consequence appointed my father freely." His son Jeremiah followed his steps in the House, and finally filled the same post there; and it was intended that his grandson, of whom I write, should pursue the same course; but this from the most generous motives he abandoned, and then resolutely and earnestly devoted himself to the Church.

When I entered the College, he had already taken his Bachelor's degree; he was, however, still a regular resident according to the College rule, and

was one of the kindly party who greeted me on my
admission into the Junior Common-room. Keble
and he were already on friendly terms, and I was
happy enough to be soon admitted to the same
privilege. Delicacy of constitution, and principle
equally made him a very abstinent man, but he
was by disposition social; his father's position, and
the society with which he associated at his home,
his more frequent visits to London, the extent and
variety of his reading, and information, might have
made him much regarded by us who were younger,
and had seen less of the world; but he added to all
these advantages such sweetness of temper, and so
much quiet humour, as made his society eagerly
coveted. Drinking tea in his room, two or three
of us at a time, was a great delight. I smile when
I remember how we thought of his tea from Twi-
nings, and his wax lights; luxuries or refinements
which in our day, or at least in our College, were
not commonly indulged in. He was very fond of
coming out late at night and pacing up and down
our little quadrangle; many and many a happy talk
have Keble and I had with him in this way; to
which, I think, he alludes in the verses which I just
now quoted.

He became a Fellow of the College; and was
elected Anglo-Saxon Professor in 1812; one admirable lecture, and one only, he delivered. He
ought, no doubt, to have done more, but in those

days the duties of such professorships were not regarded as they now are. He could not be called an indolent man, for he was always rather a laborious student ; but he had a nice, even fastidious, taste in composition, and he was very conscientious in his preparation for any work, a severe judge of his own performances, and never thought himself fully prepared to be a public teacher. He ought to have been a great ecclesiastical historian. Keble repeatedly urged him to this, and he commenced his preparations, but so conscientiously and on so large a scale that the days of health and vigour passed away in making them ; and when his pen should have been in his hand, and his work begun, his constitution gave signals of weakness, and his strength failed him.

He married his cousin, and retired to the living of Nun Burnholme, in Yorkshire, to which he had been collated by Archbishop Harcourt, a friend of his father's. The severity of the climate affected Mrs. Dyson's health, and this led him for a time to return to Oxford, as one of the Chaplains of his College. The libraries of the University and its society no doubt contributed to this choice. He exchanged Nun Burnholme finally for Nazing, in Essex, and this again he resigned in order to devote himself to the care and comfort of his father, who, in somewhat declining health, had become a second time a widower, and was then residing at Petworth.

There were family circumstances which seemed to
cast this duty on him specially, into which it is unnecessary for me to enter ; but Dyson had his scruples
as to the resignation of his living, and consulted
Keble upon it, whose answer was, " All I can say is,
I have given up my Curacy in order to take charge
of my father and sister." Dyson, however, was constantly at the service of the neighbouring clergy ;
and, indeed, for a part of the time, took a Curacy
near. His father died in the autumn of 1835, about
the time of Keble's marriage ; and I insert here an
extract from the letter to Dyson and Mrs. Dyson,
in which he acknowledges their congratulations on
his own marriage, and expresses his condolence
on Mr. Dyson's death. This letter happens to contain a fuller expression of his judgment on the
resignation of his living.

" High-street, Southampton, Nov. **5**, 1835.

" MY VERY DEAR FRIENDS,

" It is inexcusably selfish to go on so long without acknowledging your great kindness in thinking of us at such a time
so much and so kindly, and without assuring you that we
have not been unmindful of you ; though, indeed, it was
a good while before we heard the news of your irreparable
loss, for we had no letter that succeeded in overtaking us
for ten days after our flight from Gloucestershire. It is
a strange sort of feeling that one has in thus interchanging
congratulations and condolences, and the perplexity of it,
if it were not for that end to which we trust both will help

in guiding us, would be not a little painful ; as it is, I hope
we may say, without presumption, that even to our half
blind eyes the good very much preponderates.   It is sweet
to think of the rich reward you have even already received,
for coming when you did to stay where you did, and most
refreshing to hear that your dear sister bears this second
great trial so well,—a blessing which, under Providence,
you may surely attribute to your taking the step you did.
Seldom, indeed, I should think (if one may say so without
presumption), is approbation of living man's conduct more
clearly intimated.   What you say of looking for a cure in
Hampshire (for Elizabeth has sent it to us), quite makes
one ache with the pleasant fancy (one dares not nurse it
into a hope) of your coming near us."

Dyson now quitted Petworth ; he was anxious to
resume his professional duties in the care of a parish,
and was seeking for a curacy, when the late Dowager
Lady Mildmay, who had been a family friend, presented him to the rectory of Dogmersfield.   Thither
he repaired.   At his own expense he built a par
sonage, for he would not impose a burthen on a
family living by borrowing the money for the purpose ; and helped his sister, who thenceforth resided
with him, in building a new parish church.   Both
were placed in situations more convenient than the
old ones, for the larger and poorer part of his
parishioners.   At Dogmersfield he resided for the
remainder of his life.   My readers may smile at my
stating the nicknames he bore among his intimate
friends, but they were characteristic of the man, and

will re-appear, it may be often, in Keble's letters. At
Corpus he took by inheritance from his grandfather
and father the familiar abbreviation of Jeremiah, and
acquired for himself the title of the Venerable Bede;
at Dogmersfield he became the Simorg, and the Rectory was of course his Nest. And truly it was a nest,
in which the doubtful and distressed never failed to
find comfort and counsel, the cheeriest comfort, the
wisest counsel. His society and conversation were
delightful; in his talk such a happy mixture of things
old and new, enriched with so much anecdote and
literature, so grave and so charitable on serious subjects, and on all so seasoned with quiet humour in
the manner. Retiring from notice and unknown to
the world, discharging his duties in the quietest and
most peaceful spirit, he was yet to all who knew him
an object of loving veneration. Adventures in his life
there were none to tell. He was a diligent pastor,
an earnest student, a delightful host; his greatest
pleasure beyond what these things implied was in
seeing country at home and abroad. As soon as the
Continent opened in 1814, I accompanied him part
way in a tour into France, Switzerland, and Italy, with
two brothers, Nathanael and Noel Ellison. In a large
old family coach, with the same pair of horses we
went through the heart of France with great deliberation to Lyons, and thence up the Rhone to Geneva,—
happy days which I still delight to think on. Keble
was to have been of the party, but was prevented.

Arnold says in a letter to me[c], " I saw Dyson
the other day in Oxford when I went to take my
degree of B.D., and he and his wife were enough
to freshen one's spirit for some time to come," an
observation strikingly characteristic of the effect of
intercourse with him. When Keble had become Vicar
of Hursley, Dyson and he were within easy distance
of each other on the same line of railway ; the one,
however, had many engagements at home and abroad,
and Mrs. Keble's health required his close attendance
on her often, and sometimes for long periods ; the
delicacy of the other's constitution made movements
from home not easy always to him ; yet personally
or by letter seldom or never did the one take any
step of importance without seeking counsel at the
hand of the other, and every now and then they had
joyous and remembered meetings. Numerous was
the band which gathered round Dyson's grave when
it pleased God to call him home. I well remember
that after the funeral and the dispersion of the
general body of attendants on it, Keble and I
passed the afternoon until it was necessary for him
to return home, strolling together in the fields near
the house and church, conversing, as we had not
often an opportunity to do, on the past and the
future.

The last time I saw Dyson was toward the end of

[c] " Life," vol. i. p. 73.

February, 1860. I found him altered in appearance, feebler in body, and manifestly declining. Yet the approaches to death were so soft and gentle, and he contemplated his end so peacefully and hopefully, that it was not a painful subject to talk about, and we talked much of it. Among other things I remember we conversed on the intermediate state and the condition of the blessed. I asked him, "When your mind has been running on these subjects, have you ever followed the thought on as to literature or intellect? Will Shakespeare be anything there beyond humbler men?" He said, "I remember years ago we discussed this in my rooms at Corpus. I believe I was for some superiority for cultivated intellect, but I think now it is the affections of the heart that will be the test of superiority. Many a humble person of whom we know nothing now, will be called up from the lowest place to sit down on high. Abdiel was but a seraph, yet he might be an archangel." "But," I said, "David's Psalms, merely as productions of the intellect, will they be as nothing in the scale?" "Oh," he answered, "we know that such as he— Prophets, Apostles, Saints—will have their special places." "We must still," I said, "cultivate our talents, of course." "Of course we must; but you know the affections, our circumstances, our opportunities are all talents, as much as the gifts of the intellect. No doubt there will be disparities; many are called, few chosen, there are many mansions."

As we stood by his mantelpiece shortly before **I**
left him, he pointed out some old family drawings
and little relics which friends had brought him from
their travels.   I remember a fragment of rock from
Sinai, a stone from Jordan, a bit of the rocky ground
of the pathway from Bethany to Jerusalem.   He remarked how in looking on such things, and recall-
ing the scenes of his boyhood and youth, he was
moved, sometimes almost to tears.

I see him now standing at the door as I left him;
with a smile on his face, and in his old playful way
he said, "Well, Privy Councillor, good-bye ; thank
you for this.   I cannot tell you how much pleasure
you have given me by this visit."

So we parted, for this life.

I may, and I probably shall, be blamed for lingering
so long in this digression, but at whatever cost I must
yet add to it.   I cannot but in some sort acknowledge,
though I can never pay, to my friend the debt I owe
him.   He was, indeed, my friend, and when he was
a friend, he was the best of friends.   How he discharged that duty to me in the particulars, as from
time to time the calls arose, of course can never be
told to the public, but it wiii not be forgotten by some
at least in this and another generation ; and I am
persuaded his acts, and the spirit in which he did
them, are written for him in that memorial where
alone he would wish them to appear.   In the various
trials and troubles which have been sent to me in no

unusual number or magnitude in the course of a long
life, and especially during my early struggles in my
profession, he was my never-failing stay, my helper,
my counsellor. Childless himself, his paternal feelings (tender and hearty they were) flowed out on my
children. He sometimes could and did more than
fill my place. In sickness or in health his house was
to them a home, and he nothing short of a father;
he would suspend his own studies without reluctance
to direct theirs, and never seemed to feel their presence a disturbance to his own quiet. How they
gained by the love and wisdom, the quiet sympathy,
and the pleasant humour, which did not enfeeble discipline, but made its presence unfelt, it is impossible
for me to say or for them to forget. Pleasant, indeed, it is for me to feel that one and not the least
valuable of the impressions made on them still remains fresh and strong in the hearty and reverential
love they bear to his memory. Dogmersfield is still
to them in recollection a home, and Uncle Charles,
as they called him, a revered and beloved father.
The surviving member of that household must forgive me if I cannot keep back how she and her
sister contributed to the charm, which even now
makes that Simorg's Nest a hallowed place in the
recollections of us all.

I hope I may be forgiven if I print here a part of
one even of my own letters, which I have found among
a number preserved by Keble, and returned to me

by his brother. It is in remarkable harmony with what I have just written.

"MY DEAREST JOHN KEBLE,—I think I know how you must feel the blow which has lighted on us both in the departure of our most dear friend at Dogmersfield, and I cannot help writing a line to you. I naturally turn to the last survivor of the Corpus band to which I was so tenderly united, and I have been thinking over the days when, rough and rude as I was, he and you and others accepted me into that choice little circle. I have been thinking, too, how ever since, on occasion after occasion when I have wanted the advice, or the comfort, or the help of a friend, he never failed me. How wise and good he was! I do not think I exaggerate when I say he was the wisest man in the best sense I have ever been familiar with, and yet how humble and how simple! In his happy retirement, with no countenance from great people, no fame in the world, how entirely free was he from envy or repining; indeed, he was incapable of both; taking a lively interest in the important matters which stirred the State or the Church, giving out his words of wisdom about them, but not desiring to be taking any part in them. How often have I thought of that little Nest and the slender tie on which so much happiness, and the exercise of so much goodness, in that place, hung, and now that tie is rent asunder. I presume you and I shall meet at his grave."

His saltem accumulem donis.

CHAPTER IV.

FINAL EXAMINATION.—ELECTION AT ORIEL.—UNI-
VERSITY PRIZES. — SIDMOUTH. — ORDINATIONS.—
FIRST CURACY.

KEBLE passed his final examination in Easter
Term, 1810, and was placed in both First Classes.
Up to that time no one had earned this distinction
but Sir Robert Peel, with whose examination the
University was ringing when I matriculated. Keble's
youth, and what seemed, but I believe only seemed,
imperfect preparation, made his success the more remarkable. It was a joy to us personally for the love
we bore him, and a triumph, too, beyond that which
a College always feels for distinction won by one of
its members. In our little circle we had known that
he had doubted whether he should be able to prepare himself in both lines, and some of that doubt
had perhaps spread amongst us as to the result; but
both his tutors, Brydges the Mathematical, as well as
Cooke, had urged him on, and they judged his powers
more accurately than we. I now see from his letters
to his father that at the very crisis of his preparation
he was also writing both for the Latin and English
Verse Prizes. I was not aware of it at the time. He
knew, I dare say, that I was competing also, and

therefore made no communication to me. The English Verses I have never seen; some of the Latin appear in his correspondence with his father, sent to him for his censure. I wish I could have recovered the letters in which he must have announced to his father his success and his disappointment, they would surely have been very interesting. All his letters to his father which I have seen are in the affectionate and unpretending spirit of a boy, open-hearted yet deferential, considerate as to the expense he was occasioning, and shewing a strong desire to relieve him from it.

With a view to this I find him in one proposing to stand for a Fellowship at Magdalen, which it was probable some circumstances would shortly throw open. But the character he had now attained put an end to any scheme of this kind, by opening to him the prospect of the great distinction of a Fellowship at Oriel.

He was elected a Probationer Fellow there on the 20th of April, 1811, wanting then a few days of having completed his nineteenth year; and took his place at the High Table and in the Senior Common-room among that body, which even then gave the tone to the intellectual pursuits of the University, and which within a few years, by the gradual accession of remarkable men, was to acquire name and celebrity far and wide, and to originate a movement of which the effects are still felt through every part of the

Church of England. Whately entered it with him, and they found Copleston and Davison in the lead of it. I well remember being there as Keble's guest, and being struck with the remarkable deference with which these two were treated; it was such as somewhat to check the social pleasure of the party.

His progress was now rapid. In 1812 he won the Prizes for both the Bachelor's Essays, the English on Translation from Dead Languages, the Latin a comparison of Xenophon and Julius Cæsar as Military Historians of Campaigns in which they had been themselves engaged. This was an honour at that time unprecedented; indeed, the Latin Essay Prize had only been founded by Lord Grenville in 1810, but the same success has been very rarely achieved since; twice only, I believe; and in one of those instances by no less a man than my old school-fellow and friend, H. H. Milman, the late Dean of St. Paul's. Lord Grenville on all these occasions testified his sense of "the very commendable industry and exertion, as well as of the merit of the compositions," by a present of valuable books beyond the regular Prize, which was a sum of money. In one of his letters, from which I shall have occasion to make an extract, Keble refers to his Plutarch very amusingly.

Being resident, and without College office, he soon became engaged in private tuition, and in the Long Vacation of 1813 a small party of pupils gathered round him at Sidmouth, where he rented a picturesque

E

cottage (Myrtle Cottage) out of the town, the garden
being bordered by the Sid, and within a few minutes
walk of the sea. This was the property of Cornish's
father, and adjoining to the Salcombe-hill grounds,
where the Cornish family, a numerous and bright
one of both sexês, resided. He had seen the sea for
the first time at Cowes in the preceding summer,
and had given vent to his feelings in some beautiful lines ; but he had been very little of a traveller,
and the beauties even of this comparatively tame
part of Devonshire struck him very much. Writing
to an old pupil (Mr. Bliss) he says,—

"As I came into Devonshire in the dark, and consequently could not (though very *quick-sighted*) see a great
deal of the country, I was not a little delighted on waking
the next morning to find myself in a little Paradise."

At this time I had gone through my examination,
and was passing my vacation at my own home at
Ottery St. Mary. The foot-way from one place to
the other was over the steep ridge which divides the
two valleys of the Sid and the Otter, the distance not
more than six miles, and the views on the way remarkably beautiful. It was a delightful walk, and
the frequent intercourse between us was principally
kept up on foot over the hill. At the termination
of the ridge where it drops down with a steep descent
into the Sidmouth Gap, are the remains of an Armada
beacon, according to the tradition of the country.

These, at the time I speak of, were not, as now they
are, suffered to be overgrown and hidden by a planta-
tion of firs. There on the short green turf we often
rested and enjoyed a view which for beauty, variety,
and extent is not easily to be surpassed. At our feet
was spread out Harpford - wood as a grand carpet
laid on a surface here and there deeply indented,
and beyond lay the rich and wooded valley of the
Otter ; thence the ground rises in successive ranges
of hills, until you reach the higher outlines of Dart--
moor. Down deep on our left lay Sidmouth and the
blue sea ; this sea-view is interrupted by the bluff
and wooded landward end of Peak-hill, and opens
again beyond this to a wide range of sea and sea-
coast, down to and beyond the Berry Head, the west-
ernmost point of Torbay. It needs not to be said
how Keble enjoyed this, and I hope I may be excused for borrowing Wordsworth's verse,—

> "We talked with open heart and tongue
> Affectionate and true."

Those who have never known Keble familiarly or
only in later life, will scarcely be prepared to hear
with how quick a relish he entered into the gaieties
of Sidmouth. At this time Torquay was little more
than a fishing village, and Sidmouth, though a small
place, was much frequented by families seeking to
combine the pursuit of health for the delicate, with that
of amusement for the strong. It was consequently

as much a winter watering-place as a summer, and
much of social intercourse was maintained all through
the winter. No one was better received than Keble,
and no one, I may add, seemed to enjoy more heartily
the morning or evening parties, the concerts, and
dances, which were frequent ; the scenery and the
society both found him impressionable, and as was
natural they had their effect upon his poetical powers ;
he composed more often and better than he had ever
done before. I am reminded by a note of my own
to him at the time how much I was struck with this ;
in it I urged him to cultivate powers which now
seemed to me unquestionable, and, looking after so
many years with the colder judgment of age on the
poems he then produced, I see no reason to alter my
opinion. They seem to me to promise all that he
afterwards performed. I will insert one specimen
written but a few days before he was to leave Sidmouth, and addressed " Nunquam auditurae :"—

> How can I leave thee all unsung,
>   While my heart owns thy dear control,
> And heaven and love have o'er thee flung
>   The softest moonlight of the soul ?
> Oh, I have long'd for thee to call
> Soft Echo from the West Wind's hall,
>   Some notes as blithely wild to seek,
> As the wild music of thy voice,
> As the wild roses that rejoice
>   In thine eye's sunshine, on thy glowing cheek.

For not the breath of mortal praise
   Thine artless beauty dares profane ;
For thee wild nature wakes her lays,
   And thy soul feels the blessed strain.
The song that breaks the grove's repose,
The shower-drop nestling in the rose,
   The brooklet's morning melody,
To these with soft and solemn tone
Thy spirit stirs in unison,
   Owning the music of its native sky.

And when in some fair golden hour
   Thy heart-strings shall give back the sigh,
Of Love's wild harp, no earthly bower
   Shall lend such hues as bloom to die.
But earnest of the eternal spring,
Their amarant wreaths shall angels bring ;
   And preluding the choir of heaven,
Soft Eden gales shall sweep the lyre,
And starlike points of guiltless fire
From God's own altar-flame to gem thy brow be given.

It is my pride that I can deem,
   Though faintly, of that being's worth,
Who to the All-gracious mind shall seem
   Meet help for thee in heaven and earth.
Long as before Life's gale I drive,
Shall holiest hope within me live,
   Thee fair, thee blessed while I view ;
And when the port of endless rest
Receives me, may my soul be blest
   With everlasting upward gaze on you.

It is needless surely to point out how even at this

early period of his life what might have been a mere
love-song became in his way of dealing with it elevated (perhaps too elevated) and holy from the habitual holiness and elevation of all his serious thoughts.

Neither his employment nor the attractions of Sidmouth, however, prevented Keble from occasional
expeditions into the country, and I remember well
that he and one of his pupils, Mr. Gaussen, with myself, under the guidance of my father, whose good
taste and familiarity with the country made him the
best of guides, rode from Sidmouth to and through
the north of Devon and the adjoining parts of Somer-
setshire. On our return to the neighbourhood of
Exeter we parted, and Keble and his pupil went on
to Plymouth and the Tamar. He was new to scenery
so beautiful or romantic as that which he went through
in the course of this tour. It delighted him at the time,
and produced a permanent impression on his mind,
of which traces may be seen not merely in his correspondence, but in his poems. He left Sidmouth with
much regret, and was much regretted by many whom
he left; by none perhaps more than the fine family
of his landlord, with whom he contracted abiding
intimacy; and cemented more closely the friendship already subsisting between himself and George
Cornish.

Not long after his return to Oxford in December,
1813, on the proposition of Davison, and by the advice of Copleston and his father, he consented to

fill the office of Examining Master from the following Michaelmas, and he set himself diligently to prepare for the work. He had great misgivings, as
was to be expected in one at once so young and so
modest; and it was a great comfort to him that
not long after Cardwell, two or three years his
senior, was joined to him as colleague; the two
thoroughly understood each other, and agreed on
the principles which should govern them. There
was no need for his apprehensions. From several
persons examined by him, I have heard that the
simplicity and kindness of his manner, his thorough
acquaintance with the matter of the examination,
together with his entire freedom from desire of dis-
playing himself,—too common a failing, as has been
said, of examining masters,—made him very effective and popular in the Schools. It has happened
to me more than once to meet with men in after
life who were and continued personally strangers
to him, but who had carried out of the Schools
and retained through life a loving estimation of him
merely from his examination of them.

It was during his preparation for the office that I
find in his letters the first entry on a subject which
thenceforward it pleased God to give him almost
constant cause to dwell on,—the illness, I mean, of
one or other of those most dear to him. His letters
to me in the spring and summer of 1814 mention
the illnesses of two of his sisters, the eldest Eliza-

beth, Sarah the next in order of birth; the latter
was carried off by consumption in that summer;
and it must be interesting to see even at this early
period how definite and cheerful were his convictions
in regard to the Intermediate state of the departed
Christian.   Thus he wrote to me :—

   " Not that I have been so much overwhelmed by what I
have lately seen and heard as to be unable to write, or to
enter into common subjects.   Indeed, when I look back,
I wonder at my own hard-heartedness.   I do not believe
there has been one day since my dear sister was given
over, that I have not been able to go on with my reading
as usual.   Yet I do not think it is insensibility, that I have
been able to divert my thoughts from her so much, but
chiefly because I had suffered so much from suspense,
which in such cases always leads me to expect and imagine
worse than the worst.   Another thing is, that I cannot
even now persuade myself I have lost her, except out of
my sight.   That she is happy I have (blessed be God for
it !) the firmest faith, and that in her happiness she remembers us, whom living she never forgot, I fondly persuade
myself.   Whenever I think of this, (and I have now made
the thought habitual,) it checks my grief, making it seem
altogether selfish and unreasonable.   However it be, I consider it as a great mercy that my spirits have not failed
me, since they are quite wanted in the family, and that
principally on Elizabeth's account, who in her helpless
state feels the loss most of all, and has besides suffered
greatly from her lameness within the last two or three
days.   Tom does admirably well, his example has been of
very great advantage to me.
   " *Fairford, Saturday Night, July* 2, 1814."

About the same time, too, that he was first discharging the duties of Examiner, his thoughts were
much occupied about his Ordination ; he was very
desirous that I should adopt the same course of life
as that on which he was resolved ; he thought my
health, which indeed at the time seemed delicate,
would fail in the profession I had chosen ; but his
principal motive was of a higher kind.   It was thus
he wrote of that to which he pressed me in March,
1815.   After setting out his (very exaggerated) notions of what personal advancement might be in
store for me in the course I had chosen, he says :—

"I feel what it must be to forego the possibility, even
though it were but just possible, of realizing such hopes
as these ; nor do I think anything, not even the saving
health and life, would make me forego them, but for
visions far more brilliant and more certain too ; more
brilliant in their results, inasmuch as the salvation of one
soul is worth more than the framing the Magna Charta of
a thousand worlds ; more certain to take place, since temptations are fewer, and opportunities everywhere to be
found.   Can there be even among the angels a higher privilege that we can form an idea of, than the power of contributing to the everlasting happiness of our neighbour to
be especially delegated and assigned to us by Almighty
God ? I would that I were as free from worldly care and
ambition, as the thought of what I hope will be my high
calling ought to make me.   I know that I am never so free
from evil thoughts as when these things are strongest on
my mind, but how difficult to make them habitual !"

It was thus he wrote in March. On May the 20th, but a few days before his ordination, he poured out to me the genuine feelings of his heart :—

" You ask for my prayers, be assured that you have them , though cold and worthless as they are, I can hardly hope that they can do you good. But thanks be to God, there is One who can make our worthless offerings available. Pray for me, too ; pray earnestly, my dear, my best friend, that He would give me His grace, that I may not be altogether unworthy of the sacred office on which I am, rashly I fear, even now entering ; but that some souls hereafter may have cause to bless me. Pray that I may be freed from vanity, from envy, from discontent, from impure imaginations ; that I may not grow weary, nor wander in heart from God's service ; that I may not be judging others uncharitably, nor vainly dreaming how they will judge me, at the very moment that I seem most religiously and most charitably employed. Without any foolish affectation of modesty, I can truly say that the nearer the time approaches, the more strongly I feel my own unfitness and unworthiness for the ministry ; yet as I hope it is not such but that it may be removed in time by earnest and constant use of the means of grace, I do not think it needful to defer my Ordination ; but I want all the help I can get in the awful and difficult preparation ; do not therefore forget me in your prayers. I know, indeed, you do not forget me ; but make especial mention of me at this season. On Sunday next I hope to be ordained, and on Monday I go to Fairford for the summer, having engaged myself for the next six weeks to take charge of two small parishes, the churches of which are as near as Oriel and Corpus Chapels, about four miles distance from Fairford."

He was ordained Deacon on Trinity Sunday, 1815, and Priest on Trinity Sunday, 1816, both by the Bishop of Oxford, Dr. William Jackson ; and in July of the latter year, writing to me and congratulating me on an event which was the prelude to the greatest happiness of my life, and uttering words of loving advice, which I look back on now with deep and grateful interest, he says :—

" You will understand all I mean to say, and cannot. I want your prayers, too ; very much I want them, for every day I feel the dangers and anxieties of my profession increase upon me. Pray for me that I may not pollute God's altar with irregular, worldly-minded, self-complacent thoughts. Pray for me that I may free myself from all pride, all ambition, all uncharitableness. You cannot think how a little word which you dropped one day, the last we met together at Oxford, struck me, and how it has abode with me ever since. You cautioned me against Formalism ; I thought it hard at the time, but now I know you had too good reason. Help me by your prayers, your advice, if any occurs to you ; and your reproof, if you at any time think I need it, to get rid of that dangerous habit."

Little did he when he gave vent to his feelings in these remarkable passages, suppose they would ever be exposed to the light to which I am now exposing them, but I cannot believe I do wrong in publishing them ; no one can doubt that they flowed from his heart, and it may be useful to many a young man under similar circumstances to see this living picture of what Keble felt at that crisis of his life. I have more fears on another point, and yet I hope I may be forgiven for not withholding what relates to myself only. I could not separate these parts without impairing that perfect idea of him which the whole extracts now present; and I desire any one reading "The Christian Year," and the "Lyra," to bear this passage in mind when so engaged with them. I think he will see proof again and again, that these were not the passing feelings of moments of excitement, but ruling principles ever present and ever operative on his mind.

How little probably did those who with the Bishop laid their hands on Keble's head, dream at the time how holy a spirit, how powerful an agent for good, by God's blessing, they were enrolling among the ministers of the Church. On himself the impressions of the day were never weakened. Writing in June, 1827, on Trinity Sunday, to George Cornish, he says :—

" To-day I have been to an Ordination, for the first time since I was ordained myself, and I have almost made a vow to be present at one every year. I think it would do one a great deal of good, *like going back to one's native air after long intervals.*"

I must not anticipate, but I may mention in passing, that curiously enough he writes in the same letter :—

"To-morrow I correct the press of my title-page, which I need not tell you is always the last thing done in a book."

This was "The Christian Year."

There was no external manifestation of extra-ordinary or exclusive devotion to his calling in this commencement of his ministry, the sole charge of two parishes, East Leach and Burthorpe, small and contiguous, for six weeks in the Long-vacation ; nor did he afterwards, when the engagement had become permanent, think it necessary to give up his Oxford employments, or to decline the College Tutorship when called on to take it. And yet I doubt not that they were well provided for, and that scarcely any better introduction could have been had for him to the duties to which he had devoted himself. He had his father, then in the full vigour of his faculties, for his assistant and his guide. It was a peculiar delight to him to place himself once more as a pupil under that beloved and respected guide; while as generally a resident at Oxford he had probably greater advantages for the large and well-considered study of divinity, which he now entered on.

I subjoin an extract from a letter to me written from Oxford in November, 1815, because it shews not merely his views as to worldly advancement, but also how early he took up, what he seems to

have clung to through life, the necessity of discharging his duties as son and brother in close connection with, and scarcely in subservience to those
of his profession. He was never, indeed, called on
to make absolutely an election between the two;
the circumstances were always such, that at the
most it was never necessary to do more than
change the scene of his professional labours, in
order to satisfy also family claims on his time and
attention :—

" I have a great deal to say in answer to your first letter,
in which you urge the expediency of my doing something
to secure an independency if I should wish to marry. I
assure you that you quite mistake me, if you suppose that
I disavow entirely all feelings of ambition; on the contrary, I have a great deal of it, too much, I think, for my
profession. I am far from censuring ambition in general;
it were idle to blame what most people cannot help feeling : but I think I see clearly, that as a motive to my
clerical exertions, it is either wrong in itself, or liable every
moment to become so, and therefore I am sure I ought to
keep it down as much as possible. With respect to my
making some progress towards a maintenance, I have
thought much and seriously about it. I do not see anything for a country clergyman to do in that way, except
taking pupils : that I cannot do at home, nor should I like
as yet to leave my father's roof; but if Elizabeth's health,
which I hardly dare hope, should go on to improve, I think
something may be done. I may get a curacy, and take
a house, either near home, or if the sea should be recommended to her, near the coast; I have no particular re-

pugnance to the thing, and I certainly feel that there is
a great deal in what you say. I do not know what my
own prospects are ; but let them be what they will, it is
certainly right and just, that if I have opportunity, I should
do something for myself ; but as long as Elizabeth continues so helpless, I should not think I did right in leaving
home on any *speculation.* Perhaps when Tom leaves Oxford, which he will probably do in the course of next year,
we may contrive some gainful grinding scheme between us.
I was very stationary all the summer, but I am a little
afraid that you were right when you warned me against
indolence, in the shape of low spirits, or contentedness.
Yet I seemed to myself almost always busy ; but when I
look back, very little seems done. Making sermons took
up a good part of the time ; I imposed on myself a law of
writing at least one every week ; and then our school at
Fairford required a good deal of visiting, so that altogether
I am not very much *au fait* in Latin and Greek ; but my
nerves are more steeled, and my front more bronzed of
late months, so I shall bully away in the Schools as fear-
lessly as ever."

I do not attach any special importance to the
extract which I am now about to give from a letter,
which has reached me through the kindness of Mr.
Arnott, as a testimony to Keble's work in his new
sphere of duty ; but it is at least a very genuine
and unsuspicious one, and it contains an anecdote
amusing and characteristic. The writer, who now
lives in Hertfordshire, had heard of the photogra-
phical Memoir of Keble, and was permitted to see
the photographs. The first part of his letter ad-

dressed " to the gentleman with whom I had an interview this afternoon," relates to East Leach Church; then he proceeds thus :—

" I well remember Mr. John Keble coming to Eastleach to do duty when the Rev. B. Boyes, through age and infirmity, was unable to do it. A very great change took place in the village ; he commenced a Sunday-school and the Church, and at Bouthrop (*Burthorpe*) was well attended. How long he was at East Leach I don't know, but when I went some years after, the Rev. Cooper lived at the parsonage at Bouthrop, and did duty at both churches.

" Mr. Keble used to ride to and fro from Oxford, and on Sunday used to dine at a cottager's, for which he paid, and used to charge them not to provide anything extra for him ; that was the stipulation. I have frequently defended his character. In one of his visits the person had some potatoes and herring for dinner, and he remarked after some observations, that a herring relish'd potatoes. Then some one raised a report that he should say that herring and potatoes were good enough for any one. I have frequently had to set that matter right. . . . A sturdy Baptist, a shoemaker, used to attend Bouthrop Church, stating, as a reason, he there heard the Gospel. I myself have much to be thankful for on account of Mr. Keble's ministrations." . . . .

In a postscript he adds, " Mr. Keble was outside the church what he professed to be inside it."

In 1816, in the autumn, Keble was again in Devonshire, and for part of his time a visitor at my father's house, where I then was. I have no recollection of any particulars of the visit, and certainly none of that which formed the subject in part of the letter, from which I subjoin an extract. I do not know that melancholy, or despondency of spirits, was remarkable in him at any time, certainly not in later life. It has been observed, I believe, that melancholy is a common attendant on poetic genius, and good reasons may be given why it should be so. Keble, however, would have been the last at this time to think himself entitled to it as a poet; he treats it, it will be seen, as a moral fault, against which it was his duty to struggle. I have no doubt he did so, and it seemed to me through life characteristic of him that he was always ready to accept with a grateful heart and cheery disposition the blessings vouchsafed him, and to be ready to meet his trials with unfeigned resignation. His was no boding spirit, nor did he make sorrows for himself; but no one can doubt that the statement in this letter was a true account of what he really felt, and a very interesting disclosure it is. It must be added that the loss of one sister, and the suffering state of another, weighed naturally upon him, and the more because, as he was now residing at Fairford, the absence of the one, and the trials of the other, were presented to his mind more constantly :—

"FAIRFORD, *Oct.* 9, 1816.
" MY DEAREST FRIEND,

" This is to greet your return to love, law, and London, and to thank you for ten of the happiest days I have spent

F

for many years, yet those not half so happy as they ought
to have been. I do not know whether you find it, but I
hardly ever part from those that I love much and seldom
see, without a strong feeling of dissatisfaction with myself,
and feeling that I have by no means made the most of my
time, and that I have thrown away many precious opportunities for some of the greatest enjoyments of life ; and
this has been more especially the case since our domestic
distresses ; they have furnished me with too good an excuse
for indulging a certain humour calling itself melancholy,
but I am afraid, more truly entitled proud and fantastic,
which I find very often at hand, forbidding me to enjoy
the good things, and pursue the generous studies, which
a kind Providence throws so richly in my way ; then the
hours which I spend alone, owing to the distance of my
Cure from home, are many, and I have indulged myself in
a sad trick of filling them up with melancholy presages. I
have long known this to be very wrong, but I never felt the
mischief of it so much as in the midst of your happy family
party. I felt as if I was saddening everybody, and thousands and thousands of resolutions did I make that I *would*
shake off this selfish remembrance of past and distant cala-
mities, that I *would* enjoy myself wherever I went. I trust
I shall be able, though late, to accomplish these good resolutions, but it will be a long and steady course of self-
discipline alone, grounded upon high motives, and assisted
by the prayers, advice, and example of my relations and
friends, which will enable me, by God's blessing, to do so.
And to whose prayers, advice, and example, shall I have
recourse so unreservedly as to yours. My dear fellow you
cannot think how I depend on you. I have never thought
of you in my blackest dreams, without consolation and
hope ; for you, as you know, my presages were never melancholy ; and now I am endeavouring to brace myself up

to a little more activity and cheerfulness, nothing upon
earth animates me more than the brightening view which
I take of your prospects. May they never be clouded by
calamity, they will not I am sure by wilful melancholy, as
mine have sometimes been. This is not mock-modesty, I
assure you; it is the plain and simple truth, and I tell it
you because it relieves me to tell it, and because I shall
expect you to talk to me sharply, and rouse me from my
selfishness, whenever in my correspondence or conversation
you discover any sign of it. Certainly I have no hereditary
right to it; all my relations, and chiefly she who has suffered
most, are disposed to make the best of things; it is a morbid habit of my own contracting, and may, and shall, by
God's blessing, be cured. It must be so for the comfort of
all whom I ought to make happy, and still more for my
own happiness, for I feel more and more every day that I
cannot be quite happy alone, and certainly if I am a hypo-
chondriac, I cannot be happy in company. And so ends
my sentimentality, and so, like the German Baron in Gold-
smith, jumping over the stools,

" 'Sh' apprens d'être vif.' "

I will add an extract from another letter to me,
dated from Fairford, in June, 1817, in part on the
same subject, but interesting also as shewing his
judgment at that time on Jeremy Taylor and Milton.
He is speaking principally of the prose works of the
latter, but he was not a hearty lover of his poetry
even in later life. He never could separate the work
from the author, and to a great extent they are inseparable, but there is danger of disparaging good
poetry on account of a supposed bad writer of it,

and even more perhaps of overvaluing an indifferent
work, from a liking and high estimation of the author.   I do not think Keble entirely escaped either
danger :—

" FAIRFORD,
"*June* 2, 1817.

"I shall be inexcusable if I do not get into a habit of
looking at the bright side of things, and shake off entirely
a certain perverse pleasure, in which perhaps you may not
conceive how any man should indulge himself, of turning
over in my thoughts a huge heap of blessings, to find one
or two real or fancied evils (which after all are sure to turn
out goods) buried among them.

"Next to the books which it is my duty to study, I
find none so useful in helping me to considerations of this
kind, as your and my friend and favourite Jeremy Taylor.
Though I have been long acquainted with him, I never
read his 'Holy Living and Dying' regularly till this spring,
and I cannot tell you the delight it has given me ; surely
that book is enough to convert any infidel, so gentle in
heart, and so high in mind, so fervent in zeal, and so
charitable in judgment, that I confess I do not know any
other author, except perhaps Hooker, (whose subjects are
so different that they will hardly bear a comparison,) worthy
to be likened to him.   Spenser I think comes nearest his
spirit in all respects.   Milton is like him in richness and
depth, but in morality seems to me as far below him as
pride is below humility.   I have been looking into some
of his prose works lately, of which, I am ashamed to say,
I was and am grossly ignorant ; but what will you think of
me, when I own to you, that I was hardly ever so shocked
and mortified in my life ; perhaps I shall make some
amends by my unbounded admiration of many passages ;

perhaps you will attribute it all to cavalierish and episco-palian prejudices, but certainly I shut the book with an increased veneration for his abilities, and a very much diminished confidence in his opinions, and affection for his general character. But I must try to get rid of the dislike, and lay his faults, if I can, upon times and cir-cumstances, and not upon himself, for it is quite uncom-fortable to think of such a man as from some places I was inclined to do. At any rate it must be a most impressive warning to men of genius, to read, as they often may I think in his Tracts, one sentence written as if an angel had held the pen, and the next, (as it seemed to me,) more like Cobbett's style than any other I know of. One thing rather pleases me, (as every body likes to be con-firmed in his old prejudices,) that the spirit of the loyal party in those times should seem so much more candid and charitable than that of the Puritans. Where will you find in Taylor, or Hammond, or Chillingworth, or Saunder-son, or even in Clarendon, such a gross, puerile, illiberal, (not to say dishonest) invective, as Milton, evidently, *ad captandum vulgus*, has put into his Iconoclastes against K. Charles's Chaplains? How little did he dream that Taylor's name would go down to posterity side by side with his own, and the other three but a little below it.

"But enough of this declamation."

CHAPTER V.

KEBLE, having served as Public Examiner in the
Final Schools, had after a short interval undertaken the duty of Examiner in the Responsions.
This last wearied him a good deal, and when it was
performed, early in 1817, he had quitted Oxford, as
he thought, "no more to return officially." He quitted
it with delight.

"I assure you," he wrote, "it is quite a relief to me to
have got rid of my Oxford employment: I got quite tired
of the Little-Go, and more so of that prince of absurdities
"Determining,"—the very smell of the Schools sickened
me ; and I am now free to give myself up entirely to my
profession—my dear delightful profession—which I grow
fonder of every day; and yet every day proves to me what
a burden it is, and how much remains to be done before I
can be at all fit to bear it. I need your prayers, and trust
I have them ; I do assure you you are never forgotten in
mine."

Thus he wrote in March, 1817. Oxford, however,
retained a strong hold on his affections, and he was
not yet to have done with her.

"Though," says he, in Nov. 1817, "I am so near to
Oxford, and have such regular calls there, in comparison

of yours, I can yet enter completely into your feelings towards the place: every time I go there, I feel like a miser looking over his old chests, and thinking how much money he has wasted in his youth; the last time I was there, in particular, I had the temptation very strong upon me to stay and plunge myself into the walks, libraries, and cathedral services for a year: but conscience prevailed, and I came back to the Cotswolds."

It was to be expected, that if a vacancy should occur in the Tutorships of Oriel, he would be called on to fill it; and although it would be an interruption to the scheme of life which he had laid down for himself, it was pretty clear to all who knew him, that coming in the shape of a duty, which he owed to the College as Fellow, he would scarcely consider himself at liberty to decline it. At the same time, I may observe, the obligations of a Fellow to his College were not, at the period I speak of, so strictly regarded as I hope and believe they now are. Fellowships were often sought after, and obtained by very conscientious men, merely as distinctions or as helps to the pursuit of a profession elsewhere; and indeed, unless a Fellow engaged himself in tuition, or specially in some study, for which residence in the University was desirable, there were not wanting reasons enough in a great many instances, to apply to a Fellow the common saying, that his room was more desirable than his company; there being a great demand for the former, and the residence of an unem-

ployed young Fellow being often of little advantage,
or even detrimental to the discipline of the Undergraduates.

It was with mixed feelings, however, and not without scruple, that Keble gave up even for a time his
home and his curacy; but he was the more easily
reconciled to this, as it was arranged that his brother
should take his place in both, and he also looked
forward to passing his vacations principally at Fairford, and at all times still taking part in the duties
of East Leach. I find it stated in Mr. Moor's carefully prepared memoir, that he was appointed College Tutor in Michaelmas Term, 1818, but I rather
think it was very late in 1817 that he was applied to
to take the office; and that he was engaged in the
regular discharge of its duties in the very beginning
of 1818. On Jan. 29 of that year he writes to me
thus, dating from Fairford, and the letter will shew
in part the feelings which actuated him in accepting
the office.

"I am afraid you think me quite an incorrigible fellow
in the matter of correspondence: but to confess the truth
I purposely kept from writing to you as long as I hung in
doubt about migrating to Oriel; and by the time I had
made up my mind, I was got into a bad habit of not
writing; and I need not tell such a philosopher as you are,
how hard it is to break bad habits. I would not ask your
advice, whether I should turn Tutor or no, because I knew
beforehand what it would be, and I was afraid, like Noel,

of being convinced by your sophistry. However, I might just as well have done it, and then made a merit of yielding; as I have done to my friends here and at Oxford. I thought at first it would be a very uncomfortable thing to me to give up my Cure, and become an Academic again; but I get more and more reconciled to it every day. You consider Tuition as a species of pastoral care, do you not? otherwise it might seem questionable, whether a clergyman ought to leave a cure of souls for it. And yet there are some people at Oxford who seem to imagine that College Tutors have nothing to do with the morale. If I thought so, I would never undertake the office; but I feel some difficulty in settling with myself beforehand, how far one ought to carry one's interference with the general conduct of a pupil; probably it is impossible to draw a precise line."

On March 5, 1818, he dates from Oriel, and writes thus :—

"Here I am, regularly re-matriculated, and to say the truth, in many things as great a freshman as ever; I would not have believed it on anything less than experience, how much difference two or three years' absence from a place can make in one's knowledge of its ways, and fitness to live in it. But now it is no longer a wonder to me that old men should find so much difficulty in accommodating themselves to new fashions, or that they should have so little sympathy with their juniors. In both these, as in many other respects, I seem to have found myself much older than I ought to be. But perhaps I shall find the work slide more easily out of hand, when I am a little more used to it. . . . .

"You would have been delighted to have walked round
the Meadow the other day, and heard old Dyson discussing
sundry subjects for sermons, with which he means to edify
his flock. Now he has taken in earnest to Divinity, what
an admirable divine he will make. I, of course, having just
left my parish, envy every man who is just going to his;
exactly as when I go back to it again (which in process of
time I think not unlikely) I shall envy every College Tutor;
—just as we are now regretting the loss of Davison here,
having taken so little pains to improve his presence among
us. However, I shall not have done with East Leach, in
all probability, till October, and then Tom will take to it;
so that they will rather be gainers than losers on the whole
at our home by the change, for I shall be there half the
year, and Tom the whole of it.

"I live in fear and dread of some row about the first
clock or the second, or some other rebellion of ancient
standing, rising up to push me from my stool of office; in
vengeance for the part I took (by your instigation, mind)
in that 'Great Rebellion,' which, as Arnold says, secured
the liberty of the subject at Corpus. But hitherto they
have all behaved remarkably well. I am going to live in
Davison's rooms, just opposite Tucker and Cornish. I only
hope I shall not be practicalized to death.

"You must not wonder very much, if you see me come
up to London to buy furniture some time within the fortnight. Pray tell your hatter, when next you walk through
St. James'-street or the Haymarket (I forget which) to send
me a new hat, moderately fashionable, *immediately*, as the
old shovel to which Patteson paid so much respect, was
quite spoiled by the snow last Sunday week; and I am
afraid my pupils will mock me, if they see me in a bad hat.
The man has my measure."

Again, on April 30, 1818, he writes from Oriel :—

"I rejoiced to hear of your second pupil—who is he ?
I hope another Pennington : and so the long old dusky
desk is after all of some use. I used to look at it with an
eye of commiseration, as I do sometimes at my Plutarch,
with this inward cogitation : 'Oh that there were any
chance of thy being of use to thy owner.'"

This refers to the present from Lord Grenville,
which I have spoken of before : and when he speaks
of his fears of death by the slow process of practi-
calization, those who are not familiar with Oxford
should be told, that the front of Corpus faces the
side of Oriel in which his windows were, the street
between being so narrow that he was within point
blank range of a pea-shooter or any other equally
manly arm of offence from the young Tutors of
Corpus.

"Well here I am settled after a manner in Oriel, and
very comfortable I find it—not yet quite so comfortable as
my home and curacy: that was not to be expected ; but
I take to the work, and to the solitude, far more kindly
than I expected I should. We have a remarkably good
gentlemanly set, especially of Gentlemen-Commoners. None
of them, except perhaps one or two, are great readers, but
they nearly all learn their lectures, and most of them are
very well behaved. Two of the best come to me as 'peculiar grinder' (I must have a little slang, though Davison's
face should glare on me from the opposite pannel), they are
Baring, one of the banker's sons, and Fremantle, a son of
the Admiral, delightful fellows both ; and what does me

more good than anything, we get up and set to work at six in the morning; so that I can get everything done and get out for exercise at one o'clock."

I have not stinted myself in the extracts from these letters, because I am anxious above all things to present a true and minute picture of Keble in every principal stage of his life; his Tutorship at Oriel was one of these, and his letters are artless and unconscious paintings of himself by himself. I have not therefore withdrawn even so trifling a matter as his playful allusion to what he calls the "Great Rebellion," an almost incredibly childish dispute which we of the *first class* at Corpus had had with our Tutor respecting the time at which we were to commence and end our lecture. Corpus hours were regulated by the Christ Church clocks, of which there were two, the one always five minutes before the other; and I think we earnestly contended and thought that we ought to begin by the later, and end by the earlier, thus effecting *a saving* of ten minutes in the hour. It is amusing now to think of Keble and Arnold engaged in this conflict; we were indeed merely great boys in heart, though nearly all of us about soon to win our places in the Schools as First Class *men*. But though Arnold was pleased to declare that we had secured the liberty of the subject, the love of historic truth compels me to admit, that our excellent Tutor, who preserved his good humour through the whole, as indeed did the rebels also, obtained the substantial victory, enforced the standard imperial measure for the hour, and extracted from us a good sixty minutes' attendance. I have no doubt, however, that in the commencement of his Tutorship, Keble—young, modest, and sensitive as he was, and almost a stranger in his College—really felt some of the alarm which he speaks of. But this must have soon passed off: he never repented of the time which he spent as Tutor at Oriel; he felt, no doubt, that though for the time he was diverted from the main plan of his life, and to a certain extent lost what he valued so dearly, the full care of his curacies and the society of home, he was yet discharging a duty which he owed to his College; and by the view he wisely took of the nature of that duty, as indicated in these extracts, the diversion, temporary only, was never a wide one.

He was cast too on happy times for the performance of it; Oriel then stood incontestably at the head of the University; in spite of some constitutional infirmities, Dr. Copleston was an admirable Head, accurate in his scholarship, correct in his taste, studious in the acquisition of knowledge, impartial in his discipline, and, though last hardly least, liberal in his hospitality. He was, too, at this time in full vigour and activity of mind and spirits, in the commencement of his career as Provost, and entering heartily into all its duties. The rigid impartiality and good sense with which the elections to Fellowships were conducted, had succeeded in forming a very remarkable body in the Common-Room. No undue weight in the competition was given to the place which had been acquired in the Class-paper, a matter on which good fortune in many ways has, too often and yet unavoidably, great influence; but the Electors steadily aimed at finding out the candidate in whom appeared the happiest combination of scholarship, intellect, and character, and the whole Examination was conducted with this object in view.

Tutors eminent for ability and acquirements were a natural consequence of all this; and whatever may be said in disparagement of the wisdom of parents in regard to the education of their children, I believe no attraction to a College is found so invariably strong as a staff of eminent Tutors. All these circumstances made Oriel at this time the favourite College, especially, perhaps, for those who really desired to pursue the studies of the University steadily. The applicants for admission were far beyond the vacancies, so that a selection might be made from among them.

It must not be supposed that when Keble speaks of having everything done, and his going out for exercise at one o'clock, his labours for the day were over so early; he was diligent in preparing his lectures, and complains in some of his letters that he had no time for his own private reading. He attached himself affectionately to his pupils, and many of them attached themselves with equal warmth to him. His manner with them at lecture was perfectly simple and unpretending ; if he was ignorant and unable to answer a question or explain a difficulty, there was no attempt at concealment ; nor could any pupil fail to see that his well-doing was at least as great a cause of happiness to his Tutor as to himself. Misbehaviour or idleness, it was obvious, gave him sincere pain. Intimacies, of course, did not always grow up from the intercourse of the pupil room, or they might afterwards cease from separation and other causes ; but some lifelong friendships were so made ; one in especial may be mentioned in a word even here. Baring, of whom he speaks, (the second Lord Ashburton,) introduced Sir William Heathcote to him, of whom, in a letter to me in 1821, he speaks as "one of his greatest comforts at Oxford." Heathcote read with him at extra hours (as Baring and Fremantle, the present Sir Thomas, had done), and the bond which united them was never loosened. One fruit, as is well known, was his becoming in after life the Vicar of Hursley, a circumstance which, in more ways than are at once apparent, influenced and coloured the remainder of his days.

I had married later in the same year in which he became Tutor, and was very soon plunged into the anxieties of a sick house and the early struggles of a difficult profession. Our personal intercourse, therefore, was very much interrupted, but our intimate correspondence continued. He had been of course privy to my engagement, and watched its progress with affectionate interest ; now my serious anxieties caused his letters to be more frequent, and to overflow not only with affectionate sympathy, but with the most wholesome consolations. I shall be excused for making this short mention of my own affairs in order to introduce one or two of his letters on these subjects during this period of our lives. The manner in which he speaks of me must, of course, be set down to the warmth of his feelings. Once for all I may say this, and I do so most unfeignedly ; I can neither omit such passages where they occur, nor alter them ; they are interwoven with the context, and seem to me necessary not more to the accuracy of the extracts than of the portrait I seek to give of the writer. He dates from Oriel on December 6, 1818 :—

"My dearest Friend,

"Edward gave me an account the other day, which distressed me a good deal, of your Mary's health. I trust Dyson's more favourable report will be confirmed ; comfortable man that he is, he always brings cheerfulness with him. These occasional illnesses were what we reckoned on, and therefore we must not be alarmed unreasonably when they do occur. I know, however, that come what will, you and she are provided with strength and comfort beyond what I can imagine, Only bear up, and you will soon, very soon, have to rejoice. I confess I am rather glad that you have so much business upon your hands, as it will force you to keep up your spirits and take care of yourself, a most essential duty of a good nurse. Do not trouble yourself about writing to me, except you are quite in the humour for it. I shall hear of you many ways.

"After all, these anxieties are the greatest of mercies; they are, I verily believe, the only effectual means to wean us from our idols. We may make good resolutions, and do much towards keeping them, but there is something so subtle and insinuating in earthly happiness (and the more so in proportion to its innocence and purity), that one such pang, or misgiving, as leaves a lasting impression of its insecurity, will do more towards lifting our hearts where they ought to be, than all that most of us could, or at least would, do for ourselves. At least, from my own experience, I can truly say that I *know* I ought to be (I am afraid I am not) more thankful to my Lord and Master for His fatherly chastisements, than for all the comforts and indulgences He has afforded me. My dear Coleridge, do not imagine because I write in this strain that I have heard any very discouraging reports; but I have found so much comfort in some late instances in having thoroughly made up my mind to the worst beforehand, that I cannot help recommending it to my friends. But indeed I trust that your good and happy union will yet continue many, many years. It is happy for you that I have it not in my power to ensure it; for it would certainly be done, whether for the better or the worse; but I *can* pray for it, and that I will with my best endeavours, and so will they, who may better hope to be heard, all your good and kind friends, and the many who are indebted to you beyond what wealth could repay. I have particularly begged that Elizabeth would remember you both.

" My dear friend, may God bless you for Christ's sake, and may I soon see you again all well and happy. I shall write soon I hope something better than this scrawl, which I am almost afraid to send, but you know my meaning. Ever, ever yours, J. K."

It will be well to conclude this personal episode without interruption. I was mercifully spared the great evil, which I seemed to have reason to fear, when he wrote the last letter; and in July, 1819, became a father, and some months of great happiness followed; but in April, 1820, we were deprived of our child. Many who have suffered the same affliction, the loss of their first and only child, will know how bitterly it wounds young parents, and they will best appreciate the letter which he wrote to me on that occasion, and will thank me, I believe, for inserting it here.

" ORIEL COLLEGE,
" *April* 26, 1820.

" MY DEAREST FRIEND,

" It is presumption in me, I know, to pretend to comfort you on so sad an occasion as this, but I *must* tell you truly that my heart bleeds at the thought of your loss, though I know it is absolutely impossible for me to sympathize with you under it; but you have better comforters who do, not only James Coleridge and dear John Patteson, but a more effectual one than either, even Him who 'when He saw a dead man carried out, the only son of his mother, had compassion on her.' He is even now touched with a feel-

ing of the sorrow of heart which has fallen upon you and
your dear wife, whom GOD bless, confirm, and comfort for
His sake. My dear friends, think as little as you can of
yourselves, but think of the blessed infant whom you presented so few days ago before CHRIST in His earthly temple ;
think of her being even now admitted to serve Him in His
heavenly temple day and night, and knowing and praising
Him infinitely better than the greatest saint on earth can
do ; and though it is nothing in comparison of eternity, yet
it is blessing enough to assuage your grief, which, however
good and Christian, must confess itself to be but earthly,
when you consider that your darling is put into her SAVIOUR'S
arms so many years before the time that most of His servants are admitted there, *quite* safe, *quite* good, *quite* happy,
and, I dare to say it, overflowing with love for you beyond
what all your kindness and tenderness could have made
her comprehend in the longest life that parents and children
can expect to enjoy together here. And although David
said his child could not return to him, yet since we are
taught that there is a sympathy between Paradise and Earth,
at least between the saints in one and the saints in the
other, what if Christian parents, by holy living, should be
supposed to have this comfort among others, that their lost
children still watch over them, or in some way or other
know of their well-doing? The thought is not, I am persuaded, unscriptural, but thank GOD you have no need of
it. 'For if we believe that JESUS died and rose again,
even so them also which sleep in JESUS will GOD bring
with Him.' You need not look farther for comfort than
those words. May He in whom alone we can know comfort, make them and all other consolations which His Providence has in store for you, so truly comfortable to you,
that you shall be able to look backward even to this sad

time with humble thankfulness to Him for helping you to suffer as Christians; so prays from the bottom of his heart,

"Your affectionate friend,

"J. KEBLE.

"If it will be any comfort to you at all for me to come up for a day or two I shall be thankful, and can do it without inconvenience.

"Tell dear Patteson I longed to write to him, but was afraid of distressing him, not knowing till I came back here how graciously he is upholden. GOD bless him and you, through our LORD JESUS CHRIST."

The message in the postscript to my dear friend John Patteson, between whom and Keble a friendship had sprung up, had reference to the far heavier affliction, which but a little before had befallen him, in the loss of his wife.

To return from this personal digression, which has carried me out of the order of events. He was much disturbed in the summer of 1819 in the comfortable discharge of his duties as Tutor, by the alarming illness of his brother, on whom, as I have said, he had reckoned to supply his place in the family circle and in his parish. Never were two brothers more attached to each other. Of the younger, now the only survivor of that generation, I do not feel at liberty to say more than that from his great modesty and retiringness, and from his having been over-shadowed, as it were, by his brother's great reputation, the world knows much less of him than in justice it ought to have done. In May, 1819, a severe and neglected cold appeared to have settled on his lungs. Dr. Bourne, of Oxford, who was the family physician, was not very encouraging, and the symptoms did not for some time abate under treatment. Writing to Dyson about him, Keble mentions that there had been a negotiation on foot for his becoming one of the Tutors of Corpus, which of course was interrupted by this illness. He says,—

" I was afraid this might have annoyed him and pressed on his spirits, but I am glad to find it does not. He is perfectly calm and placid, wrapped up in the same thoughts which I verily believe have long taken up his whole mind, for I know he does not expect to recover. I know you will give us your prayers, my dear fellow."

It was an addition to Keble's personal trial that he could only see his brother from week to week, as he went down to take his duty for him. But he and the family were mercifully spared the great affliction of losing him. In June he began to mend, and the Long Vacation coming on, Keble was able to be with him, and regularly supply his place in his church. All this he communicated of course to me, and I must find room for his grateful and wise reflections on the event. Writing on June 15, 1819, from Oriel, he says,—

" His recovery, amendment I should say (for though his cough is much abated and all the symptoms far milder, the

complaint does not seem yet entirely removed), came upon
me, and I believe upon most of our family, almost like
a resurrection.   Without saying so to one another, I fancy
we had almost all of us made up our minds to the parting ;
and now how to be thankful enough for so great a mercy
as his being spared to us I know not.   The near prospect
of so great a loss (humanly speaking) brought home to me
a lesson which I have before now preached to you, and
shewed me how little used I was to practise it myself—
I mean the duty of preparing oneself, by constant meditation, for all the worst privations that can befall one in this
world.   My dear friend, I was and am quite ashamed to
find how utterly wanting I was at heart in what I have
been so long teaching others, and under special engagements to practise myself.   However, the example of all
at home, and particularly that of Tom himself, who took
everything with the most perfect calmness, did me a good
deal of good, and I wish and pray every day that all this
may not be lost upon me.   It certainly is, when we con
sider it calmly, and in any other case but our own,—it cer
tainly is no more than plain reason and common sense for
any one, who believes in our gracious Master and His promises, to throw his whole care, both for himself and those
dearest to him, *wholly* and entirely upon Him.   The way
of putting the thought which seemed to relieve me most
when my fears were at worst, and I was most tempted to
set my heart upon Tom's recovery, was this :—If I were
thoroughly sure of his being restored to health after a certain time, I should be most content and thankful ; now in
fact I am morally sure of his being restored to infinitely
more than earthly health, though I do not exactly know
the time.   I dwelt upon this thought, and it seemed so
exactly what I wanted, that I have just put it down for the

chance of its suggesting something to you ; though I well know, my dear friend, that your griefs are beyond the skill of any worldly comforter, yet I will say to you, 'Be of good comfort ;' for I feel that I have a right to do it. The greatness of your affliction, borne as you are endeavouring to bear it, is a sure pledge and proof that you are under the immediate hand of Him into whose hands it is good to fall because His mercies are great. You may apply to yourself, or if you are afraid of that, you may at least apply to the dear sufferer for whom you are so anxious, all those great and glorious promises which the Scripture holds out to martyrs and confessors, and to them whose souls are in the immediate and special keeping of the Redeemer. What would one not give to be quite sure of this? and I verily believe there is nothing which comes so near to assuring us of it in this life as very great affliction borne Christianly for His sake. When one has such a source of comfort as this, it is superfluous, at least it would be but for our frailty, to talk of earthly friends ; but as it is, the prayers and good wishes of so many servants of GOD as I firmly believe inter-cede for you and your's continually, that this rod may either be speedily removed, or felt as what it is doubtless meant to be, a blessing ; here is another source of consola-tion which may now and then, I trust, innocently and effec-tually be used to repress that feeling of desolation which, in spite of piety and Christian knowledge, will sometimes, I know too well, intrude itself. But you have your comforts in yourself, and I am not sure whether I have said any-thing to the purpose. Would that my prayers for you could make up for the deficiency in what I say and write to you."

In July it was still doubtful whether the Corpus

scheme for his brother could now be carried into effect, but they were in hopes it might, as indeed it was ; and after discussing this, he ends a letter to me, of July 7, 1819, thus characteristically :—

"As for myself, worthy Sir, I get on much as I used to do, always having a great load of things to do, and hardly ever finishing any thing.   Tom's plans of tuition have set us upon reading together rather more than we used to do, which I find a great comfort and, I believe, advantage; one thing is that, in reading with another, one cannot stand so long poring over a passage, doubting whether you understand it or no : or perhaps but half thinking of it, a mode of wasting time of which I profess myself very guilty.   We are reading over the Ethics together, and I propose going on afterwards to compare the Stagyrite with Plato, Butler, Paley, Smith, and others who have written more or less systematically on the subject.   I wish also to be not unmindful of your recommendation to acquaint myself better with Greek criticism, but hardly know how to set about it. I am reading Sophocles again, and marking everything that strikes me, but I do not feel any improvement.   I am afraid I shall always be σφόδρα Τεύτων in these matters.   Luckily we have got one man in Oriel that cries 'whew' at a false quantity, i.e. Tyler.   I am babbling on, and not telling you what I daresay you have hardly heard yet, that George Cornish was married on Saturday.   Tucker and I took him as far as Lichfield on his way into Derbyshire, in doing which we went over *our old* Warwickshire tour; and I was very melancholy at the thought of what an ass I then made of myself; so to keep up my spirits I made myself twice as great an ass.   All here, Tom especially, desire most loving congratulations.   Ever most affectionately yours, J. K."

His letters remind me that in 1819 I was engaged in the prosecution of some of those libels, which, by a stimulating mixture of profaneness and sedition with some humour and ability, obtained great circulation at that period, and I must have consulted him as to topics for the opening which I expected to devolve on me; the trials were to be at the Quarter Sessions: a part of his advice is so full of good sense and so characteristic, that I insert it here: he dates from Fairford, Oct. 12, 1819:—

"Of one thing, were I in your place, I should be particularly careful, i.e. how I indulged myself too far in panegyrics on things as they are; at least I feel that were I on a jury, I should be much more likely to be influenced by the representations of a man who seemed to see and deplore the too palpable occasion lent by the conduct of too many Christians and loyalists to such libels as these, than I should by the flaming panegyrics which many on the right side (e.g. the 'Courier,' and sometimes the 'British Critic') are continually trumpeting forth. To say the truth, though in a political light these agitators are perhaps as bad as anything can well be, I do not think them half so *dangerous* enemies to religion, i.e. to the souls of men, as wicked, worldly-minded Christians are."

He passed his Christmas Vacation, that of 1819 —1820, as usual at Fairford, and I have seen many letters which passed between him and the family of the Curate of Fladbury, Mr. Pruen, with whom he had become intimate in the course of his visits to his

Godfather the Rector. These shew with what heartiness he joined in the social meetings of the season, kept up as it should seem very genially in the neighbourhood. As a younger man, and before he was in Holy Orders, no one enjoyed a dance more than he; nor did he think it now at all unbecoming to take his part in those which in truth were of the simplest kind, and scarcely more than family reunions. His religion, then and to the end, was cheerful, as was his natural temperament; and it may be collected from his letters at this period of his life what a favourite he was with young and old, how much his visits were courted, and his friendship valued. I mention the Pruen family as an instance; it consisted of the father and mother, a governess as I collect, and a numerous family, principally girls of different ages, but all apparently at the time I speak of in the school-room, or, as to one or two, just issuing from it. Many letters passed between him and them, full of merriment and fun, queer riddles, familiar poetry, with sometimes graver matters insinuated; I do not publish them, and yet they exhibit in a lively way that side of his character, well known indeed to those who were intimate with him, but of which those who only knew him at a distance, or by his writings, or later in life, can scarcely be aware. Somehow, as life advanced on both sides, and graver interests absorbed him, the intercourse between him and the members of this family appears to have ceased, but

not the kindly feeling. It was when he was at Bournemouth, in the last illness of himself and Mrs. Keble,
that one of his former young friends, Margaret Pruen,
who had married and I believe become a widow,
wrote to him from Torquay; I do not know the
subject of her letter, it was probably to inquire
about his health, and to remind him of old times
and old feelings; I cannot forbear to print the answer which he wrote: the writing is in a very feeble
hand, a sad contrast to the firm and distinct character of the letters from which I have hitherto been
quoting: it may seem a sad, yet it is a very soothing
close to the correspondence :—

"BOURNEMOUTH,
Jan. 17, 1866.

"MY DEAR MARGARET,

"For why should I not speak as in the old times which
you so kindly remember? you put me to shame by your
kind, long letter, long, I mean, in comparison of what I can
write; and by your affectionate remembrance of one who
has somehow been drawn so far away from you all. It is
too good of you, but to me refreshing, to have such a report
of your dear sister and the rest who are left you. I thank
you for it; and all of you, in sight and out of sight, I thank,
for your constant kindness with all my heart, and trust to
be remembered by you at this time, especially *then* when we
all wish most to be remembered. For my dear wife's long
trial of illness seems now to be approaching its end; we came
here in October, being obliged to go somewhere, and she
feeling herself unequal to the journey further west, and she
certainly gains no strength: but thanks be to God, as far
as health allows, she is bright and cheerful as ever, and

takes all her old interest in things. I send her kind love with my own. I cannot write more at present; except that I am very sorry to hear of Henry's painful complaint, and not a little ashamed to think of my Godson, and how I have neglected him all this time. I yet hope we may have some communication, although my chance of it, humanly speaking, is fast lessening: however, assure him of my constant remembrance of him. What you say of your dear Anne's gentleness, and loving simple ways, brings her back to me as I could wish, and so does the place about Fladbury churchyard.

"God grant us all, how unworthy soever some of us may now feel ourselves, a happy meeting in the end!

"I am always, my dear friend,

"Affectionately yours,

"J. KEBLE."

"To Mrs. Billamore,
"6, Scarborough-terrace, Torquay.

It was at the Oxford Commemoration of 1820 that Southey revisited the University; he had at that time effectively overcome the prejudices which political differences, and the clever hostility, miscalled criticism, of the "Edinburgh Review," and it must be confessed some of his own peculiarities, had raised against his literary reputation. His merits as a poet, historian, and essayist, were now fairly appreciated, and the many, who approached him at all nearly, were enthusiastic in the admiration of the purity of his character, and the generous geniality of his nature. I think I have mentioned elsewhere that I had been the means of making him known as a writer to Keble in the early days of our friendship. I had now the good fortune of being able to make them personally known to each other; Southey was much pleased with Keble: writing to me a few days after upon another matter which interested us all three very deeply, he says shortly: "All that Keble says upon the subject is full of kindness and right feeling, and would make me think more highly of the writer than I did before, if that had been easy." Keble wrote of him, to me and to Dyson, at greater length; his remarks in both are striking, and I will subjoin them here:—

"MY DEAR JOHN COLERIDGE,

"Many thanks to you for this new and great kindness of making me acquainted with Southey: for I owe it entirely to you. He is indeed a noble and delightful character, and I hope to be the better all my life for what I have seen of him and heard from him. Luckily for me (though I am afraid rather irksomely for him) he has hardly any acquaintance resident in Oxford, having completely out-lived all his old contemporaries, so that I had a good deal of him to myself: and that was indeed delightful. Whatever his notions *may have been*, and however incautiously he may have sometimes expressed himself, I am satisfied his notions are now as nearly correct, meaning by 'correct,' agreeable to my own, both in religion and politics, as almost any of *theirs* whom one most loves and trusts in. The only thing which seems to me wrong in them, is a disposition which I sometimes fancy I observe in him, and which is common to him with three-fourths of the orthodox men in the kingdom, to confound the two together: I mean, to deal politically with the Church and religion. His reception in the Theatre was most flattering : not one of all the party, except Lord Hill, received anything like the same share of applause. In the evening he had an invitation from the College to dine in Balliol Hall. Reginald Heber, Miller, and Milman were there, and Noel Ellison was delightful : I have never seen four such men together in my life before. Copleston wanted him to dine with him on Thursday, but he was obliged to leave us, to my sorrow, and left a most excellent name behind him, for his kind and unassuming manners, with every one who had been in his company for five minutes."

Writing to Dyson, he says :—

" I had the great delight this last Commemoration of being introduced to the two public characters, whom of all others I should rather wish to know, Southey and Reginald Heber. I liked both exceedingly, but Heber decidedly best : he is so remarkably unaffected in his manner ; I watched him all the time they were performing ' Palestine' in the Theatre, and he did not attitudinize in the least, nor seem conscious of being the chief character in the room ; and then his style of conversation is so particularly kind and hearty. Southey has a good deal of the same excellencies ; but he gives you the idea of a man forbearing to display himself, Heber of one into whose head no such thing ever entered. Nevertheless Southey quite made good his ground in my favour, more completely a good deal than I had expected. He is now an orthodox man, and the faults of his views in ecclesiastical matters are, as far as I could judge from what he said, the faults into which such persons are most apt to fall—making religion too much a matter of politics—and the like."

Personal comparisons are too often made in ignorance or forgetfulness of the differing circumstances
under which individuals present themselves for consideration, and I cannot but think that for some such
reasons my dear friend, in this, did a little injustice
to Robert Southey. Heber was then comparatively
a young man, quite at home in Oxford, an Oxonian of
the day, in a position perfectly secure, in a place where
he was most justly and universally popular, in the scene
of all his successes and triumphs, surrounded by the
friends of his own day—the only novel circumstance of
the hour was, that he was present when his own poem
was performed as an Oratorio, in the place where he
but a few years before had recited it as a Prize : it
would be undervaluing so good and great a man to
think there was anything intoxicating in all this, anything to disturb the calmness of a really modest man.
Southey was a much older man, an Oxonian of a day
long past, who had had to win his position in the
world, fighting his way step by step against opposition fair and unfair, through poverty and hardship,
in spite of ridicule, obloquy, slander, and neglect—
slowly he had gained a great one : and where was he
when Keble met him ? at Oxford, which had been
no scene of success or credit to him as a student,
which he had left without a degree in youth, where
he found no contemporary friend, where he was now
for the first time returning in mature age, to receive
all the honour it could bestow—at the suggestion it

should seem of the very party, which had never
cheered him in his struggles, nor been over forward to greet him in his success. Did not these
circumstances tend to provoke somewhat of self-
assertion ? did they not moreover irresistibly suggest recollections and thoughts calculated to turn
his thoughts inwards, and to raise somewhat disturbing feelings ? When I asked myself this question,
I naturally turned to his letters ; there will be found
in the fifth volume of his son's Memoirs of him, two
letters, one a playful account of the whole visit written
to his three daughters, the other, which follows immediately, to Neville White ; they are at pages 38 and 41.
There will be seen, by the last, a little of what was
passing in his mind at the time. I know that the first,
perhaps in general the abiding and not unnatural, impression as to Southey was and is, that he was a vain
man ; like the great Roman Orator and Philosopher,
he was a man of great ability, and remarkable industry, and he knew it ; he knew what he could have
done, if he had been blessed with more independent
means, and he knew the value of what he had actually done ; and it is neither wonderful nor unpardonable, if such a man, when critics and wits have been
for years sneering at him, and thwarting his efforts,
should acquire somewhat of a habit of thinking and
saying what, as coming from himself, seem great
things of those efforts and their results. One thing
let me observe, a more generous soul never existed ;

generous of his money when he had it, generous always of his time which was to him money, yet who ever heard him breathe a syllable of self-applause on this?

I must add the short passage, which I spoke of, in the letter to Neville White, and hope to be forgiven for a digression, extorted from me by a sense of justice, not less than by sincere gratitude for much and most valuable kindness shewn to myself when I needed it much.

"My visit to Oxford brought with it feelings of the most opposite kind. After the exhibition in the Theatre, and the collation in Brasenose Hall given by the Vice-Chancellor, I went alone into Christ Church walks, where I had not been for six and twenty years. Of the friends with whom I used to walk there, many (and among them some of the dearest) were in their graves. I was then inexperienced, headstrong, and as full of errors as of youth and hope and ardour. Through the mercy of God, I have retained the whole better part of my nature, and as for the lapse of years, that can never be a mournful consideration to one who hopes to be ready for a better world, whenever his hour may come. God bless you. R. S."

Through life a tour in the country was among Keble's most pleasurable indulgences, and his position at Oriel now making him more at ease in his circumstances, he seems usually to have devoted a part of the Long Vacation to a ramble, often alone, and often making a circuit among his old Oxford intimates retired into the country. Thus I find him in

Worcestershire, and at Lichfield in 1819, in the summer. My manuscript copy of the exquisite stanzas
"on a monument in Lichfield Cathedral" is dated
July 22, 1819. No one who has read them can
doubt that they were suggested by a sight of the
monument, and probably commenced on the spot.
My copy I may say has but a few verbal differences from the copy which is printed in "Church
Poetry," p. 301, but it wants one stanza, so necessary
almost to the completeness of the Poem, that I suppose I must have omitted it through carelessness.
In return, mine has four stanzas at the close, separated by a few crosses, and with a very slight variation in the metre; these are addressed to himself.
The variation is produced by lengthening the fourth
line of each stanza, and is not a very happy one; and
judgment was shewn in printing the poem without
them; at the same time, they are characteristic of the
man, and represent, I have no doubt accurately, the
humble application to himself, which he would make
on such an object before him, and such a train of
thought as he had indulged in. It was no less characteristic to keep from the public this application.

In September, 1820, he made a longer tour, and
visited Ellison at his living of Whalton in North-
umberland, and Davison at his of Washington in the
county of Durham; these places he made centres
for riding excursions to the objects of interest in the
neighbourhood, among them not forgetting Stan-

hope, the residence for many years of Bishop Butler. Then coming south, he visited Dyson at Nunburnholme. His journey homeward he shall tell himself, as he described it in a letter to Dyson from Fairford, of September 11, 1820.

"Perhaps you will like to have some account of my journey. I got safe home—that you know from the date of this—and you know from Penrose that I staid at Fledborough by the way—but you do not know that I waited at Hayton half an hour for the Coach; you do not know that I travelled to York holding a drunken sailor by the button, lest he should tumble off; and you cannot possibly have the least idea of my delight, when I found myself in the Minster at sunset that most gorgeous evening; no, your low mind, debased by immoderate indulgence in Pocklington biscuits and the vulgar smell of sweet-peas, cannot enter into pleasures of so high a kind. In good earnest I reckoned myself particularly fortunate in my view of the Minster: I spent two or three hours there, and could hardly find anything to damp my enjoyment. My coffee house companion was Sir Thomas Bernard's 'Comforts of Old Age,' a very proper book for persons of a certain time of life, and very useful to me; as, though there were abundance of persons in the room, none of them seemed disposed to take much notice of me, and I was too shy (you know my usual amiable diffidence) to make the first advances. The night journey was an interchange of sleeping and grumbling, with a little sickliness now and then, by way of variety, on the part of some of my fellow-travelleresses. So you may believe that I was not sorry when it was light, and I could see the pleasant country to the north of Doncaster, and the town of Doncaster

itself, at the elegance of which I was quite surprised. But
it was still pleasanter to enter upon the rich vale of Trent;
and pleasantest of all to discern Penrose's face, half-grin-
ning, half-business-like, waiting for me in a gig, at the
place and time appointed. Right glad was I to find myself snug under another parsonage roof, and to become
acquainted with his family, who seem as well suited to
their situation, and it to them, as any group I ever beheld.
I cannot conceive how Arnold could have the heart to
disturb such a family party by taking one away. I find
by a letter which I received yesterday from Penrose, that
he has been paying you a flying visit. For this I take
some credit to myself, having taken some pains to assure
him how glad you would be to have him there. He main-
tains that yours is a more retired place than Fledborough:
but this cannot be, because you know there is a road
through Nunburnholme to Warter; whereas you have heard
of the finger-post 'to Fledborough and no farther.' Not
but that I contrived to get farther; for under Penrose's
able steerage I made my way to Lincoln, criticised the
in-, and admired the out-side of the Cathedral as busily
as I could for two hours. I really think, on the whole
I prefer the latter to that at York; but the inside architecture will not bear a comparison; if indeed one can judge
fairly of it, now it is so disfigured by yellow wash, and plain
glass where painted was evidently intended. I went up to
the top of the lantern tower, and was particularly pleased
with the view of the city, with its profusion of ruins scattered about it. I like the country for a reason more sen-
timental than picturesque—namely, that I think it like my
own. Having enjoyed myself for exactly a week, I set out
on the Friday morning by the mail for London, and got
into the Great City just in time to mount a Stroud coach,

which set me down at papa's door about six in the after-noon of Saturday."

In July, 1822, he made a tour of visits, which took in the Millers at Bockleton in Worcestershire, and his old friend, a former curate of Fairford, Mr. Richards, then residing in the neighbourhood of Aberystwith. Writing to Cornish from Malvern, on July 8, which he said he had reached, being on a voyage of dis-covery, i.e. searching out the nearest way from Fair-ford to Bockleton, he continues thus :—

" MALVERN,
"*July* 8, 1822.

" I wish you had been with me on the hill just now, and then I should not have gone to sleep in a sort of cave, which they have cut out, looking all over Herefordshire, with a telescope in my hand, reading Spenser. Do you know the ' Shepherd's Calendar ?' I think you did not use to know it, for you did not use to quote it, which you cer-tainly would. What a delightful feel it is to sit under the shelter of one of the rocks here, and hear the wind sweep-ing with that peculiar kind of strong moaning sigh, which it practises on the bent grass. I daresay you have marked it 100 times; but I was never so much struck with it as this evening. And what an air of sanctity the church gives to the place. I pick out spots (luckily the trees and houses are so grouped that there 'are a good many) where one quite loses every thing smart and townish, and then I quite enjoy it ; more I think now than when I was here before. I was not alone, but with Rickards, who was bent on visit-ing rather than scenery, and in love besides ; and when

a man is in love, you know he is a terrible touring companion to all the world, but one."

To G. J. C.

I insert this extract not merely for the amusing contrast which it presents between the Malvern of 1822,
and the Malvern of 1867, but for the passage about
the bent grass, which is reproduced in the beautiful
verses on the Twentieth Sunday after Trinity, which
Robertson of Brighton liked the best of all in "The
Christian Year" :—

> ". . . . The fitful sweep
> Of winds across the steep,
> Through wither'd bents—romantic note and clear,
> Meet for a hermit's ear."

In these years there is no doubt that he was
gradually composing the work, and these solitary
tours (for he seems most often to have wandered alone,
leaving his brother to take his place at home) were
certainly favourable to such occupation.   The dates
of such poems of "The Christian Year" as I have in
my manuscript books, are in 1819, and in 1822.

In 1821 Keble again accepted the office of Examining Master, and continued to serve until the
Easter of 1823 inclusive; but he was sighing for
a return to his home and curacy.

"We here at Oxford," says he in a letter in the spring of
1823, "go on much as usual, criticizing sermons, eating

dinners, and laughing at Buckland and Shuttleworth. I feel
as if I should be very glad to get away to some country
curacy, and yet I distrust my own powers of making good
company from myself too ; but really a man ought to be
able to do so, and one should hope one might never be
quite too old to learn that lesson."

Partly I suppose from this feeling he appears to
have entertained a notion about this time of accepting a very small living in the gift of the College, Coleby in Lincolnshire. This, however, came to
nothing, and the living was ultimately bestowed on
his and my friend Trevenen Penrose, who passed the
remainder of his life there, protracted to a good old
age, in the most exemplary discharge of his duty.

The Tutorship, however, he resigned at the end
of Hilary Term in that year, and the death of his
mother in May brought his residence in College
to a close also ; he had gone down to Fairford on
Saturday in each week as usual, and each time found
her decline more decided. On Saturday, May 10, on
his arrival he found her so much worse, that it was
clear her end was approaching, and she died very
early on Sunday morning.

"I found," says he, writing to me on the 13th, "they
were expecting her release every moment : and at 4 o'clock
on Sunday morning I may literally say she fell asleep, for
never did I see such perfect, such dovelike calmness—not
that I was by her at the time. Mary Anne was the only

one of us who had that happiness, for she had had, from extreme weakness, two or three nervous or hysterical spasms in the course of the preceding day, and it was judged better for us to keep at a distance unless she asked for us. I lay down in my clothes thinking she might do so, but she did not; so the last time I spoke to her was last Wednesday. But I thought I never saw anything so like an angel as that dear Mary Anne when she waked me on Sunday morning to tell me that mamma was just gone so sweetly, with hardly a sigh. One is apt to think too much of such things, which are but trifles after all, in comparison of the change to which they lead; but, upon earth, I can hardly conceive a more speaking call for thankfulness than for one's dearest relations to be allowed to glide in such a way, without pain, disturbance, or wandering of mind, just out of sight into Paradise. You will pray for us, my dear friend, and dear Mrs. Coleridge will, too, that we may be something like thankful enough for it: duly thankful we never can be. . . . As they were all so well at Fairford, it was judged best for me to come back and get through my business here."

Writing from Oriel at the same time to Dyson, he says:—

" I meet with so much kindness here, and feel so certain, thank God, of their being comfortable at home, that it is not at all irksome to me, at least not painfully so, as I should have fancied it beforehand if anyone had told me. As far as I can judge, the only real bitterness in parting from dear friends is having to recollect how much one has failed in one's duty to them; but it will not do to talk of that."

I have made these extracts because they are at once characteristic and instructive. Mrs. Keble was the object of the most tender affection to every member of the family, and to no one of it more so than to her son; yet he not only writes thus of his father, sister, and brother, but was himself able to leave home as usual on Monday morning, and go through his work in the Schools, returning only on Saturday to the funeral. The truth is that his faith, and I have no doubt their's, was sincere and practical; I never could find in him, when he lost the dearest objects on earth, any sign of bittter sorrow as without hope; he had no dread of death for the good, he perfectly realized the blessedness of the change for them, and he looked forward cheerfully and humbly to a re-union. It was, too, a part of his practical belief that even now the separation was not absolute; it was not merely in poetry that he expressed, more than once, this cheering thought. It appears again and again in his letters at different periods of his life. Writing of a deceased sister he says,—

> "For well I guess, and oft my spright
>   Holds tearful triumph in the dream,
>   That when Religion's holy light
>   Guides me with pure and placid gleam;—
>
> "When I do good, and think aright,
>   At peace with man, resigned to God,
>   Thou look'st on me with eye of light,
>   Tasting new joy in joy's abode.

> " But in my dark and evil hour,
>   When wan despair mine eyelids seals,
>   When worldly passions round me lower,
>   And all the man corruption feels ;
>
> " Thou turnest not thine eyes below,
>   Or clouds of glory beam between,
>   Lest earthly pangs of fear or woe
>   Upon an angel's brow be seen."

It was thus he answered the difficulty which troubles so many in believing that departed saints retain a perception of the goodness and happiness of those whom they have left behind. I do not mean, of course, that he had shaped this out to his own mind as a certain truth ; but I have no doubt that he believed, so as practically to draw consolation from it under bereavement, that the blessed in the intermediate state retained some knowledge of things on earth, some interest in those who survived ; believing this, he of course believed that Our Father would have His way, unknown to us, perhaps inconceivable by us, of so regulating that knowledge, that though it might, on the one hand, increase, it should never be allowed, on the other, to abate their blessedness ; and what that way might be, he would not even shadow out to himself but dimly, and as it were suggestively or alternately. Speaking in poetry on such a subject he would feel under as much restraint substantially as if he were writing in prose. But I feel sure that he thought the belief warranted and not unscriptural, used it for himself as consolatory, and did not scruple to recommend it to others. The exquisite poem in the *Lyra Innocentium*, entitled " Bereavement,—Children's Troubles, 8," expounds it very touchingly.

Thus ended his permanent and official residence at Oxford.

CHAPTER VI.

RETURN TO FAIRFORD, 1823.—SOUTHROP.—PUPILS.
—HURRELL FROUDE.—"CHRISTIAN YEAR."

KEBLE had now been one of the Tutors of his College for nearly five years, and had a second time served the office of Public Examiner, as well as that of Master of the Schools once, he might therefore feel justified in ceasing to be a Resident Fellow, returning to his father and two surviving sisters, and resuming the charge of his two little Curacies. His father's health and strength were still remarkable for his great age, but both were liable to sudden changes, and his spirits and sense of duty led him frequently to undertake more personal labour at Coln than was prudent for him. The health, too, of his sisters was a source of very frequent solicitude to him ; his letters again and again testify to this. The pleasure of returning to his home was greatly augmented by its combining also the return to a more regular discharge of his professional duties. The amount of these he now added to by accepting the Curacy of Southrop, a small parish very near to Eastleach and Burthorpe, as well as to Fairford. This accumulation of cures, indeed the whole arrangement in regard to them between the two brothers, seems to require some explanation, to

those especially who are familiar only with the
more orderly practice of the present day; and this
is afforded by the circumstances; their small size
and nearness to each other, their slender population,
their miserably poor endowments, and their want of
attractiveness generally to clergymen. The entire
population of the three did not exceed a thousand.
Eastleach and Burthorpe churches were within a
stone's throw of each other, there was no residence
except at Southrop. The undertaking the care of
them was indeed a labour of love, the whole receipts
exceeded very little £100 a-year, and I have no
doubt fell short considerably of what was expended
upon them. The district indeed, if I may judge
from these cures, and Coln St. Aldwyn's, was one of
shamefully scanty endowments; the value of that
being only £60 a-year. These circumstances seem
to have interested the two brothers, who took to
them as charges providentially thrown in their way
by their neighbourhood to Fairford; and their father
was ready at all times, in their necessary absences,
to provide for the calls which might casually arise.

Keble had now bid adieu to public tuition; his
pupils at Oriel had testified to their sense of his
services by a handsome present of plate, inscribed
JOHANNI KEBLE DISCIPULORUM ORIELENSIUM PIE-
TAS MDCCCXXIII.; and I observe in passing as characteristic of the degree to which he shrunk from
all exhibition, that intimate as I was with him, I

not only never saw this plate, but I was not even
aware of the fact of its having been given to him,
until I found it stated in the Memoir to which I
have more than once before expressed my obligations.   I know not whether such testimonials are
now common, but that age was not so demonstrative of affection or gratitude in silver and gold as
the present, and at that time, especially after a service of so few years, such a gift was very unusual.
It seems to shew how Keble had addressed himself
successfully to the hearts as well as the intellects of
his pupils.   It was a thing to be proud of ; he would
be sure to think it was undeserved, and therefore
perhaps he would say little about it to his friends.

But it would not the less move his affections,
and it might be an inducement the more to accept
the Curacy of Southrop, where was a good roomy
house.   To this village several of his pupils followed
him occasionally for long visits ; some received into
the house, some finding lodgings near : among these
I may name Robert Wilberforce, Isaac Williams,
Hurrell Froude.   They were visitors more properly
than pupils ; at least he would accept no remunera-
tion from them, nor would he allow them to interfere with the discharge of his parochial duties.   He
called himself an idle lounging man, and he had at
all times a desultory, and seemingly irregular way
of working ; but when these occupations are considered, and also how effectually they were disposed

of, there can be no doubt that his time was well
filled up.

Of Hurrell Froude Dr. Newman has written, " He
was a pupil of Keble's, formed by him, and in turn
re-acting upon him." This sentence is followed by
a short and striking account of this extraordinary
man, to which it would be unwise in me to attempt
any addition, except as it may bear on the object
of this memoir. I knew him from a child, and I
trace in the somewhat singular composition of his
character what he inherited both from his father
and his highly gifted mother ; his father, whom
Keble after his first visit to Dartington Parsonage
playfully described to me as "very amiable, but
provokingly intelligent, one quite uncomfortable to
think of, making one ashamed of going gawking as
one is wont to do about the world, without understanding anything one sees ;" his mother very beautiful in person, and delicate in constitution, with
a highly expressive countenance, and gifted in intellect with the genius and imagination which his
father failed in. Like the one he was clever, knowing, quick, and handy ; like the other he was sensitive, intellectual, imaginative. He came to Keble
full of respect for his character ; he was naturally
soon won by his affectionateness and simplicity,
and in turn he was just the young man in whom
Keble would at once take an interest and delight
as a pupil ; and so in fact it was. I find him

again and again in Keble's letters spoken of in the
most loving language, yet often not without some
degree of anxiety as to his future course; he saw
the elements of danger in him, how liable he might
be to take a wrong course, or be misunderstood even
when taking a right one; yet his hopes largely prevailed; and especially I remember his rejoicing at
his being elected Fellow of Oriel, thinking that the
new society and associations, with the responsibilities
of college employment, would tend to keep him safe.
That Keble acted on him (I would rather use that
term, than "formed,") is certain, and even when,
in the later years of his short life, symptoms of
coming differences in opinion may be traced in his
letters, there is no abatement of personal love and
reverence, nor indeed, in a certain sense, of his feeling the weight of Keble's influence; and though I
gather from these that there was more entire agreement with Dr. Newman as to action, yet it seems to
me that there still remained a closer intimacy and
more filial feeling with regard to Keble. I may be
mistaken in this; it is a conclusion I have come to
from reading the letters in that strangely interesting
book, "The Remains," and inferring from them the
nature of Keble's letters to him, which I very much
regret that I have not been able to procure a sight of.

I have not altered this passage, but since the
volume was printed and published, a number of
these letters have been discovered, (it would seem

by a strange accident,) and placed at my disposal by Mr. William Froude. They fully justify my anticipations as to their value and interest; and so far as I now can, I shall avail myself of his kind permission.

That Hurrell Froude "re-acted on Keble" is true also, I have no doubt, in a certain sense; it could scarcely be otherwise, where there was so much ability and affectionate playfulness, with so much originality on one side, so much humility on the other, and so much love on both. It would be idle to speculate on what might have been, when the hour of trial came, which none of those specially engaged probably then foresaw; before it arrived, Hurrell Froude had sunk under the constitutional malady against which he struggled for four years. What he would have been, and what he would have done, had his life been prolonged, no one can say; it would be unfair to judge him by what he left behind, except as rich grounds of promise. This I believe I may confidently say, that those who knew him best loved him the most dearly, and expected the most from him. This could be more truly said of no one of these than of Keble.

It was while he was thus engaged, that he received, I believe the only, offer that was ever made him of a dignity in the Church. Early in 1824 it was determined to constitute two Dioceses in the West Indies, and William Hart Coleridge, then a

I

Student of Christ Church, but who had been labouring assiduously as Curate in a large London parish,
St. Andrew's, Holborn, was selected to preside over
that of Barbados and the Leeward Islands.   He had
to appoint two Archdeacons, and he pressed Keble
to go out with him as Archdeacon of Barbados ; the
endowment was a liberal one, £2,000 a-year.   Keble
had a great regard and esteem for the young Bishop
whom he had known on friendly terms at Oxford,
and who, like himself, had achieved the honour of
a Double First Class.   He was much gratified by
the offer, and, as he says in writing to Dyson,
" I might have been dazzled by it ;" but about
a month before it was made, on his return from
Oxford, whither he had gone to preach, he had
found his father with his speech considerably affected, and with other symptoms calculated to make
his children anxious about him.

   " This," he says, in writing to me on March 2, 1824, " as
you may suppose, was a strong ingredient in my reasoning
with myself on the very kind and too partial offer which
W. C. made me.   My father was so agitated upon one's
pressing the matter in the least, that we all agreed in thinking I could not have done otherwise than I did, without
very serious injury to his health in its present state.   Under
all the circumstances, this left me of course no choice, and
I always think that is the greatest comfort, to have one's
way plainly marked out.   It is to be hoped that the recollection of such a proposal having been made will serve
a little to startle one from one's idleness, which I find by

sad experience is likely to be the besetting sin of country parsons; and not the least instance of it is neglect of correspondents and distant friends. But one lives on every day in hopes of mending, and I suppose one must not despair of oneself quite, any more than of one's parishioners."

This would seem at first sight another instance illustrating the cogency on Keble's mind of filial and other domestic obligations; but it is right to shew, from a letter to Dyson, in what light he regarded this particular call. It was not in his opinion a case in which domestic and professional duties came at all into comparison or conflict with each other :—

" Talking of Archdeacons, what do you think ? what say you to my going out Archdeacon to Barbados under W. Coleridge : would you advise me to go out, or not ? (N.B. I am ripe for asking advice). But do you remember some of the conversations we had on things in general, when we last met at Oxford ? I have often thought of them since ; indeed I may say the subject of them is hardly ever out of my mind for half an hour together. And in my cogitations on this matter, I thought of them more than usual, because they helped to confirm me in the resolution I knew I must come to. Thinks I to myself, one cannot surely think of a W. Indian Archdeaconry with 2,000 a-year, &c., &c., as a sort of primitive mission to which everything must give way. In short, thinks I to myself, 'tis a mere political thing, and I'm sure Dyson would say the same. Nevertheless, I do not say I should not have been dazzled by it, if my father had not been so decided as he was ; not so much by what he said, as by his looks and manner. We were all agreed that it was quite out of the question."

My cousin was influenced, I am sure, in making
his offer, both by personal regard, and a sincere
desire to select the most fitting person he could
find for an appointment of especial importance to
him in the settlement of the new Diocese; but I
believe every one will now rejoice that Keble declined to accept it.   Had he gone to the West
Indies, and retained his health, I have no doubt he
would have discharged the duties of his office effectively, and wherever he was, he must have been distinguished.   "The Christian Year" was so far advanced at this time, that he probably would have
completed it; indeed, according to his own theory
of poetry, which would have justified its truth in no
one more than in himself, he could not but have
written it, and we should have had it, I suppose,
with a large infusion of tropical lights and imagery,
very striking and interesting. He would have finished
it slowly however, and very probably, being in some
sort removed from the influences of his home advisers, he would have left it unpublished at his
death, according to his original intention.   But at
a distance from European influences and friendships, from the University, and the succeeding agi-
tations of the Church in England, he could not
have filled the useful and important place to which
he was now advancing; and some of his works, such
for example as the *Prælectiones*, and the edition of
Hooker, we should certainly have lost.   Considera-

tions of this kind of course did not occur to his mind, nor influence his determination ; apart from all these, however, it was one fully justified.

It was early in the following year (1825) that Keble's letters shew him beginning to contemplate seriously the publication of "The Christian Year"— silently, or only with communications to his home circle and some very few others, poem had been added to poem ; but his notion did not as yet go beyond a posthumous publication at most, when he had given the work as much perfection as he should be capable of giving it. I think at that time he would have shrunk a good deal from publishing anything— there was not, it may be remembered, the same proneness "to rush into print" which characterizes the present time—but with regard to poems of a religious character, and which affected the Church, he would, of course, feel a greater scruple about publication. Happily all his friends were against him—yielding by inches, and delaying, even when the resolution was taken, to accomplish it, the step was however ultimately accomplished. In regard to such a work, even these preliminary stages it may be interesting to observe.

March 5, 1825, he writes to me from Fairford :—

" Now they are all gone to bed, I will tell you a secret ; which is that after all my backwardness (which I suppose was chiefly affectation) on such subjects, I am in a fair way to commence *author*—' only think,' as Ellison says—Mr. Jeremiah Dyson, whose opinion on such a matter I take to

be as safe as anybody's can be, strongly recommends me
to publish some of the hymns you wot of. It is against
my original plan, which was to complete the series if I
could, go on improving it all my life, and leave it to come
out, if judged useful, when I shall be fairly out of the way;
and this is still my favourite plan—only I am afraid I am
in a way of being persuaded out of it. Do give me your
considerate, and *not partial* opinion, which way would
answer best—for indeed the matter is too serious to bandy
compliments upon—that is to say, if it is worth thinking of
at all."

As to this notion of posthumous publication, I do
not remember that he ever mentioned, or was in any
way influenced by the circumstance, that George
Herbert had formed the same resolution, and acted
upon it, in regard to the publication of the " Temple."
It is certainly at least a curious coincidence, that in
respect of two Poets, and two works so often compared together, and so standing apart by themselves,
as it were, in our literature, the same unusual resolution
should have been formed. Keble would never have
thought of placing himself in comparison with Herbert, of whose poems he was a great admirer : yet he
could hardly have been ignorant of the fact, and he
might have been moved, even unconsciously, to follow
the example of so holy a man.

To Dyson he writes on the 1st of April, 1825 :—

" I am very much obliged to you for your kind intentions
with regard to the MS. I shall certainly pump you for
more criticism, whether anything come of the printing

scheme or no. The more I think of it, the more my fancy would lead me to wait till it might be posthumous. But I must see what Johnny Davison says—I have sent him most of them—leaving out some which I think paltry, and others, which come, as it were, too near home for me to like to shew them much—some also on account of their going rather more than might be approved of upon that notion of decay in the Church, which you know I have for some time entertained. It seemed to me that this had bettei be established in prose first ; without something of that sort, the hymns of which I speak would be hardly intelligible to most readers."

To me he wrote in July :—

"With regard to my other little literary project I have adjourned it nominally till February—but I am in hopes I shall have quite persuaded my persuaders to let it stand over *sine die*, by the time February comes."

Writing to Cornish, in August of the same year, from Southrop, he says :—

"Thank you fifty times for your nice little hint about keeping back my MSS. for a good long while. I am quite sure you are right; and now there is less occasion to be in a hurry, as Tucker says the Scotch Book, which had pirated one of them, is come to another edition in which it's left out."

Cornish, I have no doubt, thought there was still much to do in the way of correction, both as to clearness of expression and smoothness in the measures, and this agreed entirely with Keble's own

opinion; and although he went on with his preparations, the advice remained impressed upon his
mind :—

"I am just now," says he in September of the same year,
writing from Fladbury to Dyson, "making up another
packet of hymns for Davison's revisal: and am coming to
a sound and judicious resolution against publishing, for
a good while yet at least."

What was Mr. Davison's advice, I have not the
means of ascertaining precisely; from the general
constitution of his mind I should expect that although his criticism in detail would be minute and
severe, and his advice in favour of great deliberation,
yet he would look through all questions of detail to
the substantial merits, and the great importance of
the work in a religious point of view; and therefore
be against long delay.   It is clear, I think, that with
Keble left alone, a degree of caution which we may
now safely pronounce exaggerated would have prevailed; this would have been dictated by his humility, which underrated the merit of everything he
did, and perhaps, even in this instance, more by his
sense of the responsibility of a work, which sought
to influence in some sort the religious belief and
practice of his readers.

On the 26th of September in the same year he
writes about "the verses" to Froude; and I the rather print what follows, because I notice in it the

first indication of the theory of Poetry, which he laid down formally afterwards in his *Prælectiones.*

" LENHAM, NEAR MAIDSTONE,
" 26 *Sept*^r., 1825.

" MY DEAR FELLOW,

" As Tyler begins, when he is in a jolly mood, these are to thank you very much for the trouble you have taken about them there things of mine, and still more for your telling me exactly what you think about them; for wch I shall hold you in greater honour as long as I live. For to say the truth, I look upon thorough honesty in this kind to be a rare thing in critic-land. I am not so partial to my own crockery, as not to be myself aware of the want of poetical depth, and fervour, wch disqualifies many or most of them from being of much use to imaginative people; but if they only serve as helps to the memory of plain, good sort of people, that is in my mind use enough; provided they do no harm by being untrue or *obtrusive,* of wch last I am a little afraid. At any rate I mean to take plenty of time, to make out the ecclesiastical year, if I can, before I publish; and I feel as if this would take up my life. It would be a great delight to do something, wch might be of use to the sort of persons you mention : but that must be left for some one who *can* do it—and probably whenever it is done, it will be done by somebody who never thought of it himself, but merely wrote to relieve his own mind. Indeed, that was the original purpose of what you have seen, and so far it has proved very useful; but there is no making a silk purse out of a sow's ear—a foolish figure, but farewell that.

" I am here on a week's visit to Tucker, before I enter on my new cure at Hursley."

There is a passage in a letter to Mr. Pruen, which, though written after the publication of the book, suggests an additional reason for the previous delay, and I feel sure this had operated strongly in Keble's mind ; a reason which I also believe caused in him all through life a feeling of sadness and dissatisfaction in regard to the book, increased rather than diminished by its popularity. I will insert the passage here, as it is necessary to complete the account of the motives which made him averse to publication, but some remarks which it suggests will find a more proper place hereafter.

"I had long ago considered about printing 'the Dedication' you speak of: but somehow or other (though Davison recommended it) I could not bring myself to it ; it seemed too much like printing one's own private confessions: and so to be sure is half the book ; and many times, when I consider what my friends would think of me if I were to print the other nine-tenths of my thoughts, I really feel quite ashamed of having printed the book at all : for though I am not blind enough to see all the good in it that you do, I am well aware there is quite good enough to make it on the whole a considerable fib on my part. But this will not do to talk and laugh about."

Keble's attention was, however, now much engaged upon a step which has always seemed to me most important in respect to himself, namely, the quitting the retirement of Fairford and his little Gloucestershire Cures, and coming more into the sunshine as the Curate of Hursley, with the sole charge of that parish.

Hursley is a Vicarage united to the Rectory of Otterbourne, and the Incumbent at the time I am speaking of was Archdeacon Heathcote, uncle to Keble's old pupil, Sir William Heathcote; he resided at Winchester, there being at that time no residence either in the Rectory or the Vicarage; he took charge himself of the former, and had a Curate for the latter; this curacy became vacant, and on Sir William's recommendation it was offered to Keble, and accepted by him in the spring of 1825, to be entered on at Michaelmas. In the mean time Sir William had found an unfinished house, which stood between the Church and his own Park gates, which he set himself to work to finish, and Keble, with the full consent of his father and sisters, made his arrangements for the change. The house would not be finished, probably, when Michaelmas came, but Keble was to take up his abode temporarily with Sir William at his mansion.

This was among the first acts of Sir William on succeeding to the property, and it is one on which I may venture to say he has reason especially to congratulate himself, both in itself, and in the train of consequences which flowed from it. Some of these probably were contemplated by no one; and perhaps at the moment little more was in his mind than the giving pleasure to Keble, while he procured for the parish in which he resided so good

and able a minister, and for himself the close neighbourhood of so dear a friend, and so wise an adviser. Yet I think it must have been obvious to
him that the time had arrived when it was fitting
that Keble, who had renounced the academical
course, and was so singularly averse to any ambitious speculations, should be called on to labour in
a larger field, and exercise his personal influence
more widely than it was open for him to do at
Fairford. Perhaps no place, and no circumstances,
could be more favourable than Hursley, and those
which attended the change when it was made.
Keble, indeed, would have said, and in strictness
truly said, that no sphere was so narrow, but that
a good man's energies might be fully and worthily
exercised in the ministry there ; and he would have
repelled the notion that he had gifts which ought
to be developed and displayed in the charge of
a more varied, and more educated population than
that of his Gloucestershire villages. Still there are
to be desired in this as in other things, where it can
be had, a fitness and proportion between the clergyman and his cure. Qualifications may be in danger
of slumbering useless in one place, which find full
scope and motive for development and exercise in
another.

But independently of this higher consideration,
there were pleasure and usefulness in what was to
be around him at Hursley, of a kind which did not
exist at Fairford ; the vicinity of Winchester Cathe-

dral, the College, and School: Robert Barter was
not then indeed the Warden of the one, nor Dr. Moberly Head Master of the other, with both of whom
he was afterwards to be on the most friendly terms.
The society of Hursley itself, however, and its neighbourhood, and especially that which would, of course,
gather from time to time at Hursley Park; the re-
newal of his familiar intercourse with his favourite
old pupil; the character of the country around him,
dry and healthy, a pleasant interchange of breezy
down and picturesque woodland, hill and valley,
the New Forest, Southampton, and the sea at a convenient distance; these are some of the circumstances
to which I allude.

Keble was not insensible to these attractions, still
it was a call on him which might seem to break in
upon the discharge of what he had always considered among the first, if not the very first, of his
duties, and he naturally hesitated to accept the offer.

I cannot do better than insert here the two letters,
addressed to Sir William Heathcote, in the first of
which he expresses his doubts, and in the second
his acceptance of the offer; the kindness of spirit in
which that had been conceived and made may be inferred from the answers:—

"SOUTHROP,
"*March* 14, 1825.

"MY DEAR AND KIND FRIEND,

"I am afraid you will think me very childish after so

many days' consideration of your too kind offer, to be still asking for more time, and yet so it is. I feel very strongly the value and the blessing of such a place as you offer me in your esteem and confidence; although I cannot help shrinking from the increased responsibility which such a change in my station would impose upon me; and then to leave my father and sisters, even for the distance of one long day's journey, is a step not to be resolved upon without a good deal of rather intense consideration, under our circumstances; the circumstances, I mean, of my father's age, and my eldest sister's health. If it were not for this, I believe I should without further delay have closed with your proposal, the friendliness and *piety* of which I do indeed most deeply feel; and whatever be the issue, shall always be most thankful to have received such a letter. Yet I feel so many doubts as to my own fitness for a charge in many respects different from my present one, that I am satisfied it is best for me to have such a family difficulty as this to hinder me from deciding too suddenly. Could you, then, and could the Archdeacon, (to whom please to offer my very sincere acknowledgments,) allow me without inconvenience a week or ten days more, from the time you receive this? In the course of that time, I think I shall be able to satisfy my mind more thoroughly than I can just now, as to what I ought to do. Do not think me cold and ungrateful, for indeed I am not so, though much weaker and less resolute in my duty than I fear you imagine me. And if you had rather have my answer sooner, pray do not scruple to tell me so. My best regards, if you please, to your Mother and Aunt, and Mr. Lovell, and believe me,

" Your very grateful and aff^{te} Friend,
" JOHN KEBLE, JUN^r."

" FAIRFORD,
" *March* 29, 1825.

" MY DEAR FRIEND,

" Having considered everything well over ' one, two, tree
time,' and having examined, and cross-examined, indivi-
dually and collectively, the several members of this my
Privy Council, I need not keep you, or the rest of my
kind friends at Hursley and Winchester any longer in suspense. I thankfully accept your kind offer, and only hope
that I may not prove unworthy of it. What I propose is,
if you can conveniently receive me, to give up Southrop to
my brother about the latter end of August, or beginning of
September, and then undertake Hursley immediately. By
that time the house might, I should think, be floored, plas-
tered, white-washed, painted, and I should think papered ;.
so that the main operations left would be to lay out the
garden, and lay in the furniture, both of which I could
superintend at my leisure. And there is this advantage in
coming while things are still rather unfinished ; that if upon
trial I should find myself more homesick than I expect to
be, it would be less of an undertaking to transport myself
home again ; or suppose my father or eldest sister, when it
comes to the point, should find it more essential to their
comfort to have me with them, than it now seems, as there
is no answering for the wishes of invalids, or in many other
supposable cases, it may turn out a great convenience to be
a little unsettled at first. But I will not anticipate anything
to disturb so comfortable an arrangement as we all think it.
My chief care now must be to endeavour, by God's blessing, that you may never have occasion to repent of your
confidence in me. My father and sisters give me good
hopes of paying me long and frequent visits, but I must
endeavour not to build much on that. I know my best

and wisest way will be to make my parish, wherever I am called, as entirely my home as possible, and to take all one sees of friends and relations as something τοσὸν καὶ ἐτί. I have been a little spoiled in this respect by the privilege of staying with my first and best friends so long; but I trust I am not too old to mend. At all events, I should like to make the trial." . . . .

Upon this footing the arrangement was made; I may seem to have been very diffuse on a matter commonly so ordinary as the acceptance of a Curacy; but it is obvious from the letters I have just inserted, that Sir William's offer was not an ordinary one, nor couched in ordinary language; and I have already stated my reasons for thinking that the change which this move made in Keble's habits of life, in the society in which he moved, and in the exercise of his professional duties, was most important; it was very happily timed too, and the acceptance met with the hearty concurrence of the Privy Council to which the letters refer. His father, indeed, was sure to consider the question with good sense, and entire freedom from selfish bias, and the conclusion was certain.

This resolution put an end, I believe, to Keble's any longer acting as Tutor to any one; and it prevented his accepting one pupil, then a lad between Harrow and Oxford, whom at the request of his father I had earnestly pressed on him to take charge of—Arthur Acland. I can hardly conceive one who would have been more congenial to him. But it could not then be arranged ; however, this did not prevent the formation of a friendship between them in after life, and it was pleasant to me to know on good information, that under the great affliction of his life, which indeed did not very long precede his own death, Arthur Troyte, as he had become, sought the vicarage at Hursley, and found substantial consolation in the sympathy which Keble manifested, and the advice he gave.

CHAPTER VII.

HURSLEY CURACY.—DEATH OF MARY ANN KEBLE.—
RETURN TO FAIRFORD.—1825—1826.

IN the lives of most men there is a period which
one would characterize, if not as the most happy,
yet the brightest, and most sunshiny; when their
hopes are most cheerful, their cares lightest, their
sense of enjoyment most lively. The year which
Keble passed as Curate of Hursley I should characterize as that period in his life; it was scarcely
a year, before he was re-called to Fairford by an
event which, with all his habitual resignation, was
yet one of the most afflicting trials he had ever
been submitted to. But of this by-and-by.

It had been arranged, as I have intimated, that
Thomas Keble should take to the Curacies, and to
the Parsonage at Southrop, on his leaving it. This
was the more agreeable, as he had not long before,
to the entire satisfaction of the family, and not least
to that of Keble, married a lady, whose sister afterwards became Keble's own wife. Before Keble settled
at Hursley, he visited two or three of his old friends,
and took Ellison's duty at Huntspill for a week or
two, and on the first Sunday of October, 1825, commenced the discharge of his duties as Curate.

Writing to me not long before he started from home, he says :—

"You would laugh if you could look into me, and read all the pretty schemes of reform which course one another over my still childish brain.   I am to be *so* regular, *so* industrious, *so* punctual, *such* an early riser, &c., &c., &c., and all to be learned, or rather picked up on Salisbury Plain, in the space of sixty-five miles from this home to my new one."

On the day of what he called "reading himself in to his new diocese," he wrote to me in high spirits ; he had found his house unfinished, and was residing with Sir William at Hursley Park ; this, too, might be called the bright period of Sir William's life ; he had not long entered on his career; his marriage was in prospect before him, and his election as Knight of the Shire.   Keble writes in the fulness of his heart, how "very very friendly" he was to him, and how "much more comfortable and more at home he was than he ever thought he should be so soon, un-Fairfordized as he was."   He likes his village, his home, his church tower, (I note his expressive silence as to his church,) and he sums up a string of likings, with the remark, that "here is a good store to set against the uncomfortable circumstances which are sure to come by-and-by."   His accounts from home, too, were bright :—

"Elizabeth's headaches are mending, and my Father is as brisk as a bee ; he has not flagged a moment about my departure, and when he keeps up himself, he keeps us all up with him."

He had come into the parish with the best of recommendations, and was most kindly received; he soon made his own way good, both socially and as the pastor of the flock; hints disclosing his industry in this last respect appear from time to time in his correspondence. Beside these, there was the Parsonage to be finished, and the garden, an especial object of interest, and the pleasure-ground, to be laid out and planted; the first of these lies between the house and churchyard on the side of the house which faces the tower and west end of the Church, the latter slopes away very prettily from the back front, and is flanked on the west by the Park pales, and some fine old elms. The house itself is rather picturesque than handsome, not commonplace, not too large, yet sufficiently commodious.

Keble's old friends were not slow to visit him in his new abode; and this was one of his greatest pleasures; among them very early was Arnold. He says :—

"I have tried the cozie powers of the Hursley air not only with Mary Anne, who has paid me a visit of five weeks ending the 9th Jan^r., but also with Tom Arnold, who ran down here like a good neighbour, and surveyed the premises and the neighbourhood presently after Christmas. How very unaltered he is, and how very comfortable

and contented ; he is one of the persons whom it does one
good to think of when I am in a grumbling vein."

Arnold was at this time residing with pupils at
Laleham, with the spirits and hopefulness of boyhood, or youth, and the activity and brightness of
early manhood ; and, as Keble says, quite unaltered
in manner from what we had known him at Oxford.
He had brought with him the opening of an Essay
on Schools and Universities, intended for a Review.
Keble says "the covering of the jar is so very
sweet and luscious, that I suspect there must be
something terribly bitter below ; but he only cackles
and crows at anything anybody can say to him."
Few survive who can remember how to the life this
paints him in his merry defiant moods in his younger
days. I may add that he had sent me in a letter
an analysis of what he intended to say ; it is so full,
and able, that I cannot but wish it had been selected
for publication in his Life.

Tucker, John Awdry, and Charles Plumer, the
two latter at that time brother Fellows with him
of Oriel, also came to him ; it was scarcely a deviation for me when on my Circuit, in passing from
Winchester to Salisbury, to go by Hursley, and I
visited him in this way both in the spring and
summer. Upon the latter occasion I was taking
my two elder boys into Devonshire, and they were
received by him during the Winchester Assizes. At

the end of these I went there and took them on
with me. I found him with his father and two
sisters in high spirits, and all four had concurred in
making the little ones happy; they on their part
had not been slow in becoming familiar with Keble,
and accepting him as their playmate; and so their
fondness for him commenced, which, combined with
the profoundest respect as years advanced, continued unabated to his death. Love for children, a
full understanding of their natures, and the power
of entering into all their ways and wishes, and interpreting their thoughts, were properties he possessed even then in a very high degree.

I have said I found his father and sisters with
him; this was a realization of the expectations held
out to him before he left Fairford. Mary Anne, as
has been stated, had fulfilled a promise she had
made for herself, on which he counted much, and
had stayed for five weeks with him in the preceding December and January. When I had proposed sending my young ones to him, I had supposed him alone, and should hardly have thought
of sending him such intruders, if I had known who
were with him; but Mr. Keble and the sisters both
concurred in wishing them to come. In announc-
ing this to me, he says :—

"You may imagine the pleasure it is to have my Father
and Sisters here; my Father so remarkably well, and so
beautifully cheerful; he enjoys the place much more than

I had expected, and will not allow that he sleeps at all the worse for being out of his own bed. Elizabeth was rather knocked up with the journey, not at first, but after a day or two; however, now she is looking up again, and enjoys our woodland drives mightily. In short, they all seem as natural almost as at Fairford; and the place being left in dishabille longer than it ought, is no great disadvantage, for it will have all the benefit of their suggestions; and I don't despair of its being quite a show parsonage by the time Johnny's eldest grandson goes his first Circuit. You will come the end of next week, and give us the benefit of your advice, there's a good fellow."

He little thought in how short a time comparatively, and in how different a sense, he would make the vicarage a show parsonage.

He and I were to dine with Sir William, and after we had set the home party down to their earlier dinner, we took a long walk in the Park, and, I remember, explored the remains of the old Merdon Castle, which stands in it. Such pleasures were now of rare occurrence to me, and the walk lives in my memory.

I dwell on this passage in Keble's life with minuteness, and with the more interest, at least to myself, from the sad close of it which so soon followed. The family visit terminated, Mr. Keble and the two sisters returned to Fairford. In a letter which I have seen, written some years before to Mrs. Pruen, in which he spoke of intending to introduce a young lady to her, he says, "not my wife Elizabeth, but my sweetheart Mary Anne." These words very happily and truly describe the shadow of difference in his feeling towards the two sisters ; both have long passed away, and I may speak of them without reserve ; while they were so identified with Keble, that those who read about him ought to know something of them. Elizabeth, the elder by several years, was almost a constant invalide ; her complaint had rendered an operation necessary, which made her lame, and she was seldom free from suffering. Her cheerful patience, her unselfishness, her strong good sense, her sweetness, and her piety, mixed up a large portion of reverence for her with the love which he bore towards her. Nor was this without reason ; in my note made at the time of this visit, and which I print because it was made at the time, and only for my own eyes, I see I say of her, " Miss Keble was with him, looking very delicate ; she had evidently suffered much from the hot weather, and looked less pretty than she used, but there is an almost angelic sweetness about her manner, and expression of countenance." Mary Anne was younger ; though not strong, yet having better health, and brighter spirits, smarter in speech, and more lighthearted, entering into all his drolleries, and answering them, walking with him, riding with him ; he constantly sporting with her, seldom addressing her but by some fond diminutive nick-name ; and in his letters to her constantly sliding into odd rhymes, or droll puns; yet with all this he had the fullest sense of the sterling qualities of head and heart, which she possessed. It would have been, I suppose, impossible to say which he loved most tenderly, "the wife, or the sweetheart."

It was the unexpected death of this dear sister which he communicated to me in the following letter :—

"FAIRFORD,
"*Sept.* 25, 1826.

"MY VERY DEAR FRIEND,

"I cannot help hoping you may in some way or other be a little prepared for what I have to communicate— a most trying visitation of God's Providence, particularly to my father and Elizabeth,—yet accompanied, as always, with many, very many circumstances of great comfort and relief. I was summoned from Hursley the morning Henry Coleridge left me, by an account of dearest Mary Anne's being alarmingly ill; when I came here, I found she had been in a state of delirium ever since Sunday night; and this continued, with very slight abatement, till last Wednesday morning about two o'clock, when she was quiet for about two hours, and then, seemingly without pain, fell into her last sleep, fairly worn down by the violence of the attack. Dear soul, I really do not think it at all presumptuous to rejoice in the contemplation of her present state. Sudden as her death was to herself, she was, I firmly believe, entirely prepared for it. Her spirits had been rather affected of late, and she sometimes appeared to anticipate something; but the only effect this had on her was to make her more cheerful and resigned in everything, and kinder to everybody. The more coolly I think of her, now the first shock is over, the more does this comfort grow upon me; and if it were not for my father and Elizabeth, I think I should feel an unmixed though melancholy pleasure in thinking of her. To them, as you may well conceive, the separation is painfully trying : humanly speaking, irreparable; but the Almighty has mercies in store which we know not of, and they are both so calm and patient,— my Father even cheerful,—that I cannot, upon consideration, be uncomfortable about them either. My brother and Bessie are with us, and are the greatest support to one another, and to us ; and the baby is like a little angel sent among us to shine in an overclouded place. Then we have our Bibles and Prayer-books at hand, and are sure of the affectionate sympathy of many dear friends, you my dear Coleridge particularly; never shall we forget the very brotherly letter you sent us the last time we were in distress, when we had just parted from my mother. I was very glad of your letter by Henry, and of the cheering account he brought of your family ; the blessing of God be upon them all. Remember us in your prayers,—me particularly, that I may make a better use of this than I have done of other visitations. And when you write to Ottery, will you let Frank and Henry know how things are, with my kindest regards. I promised to write, but perhaps he will excuse that at present.

> " Your very affectionate Friend,
> " JOHN KEBLE, JUN^r."

He wrote about the same time on the same occasion to Froude, and even had the letter been confined to this, it is so exquisite in thought and expression, that I could not have withheld it from my readers; but they will see that it has a character of its own; tenderly, and delicately, and very wisely, the former tutor suggests to the pupil, now become the young friend, how to deal with infirmities in temper, or spirits, to which he thought him constitutionally liable. I therefore give the whole letter, and for the same reason I subjoin an extract from another written later in the same year :—

" I am now in the midst of preparations to quit Hursley, and return to live at Fairford as early as I can next week ; I therefore am afraid I shall not be able to write much to the purpose, but something I must write in answer to yours, which was forwarded from home with a very comfortable account of matters there, and reached me this morning. I knew you would be very sorry when you heard of what has come upon us, and I feel that I can write freely to you about it ; but I cannot half describe to you the depth and intensity, at least as it seemed to me, of my thoughts and feelings during Mary Anne's illness and for some time since. Certainly no loss could be so great, humanly speaking, to Elisabeth and my Father; but they are both such sort of people, that I have long been used to consider everything that happens to them as a certain good : and there was nothing bitter in my grief as far as they were concerned ; much less in thinking of Mary Anne herself; but the real bitterness was when I thought of many things in which I have been far less kind to her than I ought to have been. Somehow or other I have for years been accustomed to talk to her far more freely than to anybody else in the world, though of course there were two or three whom

I loved quite as well. But it has so happened that when-ever I was moody or fretful, she has had to bear with me more than any one, and if I chose I could sit down and torment myself by the hour with the thought of it. This is the only feeling of real bitterness that I have on the subject, but I know it is wrong to indulge it, and I trust soon to get over it entirely ; indeed, I seem to have done so already, only I feel one cannot in any way depend upon one's self. I am certain no person who believes in the Atonement ought to indulge in bitter remorse, and there-fore, by God's blessing, I don't mean to be uncomfortable if I can help it, even in the thought of my past faults. I have been so too much already, and it only seems to make one lazy and weaken one's own hands and one's friends'. If you please, therefore, don't let us encourage one another in melancholy any more; but let us always resolutely look to the bright side of things, and among other helps to be quiet, let us always talk as freely to one another as we do now; for nothing relieves one so much as making a clean breast. I never was so much impressed with the value and excellency of cheerfulness as a Christian virtue as I have been since M. A.'s death. The remem-brance of her peculiar cheerfulness (for she had more of it than any of us, except, perhaps, my Father) goes so far towards keeping us all up, especially Elisabeth. We keep thinking how vexed she would be to see us annoying our-selves about her; and how she always wanted everybody to live in sunshine; and it quite makes us ashamed and afraid to feel desolate. You may easily imagine what a support this is to Elisabeth, whose thoughts, both from her temper and circumstances, are more entirely fixed on M. A. than either of ours can be. Of course, she must feel like a widow, but I trust not as a desolate one : certainly

she seems alive to every comfort, and her prevalent feeling
is one of deep thankfulness for the assurance of M. A.'s
happiness. As to my Father, he really seems to have recovered his ordinary cheerfulness: now and then he is
overcome, but tears relieve him, and he goes on comfortably
again. I am going to be his curate at Coln, where I hope
we shall yet have many a comfortable discourse, and not
find it necessary to ramble so far as the Wye in search of
'great rocks' to shelter us. I don't mean that I am to
live at Coln, but at Fairford. Betty goes to Coln. I like
your plans of reading, but don't be disheartened if you seem
to do little; only I would not indulge reveries. As you
speak of good books, do look at the Life of Mr. Bonnell
if it comes in your way. It is in the list of the Christian
Knowledge Society, and Hawkins I know can lend it you.
See p. 153. There is a passage which I have found useful,
and I suspect you may too. You cannot think how often
you come into my mind, especially now I am endeavouring
to train myself to a more thorough content and cheerfulness
than I have ever yet practised. For I fancy that you and
I require in some respects the same sort of training. At
any rate I know too well what passes in my own mind, to
think anything contemptible in you. Now I think this is
enough about ourselves, for I hold it to be a selfish and
dangerous sort of thing for people to be always turning
their eyes inward. But don't let this hinder you from
writing always as freely of what is uppermost as you do
now; only please not to let your own faults, nor anything
uncomfortable, be often uppermost. As I said before, I
am sure it is not natural it should be so in those for whom
Christ died.

"This lesson I have learned of dear Mary Anne, and
I hope not to forget it, but to have it perfect by the time

I see her again, and if I can get you to learn it too, so
much the better for us all.   She often used to speak of
you, and I dare say to pray for you, for she fancied you
not quite comfortable, and she had a great feeling for that
sort of discomfort.

  " God bless you now, my dear friend.   Let me hear from
you as often as it seems to do you any good—and don't
mind what you write.   Mention how your sister is—I have
heard nothing of her for a long time.   Ever and ever yours,
J. K., Junr." ·

" 2^d. Dec^r., 1826.

  " So much for myself, and now you.   I am bound to
thank you over and over again for your last letter, it was
and is a real comfort to me, for I am tolerably sure you
are in the right way, only don't dwell too much upon
whatever may have been wrong ; to some minds it may
be necessary, but not to those who are in danger of becoming indolent by too much thinking about themselves.
And when you find yourself, as I daresay you sometimes
do, overpowered as it were by melancholy, the best way
is to go out, and do something kind to somebody or other.
Objects, either rich or poor, will generally present themselves in the hour of need to those who look for them in
earnest, although Oxford is not perhaps the most convenient place to find them in.   However, there they surely
are, if you will take the trouble of looking for them ; and
perhaps that very trouble is in some sort an advantage in
driving away a moody fit, although I always reckon it
a great privilege of a country Parson, that his resources
in this way lie close to his own door.   Writing, too, I have
known in many cases a very great relief; but I almost
doubt the expediency of preserving journals, at least of

looking much back upon them: if one could summon resolution to do so, I fancy the best way would be to write on till one was a little unburthened, and then put one's confessions in the fire. But in all these things, of course, no one can judge for his neighbour. And whatever you do, don't throw your confessions *to me* in the fire, for it does my heart good to receive them; it makes me hope that I am sometimes *useful*, which is a sensation I don't very often experience."

It was in the spring of 1827, (March 5 is the date it bore,) that Keble wrote the poem entitled "Burial of the Dead," which is printed, No. 50, in the *Lyra Apostolica*. I hardly know whether I should not assign it the first place in all the poetry he has left behind him, for its beautiful rhythm, and most appropriate measure, the finish of its language, but above all these, for its richness, simplicity, and pathos. Its charm is increased by knowing that it was Mary Anne's funeral which it dwells on; this gives a reality and tenderness to such expressions as "cheering whispers like thine own." Here, too, we find what again and again, indeed almost uniformly, is to be found, when he wrote in verse or prose on such subjects, the expression of his belief in the communion of the departed spirits of the blest with the sorrowing survivors :—

> " The deep knell dying down, the mourners pause,
>   Waiting their Saviour's welcome at the gate :
>   Sure with the words of heaven
>   Thy spirit met us there,

> "And sought with us along th' accustom'd way
> 　The hallow'd porch, and entering in beheld
> 　　The pageant of sad joy
> 　　So dear to Faith and Hope."

I can hardly suggest why he wrote "brother" for "sister" in the stanza towards the close, perhaps it might be consideration for those who would first see the poem, whom he would not touch too closely, or it might be from his habitual shrinking from putting himself, or his own special sorrow before the public eye, that he would generalize this most touching incident in the poem. I mention the circumstance, however, as it might raise a doubt as to the occasion of the poem, for which there is no foundation.

The poem immediately preceding in the same volume is by Keble also, both bear the title of Bereavement; judging only from internal evidence, I should say this was also occasioned by the same affliction; it is most touching, but the strain of thought which makes it so interesting to those who know, or are studying Keble's nature, removes it from the province of criticism.

This event, as might be expected, recalled Keble from Hursley; he could no longer separate himself from his father and only surviving sister, and though he would have preferred, I think, their joining him at Hursley, yet he found this impossible.

"Many persons (he wrote to me) in my Father's place

would rather perhaps have moved to me, but with his turn of mind it is quite out of the question. I really think if he *had* brought himself to it, it would most likely shorten his life."

Circumstances prevented his brother, now a family man, from coming to reside at Fairford ; indeed, could that have been arranged, it would scarcely, I think, have satisfied Keble's loving heart. So he made a short visit to superintend the removal of his books and other matters to Fairford, and as Hursley, fortunately, could be provided for without much inconvenience, before the end of October he was again settled under his father's roof, and thus sadly and unexpectedly ended this pleasant episode in his life, his charge of Hursley as Curate.

CHAPTER VIII.

KEBLE returned to a home sadly changed by the death of his sister. I do not think that in the course of his life he sustained any loss which he felt more acutely; beyond the privation to himself in the death of a sister so loved, a companion at once so bright and lively, so sensible and good, he could not but be affected by the blow to his father, and even more his invalide and suffering sister, now left alone. Dyson, who visited at Fairford more often than I did, and knew Mary Anne more familiarly, wrote to me at the time, and I transcribe a part of his letter, as in a few words he does her so much more justice than I have been able to do in many :—

"Oh, Coleridge, what a sad blow to her family, the loss of Mary Anne Keble; poor I must not call her after the common usage, since she has so infinitely the advantage of all left behind. John Keble sent me word of her loss soon after it happened, and gave, as far as could be given so early after the blow, a comfortable account of his father and sister; and to be sure, if the truest piety, and most practical submission can give any comfort under such a loss, they will have it, and I dare to say, will perhaps at first feel it less, than their immediate friends will for them.

But when I think what a loveable being she was in herself, what an affectionate, gentle, guileless, and truly simple heart she had, and how little the cares and affection of the best and tenderest men can supply the unwearying, assiduous, self-denying, attachment of a daughter and sister, I must be apprehensive of the effect upon her father and Elizabeth from such a loss, a loss to be perceived not in one stunning blow, and all is over, but to be felt daily and hourly; I hope, however, and I pray for the best for them."

This was written early in October, 1826. The letters which both Dyson and I received in the following months shew that any apprehension of permanent depression of spirits would have been groundless ; all three of the survivors were strong in their common faith, and the picture which Keble draws of his aged father and sister, and unconsciously of himself, under this visitation is most cheering and instructive.

He says to Dyson early in November :—

"Amongst all the friendly letters we received, your's seemed one of the most valuable, because you both of you understood dearest Mary Anne so well, and loved her so truly. Whenever we meet or hear from you, it will seem something of an approach to her, and do not fear but by the blessing of God our meetings may be cheerful and happy enough. I am sure you would think so, if you could see how *very* comfortable both my father and Elizabeth are, and how unaffectedly they enter into the spirit of everything that is going on around them. Indeed, I don't

think you would see any difference in my father, and I am
not sure that you would in Elizabeth."

It was an additional trial to the former during
this winter, that his increasing weakness prevented
him from discharging his duties at Coln personally,
to which Keble alludes in writing to me on the 22nd
of January, 1827 :—

" You would like to see my father, how very quietly he
takes his suspension from clerical duties, which I used
always to fear would be too sharp a trial for him whenever
it took place. But it really does not seem to vex him at
all. He stays at home, and is quite contented and cheerful, in the office, as he says, of Chaplain to Elizabeth.
And Elizabeth's great delight is to do all the things that
Mary Anne used to do, and fancy her only gone away for
a short visit to a place where she is very happy, and soon
to shew herself again ; if one may call it fancy, which one
verily believes to be the real truth."

He speaks of himself as—

" Having swung comfortably back to his old moorings,
and certainly," says he, " it is more comfortable to have some
one to say 'good bye' to every night, and not to have to eat
and drink, and talk by oneself, only it remains to be proved
whether one who has been usually very idle, when he had
a good deal to do, will suddenly turn industrious, when his
sphere of action is so much diminished. Certainly the
days do not seem long, or irksome, but I am afraid that
is a very equivocal sign of industry."

But he was not idle ; he was now supplying his

father's place at Coln entirely, and as Coln was
three miles off, it occupied more of his time than
if he had been strictly resident. Moreover, that tax
was now beginning to be imposed upon him, which
in after life became very burthensome, the answering
the letters of those who consulted him in their religious doubts and difficulties. This, it is well known,
is the lot of many distinguished persons; but it is
remarkable that it should have commenced with
him at a time when he would have seemed to be
so little known.

In the same letter, from which my last extract
was made, he tells me that he had gone "through
every word of an immense bundle of papers," the
remains of a deceased convert from Quakerism, with
a view to advising whether they should be published
or not. He asks for information on the question
whether the present Quakers maintained the opinions
of George Fox and Co.; on which the answer in that
case seemed to him to turn. Again, and about the
same time, Cornish had consulted him on the conscientious difficulties of a young lady; and his answer is so sensible, that I cannot forbear transcribing
it; many persons, I believe, are occasionally in the
condition of the young lady; who may perhaps
profit by the advice :—

"I am clearly of opinion the young lady should discon-
tinue these observances which seem to fret and distract her
so much. It seems like Fasting, which no one is tied to,

even by the laws of the Church, when it is *bonâ fide* against their health : much less by any rule they can set themselves.   Clearly this is a case of melancholy from bodily constitution, and the person should be recommended to avoid all vows and singularities of every kind, as mere snares.   I seem to be speaking so positively about what I must be ignorant of, that I am afraid my opinion is worth even less than usual : but supposing the representation in your friend's letter to be correct, and Jeremy Taylor right in his *Ductor Dubitantium*, touching the management of a scrupulous conscience, (p. 158 et seqq.,) I don't think I can be very wide of the mark ; besides you have given me a pretty broad hint in what way you mean to proceed, and wish to be advised.   At any rate a person of this temperament should be cautioned, as matter of *duty*, to refrain from binding herself by anything like voluntary vows in future ; it is a mere snare, and should be repressed like any other temptation.   If she cannot be quite satisfied, (as at times I suppose she will not,) with having broken through her own rule in this instance, why cannot she add one sentence to her morning or evening devotions, relating to this particular subject ; this, if made habitual, would, as it seems to me, answer all purposes ; but she must not be fanciful, and imagine one's prayers do no good if one is uncomfortable all the time.   I am sure it would be bad enough with some of us, if we let present comfort come into our calculations on that matter.

"*Fairford, April* 28, 1827."

These are but instances ; he was busy too in his theological reading, and acquiring that intimate knowledge of the Fathers, which had such a marked influence on his theological feeling, if I may use that term, and the habitual train of his thoughts on any religious question. He was examining too, with an interest awakened by the times, the foundation and the limits of the alliance of Church and State, specially of the right of the latter to interfere with the former in matters purely ecclesiastical. In the letter dated June 22, 1827, in which he mentions the publication of "The Christian Year," he goes on to a consideration which seems to me very interesting, and which I know not whether any other writer has ever noticed or enlarged on. It was clearly an original thought to Keble :—

"The speculation," says he, "I referred to in a former letter, and on which you desired more explanation, was this. It seems clear to me, on reading over the Old Testament, that the example of the Jews *as a nation*, is there held out in such a way as to regulate and correct the religious conduct of us Christians *as individuals*. The covenant with them collectively was a type of that made with us separately ; and the faults into which they fell analogous to what may be expected, and to what we really experience, in our own private dealings with the Almighty ; this, I suppose, is what makes the Old Testament, as a whole, so useful to be considered by every Christian ; and in this I persuade myself that I see a strong auxiliary evidence of the truth of both dispensations, as well as divers other useful corollaries, if I could but develope them ; but it will take a great deal of reading, thinking, and writing, to make out the matter properly and usefully, and I have only, as it were, begun to think about it. I mention it to you, that you may tell me

if it seems absurd at first sight, or sufficiently done already.
I should like, if I could, to turn my hours to some account ;
but long habits of idleness are not got over in a moment.
I have been to Oxford once or twice lately, and it makes
one quite fidgetty to see what a bustle and business every
one is always in.   I had half a mind to go to Bishop Lloyd
and ask him to set me some task."

He had a great regard and respect for that good,
and able, and original man, and he thought his services as Divinity Professor, especially the private
Lectures which he instituted, extremely valuable.
The Bishop also was very fond of him.

Although Keble speaks of his idleness, which indeed he was fond of doing, the preceding months of
the year had brought about the completion, and
finished the printing of " The Christian Year." Pursuing my plan of giving all details which seem to
me at all interesting in respect of this great work,
I must go back a little in my narrative and my extracts from his letters.   In the beginning of February
he acknowledges to me the return of some part of
the manuscript which had been under my hands ;
he does this with his usual overflowing kindness, and
I could hardly transcribe the passage, if I had not
to qualify it by adding, that I believe after all he
rejected, and with good reason, a very large proportion of my suggestions.   The passage, moreover,
adds a fact worth preserving as to the adviser to
whom we owe the beautiful Verses on the " Occa-

sional Services," which, curiously enough, seem not to have formed part of his original plan :—

" Now I must thank you with all my might for the very kind trouble you have taken about my concerns ; you have set to work like a true friend, and I shall always love you the better for it, only I am afraid you have been taking a good deal more trouble than the affair was worth. I have set myself at work rather hardish to revise the MS., and have made a good many corrections, one or two I hope to re-write entirely ; and I also want to add something on each of the ' Occasional Services,' in pursuance of a hint I had from Davison. I have done a few stanzas for the Communion, and if I have a good spring-flow of rhyme, I hope to be ready with the others, as far as the Commination, in a month or six weeks, and then I purpose to go up to Oxford, and print without delay. I had wished to put it off for a year for the sake of the vignettes, but my father seems really anxious to have it done without loss of time, and I think one should be uncomfortable, if one did not try one's best to meet his wishes ; at the same time, I am quite aware of the defects you mention, and will do my best to mend them. I shall, however, be the more easy in not sending the rest of the MS. to you, as most of the passages you have marked were places which I was before dissatisfied with, and wished to alter ; in some few you have not caught my meaning, as I believe, through hurry, and in some I differ in grammar or taste ; but on the whole, I am exactly of your mind, and I hope to be a tolerable substitute for you in the office of criticising the rest. My theological plans, about which you enquire, are hardly plans enough to be stated on paper ; they are mere schemes floating loosely in my head. But when I have done this

job, and read one or two more of the Fathers, I hope to
tell myself something more clearly about it.   Farewell, my
most dear friend.

   " *Fairford, Feb^y* 9, 1827."

   The natural wish of his aged father to see the
work published before he died, made it now to him
an imperative duty to delay no longer ; from this
time he neither hesitated nor flagged in the prosecution of the work.   His mention of vignettes had
reference to a scheme, which he rather favoured at
this time, of illustrating the book, with the help of
some accomplished lady friends.   Several vignettes,
as he calls them, were indeed drawn ; but he abandoned this idea, which Cornish dissuaded him from ;
and thenceforward he always opposed anything of the
kind, though it was more than once pressed on him.
I rather think he did not abide by the prudent resolution he announces of sending no more of the MS.
to me for my criticism, for I possess a later and detailed acknowledgment, in which I was more surprised than pleased, to find that I had actually recommended the suppression entirely of the verses
on the Tenth Sunday after Trinity.   He meets this
very simply with the remark, that it was a special
favourite with some others of his critics.

   On the 22nd of June, 1827, he announced to me
that my copy of "The Christian Year" was on the
road from Oxford, and on the next day I received
it.   His announcement was short and simple, and

without comment, and then he passed on, as he
said, "to more interesting affairs." I am certain
that he had not the slightest idea at the time how
important was the gift he had made to the world,
nor how decisive a step he had taken in respect of
his own character and reputation. We who had
watched the work from the beginning were somewhat more enlightened, perhaps; but we had not,
I think, fully comprehended the importance of the
volume; we had, indeed, a very high opinion of it;
we thought it would gradually win its way, and would
exercise a great influence on its readers, but we were
none of us prepared for its immediate success, still
less for such a success as befel it. I have lying
before me Mr. J. H. Parker's summary of the account from the beginning to January, 1854; in this
period of less than twenty-six years I' find 108,000
copies were issued in forty-three editions. The sale
of the work never flagged through the remainder of
his life; and in the Memoir of Mr. Moor, to which
I have so often referred, a statement is made (especially remarkable considering a circumstance to which
I must advert presently), that in the nine months immediately following his death seven editions were
issued of 11,000 copies.

After what I have said above of my critical success in regard to this work in the prime of my life,
I should be very unwise if in advanced old age I
were to venture on an elaborate criticism of it here.

Indeed, it seems to me hardly the fit subject for mere literary criticism as a volume of poetry. Whatever can be desired of that kind, however, has been admirably done already by Professor Shairp, of St. Andrews, in an "Essay on the Author of the Christian Year," published at Edinburgh in 1866, and those of my readers who shall be induced by this notice to read that masterly little book, will thank me, I am sure, for having referred them to it.

Yet the publication of "The Christian Year" was such an event in Keble's life, and the work itself so interesting and important, that I venture to set down, not with any system or order, what are rather my personal experiences in the reading it, than anything like regular criticism upon it. This may, perhaps, be the way in which my remarks may be most useful, especially to young persons. I will say, then, that it is one of those volumes of poetry which no one should take up to read through at once, or as a continued study; few volumes even of miscellaneous poetry will bear this; but the very design of "The Christian Year" protests against it; it was meant, and should be taken, as an accompaniment to the services of the Prayer-book. It will be found to have a special significance, if read as such; and for this mode of study and meditation, it is particularly fitted by two among other qualities. The first that it is so wonderfully Scriptural. Keble's mind was by long, and patient, and affectionate study of

Scripture, so imbued with it, that its language, its
train of thought, its mode of reasoning, seem to flow
out into his poetry, almost, one should think, unconsciously to himself. They are always there, yet
never intruded. Many times, I may say for myself,
the meaning of what had been an obscure passage
in Holy Writ, or the true character and teaching of
an incident, has flashed on me in reading the verses,
of which it has been made the text for the day's meditation. I have heard of a clergyman in a rural
parish in Worcestershire who was in the habit of
reading, and explaining from the pulpit, in lieu of
an afternoon sermon, the poem for the Sunday ; and
I have no doubt such a practice, with proper comments, might be pursued with very good effect. It
has often struck me, what an excellent skeleton of
a sermon this or that poem suggests. The second
quality I would notice, is its almost inexhaustible
novelty ; whether this be owing to the depth of the
thought, the pregnancy of the language, or, as severer
critics have said, to the imperfect expression of the
thought, or to all combined, I will not undertake to
decide ; but speaking generally, I should say, read it
as often as you will, you will find it on each perusal
to contain or to suggest some new matter for reflection. Take it up when you will, you are never likely
to skim through a poem, as one sometimes does with
what is familiar, however one may admire it ; some

thought seemingly new will arrest your attention,
make you pause, and set you upon consideration.
This is surely a great merit in a volume of poems
intended to serve in the way of a manual.

I would further suggest to a new reader of the
book, to remark on the vivid accuracy of Keble's
descriptions of natural incidents or objects. I think
Dr. Stanley has somewhere observed on this merit
in Keble's poetry in regard to what he had never
seen, the scenery of the East, and specially of the
Holy Land; but we may all of us judge of it generally in regard to our own country. He was short-
sighted, and though he was fond of simple music,
he had not a keen or accurate ear for it. He complains in a well-known passage of the dulness of
his hearing to apprehend the full beauty of harmonious sounds; yet whether as to objects of sight
or sound, his numberless descriptions are accurate,
not only in the general, but in the slightest and
most delicate features: he seems to have observed
them all, as true poets are sure to do, with a lover-
like, and yet a discriminating interest; and his language is never more definite and distinct than in
these passages. It is hard to forbear, but I must
not indulge myself in citations. There is still another circumstance, which I have always been struck
with, the happiness with which he spiritualizes all
that he describes of natural scenery, and how con-

stantly he deals with it in this way; one stanza I
cite, not so much as an instance, but as illustrating
my meaning :—

> " He whose heart will bound to mark
>   The full bright burst of summer morn,
> Loves too each little dewy spark
>   By leaf or flow'ret worn :
> Cheap forms, and common hues, 'tis true,
> Through the bright shower-drop meet his view ;
> The colouring may be of this earth ;
> *The lustre comes of heavenly birth.*"
>   *Second Sunday after Trinity.*

I am not now unfolding the beauties, or passing
judgment on the faults, of this wonderful book ; its
great, and rapid, and not less its enduring success,
it is not at first sight easy to account for ; it certainly cannot be ascribed to its addressing especially
any one party in the Church ; although the opinions
of the author, whoever he might be, were declared
throughout with sufficient distinctness, yet the book
found favour equally with all ; it did not rest in
the beginning on the great name of its author ; for
some time its author was not known, and had it
been, he had earned no reputation in the world at
large which could have procured him such a host
of readers.   When it ceased to be anonymous in
substance, party heat in the Church, and the very
distinction he had earned, might, one would have
thought, have diminished its general acceptance.

I have no reason to believe that it has, even to the present time.

It is natural to ask to what cause especially is this exceptional success to be attributed, and will it still continue? I trust that an affirmative answer to the latter question may be given, founded on what I believe to be the true answer to the first. Of course the general success must be in a great measure attributed to the general merits of the execution; without the intrinsic beauty of the poetry, no success, or a very incomplete one, could have been obtained by the greatest excellence in the design; and, again, but for this last, the mere beauty of the poetry would, I think, after a while, have only placed the book on the library shelf with other volumes of beautiful poems in the language, a classic acknowledged and little read, exercising no daily and permanent influence. Now, as we know, a library book, or a book of the house, is just what it is not; it is rather a book of each person, and each room in the house. The design of it is very simply stated in the Preface. Keble wished to help towards the establishment of "a sober standard of feeling in matters of practical religion," and this by a work in close harmony with, and constant reference to, our Liturgy. In his title-page his motto is, "In quietness and in confidence shall be your strength." But this object, and this mode of obtaining it, both imply an appeal to a feeling, I believe, the most common and abiding in the heart of man, wherever absorbing worldliness or inveterate habits of vice have not overpowered it ; I mean the religious and devotional sentiment. This may seem too flattering an estimate of the human heart, but it must be remembered, I do not speak of practice ; I do not speak even of sentiment, that necessarily results in a good life ; but of sentiment and feeling merely. So limited, I believe the proposition to be true. How much of the pleasure we all take in works of fiction is owing to the existence of this feeling in our hearts. Those who shrink from the trials which religion may impose, and those who feel willing to undergo them, equally find their hearts excited by the lively picture of suffering, or triumphant virtue, though with regard to the former some bitterness may mingle with the sweet ; and these two classes make up the bulk of those who read. On the other hand, speaking generally, how cold are we in comparison to the story which tells us of the labours of intellect, the perseverance or ingenuity of the discoverer, the intrigues of the politician. And is not this because the former takes us more out of what is purely selfish, and brings us more close to what is religious in our nature ? Now to this feeling in the human heart "The Christian Year" makes unceasing appeal, with a voice so earnest, so manifestly sincere, so sad in its hopefulness, so unpretending as to the speaker, yet so authoritative and confident as to the cause

M

and the subject, that for the time it is commonly
irresistible; and to be so moved, as it is among the
purest, so unquestionably it is among the highest of
the pleasures which we are capable of enjoying.

This is an argument which I know must depend
for its acceptance mainly on the inward consciousness and feelings of those to whom it may be addressed.   And therefore I would ask any reader
gifted with an ordinary degree of poetical feeling,
what has been the effect of reading the verses for
the day in "The Christian Year" under favourable
circumstances of quiet and leisure? I apprehend that
although immediately on the perusal, the thoughts
which it occasions will vary much with the past conduct of the individual, in the end he will find he
has passed very much into that state of feeling in
regard to himself, which his conscience approves, and
towards his fellow-creatures and his Maker that in
which he would desire to be; he will feel soberly
hopeful as to himself; loving, grateful, and reverential towards his Maker.   And is not this the greatest
happiness we can expect in this life.   On these
grounds I explain the Volume's exceptional and
continued success, and I hope with great confidence
for its indefinite enduring.   It would lead me too far
afield, if I compared its prospects on these grounds
with Herbert's poems, which, however justly admired,
and still studied by some, have certainly lost much
of their general popularity.   In truth the two men

were more alike than their works, and what I have
said may be true of " The Christian Year," and yet
could not be truly said of " The Church."

Keble would not have assented to these conclusions : as Wilkes is reported to have said he was
no Wilkite, so Keble certainly was not a " Christian
Year" man.   Of course I do not suppose that he
could think, or would profess, that it had no merits ;
like other modest men in regard to their own compositions, he thought these over-rated ; and his taste
and judgment made him very conscious of its faults
in execution and finish ; but this does not adequately explain the position of his mind with regard to it ; it is strange, but it is certain that he
always spoke of it, and that was seldom, with
something of sadness and dissatisfaction.   I do not
think he often read it.   There were reasons for
this deeper than causes merely critical, and they
are worth considering ; the poems unavoidably paint
Keble's own heart ; they flowed out from it upon
subjects which lay deepest and nearest to it, and
no one can read them without believing all things
good of the author.   Keble felt this ; he knew what
the picture displayed ; he knew it would be taken
for a faithful likeness ; he did not indeed fear the
charge of self-display, but he thought the picture
not true ; he asked himself, was he then right in
exhibiting it ? and the good opinion of the world,
on which he knew a woe had been pronounced, was

to him with this impression a cause of real sorrow. In his poem on the "Danger of Praise," in the *Lyra Innocentium,* he says :—

> "And ah ! to him what tenfold woe,
>   Who hides so well his sin,
>   Through earth he seems a saint to go,
>   Yet dies impure within."

I have no doubt he had reference here to himself. Praise was at all times really painful to him. In writing to him on his mother's death I had used language, the particulars of which I do not recollect—but I spoke of him and his discharge of filial duties as I sincerely felt. Dyson, it appears, and some others in their letters of consolation, had written in the same strain—in his answer to me, he says :—

"I am afraid I shall be able only to send you an unsatisfactory hurried sort of letter, but I would rather do so, than let time run on, as I have done so often before, without thanking you as I do from my heart for your kind consoling letter ; kind in all respects except some partial expressions, such as I would beg it of you as a kindness to forbear ; they please me so well at first, that I am quite sure they are best not thrown in my way ; and when I come to look at them or think of them afterwards, they seem, as it were, to spoil the rest of the letter : *if you please, therefore,* do not send me any more of them."

To Dyson he says—

"Your kind letter came to me at Oxford at a moment when I needed it, and proved, I assure you, a real comfort to me ; indeed, I fear I was more delighted than I ought, both with your letter and 2 or 3 others which I received at the same time ; for it is humiliating to see, on reading them over, how much undeserved credit one's friends give one. But this will not bear talking about."

It was the one subject on which ever after I was obliged in writing to him to be very guarded in my language, even when I wrote on occasions which had excited my feelings of admiration strongly ; for though he could not write otherwise than gently and affectionately, I felt sure I had given him pain.

I have already printed an extract from his letter to Mr. Pruen respecting the Dedication. That is now very properly printed, I believe, in the Editions which have issued since his death, but he never would print it during his life. I remember when, in 1858, he allowed Mr. Parker to publish a handsome Edition in small folio, I suggested, or, rather, asked his permission for the printing it ; he would not absolutely deny me, but he yielded in language manifesting so clearly his unwillingness, that it would have been unkind to act on it, and I forbore.

In all this he was perfectly sincere, nor can I think his feeling morbid, or unreasonable, though it may have been, indeed was in my judgment, exaggerated. The more pure and holy a man is, the more odious will sin be to him ; and beside this, the more entirely will he refer every successful resistance to temptation, every good thought, all continuance in purity to the special favour of God, and feel that it calls on him for a more lively gratitude than common; so that every declension, through human infirmity unavoidable, will come to his conscience embittered with the sense of special ingratitude; sin in one who feels himself so favoured will seem double sin. This, I think, is the explanation of the declaration of St. Paul respecting himself, which I have always looked on as perfectly sincere. I am not comparing Keble, of course, with the great Apostle, but the same principle of judgment applies to both, indeed, to all good men; and when they say such things of themselves, though we may think them too severe in their judgments, we should acquit them of insincerity, and the miserable weakness of seeking for compliments.

Keble always published "The Christian Year" anonymously: at first the secret of authorship was tolerably well kept, but it was a prisoner committed to the custody of too many not to escape soon; however he availed himself always of the masque as he pleased, and sometimes he played with it amusingly enough. Not long after the publication, an old pupil, Mr. Bliss, in writing to him, mentioned the work, with some speculation as to the author; it might be, intending only to sound him; he answers, however:—

"I have seen the little book you mention, and I think I have heard it was written by an Oriel man. I have no wish to detract from its merit, but I can't say I am much in expectation of its cutting out our friend George Herbert."

I add, mainly for another reason, two notes written to a dignitary of the Church long after, who had questioned him as to the use of the word "wildering" in the verses on the Fifth Sunday in Lent :—

"Ye, too, who tend Christ's *wildering* flock."

He says in answer :—

"My Dear ——,

"It is very little use being anonymous, if one is to answer for the sense, or nonsense of all one writes just the same.

"But do you not think that such a passage as Ezekiel xxxiv. 12, in the Bible, and the mention of 'Christ's sheep that are scattered abroad' in the Ordination Service, joined with the present state of Christendom, is enough to justify and explain the word?

"You know the 'C. Y.' (as far as I remember it) every where supposes the Church to be in a state of decay.

"Ever my dear friend,

"affect^{ly} yours,

"J. Keble."

To this there was a reply which I have not seen, and to that this rejoinder :—

"Brooking near Totness,
"*April* 15, 1858.

"My Dear ——,

"As a proof that my conscience is not quite gone, I had really put your letter up to be answered among others when I left home for this place, and I now return its inclosures with many thanks. It is very pleasant to find so much sympathy with one's own travelling thoughts, such as they were in times past, or rather such as one wished them to be.

"With respect to the word which gave occasion to our little correspondence, I find that according to Johnson there is or was such word as 'wildering' or 'to wilder'— only unluckily for me it is a verb active—the same as to 'bewilder.' So it must be considered an error, and 'wandering' or some such word must be kindly substituted for it. I find it unluckily in the Oxford 'Psalter' also.

"I am always,

"My dear ——,

"Affect^{ly} your's,

"J. KEBLE."

It occurs in other parts of the book.

In spite of his concluding sentence it will be found, I believe, that the word "wildering" remained in all the editions published in his lifetime, and the line remains unaltered still. It happened to me more than once to point out some inaccuracy of language, or metre, admitting easily of correction; he used to answer not unkindly, but coldly, and intimated in effect that it was not worth while to alter it. This was the result, in great measure, of the feeling which he had grown to entertain towards the book, as well as of his constant occupation and the habit of procrastination, which, of course, did not decrease with years. He seemed to me not unconscious of the merits of the book, or of its probable usefulness;

but as if he half wished to disconnect himself from
it, and as if he would rather it had been the work of
some one else than himself. I have accounted for
this, which seems so strange, as well as I can.

In the first two editions, there were no verses on
what are called the State Services ; he did not regard
them as an integral part of the Common Prayer-book,
and I cannot now recall why he was induced to write
upon them. In the verses on the " Gunpowder Trea-
son" he wrote a stanza, which on the first reading
might certainly lead one to suppose that he denied
the Presence of our Lord's Body in the Elements after
consecration. Nobody, however, who knew his opinions on this subject, (and they were expressed openly
again and again in public, and in private, and in print,
with earnestness and uniformity,) could believe that he
intended to be so understood ; and when challenged
on the subject, he always maintained that his language was misunderstood, and that any writer whose
sentiments were unquestionably known should in justice have his language interpreted according to those
sentiments, where the meaning was not necessarily
opposed to them. He pointed out that the omission
of the word " only" after the expression " not in the
hands," raised the whole difficulty, and for that short
way of speaking he referred to passages in Scripture, which are numerous, as authority. The matter
was mentioned to him several times, but he declined to make any alteration. Some weeks before

his death, however, a member of the Upper House
of Convocation, addressing it, quoted the lines with
approbation in the sense most commonly attributed
to them; this he thought entirely altered the case,
and ought to prevent him from any longer over-
looking or acquiescing in the misinterpretation, and
he determined therefore to accept an alteration which
had been before suggested by a friend; he at once
directed that when a new edition should be called
for, this should be substituted for the old reading,
with a note, the substance of which he dictated.
At the time he did this, there was no illness upon
him which apparently threatened his life; a fortnight
later, in a note to me about Mrs. Keble's state, he
says, " As for myself, I eat, drink, and sleep heartily,
so you need be in no care about me so far." His
anxiety was entirely about her, and both contemplated that he would be the survivor. It pleased
God that he should die first. She to whom he bequeathed the copyright, naturally felt bound by the
injunction; and when she bequeathed the copyright
to her nephew, she imposed it on him,—this direction
he of course obeyed.

It cannot be doubted, on these facts, that the
alteration was Keble's own as much as if he had
written it himself years before, and that neither Mrs.
Keble, or her nephew, could properly exercise any
discretion in the matter. It would have seemed a
matter of course for the latter to make it; and in-

deed, when thus explained, to be of little importance
in itself. Keble's belief, it must be remembered, had
been long and generally known; no one could have
cited him as an authority for the doctrine which the
words were supposed to convey; and it is difficult to
understand how any one, knowing his belief, could
desire to circulate as his any verses, with the intention thereby of conveying something entirely contrary
to it, and acquiring thereby his authority for that
which he neither thought nor believed. I must not
be understood as making any insinuation of this kind
in regard to the Right Reverend Bishop, who, citing
the verse to grace the peroration of a speech, certainly was, in fact, the immediate occasion of the
alteration. Nor, indeed, do I make any imputation
against any individual, or any Body; what was said
and done in consequence—though I cannot approve
it—was, I doubt not, done upon grounds which seemed
justifiable to the doers.

To one who is familiar with Keble's diction in
"The Christian Year," there is no difficulty in understanding how an ambiguity of expression might
occur; and to one who knew him long and well,
there is equally no difficulty in understanding either
why the alteration was not made before, or why it
was directed to be made at the time it was made.
I do not think it was a happy one; but that the
direction was given under improper pressure at a
time when his judgment was obscured, or his power
of maintaining his own opinion enfeebled (and both

have been insinuated,) I am concerned strongly to
deny ; and those who impute that, I hope have not
considered how grave an imputation they cast on
his widow and her nephew, who must have known
if such had taken place. But there is the most
abundant evidence that this subject was perfectly
familiar to Keble, and had been on his mind for
years. By the kindness of a neighbouring clergyman, the Rev. Samuel Walker, who had written to
him in February, 1863, I am able to print the
material part of a letter, which sets this at rest :—

    " My dear Sir,

    " I am obliged by your kind suggestion regarding the
passage in the ' Christian Year.' For many years it has
been a matter which I have thought of at odd times, and
you will find in my dear friend Hurrell Froude's ' Remains '
that complaints were made of it near thirty years ago. I
thought of an alteration, but other friends over-ruled it.
Nor am I at present disposed to make any. Your's, I fear,
would hardly come up to what is wanted in the way of
doctrine. In a Note to the Preface of the Second Edition
of a book of mine, which nobody reads, on ' Eucharistical
Adoration,' I have given my own commentary on it : that
it is to be understood, " Not in the hands *only*," as against
a carnal presence—vide S. John vi. 63 ; and the same idiom
recurs elsewhere.

    " I have been shewn a passage in St. Bernard, but cannot
now recall it, which seemed to me to justify the expression.

    " Do you not think that if it *can* be justified, it had best
be retained, were it only to help in shewing, that such sayings do not necessarily bear such a meaning, and must be

interpreted consistently with the writer's sentiments known unquestionably in other ways ?"

Thus he wrote more than three years before his death, and thus he could not have written, had he intended to teach what those, who quarrelled with the alteration, desired he should be understood to have taught.

There is a story recorded by Isaac Walton, regarding George Herbert's " Temple," which is very apposite, and I will close what I have felt compelled to say on this painful matter, with repeating it. It is well known that in his last illness George Herbert committed the manuscript to the care of his friend Nicholas Ferrar, desiring him to publish it or burn it, according as he should think " it might turn to the advantage of any dejected poor soul," or not.

Mr. Ferrar, it is said, found that " there was in it the picture of a divine soul in every page, and that the whole book was such a harmony of holy passions, as would enrich the world with pleasure and piety :" he proceeded accordingly to publish.

" And this," says Walton, " ought to be noted, that when Mr. Ferrar sent this book to Cambridge to be licensed for the press, the Vice-Chancellor would by no means allow of the two so much noted verses—

> " Religion stands a tip-toe in our land,
> Ready to pass to the American strand,"

to be printed.

No doubt the Vice-Chancellor thought them untrue

in fact, and likely to be injurious to the Church ;
which at that time many might see reason for believing. Nicholas Ferrar, however, felt that he had
no power to enter into such considerations, and the
controversy finally ended thus : "The Vice-Chancellor said, I knew Mr. Herbert well, and know that
he had many heavenly speculations, and was a divine
poet ; but I hope the world will not take him to
be an inspired prophet, and *therefore* I license the
whole book."

Nicholas Ferrar discharged a plain duty conscientiously, and the Vice-Chancellor acted with great
good sense.

CHAPTER IX.

PROVOSTSHIP OF ORIEL.—EDITION OF HOOKER'S WORKS.—INDIA-HOUSE EXAMINATIONS.

KEBLE was called on as early as the fall of the year 1827 to prepare "The Christian Year" for a second edition;—

"But," he says, writing to me in September, "I own I am a little heartless about correcting; if things don't come of themselves, I very seldom find they come upon my calling for them. Moreover, having done admiring the print and paper, I find my own defects staring me more and more in the face as I read; so it is to be feared I shall not do much for one while."

In answer I pressed him :—

"Pray let no tædium or laziness prevent you from buckling yourself up to the task with an ardent spirit; they are so good, and may do so much, that it is a *duty* to make them as perfect as possible; *the* fault is obscurity of expression, here and there, and inadequacy in other places."

And then I went on into some particulars, but to borrow Wordsworth's words :—

> "'Twas throwing words away; for still
> The *wayward bard* would have *his* will."

But now came an event which occupied his atten-

tion considerably for a short while. Dr. Copleston was
raised to the Bench as Bishop of Llandaff, and at the
same time appointed to the Deanery of St. Paul's; he
had been Dean of Chester, and held that office with
the Provostship, a not unusual thing at that time. Indeed, there were shortly before two instances at Oxford, of Heads of Houses remaining such as Bishops.
But with Dr. Copleston this was quite out of the
question. Of course Keble's friends were anxious
to see him at the Head of Oriel, and I find both Dyson and I wrote to him; how Dyson expressed himself I do not know, but I must have written un-
guardedly and one-sidedly. He answered me thus,
after playing a little with the supposition that there
might after all be no vacancy :—

> " FAIRFORD,
> " *Dec.* 3, 1827.

"To say the truth, I should not at all choose, just at
present, to have to make up my mind on the matter you
propose to me; a thousand things would come in, of which
no one but myself *can possibly* judge, and which would
make it rather a perplexing case to me. I am not so insensible to ambition, and that sort of thing, as you seem to
think me; and many such letters as your last would, I am
afraid, help to make me more or less uncomfortable in retirement; however, in my cool and deliberate judgment,
which I am *sure* I am now exerting, this first Monday in
Advent, 1827, I must protest against the doctrine, that
a man may not be as truly and thoroughly useful in such
a situation as I am now in, or in any other which Pro-

vidence may put him into, as if he moved in a commanding sphere, and were what the world calls an influential character. I hope, therefore, if there is a vacancy, and the Fellows propose it to me, that I shall be able to see my way clearly, and come to a right decision ; at present I really do not know what I should answer, and I repeat it again, that nobody *can judge* for me. At any rate, *if you please* do not mention my name as connected with this subject till you are sure there is a vacancy. It must be very unpleasant to Copleston, if he should hear of it ; and I know the temper of Oriel well enough to be sure that any interference, even of the most friendly and delicate kind, would not be well received there. And now having, I trust, set myself up by this last sentence in your honour's opinion *as a diplomatic man*, and a *man of the world*, I must thank you for your answer to my case."

"Fairford,
"*Jan.* 14, 1828.

" My dear old Dyson,

" I have been looking to-day at your letter touching the Provostship, and have condemned myself of great ungraciousness in not having answered it sooner. You will have heard, I dare say, before now, how the matter is settled ; before I heard from you, I had consented to be voted for, but finding there was great difference of opinion, (all, however, in a friendly way,) and that I was very likely, I may say almost sure, to be left in a minority, and feeling moreover that a Headship at Oxford, though no doubt a comfortable respectable concern, would by no means realise my beau ideal of life, and most especially feeling that Hawkins would come to the work quite free and disengaged, while I should be every moment hankering after Fairford,

N

Bisley, or some such place,—all these things considered, I determined within a few days of the receipt of your letter, to abandon all thought of the offer, and wrote to my *partizans*, if I may call them so, accordingly. And I have not as yet begun to repent of doing so; indeed, the more I consider the affair, the more I am sure it was right; and I am very glad you agree with me in thinking so, for I am quite sure you do. All here, and at Bisley, take just the same view of the matter as I do; and so 'tis all just as it should be."

It was not, of course, with out-college men mainly that he corresponded on this subject. Froude, it seems, was the first who communicated to him the Bishop's resignation. Keble says:—

"I must beg a few days for consideration before I answer positively; I feel Hawkins's claim to be a very strong one, and almost doubt whether it is right for anybody in the world to be set up, when his inclinations are known."

And he closes this letter with a playful message:—

"My very kind love to old Hawkins, and tell him I think we had better put the Provostship in commission; Tyler take the red gown, Hawkins the work, and I the play. Qu'en pensez vous?"

Before, however, the end of 1827 he had made up his mind; and he writes thus to Froude:—

"FAIRFORD, ST. JOHN'S DAY.

"Since you went away I have been endeavouring (for without any proem, I think fit to enter at once into the

selfish part of this letter) to look this matter of the Provostship clearly in the face, and find out exactly what I had
best do : all being brought into a sum, to the best of my
poor judgment, I think I must, with all possible love and
thanks to you and others who think as you do, decline it
altogether. I don't act thus quite upon public grounds ;
for to say the plain truth, as far as I can fancy myself
judging impartially in such a matter, I can make out but
very little difference between H. and myself in positive
fitness for the thing ; in some respects I look on each of
us as fitter than the other. But I have great doubts whether I should be so comfortable there as I am now ; and
I don't suppose he has any doubt at all. I have calls, as
you know, elsewhere of a more pressing nature than he.
I don't fancy College a pleasant place for one's father
and sister to visit one at, &c., &c., &c. Now although
these objections might all give way, and ought to do so,
if one's College absolutely called upon one as the only
person, they come in with what I feel to be decisive force,
when there is a difference of opinion to encourage one's
natural wish of getting over things as quietly as possible.
In case any sort of unpleasant feeling should arise, one
should immediately say, 'now this is my fault ;' and in
a College, and among clergymen, a great deal should
surely be given up to ensure freedom from factions and
envy. And 'after all our superior advantages, Fellows
of Oriel are but men,' and Provosts *in esse* or *in posse*, not
many degrees superior in the scale of existence.

" Therefore, my dear fellow, don't think of me any more,
but let good old Hawkins walk over the course ; and what
I say to you, I mean to say to him, to Plumer, and perhaps
one or two more, by to-morrow's post. And I feel myself
safe in this resolution, which I should not by any means

in the opposite one.   For indeed I don't imagine my constitution at all charmed against the Oxford epidemic, rather
I should say, the Doctorial epidemic everywhere, if you
know what that is."

The kindly feeling these extracts express towards
Dr. Hawkins was, I am sure, returned on his part;
and pleasant indeed it is to see a College Election,
which is commonly so exciting, conducted between
those, who might be considered opposing candidates,
in so amiable a spirit.

Keble wrote to me after the election was over,
on the 11th of February, 1828, from Fairford.   His
letter commences with affectionate expressions of
sympathy at two family losses, with which we had
been visited :—

" In both cases I know you have the best of consolations
in remembering the kindness and goodness of those who
are gone.   It is a topic of comfort, that one feels more and
more, the longer one considers it, to be quite inexhaustible.
I dare say you were as glad as I was to meet once again
the good old Dyson, as fresh and as cordial as ever.   It
was an unexpected delight, when I went up to Oxford to
the Oriel election, to get a thorough coze with him.   How
comfortable he seems in his work of coin-inspecting and
date-hunting; and is it not rather a rare piece of philosophy, that he should take pleasure in the very expectation
of finding his work too great for him ever to finish.   By
this time I conclude his wife has joined him again ; and
perhaps I may run up and spend a day or two with them,
when Noel Ellison is there, he having promised to take
them in his way from the North to Huntspill.

" I hope you don't think I did wrong in the Oriel affair.
If there had been anything like an unanimous call of the
Fellows, I certainly should have thought it right to go;
although I am not at all clear that the change would have
been for my comfort. As things were, I felt that I was
taking the safe side in declining all thoughts of the thing;
it was not a clear *call*, and I hold it under such circumstances always best to let well alone. I do not deny that
it might perhaps be more comfortable for me to have fuller
employment than I have, yet there must surely be enough
for one to do, if one had but a little regular industry, and
common sense. For instance, one's time would be well
spent in making a sort of analytical index for the next
edition of the Ethics, or the Ecclesiastical Polity, or Bishop
Butler; therefore I have made up my mind to leave off complaining of want of work, and to keep contented with my
Father and Elizabeth, until I have, as I said, a clear *call*
elsewhere."

These letters shew distinctly under what influences
Keble acted in respect of the Headship of his College; had there been no difference of opinion among
the Fellows, he would have obeyed their call, and
been, I am sure, gratified by it; he would have
felt it a duty; and he was besides very fond of
Oxford, of literary society, and of young men; but
he would have gone there with some misgivings, and
I can hardly think without some forebodings. Within
his College, as the father and friend and pastor, in
some sense, of his Fellows and the Students, I suppose no one could have excelled him. In these re-

spects I still think we were right in pressing him to entertain the notion heartily, and to let his inclinations become known at once, and decidedly. We were fond enough of him to think that in these respects, without any formality, or pretentiousness, which might provoke opposition, or ridicule, he would exhibit a sort of model to the University, and contribute to make a great change for the better in its tone and manners. But the duties of the Head of a House in those days, even more than now, extended beyond the walls of his College; and already there were symptoms, which could hardly have escaped his penetration, of the troubles and hot disputes which not long after began to agitate the University, and not least the Governing Body, of which he would have been a member. In these it is too clear now that he would have been in a minority, and perhaps the very reputation and personal influence which I will suppose him to have acquired, as well as his great ability, might have made his position only the more painful to one of his sensitive nature. Looking back on this passage of his life, I cannot but recognise his non-election as one of those disappointments, (how frequent they are,) which one comes to regard as special blessings; disappointment I am bound to say as to this, to us rather than to himself.

In the June following he visited me in London, and I am tempted to make an extract or two from the first letter I had from him after he had left me; this was not until August 21, 1828 :—

"What a shame; it is the 21st August, and I have not written to thank you for the pleasant days you gave me the beginning of June, for indeed I don't know when I have enjoyed anything so much as my visit to you; it is a peculiar delight to find anything so domestic and comfortable, so much like a country parsonage, as your house in the middle of Law and London. I know we Curates ought to enjoy ourselves a great deal more than we do; but, as it is, we are a sad grumbling race, and I doubt whether $\frac{2}{3}$ of us get as much pleasure from the trees and shrubs we live always amongst, as you do from the *snatch* you get in your Square for $\frac{1}{2}$ an hour before dinner when you come home from chambers. . . . .

" I heard yesterday from Arnold, who seems to be fast taking root at Rugby, and will soon fill the school I dare say. I only hope he will not teach them his own notions of right and wrong in politics. He says you have got some of his Thucydides; don't sit up at night correcting it, when you ought to be asleep. I charge you, rather send it to me, if you find it an incumbrance, without minding what the book may lose (or gain) by the difference between us. I very much admire the sort of cheerful, straight-forward way, in which Tommy sets out on his new career. I am sure he is right, and much to be imitated in that, whatever he may be in his notions about some matters."

" Poor Churton, about whom I was so anxious when I visited you, gets rapidly worse, and all hope is given up. He will be a great and irreparable loss to his family and friends; but I never knew any one whom one could trust on a death-bed, humanly speaking, with more confidence,

that all would turn out well.   The only uncomfortable
thing is, that his case, (I am much afraid,) was mistaken ;
and he was sent to Brighton at a time when it was probably one of the worst things he could do to go there.
However, I do not know why one should be *vexed* at
a mistake of this kind, more than at other circumstances, in a friend's illness.   It is setting up for more
infallibility than we have any right to."

In the September of this year, 1828, he went to
Lyme, and I mention this, because this was the first
occasion on which I find the name of his future wife
introduced into his correspondence.   He went "to
convoy her and her mother" for her health :—

" She had been but drooping," he says, " ever since the
Spring, and I was not sorry myself for a bit of an excuse
to smell, taste, see, and hear my dear friend the sea, whom
I seem to like better and better every year of my life.   I
staid three Sundays, and only came home Saturday week.
. . . . . I should very much like to have gone on when I
was so far West ; but I made a kind of vow to stay quietly,
bathe, write, and read, the first of which good resolutions
I performed much more accurately than either of the others,
to the great strengthening of my nerves, and damage of my
complexion.   The Clarkes are not yet come home, but
Charlotte seemed much mended when I left them ; and we
are in good hope she will now be as well as ever again ;
she is never a very strong body.   Lyme is a beautiful bit
of coast to my fancy, one can hardly imagine oneself so
near your red cliffs at Sidmouth, the colouring, form, and
everything is so very different.   What most strikes me in
all these little absences of mine, is the amazing rate at

which Puritanism seems to be getting on all over the kingdom ; if I may judge from what I heard in church and out,
the old-fashioned way of Divinity is quite the exception,
not the rule, in that district."

This intimation of an unfavourable opinion in regard to the Party in the Church, which was then
fighting its way upwards to what I suppose it must
be admitted that it has now attained, a more than
equal share in numbers and influence, was not now
made for the first time ; his convictions on this subject were very deep-seated in his mind, and were
occasioned by no personal, or political feelings ; but
by a conviction that it was in error on some points
of belief, which to him were cardinal ; and moreover
that it was in its effects adverse to that quietness
of spirit, humility and charity, which were to him
above all price. I need not say that these differences created in him no unkind feeling towards
any individual, nor any insensibility to Christian
graces, wherever he found them.

The close of the year 1828, and the beginning of
1829, were agitated, it may be remembered, by the
vehement discussions of the Roman Catholic Question. Mr. Peel's change of opinion on that subject,
his voluntary resignation of his seat for the University of Oxford, and then allowing himself to be proposed for re-election, produced a violent division of
parties there. I am not going into these matters now,
and I only mention them as they bear personally on

Keble. He had been brought up in, and cherished from conviction, opinions hostile to the proposed concessions, and he was moreover one of that numerous body of men who thought it would be a degradation to the University to return Mr. Peel, "being in office especially," after what had happened. I had been brought up as he had, and had not then changed my convictions on the question, but I differed with him in the conclusion he drew as to the seat. I thought Mr. Peel unquestionably the best man we could elect, and that having changed his mind, as it was fair to presume, from a knowledge of facts, which we had not, and a sense of necessity, of which we could be no judges, there was nothing in his conduct to warrant our rejection of him. While for the University I thought, (as I should for individuals,) it would be wise and manly to face the groundless imputation of time-serving rather than dismiss the tried and most efficient servant for doing what he believed to be his duty. So I resolved to vote for Mr. Peel, and I would not decline to be on his Committee. My dear friend was very much distressed; he wrote shortly, and with some heat, and evidently in a wounded spirit. It must be remembered that on all such questions his opinions were "stuff of the conscience." How I answered him I do not remember; but we met at the election on opposite sides with perfect cordiality, and his letters resumed immediately their old affectionate tone. Not, in-

deed, that he changed his opinions. Writing to
Froude, in March, 1829, he says :—

"As touching politics, I am in the same mind that I
always was, that we could not do otherwise than we did
in the Election. But I am quite satisfied of Peel's good
intentions, though I cannot acquit him of weakness in giving
way for the reasons he states. Yet I give him credit now
for no ordinary virtue in keeping his place, when he *had*
given way. The upshot is, that I think well of him, and
ill of his measures ; and that I have very little hope of
his ever recovering the confidence of the Tories again."

Towards the close of the year 1829, Archdeacon
Heathcote died, and Sir William offered Keble the
living ; it was a great temptation to him ; the circumstances, and the manner of the offer touched his
heart ; he was fond of the place, and the people, and
affectionately attached to, and in point of opinions,
in entire agreement with, the Patron. Writing to
me, he says :—

"Another old friend I have lost, Archdeacon Heathcote, of whom I knew less, but have every reason to think
highly ; indeed, to reproach myself for not having thought
highly enough of him whilst he lived, now I know with
what grievous bodily pain he had to struggle in order to
maintain that composure of his. I was at Hursley a fortnight ago, considering and devising whether or how to
accept the Vicarage which was most kindly offered me ;
but after a good deal of doubt, and some anxiety, I have
written to decline it finally. I like Heathcote as well as

ever, and am quite sure he will put it in good hands. I
thought of Johnny and Henry, and our reclinings and
wheelings under the large elms, now (most of them) no
more. I have accepted a Nomination as Examiner at the
India House, mainly in hope of getting a visit to you, and
now the rogues have fixed it to the 31st March, when I
fear you will be away. But if we live till November, perhaps we may make it up."

Thus he seemed to have extinguished all hope of
his ever becoming Vicar of Hursley, because he
would not quit the care of his father; in his place
the Archdeacon's son was presented, the Rev. Gilbert Wall Heathcote, a man much younger than
himself; he was presented absolutely, and there was
no reason to anticipate another opportunity of bringing Keble there.

The India House Examinations, of which he speaks,
were instituted under an Act of Parliament passed in
1826, (the 7 G. IV. c. 56,) with the object of supplying
more Civil servants for the East India Company than
Haileybury was found able to educate. Oxford and
Cambridge were to nominate each two Examiners,
who should examine candidates at the India House
in March and October in each year, and Keble
acted in this capacity for the years 1830 and 1831;
in the former year I find among his colleagues the
name of the present Bishop of St. David's. It seems
to have been an office which the Universities filled
with men among the most distinguished of their

members, and to which such men were well pleased
to be appointed. The present Bishops of St. Asaph
and Llandaff, were among them. The appointment
of Keble was a matter of considerable interest to
me, in the hope it gave me of seeing him more often
in London.

His letters were somewhat less frequent at this
period, but when he wrote, it was in a light-hearted,
affectionate strain, as usual. Thus he begins to me
on one occasion :—

"My dear Friend,—'What unknown correspondent is
this.' say you to Mrs. J. T. C., before you break the seal.
'Oh,' says she, 'I think I have an indistinct remembrance
of the hand. Do break it open and see.' 'Well, I have,
and he calls me "dear friend ;" let's look to the end of the
letter. Oh, Keble : aye, I think I do remember such a
name, but the creature used me so ill in not answering
my friendly enquiries for half a year together, or more,
that I am almost inclined to have nothing more to do
with him.' All this, and if there be aught worse which
peremptory justice may dictate, I humbly acknowledge
myself to have deserved at your Worship's hands, for I
really have no excuse. Our health, thanks to our constant
Preserver, has continued as usual."

Then he goes on to tell me of his family, and
a visit he had been paying at his brother's :—

"Tom," says he, "and I set to work and gave little Tom
a regular lecture in Toryism and High-Churchmanship
in a large folio Clarendon with prints ; he snaps at all the
Roundheads, and kisses all the Cavaliers ; moreover, he
has a great opinion of Edward VI., but is a little perplexed

to know whether Popery is dead or no. As for his sister, she is all fat and fun, and does not trouble herself with Politics yet. And yet for all these good things, I have been too cross and lazy to write a friendly line to my kind host and hostess and Godchild, and all in whom I am interested in Torrington Square ; but I am really ashamed, so do not be too hard upon me."

According to his promise, he came to us in October for the India House Examinations. He talked, as he had written, in great admiration of Miller's new volume of sermons ; and those who are desirous of following his judgment in such matters may like to be told that his favourite sermons were three, those against judging by comparisons, on Family Worship, and on the fiftieth Psalm ; these he was desirous of reprinting in a cheaper form for the use of the poor.

This, it will be remembered, was the winter remarkable for the formidable agrarian riots in the Western counties. He had now been for years an attentive and honest observer of the condition of the labouring classes, and their feelings. I was one of the Counsel for the Crown who attended the Special Commission into Wiltshire, and had written to him my impressions from Salisbury. I will not give the whole of his answer, but it is worth while to extract a portion :—

" We have been very much taken up ever since the end of November with talking and thinking of the tumults aforesaid. I am not inclined so much as you are, I think, to lay the blame of them on the farmers; no doubt their insolence in many cases, and their extortion in some, has aggravated the tendency to riot; but I am more and more satisfied that old Malthus, hard and vulgar as he is in many things, and much as my father and Southey taught me to dislike him, has hit the right nail on the head; and that something of this sort sooner or later was the infallible fruit of the 43rd Eliz."

He was against all arbitrary or extorted increase of wages beyond what the fair market price of produce would enable the farmers to pay; and relied for improvement in the condition of the labourers on a gradual emigration, accompanied by a gradual repeal of the Poor Laws as regarded able-bodied men and children.

It will be seen how much this agrees in substance with what not long after was actually done, and no doubt with good effect ; but I cite the passage rather for the sake of shewing how he could cast aside in the pursuit of truth a very strong prejudice —and few could have a stronger than he had against Malthus. His was exactly the mind, which turned with something like disgust at one or two of the leading positions of that writer's celebrated work. He was very intent upon this matter, and I find a letter to Dyson, from which I shall have to make an extract immediately, is written on the blank leaf of a printed sketch of his " Plan for the Gradual

Amendment of the System of Parochial Relief in the Southern Counties of England ;" the principle of his scheme was the promotion of emigration, and the means were mainly the empowering of parishes to borrow money on the rates ; but I notice that he had not overlooked, what, in legislation on such matters as relief of the poor, and the education of their children, seems too commonly forgotten, the broad distinction between the South and North of England.

The letter to which I have just referred relates to a totally different subject. My readers will remember a letter written at the close of the discussion about the Provostship of Oriel, in which, among other possible and proper employments for his time, Keble spoke of the preparation of an Analytical Index to the " Ecclesiastical Polity ;" he was now called on to undertake the more worthy employment of editing for the Clarendon Press a new edition of the great work itself. What he did upon this call, and how he did it, are now well known ; but in such a matter I think it will be interesting to follow his course by steps, and to see how, from a very inadequate conception on the part of the Delegates in the first instance, he was enabled to work out to a great extent his own views, and to vindicate both the book itself and the author from much ill-usage and misconception.

Keble had been an enthusiast about Hooker from

his early youth ; the great man's connection with
Corpus, and the relics relating to him, preserved in
our Archives, (as a certain special portion of the
Library was called,) with which Keble and his brother
as early as 1816 had busied themselves, helped to increase this feeling ; partly it was what may be called
political ; partly, and I think for the greater part, it
was religious : if he could have been bitter in anything, it would have been in his condemnation of the
old Puritanical spirit, which seemed to him alien from
the better spirit of the Church of England, as he
shaped her to his own imagination. The pilgrimage
to Hooker's grave with Tucker was among his youthful indulgences ; and he wrote, in 1817, standing by
it in a silent shower, that beautiful sonnet, which will
be found among his early poems. The editions ex-
tant of the works were quite unworthy of them, inaccurate in the text, and inconvenient in the use ;
moreover, he had reason to believe, on better than
the common evidence, that they were, as to important parts, very corrupted. I have no doubt it
was a delight to him to be invited by the Delegates
of the Press, through Cardwell, one of them, to undertake the office of Editor.

On Dec. 18, 1830, he writes to Dyson thus :—

" I heard from Cardwell the other day that a new edition
of Hooker is in contemplation at the Clarendon, and he
wants me to undertake it ; I don't very well know what
such an undertaking implies ; but he says it will be a mere

O

reprint, he thinks, if I decline it : so I think of trying it, if
I can get you and Tom to help ; or rather I should like for
you, most venerable, to be *the* editor, and for Tom and me
to be under-strappers ; and if you will allow me, I will propose this to Cardwell.   At any rate, I wish you would give
me your opinion as to what is wanted for a good edition of
Hooker, and then I shall be able to judge whether I can
decently undertake it.   I am still in abeyance about the
Psalms, and waiting for a good opportunity of communicating with the Archbishop, or rather, I should say, I shrink
from writing to him, because I feel sure that in his extreme
caution he would damp my project at once.   However,
I suppose I shall take courage some day.   We are full just
now of political, or rather rural economy ; and emigration
seems the order of the day among us.   I have got a little
scheme with regard to that, which I should like much to
have your opinion on.   In short, there is no end of the
things I have to talk over with you ; indeed, how should it
be otherwise in these times with two such great politicians.
I was much amused at Oxford to hear the old Liberals
talking rank Jacobitism the other day.   L—— L——, I understand, wishes for a military government.   And to conclude, be the constitution what it may, you are hereby
wished a merry Christmas and a happy New Year, and
may it not pass away without our exchanging visits.   And
so we all rest your's and your Lady's very affectionates,

"The Kebles."

He writes again to Dyson on the 18th of January,
1831, very shortly :—

"The purport of this is rather to ask you, *bonâ fide, will*
you help me about Hooker ? And if you won't, will you

give me a little hint or two, what one had best do? You see I have accepted Cardwell's proposal, thinking I could not do worse than nothing, and he said the choice was between us two—me and nothing. The smallest donation in the way of advice, &c., will be thankfully received. I must be ready with a proposal to lay before the Delegates by the end of this month, when I go to Oxford to preach ; *verbum sat sapienti.*"

I do not know what answer Dyson had sent him to the first of these two letters ; but it is clear from that which now follows, that to the second he had sent one full and well considered. And it is satisfactory to know that in the end both the haste and the scruples of the Delegates were overcome, and Keble was allowed to pursue his own course, and produce an edition worthy of the subject-matter, and of all the parties concerned in the publication.

"*Feb.* 10, 1831.

"MY DEAR DYSON,

"Many thanks for your welcome letter of 'Advice to a Middle-aged Editor,' full of most useful hints, and many more thanks for your kind offer of assistance. I drew up a proposal which Cardwell laid before Messrs the Delegates (a most disagreeable word, for it puts one in mind of Paris, Poland, Brussels, Ireland, and everything that's whiggish and disagreeable), and being constructed in a great measure from your hints and Tom's, it was for the most part approved ; but they are in a hurry to get out the book, some varlet of a dissenting edition being now in possession of the public ear, with notes about as apt for Hooker as Voltaire's are for Pascal : for which reason they demur

to the enquiry into the genuineness of the last three books,
which they think would take up too much time ; and this
I mind the less, as I am not sanguine in expecting to make
anything out on the subject.   Moreover, whoever ventures
to question the said genuineness must be prepared to do
mortal battle with Henry Hallam, Esq., of Constitutiono-
Middle-Ageo celebrity ; who I find fancies he has settled
the matter in one round sentence.   And this I take to be
one reason why those cautious mortals decline the subject ;
though they say nothing about it.   If one could make out
anything, it might come in an additional volume, with
a thorough good index ; which, as things are, is more than
they must expect.   Now the drift of all this is, to tell you
how much you will help me if you will only put down any
historical matter which strikes you as useful to illustrate
any passage.   I say 'historical,' because I think that is
what you will like best : but contributions in any other
kind will be most thankfully received.   Tom has begun
an index to the Scripture quotations, and I am correcting
the text, and verifying quotations as far as I have the
means of doing here ; also dividing the whole into paragraphs ; this Tom has done long ago ; and if we agree we
shall think ourselves correct.   As to 'the Christian Letter
of certain English Protestants, with Hooker's MS. Notes,'
which you wrongfully detain from Tom, and about which
you keep such a determined Old Bailey sort of silence in
your last epistle to me, I am disposed to think the best
way will be to embody the valuable part of the said notes
in our lower margin, as occasion may require.   I quite
agree with you on the desirableness of a general view of
the Writers and Books against which Hooker had to write
(and perhaps of those who preceded and immediately followed him in the controversy, Whitgift, Bridges, Covel,

Bancroft, &c.), but will *you* write it for us? I much fear it will be beyond our calibre. Well now, my dear Mrs. Dyson, I think you must be perfectly satisfied with the quantity of work we have assigned to that lazy Vicar of yours. I am not without hopes that the mere anticipation may serve as a saline draught to drive away his cold, and clear his head; but we shall be glad anyhow to know how he is going on."

I perceive towards the close of the same letter he indicates in a playful yet determined word his opinion upon the holding a living on the term of resigning it in favour of another—an opinion he had probably derived from Bishop Wilson, a great authority with him at all times,—and I will insert it in a parenthesis, though foreign to the present matter. He says, "I hear that ·Noel has been accepting a living to hold; please to bite him well when you write, there's a good Jerry."

From this time he was fairly engaged on the work; what assistance he received from Dyson from time to time I am not able to state specifically, though I do not doubt it was very valuable; but it is certain that from his brother, whose zeal in the matter was equal to his own, he received much, and important. But it was a work of years. The publication was not until 1836; and this could scarcely be otherwise, considering the absolute necessity he was under of frequent reference to public libraries, and the difficulty he experienced in leaving home for the purpose: this he never liked to do, and

scarcely ever did, unless his brother, or some intimate friend of his sister's, could take his place during
his absence.

In the letter from which I have last extracted, he
makes a free and playful allusion to Mr. Hallam, who
had pronounced a clear opinion in favour of the
authenticity of the three last books as we have them.
It will be seen by Keble's Preface, that at last in
substance, though not professedly, he did not shrink
from "the mortal battle," which he speaks of, with
that great authority. He was in possession of evidence, in particular as to the sixth book, which
Mr. Hallam, it is clear, had never seen, and which
was really all but demonstrative. To this, indeed,
he yielded in later editions of his History. I must
refer to Keble's Preface for a full account of this evidence, but this part of it may be shortly stated thus :
—Hooker had sent the Sixth Book in manuscript
to Cranmer and Sandys for their criticisms ; they
made and returned them ; these shewed, both by
the catch-words prefixed to nearly all the notes,
and by their own tenor, that they were written upon
a text different in itself, and on a different subject
from the Sixth Book as we have it. But the controversy, if so it may be called, furnishes an instance
how dangerous it is to rely in matters of this sort on
conclusions drawn from intrinsic evidence only. Mr.
Hallam says, "The intrinsic evidence arising from the
work itself, on which in this branch of criticism I am

apt chiefly to rely, *seems altogether to repel every suspicion* [a]." Keble, to the credit of his critical acumen
be it said, before he had seen the document to which
I refer, " had always suspected" that other papers,
which Hooker had left behind him, had been substituted for the genuine Sixth Book ; " seeing it is so
little to the purpose, the last fault with which one
should suspect anything of his to be chargeable."

It will be worth while to trace him in his progress
in this important work from his letters.

As early as July 6, 1831, writing to me from
Fairford, after describing the difficulty under which
he laboured as to leaving home, he communicates
to me the discovery of the document I allude to
above :—

"I have met with one thing in C.C.C. Library, which
has proved to be more interesting than I expected, viz.
some notes by Hooker's friends, Cranmer and Sandys, on
the MS. 6th Book of the E. Polity, which he had sent to
them to criticize. They are many of them merely verbal,
but even those have their interest, not merely as reliques,
but also from the sort of light they throw on the tempers of
the three friends, and the terms on which they mutually
were. But some few of them are full of matter and very
sensible, and they prove to demonstration, I think, that the
6th Book, as we have it, is by no means R. H.'s ; at least, if
it be his, it is a mere collection from other papers, which
he may have left, substituted for the genuine 6th Book. This
I have always suspected, seeing it is so little to the pur-

[a] Constitutional History, vol. i. ch. iv. p. 237, 1st edit.

pose, the last fault with which one should suspect anything
of his to be chargeable : and to my mind these papers entirely prove it."

On Oct. 29, 1832, writing to Dyson, he says :—

" Did I tell you that Cotton (of Ch. Ch.) is collating the
Hooker MSS. in Dublin Coll., and pronounces them very
valuable? Have you any friend in London who could help
me at the State Paper Office? I think it possible there may
be some correspondence about the latter years of Q. Eliz.,
which may throw light on the history of the book.   Also
how am I to find out what became of Lord Conway's
Library, or Bp. Andrewes', or any other of the Libraries,
which Isaak Walton mentions as having contained copies
of the missing books.   In consequence of Cotton's statements, the Delegates have allowed an indefinite time to
go on with Hooker ; which is very convenient, as I have
only bits and snatches of time to employ on it."

In December, 1832, writing to Cornish, he says :—

" I don't seem able to tell you much of our old friends.
Our *very* old friend Dick Hooker grows more slowly than
one could have expected ; the fault whereof I am willing
to throw not so much on my own indolence as on Tom's
occupations, which hinder him from coming here, and
therefore hinder me from going to Oxford, and I am now
at a point where I cannot get on without libraries."

On Dec. 3, 1834, he writes to me from Fairford :—

" As for Hooker he plods on, rather slow than sure : we
are just now at the Athanasian Creed, i.e. not half through
the 2nd volume.   It would be pleasant work if one had the

command of libraries, but as I have been forced to do it by fits and snatches, it is anything but satisfactory."

In January, 1835, writing to Cornish, he says :—

"My friend Dick H. gets on much more slowly than I could wish. I am only as yet in the part about Baptism, in Book V. ; and let me advise you, as a friend, not to undertake editing Hooker, till you have read a good lot of the Fathers."

In August, 1835, writing to Froude, he says :—

"As for myself I am now all through Hooker, except about ½ a dozen references in some of the *Opuscula*, and must begin forthwith to discuss the Prelim. Dissertation, in which N. says I must give a view of Hooker's views. But this will go terribly against the grain ; and, indeed, I sometimes feel as though I were utterly incapable of it. Such is my feeling this very evening, owing in part, I imagine, to the oppressive drought and heat of the day : but I must set doggedly to work, if I can, to-morrow. I am more and more satisfied that Richard was in most things a middle term between Laud and Cranmer, but nearer the former ; and also that he was in a transition state when he was taken from us ; and there is no saying how much nearer he might have got to Laud, if he had lived twenty years longer. His notion of Regal, or rather State, power would rather have stood in the way, and so *perhaps* would his dislike to anything approaching to Justification by inherent grace. But in the great point of the Sacraments, as I conceive, he was almost or entirely with us ; if such an expression be not ludicrously presumptuous."

In Sept. 1835, he writes from Oriel to Dyson :—

"I have been plodding on with Hooker, and have at

last, after a sort, finished the notes, and begun the Editor's Preface, in which I am now got to the eighth Book, and therefore shall soon, I hope, have finished the critical part of it ; but I am doubting whether or not to attempt a theological part, i.e. a kind of *precis* of Hooker's views on the great subjects ; after the manner of those which the Benedictine Editors, I believe, adopt in their edition of the Fathers. Newman says I ought to add something of this sort ; I doubt both my ability and my leisure, but one can but try ; and it is a satisfaction to think, that if the trial fails, it is but putting so much of the MS. into the fire, and the rest will do."

Finally, on March 17, 1836, he tells Dyson :—

" I have this day sent my last sheet of the Hooker Preface to the press, i.e. the correction of it, so that nothing remains but the index, which will take a few days licking into shape ; the matter of it is all ready : wish me joy of this, although I expect to be pelted with plenty of hot water, for certain views which I have given in the Preface."

I have thought it well to be thus minute as to his progress in this labour, and the difficulties which beset it. Its importance to the Church of England can scarcely be over-estimated. All will agree, I presume, in the advantage of having the text of this great work diligently collated with the best editions, briefly and carefully annotated, with a verification of the references, and made more conveniently readable by the breaking it up into numbered paragraphs and sections, with a running title of the chief topics. No Father of the English Church has now had more justice done to him in all these respects and no one, I believe, more needed it, none more highly deserved it.

But it would have been discreditable to the University, if the Delegates, when they were reprinting Hooker, had limited the Editor, as it will have been seen was at first proposed, either as to the extent of his labours, or the time within which they were to be accomplished. They made an excellent choice of their editor; and although, it must be admitted, he tried their patience considerably, they made allowance for his difficulties, and never withdrew their confidence. In a series of English Classics which they are now printing, the first book of the "Ecclesiastical Polity" is rightly included, and I have had the pleasure of reading the masterly Introduction of the editor, Mr. Church : it seems clear from this that the lapse of thirty years has brought to light little, if any, new matter, and detected Keble in no substantial error. His edition, the Clarendon Edition, still remains, and probably will remain the standard one; and this is a distinction which Oxford cannot lightly afford to lose in regard to the works of her great son.

It has been seen how Keble speaks of his Preface ; when one considers the difficulties under which he wrote it, it is a really astonishing work ; and it shews how much knowledge, and in how many various

ways, he had not merely acquired, but assimilated
and made his own.   It was not to be expected that
in one part of it he would please all parties in our
unhappily divided Church ; and it would be presumptuous in an ignorant person, as in these respects
I am, to pronounce a judgment on the controversies
he dealt with, or his account of the agents and movements in it.   But looking on it only as a narrative,
and as a piece of reasoning, I cannot suppress the
feeling of satisfaction I have as an old Scholar of
Corpus, that it fell to the lot of another Scholar
of the same House to do this act of justice to the
greatest name upon our list, and that he was enabled to do it so consummately.

CHAPTER X.

PAIGNTON. — POETRY PROFESSORSHIP, AND LEC-
TURES.—ASSIZE SERMON, 1833.—THE TRACTS.—
DEATH OF MR. KEBLE.—1835.

I HAVE thought it better to set down in one
place all that it seemed desirable for me to
state in regard to the Edition of Hooker's works,
and in so doing, I have necessarily departed from
the order of time in my general narrative; to this I
now return.

I am entirely indebted to the Memoir to which I
have so often referred, for my knowledge of the particulars of the incident which I am about first to
speak of, and I take the liberty of transcribing the
passage[a]. Mr. Moor says :—

"In the year 1831, when Mr. Keble was living with his
father at Fairford, the present Lord Bishop of Exeter offered to him the valuable and important living of Paignton
in Devonshire, considering him even then to be 'the most
eminently good man in the Church,' as his Lordship has

[a] I may state here that this Memoir is not, I believe, printed separately, but is included with other matters in a handsome volume published by Mr. Savage at Winchester, entitled "The Birth-place, Home,
Churches, and other places connected with the Author of 'The Christian Year,' illustrated in Thirty-two Photographs." 2nd. Ed. 1867.

kindly informed the writer of this Memoir; adding that 'the conscientious scruple of the Patron, who had purchased that presentation, and who felt doubtful of the propriety of his acquiring Church patronage by such purchase,' made him feel it his 'duty to use the utmost caution in selecting a person to fill it.'"

Nothing could be more flattering than this offer, but the circumstances I have already stated, of which it is to be presumed the Bishop at the time was not aware, of course made the acceptance of it out of the question. In after life, when a warmer climate than that of Hursley, and close vicinity to the sea became necessary for Mrs. Keble's health, and very useful for his own, a residence on the shores of Torbay might have been very beneficial; but it is still impossible to regret that he could not accept Paignton.

In the same year he was without any opposition placed in the vacant chair of the Poetry Professorship. This is usually held by two successive elections for ten years, and when it was vacant in 1821, his friends were very anxious that he should be elected, nor was he indisposed to it; but as soon as he heard of the intention of the late Dean of St. Paul's to become a candidate, he would not permit his claim to be pressed. It would have been difficult to persuade him to be a candidate in any contested election; but Milman and he were on very friendly terms, and Keble felt that his talents, acquirements, and distinction, entitled him to any honour of that kind which the University could confer.

Keble now was not without scruples as to his own qualifications for the office, and the passage I am about presently to cite from one of his letters seems to shew that a chance expression of mine, favouring, I fancy, his own disposition to undervalue himself, may have contributed to create, or increase these scruples. However they were wisely overcome. In December, 1831, dating from Fairford, he says to me :—

"I am not very particularly sanguine about this Professorship, to which my friends have been so kind as to nominate me; I feel as if the Latin wouldn't come; and what is worse, I have not yet come to any resolution on the subject to lecture on; if anything occurs to you, the smallest donation will be thankfully received. I imagine I don't begin 'till when I please in Lent Term.'"

It was perfectly well known when his predecessor's term of office would expire, but it should seem that Keble had thought so little of the succession, as to be still at sea as to the subject on which he would lecture, if elected. However he must have made up his mind without much delay, as he delivered his first lecture in February, 1832, and on the 13th of that month, in the letter to which I have already alluded, he gave me this account of his design for the whole course :—

"I was at Oxford the beginning of this week 'reading

in,'—it is uphill work to me, and you never said a much truer thing than when you told Tom I was ten years too old for the task. However, I must do my best now. My notion is, to consider Poetry as a vent for overcharged feelings, or a full imagination, and so account for the various classes into which Poets naturally fall, by reference to the various objects which are apt to fill and overpower the mind, so as to require a sort of relief. Then there will come in a grand distinction between what I call Primary and Secondary Poets; the first *poetising* for their own relief, the second for any other reason. Then I shall βασανίζε, one after another, each of the great Ancients, whom in my Royal Authority I think worthy of the name of a Primary Poet, and shew what class he belongs to, and what sort of a person I take him to have been. From which will arise certain conclusions as to the degree in which the interest of poetry depends on the character of the writer, as shewn in his works; and, again, as to the relation between this art, and practical goodness, moral and religious. In the whole affair, I *think* I have hit on the truth, and I expect to interest myself; but there my expectations pretty nearly terminate; and as to Latin, it will be ἀγαπητόν, if I do not disgrace myself. However, I do not like the notion of making it English, even if the Doctors would allow it; because of the moral certainty of a large importation of trash, which ought not to be on the University account; and also because I think Latin would suffer more than Poetry would gain."

I venture here to remind my readers of the letter to Froude of September, 1825, from which I have made an extract, in which he speaks of "The Christian Year," and glancing at this Theory of Poetry, shews that it was not only then in his mind, but that, in fact, that Collection of Poems had grown up under its influence.

In May, 1832, writing to me from Fairford, he says :—

"My Lectures have hindered me sadly in my Hooker, neither thoughts nor words will come neatly as I wish. But I am more and more satisfied that my theory in itself, *as far as it goes*, (for it is not so absurd as to pretend to explain all phenomena,) is a good, and useful, and true one. The point I am now upon is making out what people mean when they talk of the Poetry of Painting, of Music, of Sculpture, &c. ; if you know of any good book on the subject, it will be a charity to mention it. But after all, I believe the best way, especially in Latin, is to make the most one can of some one or two popular examples."

Since I undertook the task I have in hand, I have thought it right to refresh my memory as to the *Prælectiones*, and have read them through again with attention. I must say, in the first place, that I entirely retract the observation that he was ten years too old when he was elected to the Professorship ; he was not in my opinion a day too old. I presume I must have been thinking principally of the Latinity, and no doubt the ten years' disuse added much to the difficulty of which he complains, and the danger which he feared. I will not presume to pass the judgment of a scholar on his Latinity, but I may venture to say that while there is no affectation of Ciceronianism, nay, while you sensibly miss the inimitable rhythm and roundness of the

great Master's periods, Keble seems to me almost
always to have what is after all of the highest value,
a sufficient command of the instrument he is using.
The common failing of modern Latinists, those especially who covet most to be Ciceronians, is that
they trim their conceptions, and limit their thoughts
to suit their powers of expression ; they do not so
much write what they think in all its extent, as set
down what they can find apt clothing for in Cice-
ronian language; as if one should omit the operations of the artillery in describing a modern fight, because Cicero supplied no word for a cannon.   Keble
never falls into this error; he always says, and with
sufficient clearness too, what he wishes to say, and
never leaves anything unsaid from want of words
to express it in.   But, passing from the language to
the matter, the subject he chose demanded a full-
grown man for its exponent, one who could bring
forth "things new and old" from his storehouse,
and who without presumption might claim to speak
with authority.   The ten years of interval between
the two Elections had been to him years of mental
enrichment, ripening, and consolidation ; yet had not
diminished, perhaps increased, his conscientious consideration of what he might say, and the modesty
which was an inseparable part of his whole nature.
They had been years too of considerable progress
and activity generally in poetic and artistic studies ;
in this he had participated, and he had seen more
of nature, and studied her intensely with a true

poet's feeling. Moreover attentive readers will not fail to perceive that all through his analyses of poems and his criticisms, and especially through the hortatory parts of the Lectures, there run the golden threads of a religious spirit; never obtrusively, never patchily manifested, but uniformly, and as it were imperceptibly shedding a mellowness and glow of colour over the whole texture. Certainly he had the feeling, which was the source of this, in 1821 equally as in 1831; but I think it came out with more grace, consistence, and power, with the years added to his course. Such a man, especially one so diffident of himself, would be able to say at the latter age what he might perhaps have shrunk from saying, or said with less authority at the former.

The late Professor, Mr. Arnold, with somewhat of hereditary boldness, cast off the yoke of a foreign language, and defied Keble's prophecy, which for himself he might safely do ; and he came to the office in a different state of the public mind, and under an altered constitution of the University.

I may, however, freely express my hope that his successors will revert to the ancient practice of selecting a subject, and giving a course upon it, which shall form an entire and complete work. It seems to me to let down the office, and to be a great temptation to clever and ready men, who may shrink from sustained labour, and the mental effort of grasping all parts of a great subject, to make the Terminal Lectures opportunities for delivering merely brilliant essays, which find their not inappropriate future in fashionable Serials. The Poetry Professorship is a great office, and ought to exercise a sensible influence on the national taste. Great subjects will never be wanting, at least, we have at present a long list of such unexhausted. Chaucer, and the early English Poets,—Shakespere, and the Elizabethan Dramatists,—Spenser, Milton, Dryden, and Pope,—Wordsworth—occur at once. And if our own poets failed, the great Italian and German masters might be taken up. These, and such as these, are noble subjects, which would tax the intellect, the learning, and the industry of great minds. Thoroughly to inform the English mind on these, and to educate its taste in regard to such models, would be not merely to reflect credit on the University, but to confer wide and lasting benefit on the nation.

Whether Keble could have done as Mr. Arnold did, without permission of the governing body, and if that were necessary, whether he would have obtained it, I do not know; but I do regret extremely that the Lectures were not originally composed in English; and it is a great gain that, as I presume, all future Professors will follow Mr. Arnold's example in this respect. We boast nationally of our Scholarship, and there is no doubt for a Scholar much pleasure in composing, and not a little in reading good modern Latin; but after all to write in Latin is to write for readers comparatively so

few, that when we do so, we may be said almost to
seal up our thoughts from the public. But the Professor of Poetry at Oxford has a duty of a popular
character; he has not indeed to make poets, or even
scholars, but to improve poetical taste, to regulate
critical judgment, to enlarge and systematize knowledge as to the great poems of the world, and all
this demands the freedom of a native language both
for the lecturer, the audience, and readers. Mr.
Gladstone has happily characterized the *Prælectiones*
in one point of view, when he calls the course a "*re-
fined* work," and he has truly said that it "criticises
the Homeric Poems in the spirit of a bard, setting
an early example, at least to England, of elevating
the tone of Homeric study [b]." One regrets to think
that such a book on such a subject should not be
accessible, without difficulty as to the language, to
every educated woman as well as man.

It may be said, Why not translate it? a question
natural enough to be asked, before one has considered the difficulty of making any Latin book
into an original, idiomatic English book, enhanced
in the present instance by the vast number of citations, of which translations would have to be made
or found. Yet the purpose was floating for a long
time in Keble's mind, and if any one could do
such a work successfully, it would be the author of
the original, as he might properly indulge in modifications or alterations not allowable to a third

[b] Homer, vol. iii. p. 374.

person. More than once I believe I was myself tempted by my fondness for the work, and my opinion of its possible usefulness in an English dress, to offer my services ; he answered me thus on July 5, 1844 :—

"I never thanked you for your partial pat on the back touching the *Prælectiones*. I have sometimes thought whether any kind of translation or adaptation might be useful, though of course no such vision ever crossed my mind as one of Her Majesty's Puisne Judges engaged in such an operation. If *it took no time,* I should like to substitute modern examples for the Greek and Latin."

This substitution might have been effected ; and very usefully, where the example is used only to illustrate some general position in the text ; but in far the greater number, where the Greek or Latin Poem is the special subject of remark, that and the example are necessarily so wedded together, that it would have been impracticable. However, the notion was not wholly abandoned, and in March, 1847, in answer to some proposition from me, he writes thus :—

"I am really sorry not to have thanked you sooner for your kind thought about the *Prælectiones*, but I would not for a very great deal have your energies and scanty leisure wasted on anything so very unworthy. If they are at all likely to do any good in English, it must be, I think, by some reform more radical than any translation ; and if I were industrious enough ever to have a little leisure, I should encourage a thought, which has sometimes come into my mind, of Anglicizing the substance of the poor book in a kind of dialogues, which might be touched up with a little scenery, and made semi-dramatic. But it would take a good deal of time and trouble, especially as I suppose modern examples must be substituted in many cases for the classical ones ; and then it will be matter of many a weary chase to hunt out the fugitive glimmer of a meaning, which may or may not be lurking in the folds of a long Latin sentence. What a prose I am getting into."

One cannot but regret that he never found time to carry into effect this last idea, suggested to him probably by Southey's Colloquies. It is easy to see how the work would have lent itself to lively discussion in dialogue. He was powerful in local descriptions in prose and verse, and at this period of his life he had seen a great deal of beautiful country ; but even if he had confined himself to the scenery at and about Hursley, with every nook and alley of which he was familiar, he would have found scenes enough for his purpose, which he would have stamped thenceforward with indelible associations.

Will my readers forgive me if, upon a favourite subject, I venture to add an extract from my answer to his last letter, which I have found among my returned letters :—

"If you can accomplish *your* design with the Lectures, it will be indeed excellent ; and now you have surmised such a thing, I shall not let you rest without putting it in execution. But I think you will not only incur unnecessary labour, but very much impair the general utility of the book, and also interfere with its peculiar character, by seeking for modern instances. How can you sponge out Homer, Achilles, &c., without making it a new work, and at the same time destroying the happy peculiarity which your book would have of at once teaching a true and novel theory of Poetry, and illustrating it from the Classic Poets. Sprinkle here and there, if you will, modern examples, without confining yourself to English poetry for them, but make your present instances *the staple;* print the originals with translations, which last I should without scruple *adapt* from the best I could find, altering wherever I liked, so as to make them reflect the very matter, for which I had selected the originals. And as the passages are not very long, this would not be so troublesome as it might seem ; and you would do them in your walks, and at all odd times. In this way your argument and stuff being already provided, I think you would find the work not very laborious, and full of interest. Your scheme of dialogue and scenery is excellent ; it is long since I read Southey's Colloquies, but I remember how the framing of the pictures there interested me. Euge-macte.

"*March* 5, 1847."

It was not to be; singularly enough the subject was renewed so late as January, 1866, when he was at Bournemouth, by an offer made to him by a gentleman who was a stranger to him. He consulted me about it, and reminded me of what had passed between us on the subject many years before, and asked if I still retained my former notion of undertaking it myself ; but the time for such things with me had passed away.

No short analysis of the work, (and a very short one only would be suitable here,) would give so true an account in general of its plan, as that which I have already cited from his own letter.

The peroration of the series so illustrates the spirit of the whole, that I am tempted to give it, and "done into English ;" though I fear this may prove too clearly the justice of Keble's reluctance to entrust me as his translator. Something grandiose must be allowed for in a peroration.

" This would I desire most earnestly to deliver and commend to the thoughts of our young men, that it will be well with the pursuit of Poetry so long only as her lovers shall remember that she is a gift vouchsafed to man, to minister as a specially honourable handmaid to true piety; so that they should serve her, not in word, but in deed and in truth, with all reverence, constancy, chasteness of spirit. On these, indeed, will depend entirely the hope, which at length we dare conceive for the future, that that grander and loftier voice of Poetry, which now for several years hath been heard among us, shall have good end and issue, through the happy increase of those studies which are peculiarly and properly termed Divine.

" May God, Best and Greatest, vouchsafe that if He shall haply have ordained for us so great a blessing, it may not in the very smallest particular fail, and be of none effect through the fault of any one of us."

I have noticed in passing the interest which Keble

took in public affairs, as they concerned the labouring classes ; his faith, for so I must call it, as regarded
the Church, and his opinions in respect of the two
parties which have divided her ever since the Reformation, have also appeared incidentally in the
course of my narrative. With him these interests
were living realities : gentle as he was by nature,
and loving-hearted to individuals, he was very sensitive in regard to them, and it was not in his nature, nor according to his conscience, to be inactive
when he felt deeply. He was appointed by the
Vice-Chancellor to preach the Summer Assize Sermon at Oxford in 1833 ; he was glad of the opportunity, and he published his sermon with the title
of National Apostasy, his text being the noble declaration of Samuel as to the course which he will
continue to pursue in regard to his countrymen,
when they insisted on renouncing their Theocracy,
and on being governed by a king, as the Gentiles
were. Among other things the measures then in
progress in regard to the Irish Protestant Church,
which had ended before the publication of the Sermon in what I scarcely think he accurately termed
the *suppression* of ten bishoprics, moved him very
deeply ; and his Sermon, though the language is
measured, and the recommendations, such as most
Churchmen would approve of, is evidently written
under deep though suppressed emotion of heart.

I may state while I am noticing this Sermon, that

in it he lays down as the ground on which he thinks the events in Jewish history applicable to Christian teaching, the principle which my readers will remember him to have stated in a letter I have before extracted from. He says, "As regards reward and punishment, God dealt formerly with the Jewish people in a manner analogous to that in which He deals now, not so much with Christian nations, as with the souls of individual Christians."

We have long as a Nation passed by Keble's principles in these matters, and I am not about uselessly to re-agitate them, but I have made this particular mention of the Sermon, because out of the same feelings, and about the same time, arose that concerted and systematic course of action, of which the first-fruits were the celebrated Tracts. Dr. Newman says in his *Apologia*, that he has ever considered and kept the day of the publication of the Sermon as the start of the religious movement of 1833.

I have prepared my readers not to expect in this memoir the history of that movement. But one who ought to know, has said in regard to it, that John Keble was its true and primary author, and I shall therefore supply such personal and incidental mention of it as my means enable me.

Writing to Dyson on the 26th of August, 1833, very shortly after the preaching and publication of the Sermon, he says :—

" If I had not hoped to see you so soon, I should have

sent you, I think, what I now reserve for you, if you will
accept it, a sermon which I have ventured to preach and
publish ; and at the same time I should have asked you,
What think you of a kind of association (as quiet and unpretending as may be, if possible even without a name) for
the promotion of these two objects ? first, the circulation of
primitive notions regarding the Apostolical Succession, &c.;
and secondly the protection of the Prayer-book against profane innovation. We have as yet only written round to
a very few intimate friends, Davison, Ogilvie, Tom, &c.,
and as far as they have answered me yet, they seem to
think it may do good. To give you a notion of the kind
of thing, the first Tract we propose to print will be a *Penny*
account of the martyrdom of St. Ignatius, with extracts from
his Epistles. *Pray* do not blow on it as being all Ultra."

In the same month, and a few days earlier, writing
to his father's old friend, Mr. Richards, he says :—

"Some of my friends at Oxford, persons worthy of much
confidence, are wishing for a kind of association, to circulate right notions on the Apostolical Succession, and also
for the defence of the Prayer-book against any sort of profane innovation, which seems too likely to be attempted.
Might we hope for your countenance and support if such
a thing should be set on foot ? Isaac Williams, I think, has
been written to, and can give you all particulars about it.
I cannot help hoping that there is still a good deal of
cordial Church feeling about the country, which it is very
desirable to encourage in a quiet way, and to get people to
dwell on it a little more."

In October, 1833, writing to me, he says :—

"Dyson and I had a great deal of talk on a plan

which he may have mentioned to you, and which at any rate I must,—the more boldly as you speak so kindly of the tone and temper of the sermon I sent you. Considering the helpless state of the Church in England, and the very inadequate ideas entertained by most of her children, lay and clerical, of her claims on their allegiance, certain intimate friends of mine at Oxford have drawn up a paper or two, of which I hope you will in a day or two receive certain copies through the Parson of Plymtree, who has promised to convey them so far. Now if you approve and would like to assist us, give me one line to say so within this fortnight ; and put down and send me at your leisure any memoranda that may occur to you of the best and most effectual way of proceeding, e.g. on what subjects tracts may be usefully provided, either for the clergy or the laity, what you hear said against us that you think deserves notice, in the way either of amendment or justification, whom you think we might serviceably apply to," &c.

Such was the original design of the small knot of zealous Churchmen, who projected this celebrated series of Tracts.

It is impossible to impute disloyalty, or a mischievous intention concealed under the avowed design, or in the means adopted to promote it ; those who will read in Dr. Newman's *Apologia* the names of the parties concerned, will never, I am persuaded, think that the real object or means were other than those avowed. Names more free from question as to their general honesty, and their unquestionable loyalty to the Church of England, could scarcely be found. Still both imprudence in the execution, and an advance upon the original purpose are possible ; matters to be considered hereafter. For myself, I had not, or fancied I had not, leisure at the time to read many of the Tracts as they came out, nor have I read them at any time since ; a predicament in which I believe to stand a large number of those who have borne the name of Tractarians, as well as of those who have objected to them as mischievous. From the letters I have seen, I find that the bishops were not invited to sanction, or interfere in the movement in the way of regulation ; good reasons may be assigned for this resolution, beyond the caution of one individual, from which however I believe it proceeded ; although Keble, I think, would simply and heartily have invoked the countenance and influence of the Fathers of the Church ; from similar motives a too careful or rather a formal organization was avoided, and this perhaps, under the circumstances, was to be regretted ; when every move would be so vigilantly watched, and when a false move might be so prejudicial.

It is, in my opinion, mere prejudice to deny that the cause of true religion, and of the Church of England, reaped great advantages from the circulation of the Tracts ; one must have been a quiet and attentive observer of the state of the parochial clergy, and of the English Church generally before they issued, to be a competent judge of this. Making every allowance for exaggeration, the change for the better is great, and to be observed not so much in bright instances here and there, as in the general tone of feeling and conduct, in the higher appreciation of what the profession requires of its members, and the larger and more distinct acknowledgment' of duty. In these respects I think it may be said, comparing the two periods, that the rule has become the exception, the exception the rule. But it will be equally prejudice, as it seems to me, to deny that incidentally some evil flowed from them. I remember on occasion of some early secessions to Rome, it was reported to have been said by Dr. Pusey, that however much he regretted it, he could not deny that some were to be anticipated,—it was a sensible remark, if I may be allowed to say so. The Tracts came at a time when we were (speaking of the generality both lay and clerical) wholly untrained in dogmatic theology, wholly unversed in the questions which lay between the Roman and the English branches of Christ's Church. Elderly men will remember the time, when for students to go into the controversy with Rome was thought nearly superfluous, and for clergymen to preach on it a mere waste of time. The Tracts stirred this tranquil, perhaps stagnant, lake ; and the stir of men's minds, especially among the younger and more ardent, naturally produced enquiry, under circumstances not at all favourable to a just result ; the imperfect practice, and the theory in some instances not strictly logical or complete of our Church, were arraigned without that diffident reverence, or that due allowance for circumstances, which might have been reasonably expected ; and there was the crowning fallacy, " if not England, then Rome ;" on behalf of which latter every assumption was made.

I am far from saying that this explains every instance of secession ; certainly, as at the Reformation great men of unimpeachable holiness, vast learning, and powerful intellect, remained with Rome, so now some few of whom no less can be said went to her : such is the character of the controversy in which Bellarmine and Andrewes are opposed champions, that this must in all time be expected.

But after all, and now that one can look back in comparative calm on the movement, I believe that its general effect on the Church, in its clergy as well as laity, often to be seen operating on those who are least conscious of it, and least willing to acknowledge it, must be pronounced a subject for the deepest gratitude to its Great Head.

Keble's direct contributions to the Tracts were few ; in a list of his writings to be seen in Mr. Savage's work, p. 52, four Tracts only are set down as his, Nos. 4, 13, 40, 89[e], and I am not aware that to anything in either could objection be made by any critic with ordinary

[e] To these I find now on the best authority ought to be added, Nos. 52, 54, 57, 60, four Sermons on four Saints' Days. These on the same authority were to have been parts of a course.

pretensions to Churchmanship. The series is now
unwisely and undeservedly consigned to such entire
oblivion, that it may be as well to state shortly the
subjects of these four. No. 4, is an argument in
the manner of Butler, Keble's favourite mode of reasoning, to shew that adherence to the Apostolical
Succession is the safest course. No. 13, is on the
Principle which regulated the Selection of the Sunday Lessons. I think he owed the original suggestion
of this to Miller, as I find him stating it in one of his
letters, in which he speaks of a visit from Miller, and
the conversations they had had together. At the present time the Lectionary of the Prayer-book is coming
it is said under the revision of a Royal Commission,
and it may therefore not be wrong respectfully to urge
his caution ; that before fault is found with the present selection, those who alter it " ought to be tolerably certain that they understand the principle on
which the Lessons in general were selected." It is
to be observed that he is speaking only of the Sunday Lessons ; and as to the First Lessons, his theory
is an application of that which I have mentioned before as a favourite one with him, " that the arrangers
desired to exhibit God's former dealings with His
chosen people *collectively*, and the return made by
them to God, in such manner as might best illustrate
His dealing with each *individual* chosen now to be
in His Church, and the snares and temptations most
apt to beset us as Christians." This was an argument which of course was applicable only to the

First Lessons on Sundays; but he fails not to assign ingenious reasons for there being no selection for the Second Lessons; one of the advantages which he finds in this is, "that it presents the Old and New Scriptures in endless variety of mutual combinations, the more striking because they are unforeseen, and in a certain sense casual." "The thought," he goes on to say, "is happily expressed by Herbert, thus addressing Holy Scripture:—

> "'O that I knew how all thy lights combine
>   And the configurations of their glory:
> Seeing not only how each verse doth shine
>   But all the constellations of the story.'"

He had referred to this stanza in the letter to which I have just alluded. It will interest those who should be induced to read this Tract, to collect from it indirectly, how diffused and how earnest at the same time was the attention which he gave to every part, the most ordinary as well as the most rarely recurring, of his duty.

In the Tracts are several entitled "Richard Nelson;" these are dialogues, in which a mason by that name bears a principal part with the clergyman of his parish on different religious questions then much agitated; they are very pleasantly written, and afford good specimens of the manner in which information on grave subjects may successfully be conveyed to the middle classes of our people. The subject of No. 40 is the marriage of Nelson's ne-

phew and godson, whose father is dead, to a young
woman who has not been baptized, and of course is
not a member of our Church. Nelson is much opposed to this as well as the clergyman; the argument, therefore, is not a contentious one, and to
the spirit of the present day it would seem to relate to a very old-world matter; yet I will own it
has interested me in reading it over again, and it
can never be out of season, I suppose, to read what
tends to elevate and sanctify that which the Church
calls the state of Holy Matrimony.

One of the points in which Arnold and Keble
differed very widely was in their general estimation
of the Fathers. It was not unnatural that Arnold
should have a quick eye for occasional looseness in
argument, and the absence of that critical judgment
in history which may almost be said to have only
come into being since the death of the latest on
the roll. But Arnold had not (indeed how should he
have acquired?) the extensive knowledge of them
which Keble had, and he was scarcely competent to
set a due estimate on the scriptural feeling, and
habit of reasoning for which they are remarkable,
or the weight of their direct, and perhaps even more
their indirect, testimony on the belief and practice
of the early Church. Keble had had time, which
Arnold with all his wonderful industry and quickness
of apprehension had not, for a general and very considerate study of them; it had been his duty as the
editor of Hooker to deepen that study, and while

perhaps he might a little underrate the importance of those defects on which Arnold insisted, he dwelt with just admiration and gratitude on their merits. His was a nature, too, in this respect directly opposed to Arnold's, and he loved the study, which Arnold perhaps too much despised.

No. 89 was the result of this, an Essay on the Mysticism attributed to the Early Fathers of the Church, and I cannot but regret that it remains a fragment only.

Such were Keble's direct contributions to the Tracts, which I have thought it right to mention in detail; but it is not to be doubted that his interference in regard to them went much further, not merely in suggesting subjects, and reviewing the essays of others, but in personal influence elsewhere than in Oxford, in procuring contributions, and extending the circulation; this, however, it will be more in order to notice when I come to the period of the abrupt termination of the series in 1841.

He seems to have been fully occupied between home and Oxford during the year 1834, — with Hooker, and his Lectures, and the other duties of the Professorship; he was also at this time busy with the version of the Psalms, of which I delay to speak until its completion. Towards the close of the year it was evident that the object of his tender care for so many years was about to be removed from him; his father's infirmities had compelled him to take to his bed in November :—

" For a bed-ridden person of 89" (he writes to me on the 3rd of December) "he is I trust no very great sufferer; he has infirmities, which give him often a good deal of pain and distress, but he sleeps a good deal; his appetite is tolerable, and he seems to have no thought but that which one would wish to be taken up with. Elisabeth has been able to do much for him."

Elisabeth, writing to a friend, says :—

"We have every comfort in seeing, and you will have the same in hearing, that the same peace of mind and trust in God still attend him in the near approach of death, as have been his comfort through life; he sleeps a great deal, and wakes to repeat prayers and psalms, and it seems to us who stand by, that he is only uncomfortable when his attention is called away from that happy world towards which we trust he is approaching."

To Mr. Richards Keble writes :—

" Whether wandering (which is the case occasionally) or collected, I may almost say that what comes out of his lips is one continued prayer."

The venerable patriarch fell asleep on the 24th of January, 1835, closing his blameless life in peace, with his family and faithful servants all around him :—

" His memory for prayers and psalms," says Keble, " did not desert him all through his illness, and it was remarkable how he made out the prayer, when he could not exactly remember it, by adding the words of some other prayer, hardly ever becoming incoherent, and always in the same clear silver voice."

As on all the preceding occasions, so on this, the
survivors accepted the bereavement with the cheerful
resignation of real Christians ; they found comfort in
all the circumstances of the illness, and the departure.
Yet on John Keble, and Elizabeth especially, the
blow was heavy ; to them their father had long been
the, object of tenderest care ; their ardent love for him
(no distinction can be made between the two) had
a mixture in it of filial pride, and veneration for his
great qualities of head and heart ; the feeling naturally descended to smaller matters,—John delights
to speak of " his silver voice," " the clear and peculiar tones of his voice," and how in advanced old age
the flock at Coln admired his manner still of performing the duty ; and now they two were bereft of
that object, and alone.

Yet as at his mother's death all his usual cheerfulness and readiness for duty were what the standers
by would have noticed. My readers will see no in-
consistency in this : an incident has come to my
knowledge since I spoke of his mother's death, which
is worth introducing here ; it was told me by one who
was present when it occurred. Keble returned, it
will be remembered, from his mother's death-bed to
the Schools at Oxford, and continued in the discharge of his duty as Examining Master through the
week until the day of her funeral. A young man
had given in among his books some plays of Euripides, including the Alcestis. Keble happened to

be conducting his examination; and whether inad-
vertently, or, as we sometimes do, humouring the
sorrow at his heart, had set him on at the part, (ver.
395 *et seqq.*,) in which she dies in the presence of
her husband Admetus, her son Eumelus, and his
sister. Much of the tenderness and pathos of the
passage arise from the wonderful simplicity of the
language, which it is almost impossible to reproduce
in a translation; but I think my readers will be glad
to see the passages in a rendering, which my son,
Mr. Coleridge, has been good enough to supply me
with:—

ADMETUS, ALCESTIS, CHORUS, EUMELUS.

ADMETUS. Turn thy face hither; leave not thy children so.
ALCESTIS. Not with my will; yet fare ye well, my babes.
ADM. Look, look upon them!

      ALC. I am nothing now.

ADM. What? goest thou?

     ALC. Farewell.

       ADM. Let me die too!

CHORUS. Thy wife hath past away, she is no more.

EUM. Ah, for my fate! To shades below,
   My father, see my mother go!
   She is no more beneath the sun,
   Leaving me here my race to run,
   An orphan boy, till life be done;
   Ah, see her stiffening eyelids!
   Look at her nerveless hands!
   Hear me, oh hear, sweet mother,
   The child who o'er thee stands.

I call to thee, my mother, yea, I call;
A callow nestling on thy lips I fall.

ADM. She hears thee not, nor sees thee ; thus am I
And ye two smitten down with heaviest sorrow.

EUM. Ah, father ! I am left alone,
So young, forlorn of mother's care,
The harsh things of the world to bear ;
Thou, maiden, too my lot must share,
My sister ! for her love is gone.
Father ! all vain
The nuptial strain ;
In vain her bridegroom didst thou stand,
Hoping in vain that hand in hand,
With her thou might'st attain old age,
The bourne of earthly pilgrimage.
For, she first withering, in her swift decay
The whole house perished as she past away.

Keble, as was then usual, was standing ; he heard
the passage out with fixed attention, and unchanged
countenance, then dropped on his chair, and burying
his face in his hands on the table, remained for some
time silent, overcome with emotion.

CHAPTER XI.

COLN ST. ALDWYN. — ENGAGEMENT WITH MISS CLARKE.—ACCEPTANCE OF HURSLEY VICARAGE. —MARRIAGE, AND SETTLEMENT AT HURSLEY.— VISITATION SERMON. — HURRELL FROUDE'S RE- MAINS.—A. KNOX.—VERSION OF PSALMS.—CREWE- IAN ORATION AND WORDSWORTH.—1839.

KEBLE and his sister had cast in their lot toge- ther, and were now left with the world before them. I do not know what the disposition of the family property was, but no thought seems to have occurred to them of continuing at Fairford. One discomfort there had been during all his long re- sidence there, felt even while his father and mother lived, and important enough to have decided him now of itself against choosing it as his residence when his choice was free; the views of the Incum- bent in Church matters were of the kind to which he was very averse, and he felt that between him- self and this gentleman there could be no cordial co-operation. Most of us, I suppose, would feel such a circumstance to be one which would mar the per- fect enjoyment of any residence, however delightful in itself, or endeared to us by circumstances; with one who felt so strongly on these points as he did, it would be conclusive.

But with both the brother and sister Coln St. Aldwyn had always been the favourite residence; it was
a great delight to them when the family moved, as
they sometimes did, for a fortnight or three weeks to
the Cottage Parsonage at Coln. I do not remember
ever to have seen the place, but the photographs,
three in number, devoted to it in Mr. Savage's work,
create a favourable impression of the church, and of
the river scenery. Keble delighted in walking on
the banks of rivers, and no features or incidents of
natural scenery does he describe in poetry more
faithfully and imaginatively than those with which
rivers, and their banks, the flow of their waters, their
flowers, and their trees abound. In the chapter
which these photographs illustrate are some citations from "The Christian Year" and the *Lyra Innocentium,* which the writer seeks to trace to the
Coln. It is probable that he does so correctly; the
whole chapter is interesting. Keble had a special,
a sort of filial fondness for this river. Writing to
his brother in June, 1815, on his return from some
summer expedition, he says :—

"I got to Bibury about $\frac{1}{2}$ p. 6, and walked leisurely home,
and really some of the spots which I passed on our jolly
river Coln are quite beautiful enough to recompence one for
a much longer walk."

I was not surprised to see him date from Coln St.
Aldwyn's soon after his father's death. I had hoped

to meet him at Oxford on my first Circuit as Judge ;
he says :—

" Very much disappointed am I that I cannot have the
pleasure of meeting you at Oxford this week. I fixed my
Lecture on purpose for last Tuesday, intending to stay all
the week, but I had quite forgotten that it was the first
week in Lent, when I could not well be absent from the
parish ; so I was obliged to mount my horse and ride home
on Tuesday evening. After all, I imagine I should only
have had very scanty fits and snatches of you, and that I
shall be better off on the whole by considering this disappointment as a good excuse for coming up to London and
spending a few days with you, and the Museum, some time
after the Circuit is over. At present I cannot look forward
with any great certainty to my own movements, for this
vicarage is not yet disposed of, and I do not like leaving
the people till they have some one to take care of them.
It will be with a heavy heart most likely when I do go.....

" I think it likely that I shall continue bobbing back-
wards and forwards between Oxford and this place till
after Easter, and then probably come to Oxford for the
whole Term to look after my professional duties, and, as
I hope, put Hooker fairly out of hand. Eliz. by that
time, I dare say, will be reconciled to moving on Bisley
for a while."

They did not in fact leave the little vicarage
until June, and left it with much regret ; it was like
a second loss of their father to quit for ever the
home and the church, where the recollections of
him from their earliest childhood were so deeply
impressed, where they might still seem to see his
venerable countenance, and hear the clear tones of

his silver voice in the discharge of his duty. I need not say that the day of their departure was a sad one for the villagers; far the greater number of them had grown up under the care of the old man; his children had always identified themselves with him in visiting and loving carefulness for the sick and poor; these, and cordial assistance in the schools, and latterly Keble's ministrations there, had endeared them to the whole population.

They returned to Fairford to prepare for their final departure, and about the same time two events occurred, which determined the course of his whole future life; his engagement with Miss Charlotte Clarke, and his acceptance of the Vicarage of Hursley, again offered to him by Sir William Heathcote. The engagement, indeed, had been made some years before. None could be more natural : they had known each other well from childhood ; their parents were old and intimate friends, and the marriage of the sister of the one with the brother of the other must have added to the familiarity of their intercourse. At first sight the only wonder would be that the announcement and fulfilment should have been so long delayed ; but, on the one hand, Mrs. Clarke, a widow, was loath to part with her daughter, and Keble, on the other, was very unwilling to leave his father, and so from year to year the marriage was delayed.

Perhaps it might have been expected that his very intimate friends would have been let into his secret

earlier. His communications, when at last they came,
to Cornish, to Dyson, and myself, were characteristic;
and when I read them over now, I cannot help re-
calling to mind his exquisite verses on the Fourth
Sunday in Lent :—

> " But there's a sweeter flower than e'er
>   Blush'd on the rosy spray—
> A brighter star, a richer bloom
> Than e'er did western heaven illume
>   At close of summer day.

> " 'Tis Love, the last best gift of Heaven ;
>   Love, gentle, holy, pure ;
> But tenderer than a dove's soft eye,
> The searching sun, the open sky,
>   She never could endure."

To me he said, writing on the 4th of May :—

" As for me, I don't like talking of such reports so soon
after our great loss, but surely you have a right to know
all about me, and I will not affect to deny that I hope
they may prove true in time ; but I am sorry to say that
I cannot speak highly of the health of the dear person in
question, and that alone is a reason for not talking much
about things."

To Cornish, from Fairford on the 12th of June, he
writes in the same way :—

" I dare say Hubert has told you about me, and therefore I am not going to make a regular announcement, but
only to beg your blessing as *young* people ought on such
an occasion ; but so shortly after my dear Father's death,

I do not much love being forward in telling my friends about things, and this I hope you will take as a receipt in full for all apologies due from me on the score of un friendly silence."

I give the letter to Dyson in full :—

                                        " FAIRFORD,
                                   "*June* 12, 1835.

"MY DEAR DYSON,

"I must allow, without any violent exertion of humility, that Mrs. Dyson, this time, has some ground of complaint in respect of the word 'soon.'   And yet, considering how wonderfully quick the weeks and months move when once folk are got to our time of life, I hope she will make allowances.   But as touching the news, (if uncertain futurities can be called news,) which Sir John communicated to you, I am not going to be coy, nor to argue against the propriety of such things, *as a friend of mine did in Yorkshire some years ago;* but only to say that whereas it is a project of some standing, I hope you will not think it any unkindness that nothing was said to you before ; for surely, if any one out of the family, you and Mrs. D. have a right to be told of things ; but you see it was all so very uncertain and contingent, and seemed somehow so made to depend on what of course we did not like to think of, that one could hardly say it had assumed the shape of a project; and since my Father's departure the time has been full short for talking of such things ; and I dare say you will agree with me that few things not immoral are more disagreeable than the hurry people now-a-days are generally in to get out of the house of mourning.   Well, now hoping I am forgiven, I proceed with the plans and projects.   First comes the melancholy reality that we are finally parted from dear little Coln.

"I think Elisabeth has behaved very well considering; but what with the hot weather, what with the packing up, and what with the people coming in to say good-bye one after another, the two or three days last past have been very trying to her, and I shall be rather glad to-morrow evening to think of her safely landed at Bisley. Our nephew has been with us all the time, and has been of the greatest use to her as well as enjoyment. When she starts West, I start East, having to visit Oxford for as long a spell as I can, to finish my Term's work, and break the back of the 3rd vol. of R. H., which is now in the press. At Michaelmas I have engaged at last to accept the Vicarage of Hursley, which Gilbert Heathcote is desirous of vacating. This house will probably be let to Cornwall, who, as you may remember, is our Doctor at Fairford, for a term of years. He wishes for it, and I suppose there is no person at all likely to seek it whom my Father, if we could ask him, would more desire to have here. Dearest E. will spend her time between me and Tom. My notion is Hursley in the winter for her, and Bisley in the summer. The distance is the great objection. . . . ."

Mr. Heathcote's health had failed very seriously at Hursley, and he was desirous of resigning the living. Sir William again and immediately offered it to Keble, who agreed to accept it, and it was arranged that he should come to it at the Michaelmas following; he was not in fact instituted until March 9, 1836. It is at least a remarkable circumstance, that Keble should have become the Incum-

bent of Hursley after the circumstances which have
been stated ; he had obeyed the calls of a sacred
duty ; these were now satisfied, and the vacancy
was announced exactly at the time when, with the
prospect of marriage before him, he must have been
considering where he should settle down as a married man.   And I believe that even with the objection to which he alludes at the close of my last
extract from his letter to Dyson, (the distance from
Hursley to Bisley, not great in itself, but inconvenient in days when there were no railways, to two
busy clergymen, with not overflowing means,) Hursley was, of all the incumbencies he had known of, the
one he would have most delighted to be placed in.

The marriage took place at Bisley on the 10th
of October, 1835, and the newly-married couple
went to Southampton, where they remained, I believe, until they took possession of the parsonage
at Hursley.   Southampton was convenient from its
vicinity, and it was thought favourable for Mrs.
Keble's health.   Keble, it will be remembered, had
mentioned in his announcement to me the delicacy
of her health ; this reason always for care, and too
frequently for anxiety, was in operation from the
very commencement of their married life, and continued until its close.   It did not find him unpre-
pared.   It is remarkable that so early as the year
1816, when I had, I presume, mentioned in writing
to him the delicacy of health of the young lady

to whom I was engaged to be married, he wrote thus in answer ; and had I shewn him his letter in 1835, or indeed at any later and less romantic period of his life, I feel sure he would have adhered to every word in it, and applied it to his own feelings :—

"One part of your letter did indeed make me very sorry, it is that where you speak of Miss B.'s state of health. I think I can enter into your feelings on that subject; I have often thought why it is that illness attaches us more to people whom we love, and though I cannot analyse it, I feel that it is both a merciful and trying dispensation : merciful, because it makes us more useful to them, and attracts us towards another world; trying, even to heart-breaking, because it gets stronger as hope gets less. But I would not advise any man to encourage it who has not an habitual sense of religion, and dependence upon God. I have often thought how miserable it must have been to heathens to lose a relation, and it must be still worse, methinks, to heathenish Christians. But since we are Christians, I do not think the chance, or even the moral certainty of ill health should be considered as an objection to a marriage well considered in other respects.

"*Jan^{ry} 9, 1816.*"

Keble had abundant opportunity of testing the soundness of this opinion in his own married life. As he seldom wrote a letter to me before his marriage which did not contain some words about the varying health of his parents, or sisters; so during

R

his after life there was seldom one in which that of
his wife was not an important topic.　Beside all
other comforts, one he had in a remarkable degree,
in the patience, good spirits, and energy of Mrs.
Keble; she bore very trying and long sicknesses
not merely with cheerful resignation, but with bright
spirits, and when one would have thought her unfit
for anything but rest on her sofa, she would be up
and at work in or for the parish almost as if she had
been in strength and health.　It may give some little
notion of her in the early part of her married life,
if I extract parts of a letter from her to Elisabeth
Keble, then at Bisley.　It is dated from Hursley,
March 9, 1836 :—

　　" My dear Eliz[th],

　"Every now and then, when I propose to a gentleman
to write a little scrap to you, he says he is going to send
you a whole letter; but as even poor Hooker's departure
doesn't seem to have made a gap in his occupations, I
dare say this intended letter will be some time before
it reaches Bisley, so I must say 6 words to you in this.
I dare say you are thinking as much about Oxford as
we are."

This was the period of the agitation which existed
there on the appointment of Dr. Hampden to the
Regius Professorship of Divinity :—

　"Some of the clergy about here seem to take a real
interest in the subject, but those at Winton are not easily
moved ; at least, I suppose those who are much influenced

by the Bishop do not feel very sure of his concurrence ; but perhaps, as Mr. Newman says, the example of Bath and Bristol and other places may give them courage; and if the Bishop knew that the Archbishop really wished for such support, I should hope he would sanction it. John is gone to meet him to-day, and I dare say he will have some talk about it.

" I do not at all like the thoughts of letting him go again by himself to Oxford, but I suppose it must be this time ; and to comfort myself, I have been thinking that it would be very nice, (if nothing prevents,) to be there with him when the Prize time comes; he must be there longer then ; and if you could get your visit to the Edwards' over, and meet us at Oxford, and come back with us, I think it would do beautifully. I'm afraid the poor Lecture is rather behindhand. There have been so many things just lately to take his thoughts another way ; but after the last, which was only just finished in time to be *preached*, and yet turned out so well, I shall not be much in a fidget. The chief vexation is that one can't help him at all.

" By the end of this month I think we shall begin to look very pretty here. Even now there is a delicate tinge of green coming over the underwood and hedges, as I see when I take my walk up and down the south end of the Terrace. All that we have done as yet is the walk under the trees, which Churcher was gravelling yesterday, and which I hope will be in good order by the time you come. We have plans in our head about making flower-beds, and putting in some shrubs, but the ground is too wet to do anything.

" The daily service goes on very quietly and comfortably ; the number of persons continues about the same ; but to have this daily sacrifice at all seems every day to be more valuable. I shall be very glad for poor Mr. Newman to have the comfort of John's being in Oxford. He seems very much to need it; and nobody, I suppose, can so entirely sympathize with him both in his distress for the loss, and also in the views and opinions which knit them all three together. I can't help thinking, at least one doesn't know, but that Mr. Froude may in some way or other be of more service now, than if he had been kept here longer.

"Mr. Wilson seems to set in to his work with very good heart, though Mr. Norris of Hackney tried to frighten him by saying, 'Do you know what you are going to undertake —daily services, &c.?' He has been a good deal about the parish, but he can't do much in the way of reading or writing on account of his eyes. My best love to the children, dear. I shall leave the outside for another hand.

"Dear Elizabeth,

"Your affect^{te} sister, C. K."

Then *John*, later in the day, has taken up the pen and says :—

"Charlotte has just wakened me out of an afternoon's nap to say I must write a line to you dearest Eliz., and I say I have nothing worth writing, but it may be good to have her favourable account of herself confirmed, for she is certainly better and stronger than she was. . . .

"I most wish my lecture was done, it makes me feel so stupid. Your lovingest, J. K."

Let it not be supposed (I add in a parenthesis) that my old friend Mr. Norris was averse from daily services, which from the time he had a Church of his own he constantly celebrated.

It is not waste of time thus to make my readers acquainted with the person whom Keble had chosen for the partner of his life ; his was a nature which delighted in sympathy and intimate communion.; he had chosen well. Mrs. Keble, without going out of her subordinate place, and in spite of her delicate health, was his very helpful and affectionate fellow-worker, comforter, and support to the end of his days. I need not point out the features of her character in this picture so unconsciously drawn of herself by herself, but I will add a testimony to myself from Dyson, who says, writing to me in October, 1836 :—

" At the end of August we paid a visit to Keble at Hursley, where he has a pretty home and garden, and a charming wife, not omitting a most excellent Squire ; so that our dear friend has many happy appliances about him with only one great drawback, the delicate state of his wife's health. I find he has advanced higher up the hill of Ecclesiastical Orthodoxy than I have reached as yet. I require more time, being of a sluggish constitution of mind and body. · If I had the same purity and singleness of spirit, and something of the same depth of thought and feeling, as he happily has, perhaps I should strive more to keep up with him."

Again he says in February, 1837 :—

" Also I have a letter from J. Keble, who says his wife has been attacked by the Influenza, which has thrown her back much, bringing on her cough, &c. This I grieve to heat, being anxious about her both on her account and his. For bating her ill health, I do not know that our dear friend could have been more happy in his choice in all respects. And indeed this thorn in the side of ill-health has little venom in it, from her sweetness of temper and patience ; and may be wanting as a trial to make him more perfect."

In the autumn of the year 1836, Keble was called on (I suppose as the junior Incumbent) to preach in Winchester Cathedral the Visitation Sermon, before Chancellor Dealtry and the clergy of the Archdeaconry ; his subject was " Primitive Tradition recognised in Holy Scripture ;" it was published "in deference to the wish" of his audience, and was afterwards included in a volume of Academical and Occasional Sermons, which he published at a later period. But it had reached a third edition before that, and he had then subjoined to it an Appendix, and also a reprint of the seventy-eighth Tract for the Times, being principally a Catena Patrum collected as authority for the view he had taken. The sermon seems to me to put the important matter of the true and allowed authority of Tradition in the right light, and to have been a very seasonable contribution to our theological libraries. For himself he said to me :—

" I am glad you do not think I have gone too far in the view I have taken of Tradition. It appears to me such plain hum-drum common sense, that I am sure no one would think of urging such a truism, if Romanism had not brought it into discredit."

Cornish, through his brother Hubert, had intimated a doubt as to the correctness of his view of Tradition, in answer to which he says :—

" Hubert (who is a good fellow) says I am to tell you the meaning of Tradition, and reconcile myself with my Master, Hooker: to which I answer first he is not my Master, as I have dared to differ from him widely in my Preface; and secondly, if you compare what he says in B. i. c. 13, about Tradition, with the place in B. v. about the Tradition of the Cross, you will see that he does not deny the *principle*, that *if* you could make out such things to be Traditions, you ought to receive them, but only *the fact* that such things are Traditions. In the fact I am at issue with him, and so (among others) is St. Basil ; who says some of the chiefest and most universal rules of Christian worship are known by Tradition only without Scripture."

I make a further extract from the same letter, which presents a pleasant picture of the life at the Vicarage at this time, and adds an interesting incident or two on other matters. Dr. Newman will excuse, I think, my introduction of what relates to him. The letter is dated Oct. 16, 1837 :—

" My wife, I am thankful to say, continues on the whole a little stronger then she used to be at Cirencester ; but the autumn makes itself felt a little both by her and the trees, gently as it is coming on. Elisabeth is with us, very comfortably well, keeping up our spirits on the departure of my brother and sister and their three daughters, after a visit of a full month, the first they have ever paid us. It answered remarkably well, all parties enjoying themselves; and Tom seeming quite set up after his trying campaign with the Beggars and Guardians right hand and left at Bisley. Newman came among us for a week when we were all together: I wish you could meet him here some day; I think you will find that his demeanour answers reasonably well to the impression made by his writings and preachings. He has now in hand a work on Justification, of which I have seen a very little; those who know more of it, say that it is as striking or more so than any thing he has yet put out. While he was here we were very busy correcting some sheets of the 'Remains' of dear H. Froude, which N. is bringing out: if my partiality does not deceive me, it will be a most original and interesting book. His Journal has taught me things concerning him, which I never suspected myself, as to the degree of self-denial which he was practising when I was most intimate with him. This encourages one to think that there may be many such, whom one dreams not of. . . . I sent Newman what you said concerning Oxford Statutes, and found that he had been turning his mind to the subject; he has made a copy of the Oriel Statutes, and finds only two things which are not in substance (he thinks) observed; the Provost living with the Fellows, and the Fellows residing. This excepts of course the great deviation common to all the Catholic Foundations: the cessation, i.e. of Prayer for the Founders; of which the more I think of it, the more I regret it, as a most lamentable concession to Ultra Protestant fears and jealousies; nor do I think we shall ever be quite right till it is restored. In the meantime I am for

holding back as much as possible from all State interference; my notion of the Constitution (of course under
your correction) being that all such foundations ought only
to be controllable by Chancery, and that Parliament has
nothing to do with them."

A notion, I may subjoin, in which he was soon
to be somewhat rudely corrected; he lived to see
the principle insisted on that the Universities and
their Colleges were National property, and the consequence followed of course that it was within the
competence of Parliament to regulate their Government. And these principles established, I think he
would have admitted that on the whole they were respectfully and moderately dealt with by the Oxford
University Act of 1854, and the Executive Commission appointed by it. He certainly had no reason to
cling with regret to the Government of the Hebdomadal Board. It is easy to form an opinion as to what
he would have thought of the measure apparently
in contemplation at the time I write. On questions
of this kind especially his principles were uncompromising; if a measure offended against what he
thought honest, or violated what he thought sacred,
good motives in the framers he would not admit
as palliatives; nor would he be comforted by an
opinion of mine that measures mischievous in their
logical consequences were never in the result so
mischievous, or beneficial measures so beneficial, as

had been foretold. So he writes playfully to me at an earlier time :—

" Hurrell Froude and I took into our consideration your opinion that ' there are good men of all parties,' and agreed that it is a bad doctrine for these days ; the time being come in which, according to John Miller, ' scoundrels must be called scoundrels ;' and moreover we have stigmatized the said opinion by the name of the Coleridge Heresy. So hold it any longer at your peril."

I think it fair to set down these which were in truth formed opinions, and not random sayings ; but it would be most unfair, if one concluded from them, written or spoken in the freedom of friendly intercourse, that there was anything sour in his spirit, or harsh or narrow in his practice ; when you discussed any of these things with him, the discussion was pretty sure to end, not indeed with any insincere concession of what he thought right and true, but in consideration for individuals, and depreciation of himself.

I give, from a letter to myself, dated Hursley, Oct. 23, 1838, an extract more considered, and not unimportant. I had been reading Alexander Knox's Remains, and been much struck by them, and mentioned them to him. He says in the course of a long letter, (and I desire to draw attention to the close of the extract) :—

" As touching Mr. Knox, whom you have been reading, I admire him very much in some respects, and think he

did the world great service by his 'Treatise on the Eucharist;' but I cannot admit his symbolizing with Methodists
to be at all Catholic; quite the contrary, for Catholic
means, 'according to the rule of the whole uncorrupt
Church from the beginning;' and Mr. Knox's admiration
of Wesley and Co., was founded first on his own private
personal experience, and then justified by his own private
personal interpretation of Church History. Surely it was
a great fallacy of his, that where he saw the good effect of
a thing, the thing itself is to be approved. You know how
it issued in the case of his friend Mr. Forster, that he
made out Mahometanism to be a kind of Divine dispensation: and in itself surely it is rather an arrogant position in
which Mr. K. delighted to imagine himself, as one on the top
of a high hill, seeing which way different schools tend—(the
school of Primitive Antiquity being but one among many,)
and passing judgment upon each how far it is right, and
how well it suited its time—himself superior to all, exercising a royal right of eclecticism over all. It does not seem
to me to accord very well with the notion of a faith 'once
for all delivered to the saints.' I speak the more feelingly
because I know I was myself inclined to eclecticism at one
time; and if it had not been for my father and my brother,
where I should have been now, who can say?"

If it should seem to any enthusiastic admirer of
Alexander Knox (and although I believe he is much
less read now than he deserves, there may be many
still,) that Keble speaks with too great freedom of
one so justly remarkable as he was, it should be remembered that he was writing to me whom he was
perfectly entitled to advise on such a subject, with

the freedom and unreservedness of friendly correspondence. It was therefore natural to pass by the
qualifications which he might have thought it right
to express under other circumstances.

My readers will have observed how Keble writes
respecting Hurrell Froude and his "Remains ;" his
death was a heavy blow to him, and no wonder ;
those who knew him, but were not on terms of intimacy, could not but regard mournfully the end of
one so accomplished, so gifted, so good, and so pure ;
a man of such remarkable promise, worn out in the
very prime of life by slow and wasting and long
hopeless disease. But it was much more than this
with Keble—they were more like elder and younger
brothers ; reverence in some sort sanctified Froude's
love for Keble, and moderated the sallies of his somewhat too quick and defiant temper, and imparted
a special diffidence to his opposition in their occasional controversies with each other ; while a sort of
paternal fondness in Keble gave unusual tenderness
to his friendship for Froude, and exaggerated perhaps
his admiration for his undoubted gifts of head and
heart. And these were greater than mere acquaint-
ances would be aware of ; for he did not present the
best aspects of himself to common observation.

I must say a word upon the book : it was published
in 1838 and 1839 in two Parts, and to each is prefixed
a well-considered and able preface, written by Keble ;
with the exception however as to the second of a few

formal lines at the close, but as to the first, of the
portion from p. ix. to p. xv. This last vindicates
Froude from the imputation of Romanism, in the
sense either of favouring the Roman Catholic Church,
or of being disloyal in any true sense to the Anglican, by citations from the "Remains" themselves.
These excepted parts are, as I now learn, by Dr.
Newman, who was the publisher of the work; Keble,
however, shared largely in the preparation, and
insisted on partaking of the responsibility. I had
the misfortune of giving him pain, not only by differing from him on the subject; but, owing to mis-
information, or misapprehension on my part, by what
turned out to be a fruitless and ill-timed interference
to prevent the publication. I need not now explain
how this arose; but I must confess that my opinion
remains unchanged. It is a deeply interesting book,
not only perfectly harmless now, but capable of instructing and improving those who will read it
calmly and considerately; still I think that it was
calculated at the time to throw unnecessary difficulties in the way of the Movement; that it tended to
prevent a fair consideration of what the movers were
attempting, to excite passion, and to encourage a
scoffing spirit against them. Some part of the anger
and bitterness with which the Ninetieth Tract was
afterwards received, may fairly be traced to the feeling created, unjustly indeed, yet not unnaturally, by
the publication of the "Remains;" the one seemed

to be the result of the other: and the sequence of
the two was held to shew a deliberate hostility to the
Anglican, and an undue preference of the Roman
Church.

It was in May, 1839, that Keble published his
metrical version of the Psalms; he had prepared
this some time before, and it lay among his papers;
until an intimation reached him that the Bishop of
Oxford (Dr. Bagot) would, if it were published, license
it formally for use in his diocese. A sanction of
this sort he particularly desired; he had determined
not to publish it under his own name; and now
having this encouragement from the Bishop, under
whom, in a certain sense, he considered himself to
be as an Oxford Professor, and being also more
directly related to the Bishop of Winchester as Vicar
of Hursley, he was desirous of the same sanction
from him also, and to be allowed to call the work
the "Winchester and Oxford Psalter." He accordingly applied, and some delay occurring in the receipt of an answer, he became apprehensive that he
might have done what was wrong in making the application. By his desire I wrote to the Bishop, my
old and intimate friend. I speak from recollection
now only; but I think the delay might have been in
part occasioned by his disappointment at the execution of the work, and his consequent unwillingness
to connect himself with it so closely as he might
seem to do, if he formally licensed its use in his

diocese. He had, however, another ground; for it seemed to him, at least, very doubtful whether he had any authority as diocesan to issue such a licence: and he accordingly contented himself with leaving Keble and any other incumbents in the diocese at liberty to use it at their own discretion without his inquiry or interference.

Keble was content with this, and the version was published, with a dedication to the Bishop of Oxford.

Writing to me on May 1, 1839, he says :—

"I do not the least wonder at the Bishop's or any one else feeling disappointed at the execution of the work. I am sure I should be so most exceedingly, if I could come to it as a reader. The truth is, I really believe it impossible, and intended to be so, for reasons which I shall endeavour to explain in the Preface, if the book ever comes out."

Accordingly in the Preface he says :—

"The Version was undertaken in the first instance with a serious apprehension, which has since grown into a full conviction, that the thing attempted is, strictly speaking, *impossible.*"

This Preface is well worth reading, in which he gives the reasons at length for this assertion. Archbishop Howley is said to have pronounced, with his peculiar neatness of expression, a criticism at once conclusive, and yet personally flattering: "Mr. Keble's work has demonstrated the truth of his position."

The general substitution of hymns in the Church

service for metrical versions of the Psalms might
have been alone conclusive against the general introduction of this version into our parish churches.
But I think in the remark which I have cited from
Keble's letter a fallacy exists, which has operated
unfairly on the general opinion as to the work; he
says, "I should have been exceedingly disappointed
myself if I could come to it as *a reader.*" Now it
seems to me that a version of the Psalms should
never be considered as a book of poetry to be *read*,
but as a collection of hymns, or sacred songs to be
sung congregationally; and after satisfaction as to
its faithfulness, the only question is whether it is
that which lends itself to effective and harmonious
congregational singing. It must be familiar to all
of us how in some of our grandest oratorios we lose
all sense of the tameness or poverty of the verse
where it fits itself well to noble music. He who
versifies the Psalms, therefore, for choral singing,
should have some musical science, and much musical
taste. Keble was not well qualified in these respects,
nor am I competent to say how far he has succeeded.
But I have confidence in his version being faithful,
and I think I find it useful to refer to when I want
to extract the meaning of an expression in our autho-
rized versions, or to trace the sequence of the argument. I trust the version will not be omitted, though
I suppose it may not be largely read, in the complete collection of Keble's "Poetical Works," which
is promised us.

This year it was Keble's turn as Poetry Professor
to deliver the Creweian Oration at the Oxford Commemoration ; and among the select few on whom
it was proposed to confer honorary degrees was
William Wordsworth. The Poetry Professor and the
Public Orator deliver this Oration in alternate years,
but it is the duty of neither, as such, to present for
their degrees those distinguished persons on whom
they are to be conferred. I believe this office is
always performed by the Regius Professor of Civil
Law ; and certainly Keble did not present the Poet
on the occasion in question ; as Dr. Wordsworth
(who, being a Cambridge man, may well be excused
for inaccuracy in such a matter at Oxford) states
in his life. But Keble would know of the intention
to confer the degree, and it would be easy enough
to introduce the incident into the speech which he
had to deliver ; having the manuscript before me,
I see that the passage originally formed part of it.
He would gladly embrace the opportunity of paying him honour ; he had been for many years an
enthusiast in his admiration of the man and the
poet ; though I believe he was first introduced to
him personally at this Commemoration, by the Rev.
F. A. Faber, at whose rooms in Magdalen College
he met him by invitation. The Oration commences with pointing out a close analogy between
the Church and the University as institutions, and
after tracing this out in several particulars, notices

S

a supposed and very important failure of the analogy in respect to the poorer classes, to whom the gates of the latter are not practically open, nor instruction afforded. This failure the orator then proceeds to explain and neutralize so far as he is able, and towards the close he is brought in very natural course to the passage in question: Dr. Wordsworth has printed it in the original. I am tempted to add a poor but tolerably faithful translation :—

" On this also I might insist, that the University, and so Letters themselves, cannot well be without that austere and solid sweetness, with which youth well and wisely spent in poverty is wont to flavour those who are submitted to its training. But I judged, Gentlemen of the University, that I should satisfy, and more than satisfy, what this topic demands, if only I should recall to your recollection him, (specially now as in this honourable circle which surrounds me he is himself present,) who of all poets, and above all has exhibited the manners, the pursuits, and the feelings, religious and traditional, of the poor,—I will not say in a favourable light merely, but in a light which glows with the rays of heaven. To his poetry, therefore, they should, I think, be now referred, who sincerely desire to understand and feel that secret harmonious intimacy which exists between honourable Poverty, and the severer Muses, sublime Philosophy, yea, even our most holy Religion."

Wordsworth was exceedingly gratified by this unexpected tribute, which was received in the crowded Theatre with hearty and general applause, according well with the universal shout with which his name was received, when announced by the Professor in presenting him.

Dr. Wordsworth well remarks :—

"What a contrast was this to the reception which, a few years before, Mr. Wordsworth had experienced from the most celebrated critics of England, and from the literary world at large."

When the *Prælectiones* were concluded and published, Keble sealed his testimony by dedicating the volume to Wordsworth, with an inscription very beautiful in itself, and peculiarly gratifying to the Poet, as describing very correctly what it had been his object, as a Poet, to accomplish by his writings.

CHAPTER XII.

1840.—LIBRARY OF THE FATHERS.—CHARLES MAR-
RIOTT. — DR. ARNOLD. — TRACT 90, AND SUBSE-
QUENT PROCEEDINGS.

PERHAPS I ought to have mentioned earlier
an undertaking in which Keble began to be
engaged as early as 1838, and to which he attached
much importance, the Library of the Fathers. It
was this, I think, which first brought publicly into
connection the three names which for a long time
thenceforward, through good report and evil report,
were intimately associated together,—those of Pusey,
Keble, and Newman ; two of them still survive, of
whom it is no part of my present duty, and might
be a breach of another, to say more than what is
inseparably connected with my memoir of the deceased.   All three were of the same College, and
though of different standings, had been brother Fellows ; they were specially bound together by a common zeal for the Church of England, and a general
agreement of belief and opinions.

The undertaking just mentioned was one fruit of
this zeal and agreement ; they proposed to edit
translations of the whole or of selected works of
certain of the Fathers who had flourished previously
to the division of Christendom into East and West,

and also in certain cases of the original texts. They constituted themselves editors, and made themselves responsible for the selection of the works, and the faithfulness of the translations, and it must be added, for the general management of the whole publication ; but they relied for the execution of the parts on the help of a considerable number of gentlemen, whose names appeared either in the prospectus, or in the course of the issue, many of them men of mark, and well known in both Universities. They themselves declined all pecuniary profit.

It is an impediment to the success of all such undertakings almost inseparable from them, the obvious risk that what requires so many hands, and so much time, will never be carried on to completion ; the Editors sought to extenuate this as much as possible by allowing subscriptions for separate works, and by making these separate works of convenient and inexpensive magnitude. But they could not foresee, or provide against the calamity of losing the services of one of the most active and able of their own number ; or the troubles and differences which were before long to divide the University,—and the Library still remains incomplete,—a disappointment to those interested in possessing it ; yet it is still for use very valuable to any one who wishes to read, or consult, some of the most important of the Fathers, especially I mention Chrysostom and Augustine, in the course of his study of the Scriptures. It was scarcely to be expected that the translations in general, though they might faithfully render the opinions and arguments of Augustine and Chrysostom, should give us to the life the short, close, epigrammatic manner of the former, or the luxuriant eloquence of the latter. Keble was conscious of this; in a letter to me he says :—

"Have you looked into any of our volumes of the Fathers? I am just finishing the Revisal of S. Chrysostom on the 1st Corinthians, which is hardish work. I fear we are too literal, but it is the best extreme."

To which opinion I think all would subscribe.

The loss of one of their own number, to which I have alluded, was supplied by them as well as they were able by the accession of Charles Marriott, also a Fellow of Oriel. I recall the name of a man justly dear to many, and too early taken from us; a man of great learning and ability, but more remarkable for his rare simplicity, zeal, and purity, of a charity in one sense bounded only by his means, in another and higher unbounded. He died in the prime of life, still a Fellow.

Keble was greatly interested in this undertaking, as might be supposed, but, judging only from the initials affixed to the Prefaces, (some of which I may observe in passing have a considerable independent value,) he does not appear to have taken a very active part in it, compared with Mr. Newman, so long as he remained one of the body ; or Dr. Pusey, who laboured throughout with his accustomed industry. His most important contribution, however, has not yet appeared, a translation of S. Irenæus; which, I am told, is now being carried through the press by Mr. Liddon.

In the course of 1839 Cornish had been making a tour in different parts of England, and among other friends had visited Arnold at Foxhow. He must have written to Keble mentioning this. Keble answers him on "Old Christmas Day, as the folks call it," 1840 :—

"I am glad of your account of Arnold, which quite agrees with what I had been led to hope. His feelings seem much mitigated towards his old friends; but I wish I could see some fair sign of his taking a better view of great questions. In consequence of your letter I wrote a line to him to-day, with a proof leaf of a new Tract for the Times, in which it came in somehow to find fault with some of his speculations. How he will take it I don't know, but it seemed to me kinder that I should let him know, than that he should light upon it in print without notice. It does not name him, nor is it, I hope, very severe."

On St. Mark's Day following he had to write again to Cornish upon the death of his youngest sister, an event which for particular reasons moved him very tenderly; in the course of his note he says :—

"One surely feels more and more the privilege of being allowed to remember one's departed friends in private prayer, and secretly at the altar."

And at the close he adds :—

"I have had a very kind and comfortable Easter Letter from Arnold."

I find in a letter from Arnold to me, written soon after, the following passage :—

"I have heard from old Keble, to whom I could not help writing in the hope of getting some friendly communication with him once again. And his answer was such as to make me heartily glad that I had written to him."

In the summer of this year Mrs. Keble, who had again been very unwell, was so far recovered as to be able to accompany him in a tour which he made in North Wales ; it was made indeed in great measure to give her change of scene and sea air, her great specific. He wrote to me from Barmouth, where they were halting in a lodging on the level of the sea, and with great convenience for boating, the best of exercises for her. He was at the time helping Mrs. Davison, then a widow, in publishing the scattered *opuscula* of her deceased husband, and he wrote to me for some help. This subject was renewed in a letter which I received from him early in December of the same year, from which I must make some extracts on two or three different subjects. Mrs. Keble had again become ill, and was very slowly recovering when he wrote. After describing this illness, he goes on :—

"I was thinking of writing to you when your letter came,

for Heathcote told me he had heard not a good account of Mary."

She was his godchild, and he seldom failed to mention her with affectionate interest in his letters :—

"He did not say any thing of your wife being unwell. I trust both are now better, and that you are yourself enabled to nurse your winter cough a little. I expected to hear you were at Oxford, from what John said, when I just hailed him there ; and I very much regretted at the time that I had not paid my visit one week later ; it would have been a great and peculiar pleasure to walk about with you, and gaze on some of the old places. I missed seeing M. Arnold, (who was also his godchild,) but had a very kind note from him, in answer to one that I sent. I live in hopes of coming into full communication with Rugby again one of these days. As to dear old Dyson, I hear from him to-day an improved account, both of himself and of his two wives.

"I am rather busy just now, having sent a bundle of papers to the Tract Press on the Mysticism of the Fathers, a subject on which I feel that I can only just make a beginning ; but if one can draw attention, I shall be satisfied. Moreover, we are just putting the last hand to the volume of Davison's 'Remains.' (By-the-bye, I never thanked you for your kindness in that matter.) I am just now puzzling myself how, in the quietest and best way, to counteract the ill and false impression which the Bishop of Llandaff and poor Lord Dudley have been spreading abroad concerning his conversation. Mr. Markland kindly got Murray's leave to reprint the articles from the Q. R., and he has also procured the suppression of the unworthy sentences in the new Edition of Lord Dudley's Letters. . . . I love to think of your little Church, and it shall go hard, but I offer a small trifle, (I fear very small,) to it, but I shall know better after Christmas."

It is not material now to ascertain what "the unworthy sentences" were to which Keble refers, but they undoubtedly had given Mrs. Davison much pain, and he was very sensitive in regard to Davison. There certainly was in Davison's manner and talk something not exactly finical, yet over precise, and constrained, something of a want of ease and naturalness, which, in the freedom of private correspondence, might provoke a sarcastic remark from Lord Dudley; and there was a difference moreover in the natures of Davison and the Bishop, which might make the latter, good-natured as he was, and certainly esteeming the former highly, somewhat less careful than he might have been in regard to such passages as Keble regretted.

My principal object, however, in printing these extracts, was to give my readers a glimpse in passing of the real state of feeling which existed between my two dear friends; both of whom in a true sense I may call great men.

There is a very interesting letter from Arnold to myself, printed in the second volume of his Life by Dr. Stanley, which, in tracing the formation of his opinions and character, shews what they were during the greater part of his residence at Oxford; then and there it was that the intimate friendship between him and Keble commenced; and this explains what might seem at first a difficulty, how they became so closely united. Radical differences of opinion subsequently arising upon subjects which each held to be of vital importance, had interrupted their intimate intercourse, and that intercourse had been too intimate, and their love for each other too deep, to admit of their putting themselves on the footing of mere friendly acquaintance. It was to be expected, too, that as each advanced, (and each certainly did advance,) farther and farther in his own line, the difference between them would become wider, and the condemnation, by each, of the other's opinions, more intense. If Keble's language respecting Arnold had been occasionally stronger than that of Arnold respecting Keble, (and I really do not think it was,) it would have been no more than was to be expected ; for in his view the difference was on things sacred, his nature was very sensitive, and his attention was not, like Arnold's, occupied on a variety of subjects, a circumstance of course tending to diminish its intensity on any one. But all the time in the hearts of both the early love remained ineradicable ; these extracts are little indications of that, of which I can speak beside from personal knowledge ; and I feel sure that had it not pleased God to take one away in the very prime of his life, they would have learned to look through their differences, and to have set against each other's supposed errors that greatness

of mind, goodness of intention, and loving-hearted-
ness which they could not but recognise in each
other ; each might have admitted a salutary distrust of his own very strong opinions, and indulged
finally in what both so longed for, their old affection for and admiration of each other.   If this be
a piece of what Keble and Froude called the Coleridge Heresy, I hope it will be forgiven.

It appears in the course of these extracts that
Keble was not in 1840 at all contemplating what
was so soon to burst out at Oxford in respect of
the Tracts.   He was evidently intending to finish
the essay which he had commenced in the 89th,
when the publication of the celebrated 90th brought
the whole series to an abrupt termination.   The part
which Keble took as to the tract itself, and the proceedings which followed, make it unfitting for me,
however much I might wish it, wholly to pass over
these transactions in silence.

The Tract is dated " The Feast of the Conversion
of S. Paul, 1841 ;" shortly after appeared what has
since been called the Letter of the Four Tutors
reflecting upon it, addressed to the Editor of the
Tracts for the Times, and requesting him to make
known the name of the writer of the Tract.   Mr.
Newman answered them at once, and his letter professed at least to remove one principal ground on
which the censure in their's was rested ; he also
commenced immediately the preparation of a **Letter**

to Dr. Jelf, in explanation and justification of the Tract. But both of these measures might for any immediate purpose have been spared, so rapid were the proceedings of the Hebdomadal Board. The Letter of the Tutors was published, I believe, on a Monday; it was laid before the Board, with the Tract, on Wednesday; a censure was agreed to on the Friday, and on the following Monday in form pronounced and published. In the meantime Keble had communicated to the Vice-Chancellor that he was responsible for the Tract, having seen it in type, agreed to it, and desired it to be published. Dr. Pusey had written to the same effect. Mr. Newman had applied for a delay of twelve hours, that he might complete the defence he was preparing in his Letter to Dr. Jelf; which in point of fact issued from the press on the Tuesday, the very day after the publication of the censure.

These are the facts relating to the Tutors' Letter, and the censure of the Hebdomadal Board; but it will be convenient for the right understanding of their character, and the part which Keble took, if at the cost of anticipating events I add a few more particulars. Keble, as I have said, had at once, and before the censure was determined on, communicated to the Vice-Chancellor, that he held himself to be a sharer in the responsibility for publishing the Tract; and he was by no means satisfied that the whole blame, whether deserved or not, should rest

on Mr. Newman's shoulders. He accordingly prepared and sent to me a letter, with a request which
it may be as well to give in his own words :—

> "HURSLEY,
> "*E. Tuesday*, 1841.

"I AM going to make a request, quite depending on
your declining it, if it is unpleasant to you, with or without giving any reason. It is that you will let your name
be inserted in the blank of the title-page of the pamphlet
whereof I send you a proof. You will see that it is not to
be published, but only printed, and some copies sent to
those whom it is most supposed to concern. . . . . You see
I am a good deal concerned in this matter, and have all
along felt as if I was doing wrong in not taking my share
of the annoyance ; and I thought if one could calmly put
one's case before Archdeacons, and those sort of people,
which this mode of printing without publishing enables
one to do, some might be less likely to commit themselves
to what they would be sorry for by and by."

I did not agree in all respects with the course
which had been pursued ; nor indeed had I knowledge enough of the whole series of the Tracts to
pronounce an opinion upon them. But I did not
think either of these circumstances sufficient to warrant me in refusing Keble's request ; the granting
such a request does not seem to me to import entire assent to all which the letter may contain. Accordingly, the Letter was printed addressed to myself, and although not published until 1865, or 1866,
it was largely distributed in the course of the con-

flicts which disturbed the University in the three or four years immediately following the printing.

After stating as one motive for writing it, the personal one, "that he is himself responsible, as far as any one besides the actual writer can be, for the Tract on which so severe a condemnation has lately been pronounced by the Heads of Houses at Oxford, having seen it in proof and strongly recommended its publication," Keble goes on to mention a few instances, as examples only, of the need there was for some explanation of expressions in certain of the Articles ; and then in the two following paragraphs he states what he took to be the object and justification of the Tract :—

" On all these and similar points explanations had been given in various works, and it seemed desirable to collect them in one as a kind of manual to assist in what was believed to be the true legitimate catholic exposition of the Articles, whereby the scruples which were known to exist, and other similar ones, which may be expected to arise from time to time, in the interpretation of them as of other formularies, might be removed, or allayed, and our adherence to primitive antiquity, so far, thoroughly reconciled with our allegiance to the Anglican Church.

" Looking in another direction, one seemed to perceive an additional call for some brief and popular treatise to the same effect. From various quarters the cry of insincerity has been of late more and more loudly raised against those, who, subscribing these Articles, professed uncompromising reverence for the Ancient Church ; and it was supposed neither unreasonable nor uncharitable to put within the reach of persons who might find something plausible in such an outcry, the true account of the several points of detail, which at first sight would naturally tell in its favour."

The whole letter is carefully and ably written, very temperate in language, and charitable in spirit, its argument more easily brushed away with a contemptuous word, than answered point by point. It was, I believe, pretty largely circulated, though with little immediate success ; three or four years, dreary years as regarded Oxford, of repeated conflicts ensued, in which those whom, for want of a better name, I call the High Church Party, fared but ill against the bitter hostility and concentrated vigour of their opponents. Among other fields, on which the battle was fought, was the Poetry Professorship, the chair of which, in 1841, Keble ceased to fill, and was extremely anxious that his friend the late Isaac Williams should succeed to it. In more peaceful times it would have seemed a matter of course to elect him, at least as against his successful opponent ; but he was known or believed to have contributed to the Tracts, and the prejudice created by this circumstance prevailed. At length the contest was in some sort brought to a head by the announcement of an intention on the part of the Hebdomadal Board to submit to Convocation a new test as to the XXXIX Articles, in the form of a declaration to be made

before subscription, of the sense in which the sub-
scriber was about to make it ; strange to say this
was to be the sense in which he should believe
them to have been originally published, *and to be
now proposed ;* the identity of the two being, I suppose, in all cases assumed. Upon this issue the
numbers on either side were preparing to be mus-
tered ; and whether the objections appeared on consideration to be too many, and too serious, or the
prospects of success too uncertain, this was suddenly withdrawn ; and not long afterward, with only
eight days' notice, a statute was propounded to Convocation in substance, if not in terms, the same as
the Censure of 1841, including however the defenders
as well as the authors of Tract 90. An eye-witness
has described to me the scene which the Theatre displayed, where, by reason of the numbers assembled,
the Convocation was held, when the sense of the
House was to be taken. The great area and the gal-
lery were crowded, those who filled them much excited, yet all in suspense ; for a rumour had spread
abroad that the Proctors might perhaps intercede by
a veto ; but few, if any, knew what their intention really
was. The *Placetne vobis* was at length put, and then
in a still silence which at once pervaded the whole as-
sembly these two officers rose from their seats, and the
Senior declared *Nobis Procuratoribus non placet.* And
so the test fell ; the Proctors, who had wisely exercised their prerogative power, quitted office in a few

weeks, and the measure might have been renewed; but counsels more wise and perhaps more generous prevailed; and happily it was heard of no more.

This narrative of the leading facts, as relating to Keble, has run to greater length than I anticipated, but it will still be proper to subjoin one or two general remarks. It was Mr. Benson, who had preached and afterwards published some able sermons on the controversy, in the Temple Church, who gave the authors and favourers of the Tracts the perfectly inoffensive name of Tractarians. In the sense of entire agreement with them I never was a Tractarian; but I have already said how much upon the whole I think we owe to them; what I now proceed to say will be found, I hope, if not entirely agreeable to either party, yet not partial, nor such as ought justly to give offence.

There is no evidence of indirect motive, or want of perfect honesty of purpose, in either party in the commencement of the dispute. From the beginning to the end the Editors seem to me to have been actuated by the purest principles; they were labouring, as they believed, in support of the Church to which they belonged; they sought to elevate and purify the principles and practices of her children, clerical and lay; of course according to their belief of what those, rightly understood, were and should be, — but still in perfect loyalty to her. But this necessarily called on them to pursue a course which must wound the honest and sound convictions of many, and the strong prejudices of more, and which must condemn the indefensible habits and practices of not a few; they were therefore bound to exercise in an especial degree the virtue of Christian prudence, if only as a necessary condition of success. I own I think that the 90th Tract, (to go no farther,) failed in this respect; and that what ensued upon it might to some extent have been foreseen. It is true that there is much justice and much reasoning not easily answered in the defences and explanations which were then and have been more recently put forth in its behalf; but it must be remembered that it came after a number of essays, some at least, probably not a few, of which had tended to give offence and excite suspicion. And it is strange that it should have been apparently forgotten that the feeling which it was likely to rouse, was just that of which the English mind is most acutely susceptible, and under which, when excited, it is most indiscriminate and bitter. It is true that it is a prejudice, and for Anglicans especially the silliest and most suicidal prejudice, to confound the Ancient Church with the Roman Catholic; Keble read the Tract, as it was written, with other lights, and after a long education of the mind to discriminate between the two; but it was not to be published for such as he; and when it came before prejudiced or careless minds, it was calculated to create the impression that after all the object of the writer

was to lead men unawares to Romanism; and they
who thought this would naturally think him dishonest; while men neither prejudiced nor careless
might fairly object to a publication which they believed to have that tendency, though, strictly speaking, not by his intention.   It is not of course for me
to say how it might have been written, and when
I consider from what a clear thinker and perfect
master of language it proceeded, I do not acquit
myself of presumption in venturing to express my
opinion that, with proper guards and limitations
carefully and avowedly set forth, the legitimate end
might have been gained, a useful element imported
into our theology, and the great offence which it
gave avoided.   If this were impossible, the serious
question arises, should the Tract ever have been
issued?

To this extent, then, the Editors seem to me to
have been blameable; they had made what lawyers
would call at least a *primâ facie* case against themselves; but were they treated properly? that is, with
strict justice; even if a tender consideration was not
to be had for them?

I consider the Letter of the Four Tutors as of no
other weight than as the accusation; or, to speak
again in the language of a lawyer, the indictment
preferred by four individuals, acting unofficially, but
holding such offices in their Colleges as justified
their interference.   The Hebdomadal Board was substantially a Court before which this indictment was

brought for trial. We all know to what any person accused before any judge is entitled; to all this the Editors were of course entitled. Here, when the Letter and the Tract were laid before the Board, it had both the charge and the evidence offered in support of it, and no more. It may be taken that it was not the usual course in such a case to summon the party, or even to give him any notice of what was impending, and therefore, however strange such a practice may be, it cannot fairly be said that any *especial* unfairness is to be complained of for the want of these. But the Board knew and were indeed directly informed that three individuals, among the most eminent in the University, and most blameless in character, were substantially the persons to be affected by their decree; nor could the Board be ignorant how heavy was the blow which it proposed to strike by its sentence. The barest justice therefore required, that if any one of them desired to be heard in explanation or mitigation of the charge, reasonable time should have been afforded for the purpose; the more plain the case, the stronger seemingly the evidence, the more imperative in a judicial proceeding was this duty. One can hardly believe that five days only elapsed from the commencement of the proceeding to the publication of the sentence; and twelve hours of delay were respectfully solicited for the defence and refused; on the sixth day the defence appeared. It is obvi-

ously quite immaterial to consider whether that defence would have availed, or ought to have availed ;
a judgment so pronounced could have no moral
weight.   The members of the Board must have
been familiar with and should have remembered the
weighty lines of the Roman Tragedian :—

> " Qui statuit aliquid parte inauditâ alterâ,
>   Æquum licet statuerit, haud æquus fuit."

But from judges they had unfortunately made
themselves parties ; and it was impossible after this
that in the course of the subsequent proceedings
in the progress of the controversy, they could be
looked up to as just or impartial.   In proportion
to the goodness of their cause, (and no doubt they
believed it to be good,) it was a great opportunity
lost.   The subsequently proposed statute was a fitting sequel, the same indecent haste prevailed, and
the strong measure of the veto was provoked and
justified.

It has been said that the proceeding was not judicial, that the sentence was against no person ; this
seems to me mere trifling with common sense ; they
who pronounced it must have known that through
the Tract they were striking at the author and defenders ; and that it was only as it affected them
the sentence could have any meaning or weight.
The consequences of it were indeed weighty, but
with these I have now no concern.

A Memoir

OF THE

REV. JOHN KEBLE, M.A.

LATE VICAR OF HURSLEY.

BY THE RIGHT HON.

SIR J. T. COLERIDGE, D.C.L.

"Te mihi junxerunt nivei sine crimine mores,
Simplicitasque sagax, ingenuusque pudor ;
Et bene nota fides, et candor frontis honestæ,
Et studia a studiis non aliena meis."
Joannes Secundus.

VOL. II.

Second Edition,
With Corrections and Additions.

OXFORD and LONDON:

JAMES PARKER AND CO.

1869.

CONTENTS.—VOL. II.

———◆———

CHAPTER XIII.

PAGE

Otterbourne Church and Parsonage.—Ampfield Church and Parsonage.—Hursley Parsonage.—"Lyra Innocentium."—Keble's Resolution as to the English Church.—"Mother out of Sight." 279

CHAPTER XIV.

"Lyra Innocentium."—Charles Marriott's College.—Gladstone Contests 319

CHAPTER XV.

Should Keble have been preferred to Dignity in the Church?—Tour in Wales, and Visit to Ireland, 1840.—Tour in Scotland, 1842.—Undertakes to Write Life of Bishop Wilson.—Visit to Isle of Man, 1849.—Marriages with Sister of Deceased Wife, 1849.—Second Visit to Man, 1852.—Trip to Skye, 1853 . . 350

CHAPTER XVI.

Death of W. C. Yonge, 1854.—Oxford University Reform . . 377

CHAPTER XVII.

1854, Bishop of New Zealand at Hursley.—Francis George Coleridge's Death.—Visit to the West.—The Vineyard and Dartington Rectory.—Archdeacon Wilberforce.—Service for Emigrants.—North of Devon.—Professor Reed.—Decision of the Denison Case.—Tour in North Wales.—Argument on the Divorce Bill.—Departure of Mr. Young and Family.—1857, Tour in Switzerland.—Eucharistical Adoration 402

CHAPTER XVIII.

PAGE

1857, Death of the Rev. J. D. Coleridge.—Building of School Chapel at Pitt, 1858.—Death of Mrs. T. Keble, Junior, 1858.—Troubles in the Scottish Episcopal Church.—Stay at Oxford, 1859. — Tour to the North. — Visits to Edinburgh, 1860. — Death of Elizabeth Keble, August, 1860.—Death of C. Dyson.—Visit to Devonshire.—Death of J. Patteson, 1861 . . . 439

CHAPTER XIX.

Keble's Self-dissatisfaction, and Thoughts of Resignation.—Oxford Local Examinations.—Mrs. Keble's Alarming Illness.—Move to Sea View.—First Visit to Penzance.—Bishop Wilson's Life Completed.—Church Discipline.—Court of Final Appeal in Cases of Doctrine.—Bishop of Winchester's Charge.—Commentary on the Bible.—First Stay at Penzance.—Return to Hursley.—Judgment in Long v. Bishop of Capetown.—First Visit to Torquay in January, 1864.—Second Stay at Penzance, April, 1864 465

CHAPTER XX.

Subscription and Oaths of the Clergy.—Return from Penzance.—Practice as to Confirmations.—Paralytic Seizure, November, 1864.—Second Visit to Torquay.—Removal to Penzance.—The Colenso Appeal.—Pastoral Letter to the Confirmed at Hursley.—Visit at Heath's Court, May 10.—Return to Hursley.—Abolition of Tests at Oxford.—Mrs. Keble's Severe Illness.—Visit of Dr. Pusey and Dr. Newman 500

CHAPTER XXI.

October 11, 1865, Leave Hursley, and go to Bournemouth.—Letter on the Ritual Question.—His Life at Bournemouth.—Illness.—Death, March 29, 1866.—Burial at Hursley.—Remarks on Person and Character.—Mrs. Keble's Death, Burial, Character 532

CHAPTER XIII.

OTTERBOURNE CHURCH AND PARSONAGE. — AMP-
FIELD CHURCH AND PARSONAGE.—HURSLEY PAR-
SONAGE.—"LYRA INNOCENTIUM."—KEBLE'S RESO-
LUTION AS TO THE ENGLISH CHURCH.—"MOTHER
OUT OF SIGHT."

IT is pleasant to come back for a while from the
troubled scene at Oxford to the quiet of Hursley,
a quiet which however was full of hope and activity.
I have already given a general account of what the
benefice, which Keble was now the incumbent of,
consisted. The Vicarage of Hursley is of large extent, including several hamlets, and having a scattered population. Otterbourne is less in size and population, but its population also is scattered, and for
the most part living at a distance from the church,
which was far too small for its numbers. When
Keble entered on his charge, he found the inhabitants of Otterbourne busy in endeavouring to add
to it an aisle ; the Bishop had recommended them
to wait until the new Rector had been instituted,
and they had done so. When the matter came before him, their views had enlarged, and in consideration of the great inconvenience of the situation, aggravated now by the Railway having been

carried near to it, they desired, and he with some
regret acceded to, the erection of a new church on
a more convenient site; he was unwilling to separate the church and churchyard, from a feeling which
one cannot but sympathize with; but he yielded to
the general wish, preserving, however, the old chancel
for the performance of the Burial Service. He contributed £400 towards the erection of the new church,
on a site which was given for the purpose by the
President and Fellows of Magdalen College, Oxford,
who are landholders in the parish.

Keble had the good fortune to find among the residents in Otterbourne a relation of mine, William
Crawley Yonge, who having served in the Peninsula
and at Waterloo in the distinguished 52nd, had retired from the army upon his marriage at the re-
establishment of the general peace; though a Light
Infantry officer only, he had been a diligent student
of military engineering, and had made himself a good
military draughtsman. He became Keble's architect : for his designs he had recourse to the great
examples at Winchester, and in its neighbourhood,
and worked out his drawings with infinite care and
patience; he brought his stone from Caen, at that
time a rather unusual thing; was acute and intelligent in making his contracts, and vigilant in seeing to their faithful execution. The result was a
church not without its faults, and thirty years ago
few churches were built without them, (not many

indeed now,) but effective in its architectural character, and on the whole, with reference to its date,
convenient in its arrangements. Keble of course
considered a parsonage necessary to complete his
designs for the parish ; accordingly he purchased
a site, and, with the same help from the same architect, erected a handsome and commodious residence
for the Curate whom he placed there ; these last
measures were at his sole expense.

While the Otterbourne Church was in course of
erection, Sir William Heathcote was busy in preparing for building, entirely at his own expense,
a second church in Hursley parish, at Ampfield ;
and this was also undertaken and executed by the
same volunteer architect, with at least equal success. I take pleasure in recording these labours
of the retired soldier, performed at a time when
regularly trained architects were not so numerous
as now, and when the principles of architecture, and
their application, were comparatively little studied.
The works too were performed without ostentation,
and with most commendable patience and zeal. I
should add that in respect of both these churches,
W. C. Yonge was assisted as to some details by
Mr. Carter, now deceased, then an architect residing
at Winchester.

The situation of Ampfield Church is very beautiful, and that of the churchyard remarkably so,
sheltered on the north and east by wood and wood-

land, open on the south and west, and commanding
a beautiful and extensive view; flourishing ever-
greens adorn it; the road from Winchester to Romsey runs by the open side, which gives a special ap-
propriateness to a fountain surmounted by a cross,
which is close to one of the entrances to the churchyard; it bears the inscription following:—

> " While cooling waters here ye drink,
>   Rest not your thoughts below;
>   Look to the sacred sign, and think
>   Whence living waters flow;
>   Then fearlessly advance by night or day,
>   The holy Cross stands guardian of your way."

Many years have passed since I stood on this
spot, but I remember well, that even with the close
neighbourhood of a turnpike road, the prevailing
character of the whole scene was one of solemn
rest, and almost seclusion; the dark background of
foliage perhaps helps to produce this effect.

A very short inscription on the basin into which
the water pours, in German character, and German
words, headed with the initials of three names, hardly
serves to convey information to the common way-
faring man, that it was placed there in memory
of a holy fountain seen by the three friends when
on a tour together in the Tyrol. One of these three,
Lady Heathcote, for I will take leave to add her
name, furnished the inscription which I have printed
above.

Mr. Savage, from whose work I have freely refreshed my memory, mentions the placing in the church of a stained-glass window in memory of John Keble; it is the gift of the parishioners, and records their grateful remembrance of his services; the design was *given* by Mr. Butterfield, and £25 out of £33, the cost of the window, were returned by Mr. Wailes to the Keble College Fund. These are, it may be, little facts, but I do not like to pass them over in silence.

The building of Ampfield Church, and the constitution of a separate district for it, relieved Keble from a considerable part of his burthen, the whole of which was too heavy to be borne by a single pastor; and he no doubt gladly consented, by the apportionment of part of the rent-charge of the Vicarage, to lay the foundation of an endowment for the new district. This was completed by a grant made from the Great Tithes by the Dean and Chapter of Winchester, and a fund subscribed by the parishioners; to which a single individual, Mr. White, of Ampfield House, contributed £500. Sir William Heathcote gave a pleasant parsonage and field, and Mr. Wilson, Keble's first Curate, became the first Perpetual Curate of the new district.

I may add here that Sir William had also before this conveyed to the Vicar of Hursley, as the Vicarage, the house, which he had in the beginning occupied only as tenant.

The particulars of this narrative are surely pleasant to think upon; it was in this spirit, I conceive, that our Parochial System first took its beginning; a liberal landholder, a zealous tenantry, an earnest Priest, all concurring to raise in a certain district the first daughter church to the great cathedral mother; and the system itself furnishing facilities, as time passed on, and the population, cultivation of the land, and wealth increased, for subdivisions to be made, and new daughter churches to spring up. Such a system, so favourable for the maintenance and growth of religious feelings and practices, we should surely cling to; where it is possible, as in the country it generally is, even in its details; and where not so, as may be the case in our overgrown towns and cities, in that which is more important, its principles.

The erection of these two churches in his cure was matter of deep joy and gratitude to Keble. The remainder of his scattered flock, with an exception as to a hamlet called Pitt, which was provided for afterwards, was now within more easy distance of Hursley Church; but their erection naturally turned his thoughts more actively towards that church which was daily under his eye. It was, according to the fashion of many in Hampshire, of brick, well and solidly constructed, and it was in good substantial repair. It had been built by Sir William's great grandfather towards the end of George the Second's

reign, probably on the site where one of stone had
stood before, for it was attached at the west end
to a massive tower of flint and hewn stone, surmounted by a brick parapet ; it was arranged and
furnished within after the fashion of the eighteenth
century. Within and without the whole was painfully unsatisfactory to Keble. It may be remembered how, in a letter from him on his first coming
to Hursley as Curate, when he enumerated the objects which he found there to his liking, he mentions the tower, and is silent as to the church. He
was at the time fresh from the noble church at Fairford ; but the feeling grew on him ; nothing that
was appropriate could be to his mind too beautiful
or rich for God's house. I find him, in a letter to
Cornish, dated Oct. 19, 1846, writing thus :—

"We are stirring about our church, under the patronage
of the Venerable Bede, and next spring I trust we shall
really go to work ; you must come and see the plans first,
or else hereafter for ever hold your peace, in respect of
alleging impediments. One feels that one's advanced age
has not rendered one fitter to set about such works ; but
really the irreverence and other mischiefs caused by the
present state of Hursley Church seem to leave one no
choice."

Two or three subjects of course engrossed his attention at once in consequence of his resolving upon
this undertaking, and it will be better for me to follow
him throughout in regard to these, postponing for

the time other matters which I shall have to mention, and which occurred before and during the prosecution. Scarcely anything seemed to him of more importance; and his frequent letters to Dyson, shew that he spared neither money, nor time, nor thought, nor bodily labour, in doing as well as he could what he had set about.

He was first to determine as to an architect: was he to call on William Yonge to do for Hursley what he had done for Otterbourne and Ampfield? As to this he might have felt some little delicacy, but William Yonge at once removed it; he not only cordially concurred in the desire to employ a professional architect, but advised it strongly in consideration of the much more varied and complicated work now to be done. Keble accordingly wrote to Mr. Harrison, of whom he had heard well "from various quarters independent of each other," and who was beside a relation of his old friend of the same name, the Archdeacon of Maidstone. He accordingly became the architect.

The procuring tenders, and contracting with builders, were matters to come on subsequently; but at once, of course, he was to consider his funds. He had determined to meet himself the whole expense of the building, and it was clear, without waiting for specification or estimate, that the money at his own disposal would be inadequate; it occurred to him at first to sell the copyright of

"The Christian Year." As soon as two or three of his intimate friends heard of this, we opposed it very strongly. We had a strong opinion as to the great pecuniary value of the copyright, and thought it very unlikely that any publisher looking on it as a mere trade speculation, would be likely to offer a full equivalent; but we thought further, that it was exactly the kind of work which ought to remain as long as possible in the Author's own hands, and under his own control. Three of us, therefore, Dyson, Patteson, and myself, proposed to supply him with money as he should want it for the building; "The Christian Year" to be our security. There was no thought or talk of any legal security by assignment to us; but I was to arrange the terms for each edition as it should be called for, and to receive the price. No doubt this was a convenience to Keble, and set his mind free from all anxiety; but it was no inconvenience to us, nor ultimate loss. Keble sacrificed for the time the income he had used to derive from this source, but he never lost the ownership of the book, while it was nominally in our hands; and the beneficial property returned to him, when the account was cleared, to be the means in his hands of supplying comforts which age and infirmity might make necessaries, and of feeding that stream of bounty which was constantly flowing from him. So much has been said of this arrangement, and sometimes with so much exag-

U

geration, that it seemed to me right to state the simple truth regarding it.

I do not know what funds Keble had at his disposal beyond the yearly proceeds of " The Christian Year," but it was certain that some further addition would still be desirable ; to this we owe the completion and publication at that time of the *Lyra Innocentium.* On the 26th of May, 1845, he wrote to me thus from Hursley Vicarage :—

" I have got a scheme for raising money for the Church, in which perhaps you can help me ; (perhaps the Dysons may have mentioned it to you ;) to publish a set of things which have been accumulating for the last 3 or 4 years, under the title of ' *Lyra Innocentium,* or Thoughts in Verse on the Sayings and Doings of Little Children, and the Revelations of God's Will concerning them,' or something to that effect. As far as I can judge, it may stand as fair a chance of being profitable as its predecessor. Will it be asking too much of my kind Committee Men to suggest that they should make the bargain for me with Parker, if they approve it. I could wish to stipulate that Mozley of Derby should be the Printer. It will be nearly, but not perhaps quite as big as the C. Y., and will admit, I think, more easily of illustration by the pencil. It has been a great comfort to me in the desolating anxiety of the last 2 years, and I wish I could settle at once to some other such task."

The sorrows and troubles to which he refers under the touching term of " desolating anxiety," I have already in part stated ; but he also included that of which he had now the certain prospect before him,.

the loss from our Church of that most dear and honoured friend, with whom for so many years he "had taken sweet counsel, and walked in the house of God," heart to heart and mind to mind locked closely. This was the sorrow of his life, from which I think he never wholly recovered.

He goes on :—

"I can already judge a little of the perplexity and distress which will ensue. Did I tell you that Pusey wrote some time since to ask whether one could think of anything to be done by way of preparation for the blow. Does anything occur to you? I wish P. himself, Moberly, Marriott, and Manning, &c., to apply themselves to the study of the controversy, for I am sure there will be great need of them."

I shall have occasion soon to enter more into Keble's own thoughts on this matter. I pursue at present the subject of the *Lyra*.

Specimens were sent very soon after both to Dyson, (or I should rather say to the Dysons, for the ladies there were always most properly included in the council,) and to myself. We all agreed in our admiration of them, and also in the token they gave that Keble had advanced considerably in his religious opinions. On grounds partly of actual disagreement, and partly of the imprudence, at all events, of publishing them at that critical time, we objected to the insertion of two or three of the poems. There was one especially, perhaps the most beautiful of the whole, upon which we wrote to him, after I had been to Dogmersfield to confer upon it. This poem, as commonly happens in such a case, has been much talked of, and has been seen by many people; and it seems to me both just to Keble's memory, and a part of the duty of an honest biographer, to publish it now at a time, when, even if it might have been harmful originally, it can do no harm, and may help to establish that legitimate, and as I believe, Scriptural reverence which is due to the object of it.   He wrote to me respecting it thus :—

"H. V., 18 *June,* 1845.

" MY DEAR COLERIDGE,

" You may believe that as far as trade is concerned, your opinion and Dyson's is very welcome to me, and I am quite willing to make the bargain with Parker which you think equitable.   I of course rather expected that some would demur to the things which you mention, and indeed I selected on purpose the three which I thought most likely to attract such objections as part of the specimen.   But to say the truth, I did not expect that Mrs. and Miss Dyson would have objected on their own account ; and it makes me even sadder than I was before, as shewing how very very far even the purest specimens of the English Church are from the *Whole Church* everywhere else.   You see when I recommend the Ave, I mean merely the Scriptural part ; but if such persons have this feeling, I suppose even this must be given up.   With regard to the verse

' *He* calls thee Mother evermore ;'

if the Gospel is His word, and if the Gospel calls her His

Mother, and if the doctrinal decisions of the Whole Church are His words, and if they call her Θεοτόκος, how can it be other than true, and so true, that to deny or doubt it is touching a very vital part of the Faith. Indeed, when I think of it, I am sure I must misunderstand your objection; would it be removed if the word 'owns' were put for 'calls.' This, however, I only ask for my own satisfaction, for I see that it is quite impossible to print those verses in the face of such a feeling as you express on the part of the Dysons, and I cannot see my way to any decent abridgement or modification. I have made up my mind also to the omission of the other two. I only wish I had some good substitutes.

"No doubt there would be the difference in tone which you take notice of between this and the former book, for when I wrote that, I did not understand, (to mention no more points,) either the doctrine of Repentance, or that of the Holy Eucharist, as held e.g. by Bp. Ken ; nor that of Justification : and such points as those must surely make a great difference. But may it please God to preserve me from writing as unreally and as deceitfully as I did then ; and if I could tell you the whole of my shameful history, you would join with all your heart in this prayer. Pray do so, dear friend, for indeed there is great need.

"But not now to talk of myself; if the verses are less comfortable, perhaps they may be of more use as making their readers, the younger ones especially, familiar with some of the great truths ; and I suppose I had some fancy of this kind in the one which you so much doubt about. If we come when we hope, we will bring up the whole batch, and you will be better able to judge.

"In the Lifting up to the Cross, (which was suggested by a drawing of Miss T.'s, taken from the life,) the 'believing Isle,' is Ireland; the scene should have been Belgium, but I made it Italy by mistake.

"I thought that case of Simeon was an illustration of the principle I was laying down, that great spiritual favours must expect to be accompanied with suffering; and I suppose death is in itself so awful a thing as to warrant the expression, 'deep agony.' But this might be easily changed."

Then, after writing on entirely different matters, he adds these very touching words :—

"I am sure I ought quite to share in your feeling, that it is not for those to be judging between different Churches who have made such ill use, as I for one have, of present helps to holiness. (This is not humility, mock or real, but plain and sad truth, as you would say, if you knew all.) And with this thought I suppose I should content myself, if a Layman, as far as controversy is concerned; but it keeps coming unpleasantly before me that this is hardly consistent with the Priest's office; and especially when, as sometimes happens, I am asked for advice, then indeed I have had to think of the blind leading the blind. And yet I suppose I am not really uncomfortable, I eat, drink, and sleep, as if nothing was the matter.

"I hope Charlotte is rather better; with all love, again your's ever dearest friend,

"J. K."

It will scarcely be supposed that I publish a letter, however deeply interesting in itself, so liable to misconstruction, without much consideration. I am to represent my friend for good and for evil truly, if I undertake to write his life at all. This

is a part, and sometimes a painful part, of the com-
pact which a biographer makes with the public, when
he undertakes to write a life. Keble I am sure
needs no panegyric at the expense of truth, nor do
I think that when what he says of himself in this
letter is fairly considered, it will be found that he
needs an apologist. He writes indeed bitter things
against himself, we are bound to believe sincerely,
and I am sure without any intentional exaggeration; but I am as certain as I can be in a matter
which does not admit of demonstrative evidence,
that there is all that exaggeration, which is, I may
say, the natural growth of remarkable purity of
heart, and the most unusual humility. Something I
have said on this subject before, which I need not
repeat : but this I must add, that had there been
any reasonable foundation for the language which
Keble uses in regard to himself, he ought to have
added something more to it to make it the whole
truth; he ought indeed to have spoken of himself
as also the most consummate of hypocrites. I say
this not with reference to the world in general, but
he and I lived on terms of such entire intimacy, that
if there were any foundation for his strong expressions, nothing but the most artful and systematic
hypocrisy could have prevented my knowing something of it; yet on me he has left, and he must
have known that he was leaving, the deepest and
simplest impression of the most spotless purity in

words, thoughts, impulses, and acts from youth to
old age, of any human being I have ever seen or
known of. How I answered this part of his letter at
the time, I do not now recollect ; probably I passed
it by in silence, for I had long learned that he took
nothing so ill as words of praise, or vindication of
himself from himself.

I rather fear that I have been induced by the remarkable intensity of his language to say more on
this subject than was needful. It is, indeed, an
awful consideration that such a man should be able
to write of himself sincerely in such language. We
are not often allowed to see into the inward thoughts
of holy men respecting themselves, and surely when
we are, it should not lead us to think ill of them,
but should serve to rouse us out of our own easy
goings on. Let my readers turn to the strong language of the Private Devotions of Bishop Andrewes,
said to have been printed from a manuscript wet
with his frequent tears ; no one can doubt their sincerity, yet no one ought to doubt the purity of his
spirit, or the holiness of his life.

Now I pass to the other matter discussed in the
letter, or rather suggested by it. Here, again, allowance must be made for the same humility which extended to his notions of himself intellectually, and
in regard of his acquirements and knowledge, as
well as to all his considerations of himself morally.
In truth he had been a more than commonly well-

grounded student in theology; his reading was
extensive, and his recollection very accurate; and
although circumstances had for some years directed
his attention more to the divisions in the Reformed
Church, than to the great controversy between Rome
and the Reformation, he was by no means ignorant
in this. I believe his position to have been of this
sort. All his associations, early and late, were with
the Church of his Fathers; the loyal and affectionate language in respect of her to be found everywhere in "The Christian Year" was not merely poetical, it was sincere. But he had grown up in the
High Church School, and as a High Churchman
naturally will do, he looked upwards through the
Reformation to the Primitive and the Undivided
Church; he loved his own Branch as, on the whole,
a faithful representative on earth of that Church;
the more truly and exactly she represented it, the
more did he think her excellent, and to be loved;
the more she admitted what he called Puritanical
Doctrines or Practices, the less loyal and dutiful
could he be. Coln and his father on the one hand,
Fairford and its incumbent on the other, were ever in
his recollection; and he saw with the greatest grief
the uprising and growth of the latter school, from
a state in which it might be thought to have needed
greater tolerance than it received, into equality first,
and then predominance, not always used with perfect charity or fairness. Again, he was troubled with

the entire want of discipline in the Church; and it seemed to him, from his own experience as a Pastor, that this, coupled with the disuse of Confession, left him without the means of acquiring a proper knowledge of the condition of his flock, and without power of enforcing upon them amendment of life. He was moreover much dissatisfied not only with some of the decisions, but with the jurisdiction of the Final Court of Appeal; did its decrees respecting Sacraments bind the Church? had She the means of protesting against them, and did She by her silence acquiesce in them?

These were troubles on one side; on the other he could not but know of the doubts, in favour of Rome, which were arising in the heart and head of one whom perhaps of all his intimate friends he most loved, and leaned on in such matters; doubts the more perplexing to him, because he knew they were not invited wantonly, and yet continued to increase in strength, until they issued, to use that friend's own language, in "a strong intellectual conviction that the Roman Catholic System and Christianity were convertible terms." There may be many, not perhaps those who have read or thought most deeply on the controversy, who can see in all this no reasonable, or even excusable grounds for doubt, or trouble of mind. Keble, however, was not one of those; he had both; and it is matter for the deepest gratitude that he was supported under them, and guided safely through them. The process through which he passed may be traced in his letters which lie before me. In the first place, and from the beginning to the end, he had a deep conviction that, let what would happen in England, there was that in Rome to which he could not reconcile his belief :—

" I cannot go to Rome," he wrote to me in 1841, " till Rome be much changed indeed ; but I may be driven out of the English Church, should that adopt the present set of Charges and Programmes ; and many will, I fear, not be content to be nowhere, as I should feel it my duty to try to be."

And, again, in the same year he writes :—

" As to Rome, I thought I had said in my letter to you, that come what will, it would be impossible [twice underscored] for me to join it until it is other than at present ; Archbishop Laud's saying as I think ; and I suppose you would not yourself say, that if Rome altered her terms of communion to a certain extent, such communion ought not to be sought. The contingency that I contemplate, a very dreary one, but such an one as I, ought not to think it strange if I incur it, is, not going to Rome, but being driven out of all communion whatever. I cannot hide it from myself that two Prelates have distinctly denied an article of the Apostles' Creed, the H. C. Ch. ; and that while no notice is taken of them, attempts are being made in Oxford, and in many Dioceses at once, to enforce a view equivalent to theirs ; which view, if it were adopted, would drive me, and, as I suppose, all Catholic Christians, out of Communion. If I were like some whom I could name, I suppose I should look at this more calmly, but it would take a long time to prepare me as they are prepared. Pray think of me as kindly as you can, and do not forget me when and where you know one would most wish to be remembered."

In this state of mind he continued for some time : it is indicated in the touching passage I now extract from a letter to me in June, 1843. This had been a year of trial for myself, and I reluctantly pass over the touching and affectionate language in which he consoled me under great sorrow ; but I will not interrupt the present consideration by anything personal to myself :—

" What a comfort," says he to me, " in your late deep affliction, must it have been to be so sure as you all are of sympathizing entirely one with another ; and by this time I hope the bitterness has passed away with you all. Of course I cannot tell how a parent feels, but it seems to me that the unsettled state of our Church tends to make me think more of the joy and comfort of those who are in peace out of sight ; and as things get more perplexing, I keep saying to myself, it ought to make me more charitable, and then the next minute I go away and rail at those unhappy . . . without mercy. I suppose we all want to learn how to act, when in doubt ourselves, and how to make allowance for others who feel certain when we are doubtful."

Again, in October of the same year, he writes to me :—

" I suppose from some part of your letter that you have been told of my speaking to friends occasionally, as if I was perplexed about continuing where I am. My perplexity is rather what to say to others, who may ask my advice, than how to act myself. Few persons have a stronger feeling than I of the duty of continuing where one's lot is cast; except where the call to go elsewhere is very plain. It may be that I do not see my way clearly in the controversy between us and Rome ; but as long as I was in doubt, and perhaps a good deal longer than I might seem to myself in speculation to be so, I should think it my duty to stay where I am. Nothing could justify one's quitting one's Communion, except a long, deliberate, unwilling conviction, forced on one's heart and conscience, as well as intellect, that it was incurably fallen from being a Church. No private judgment of the comparative perfection of another Church, did such exist, would at all justify such a change. This, as far as I understand myself, is my present judgment in this awful matter ; but, believe me, my dearest friend, I want prayer and help quite as much as N., though for very different reasons."

On St. John's Day in the same year he writes to me :—

" You will find a good deal of my feelings in an article which has been reprinted from the ' Christian Remembrancer,' I mean especially when that speaks of the *practical failure* of the English Church, which I feel more and more deeply every day ; chiefly in that I find myself more and more oppressed with the consciousness of my own ignorance, and how blindly I go about the Parish, not knowing what men are really doing ; and whenever I do make any discoveries, they disclose a fearful state of things ; and even when there is some seriousness, of respect and confidence towards the Priest as such there is none, or next to none. In short, our one great grievance is the neglect of Confession. Until we can begin to revive that, we shall not have the due severity in our religion; and without a severe religion, I fear our Church will practically fail."

He pursues the same subject in a letter dated on the Purification, 1844 :—

"Another reason for my being a worse correspondent than usual, is that somehow or another the Parish takes up more and more time; as one gets more acquainted with the people, more and more things occur, which make me think a visit worth while. This is a reason for which I ought to be very thankful, though it is sad to think after all how very little one knows of one's people. We go on working in the dark, and in the dark it will be, until the rule of systematic Confession is revived in our Church. This is one of the things which make persons like Mr. Gladstone, however competent in most respects, yet on the whole incompetent judges of the real working of our English System. They do not, they cannot, unless they were tried as we are, form an adequate notion, how absolutely we are in our parishes like people whose lantern has blown out, and who are feeling their way, and continually stepping in puddles and splotches of mud, which they think are dry stones. Then the tradition which goes by the name of Justification by Faith, and which in reality means, that one who has sinned, and is sorry for it, is as if he had not sinned, blights and benumbs one in every limb, in trying to make people aware of their real state. These are the sort of things, and not the want of handsome

Churches, and respect for Church Authority, and such like comparatively external points, which make me at times feel so disheartened about our System altogether, and cause a suspicion against one's will, that the life is gone, or going out of it. And this is why I so deprecate the word and the idea of Protestantism, because it seems inseparable to me from 'Every man his own absolver,' that is in other words the same as Peace where there is no Peace, and mere shadows of Repentance. And this objection is over and above the great doctrinal grounds, which, I see, are pretty well stated by some one in the 'English Churchman' of this week. But enough of this which I inflict on you, because I think I made some such promise, and which I know is too vague and common-place to be worth writing down, only I seemed to feel it at the moment."

On the 31st of December in this year he wrote to me a New Year's Eve letter, much of it on the same subject, but I do not like to omit other parts so full of affection, and so characteristic of him :—

" MY VERY DEAR COLERIDGE,

" I must write you a line on this New Year's Eve, though you will not get it to-morrow; but you will have our best wishes, one and all of you, just the same. Among many blessings most undeserved, and enough to make one sink in amazement, if one's heart was not so much harder than it ought to be, which come crowding on one's memory at such a time, I seem this year particularly to feel, that surely nobody ever had so many kind affectionate letters as I have this year received, and especially from Montague Place and Ottery ; and one's neglect of them, I fear, is a faint sample of how one stands for thankfulness in a Higher Quarter. Well, as poor old Latimer used to say, God mend all. Now I must touch on one or two things in your late letters. First, on that which seems to be nearly heaviest on your heart, as it has long been on mine, the danger we are in of losing dear —— from our branch of the Church. I wish I could say that my sense of it at all abates; but my comforts (some of them) are these; with regard to him, really whatever happens, I believe him so pure-minded and self-denying, and so on the watch against intellectual pride, and other such temptations, that I shall think he probably does right *for himself* whatever he does. Yet with regard to the Church of England, I cannot but think, that if it were the duty of ordinary persons to leave her, the marks of reality would be more decidedly wanting, so that persons like some whom we know would not be left in undoubting adherence to her. Intellectually I fear I should be myself in a state of doubt, were I to give my mind to that controversy, but such doubt as, according to the principles of Butler, would make it my duty to stay where I am. This being so, however, I suppose it is one's duty to long for and aim at a kind of neutrality in one's judgment and demeanour towards Rome; and this I imagine to be really consistent with the English system, and by all accounts intended by Q. Elizabeth's Government for the first thirteen years. Then I seem to myself to see Scripture authority for this, both in the O. T. in respect of the relations between the Ten Tribes and the Two, and in the N. T. in Our Lord's often-quoted aphorism, 'Forbid him not, for he that is not against us is for us.' You know it is often applied to Dissenters, but surely it applies *à fortiori* to other branches of the Church. Now how this view would act is a great question. I fear it is unreal, but if real, it seems to

me most consoling, and as if it would help one to see one's
way both in Ward's matter, and a good many more."

Keble and Mrs. Keble visited us in Montague
Place in June, and at Heath's Court in September,
1845; we had of course some talk, and some differences on religious questions, but on neither occasion could I perceive anything which indicated
any danger of his secession from the English Church.
The first visit was at the time when the controversy
was going on between us as to the Poem which
Dyson and I desired to keep out of the *Lyra ;* and
of course much of our talk was respecting the honour
due to the Blessed Virgin, which it seemed to me he
was desirous of raising as much too high as many
among us were of reducing it too low.   I remember
I was fresh from a talk with my dear relative Sara
Coleridge, who would not admit there was any evidence to warrant our holding her to be even a saint,
that is, no clear evidence that she was even remarkably holy in her life.   In this I thought her, I may
say, outrageously wrong; but Keble, who was as
clear as I could desire from thinking her an object
of worship, still would have been glad to go farther
than our Church has deemed safe in the honour to
be paid to her.   With him the Primitive Church
gave the rule, and he allowed great weight to clear
ancient tradition in ascertaining what she held.   I
have before me my notes made at the time of our

talks on both occasions, and I see how I was struck
with the kindness with which he received even rebuke when he had seemed to me to speak with too
much severity, as well as with his sweet humility,
and his deeply reverential manner, lowering the tone
of his voice, when he spoke on these religious questions. On both occasions he parted from me leaving
me in full confidence as to his loyal adherence to
our Church.

This last visit was paid to us when they were returning from a tour which they, together with a party
from the Bisley Parsonage, had been making in Cornwall, and although some of them had been unwell at
Bude, yet on the whole it seemed to have been a restorative to all of them. Mrs. Keble especially had
nearly reached Hursley in better health apparently,
and with more than her usual strength. But immediately after, Mr. T. Keble at Bisley, and she at
Hursley, were attacked with very severe and alarming illness; the danger at Hursley seemed so great
and imminent that a physician was summoned from
London twice, and he (it was the late Dr. Southey)
kindly volunteered a third visit, on pretence, as Keble
said, of paying a visit at the Park. It will be seen
why I mention this illness, its bearing namely on
my present topic. It was just as the agony of this
trial was passing away, that the news reached him
from Oxford of that having actually been done by
his most dear friend, which had so long been im-

pending. He speaks thus of both trials in writing to me and to Dyson. Thus he expresses himself on September 27, 1845 :—

"MY DEAR COLERIDGE,

"Since I wrote we have had some fearful ups and downs. She was nearer sinking on Saturday than ever I knew her. So much so that she took regular leave of us, and *such* things as she said and looked, my dear friend ; you must really pray that they may not be thrown away upon me. You see the feeble frame exhausted by intense pain seemed unable to resume its functions, and we feared she would sink of mere exhaustion ; in our distress we telegraphed Dr. Southey a second time from London, and by the time he came she was beginning a little to revive ; she had received the H. C., and sent directions and messages to different friends, but it pleased God that she should, for the time at least, be brought back from the very gates of Paradise. During the night, and through Sunday, and the first part of yesterday, she was reviving ; but just after Dr. S. went away yesterday, about noon, she seemed sinking away again, and the alarm returned. . . . .

"The friendliness of the Heathcotes is unspeakable, and all the people about are very kind.

"It is remarkable that at Bisley they are quite as anxious as we are, Tom having been very seriously ill ever since he went away, but he too has now I trust only debility to contend with, of that however far too much. On the whole it is a sore season with us, and you and other dear friends must help us."

Another letter followed of much the same doubtful character, and then on October 16, he wrote

communicating more confirmed advances towards recovery as to both the sick ones, and he continued
thus :—

" These are great mercies, indeed, and most mercifully
are they given, as if on purpose to keep one's heart from
quite breaking at the bad news from Oxford. I thought I
was quite prepared for it, but it came on me like a thunderbolt at last ; I had not expected it so soon, and I clung to
the respite of a few weeks or months. And yet, though I
talk in this tragical way, I go on eating, drinking, and sleeping, just as if nothing had happened, or was happening. It
is my reason that tells me how low I ought to live, my
whole self keeps as hard and as cold as ever. It has been
a sort of relief to write to ——, and tell him how unchanged I hope to be both toward him and the Church
of England ; but sometimes I feel as if I could do nothing
but sit astonied for the rest of my life."

To Dyson he wrote on the 12th of October :—

" But what shall I say to the Oxford news, so long expected, yet it came like a thunderbolt at last. One can
but be still and pray ; I scarce know anything else that
can be done. I have written to him to express as well as
I could two feelings, one, continued love and affection towards him, the other, that every day things are happening,
especially in our two sick rooms, which make it more and
more impossible for me to do as he has done ; it would
seem like impiety to reject such warnings as have been
sent to me in that manner ; I mean things which dear C.
said at a moment when she thought herself dying. I have
some fear whether —— himself will not be unsettled again

before long. He wrote now to —— to announce his profession, and the tone of the note seemed to me a little excited. God bless him wherever, and with whomsoever
he is. Ever your aff^te,   J. K."

There remain but a few general words to be said
to complete this part of my subject. Keble's course
was henceforth clearly laid down in his own mind
for his own guidance; and, as far as regarded himself, he would have abstained from the controversy
entirely. When Dr. Newman's " Essay on the Development of the Christian Doctrine" was sent to him,
I presume from the author, he declined to read it;
and, having done so, when Dr. Moberly sent him
his " Sermons on the Sayings of the Forty Days"
with a Preface containing Strictures on that Book,
he equally declined to read that. But what he would
not do for himself, he could not refuse to do for
others. There were some, who, either in their own
perplexity applied to him for counsel, or who challenged him, having themselves taken, or resolved
to take the step of secession, on his own resolution.
He might perhaps have declined to answer, but it
was not in his nature to do so, and in order to do
this properly, he read the book; and with the same
result. Some of these papers are before me, and
testify to the care and candour with which he considered the questions he had to answer.

Some there are undoubtedly, I believe not many,
who have carefully and honestly sounded all the

depths and the shallows of this great controversy, have ascertained the bearing and the importance of the rocks bare or hidden on either side, and have come out with their minds in a clear undoubting conviction as to the haven in which alone the truth, the whole truth, and nothing but the truth, is to be found; whichever be the port in which they are anchored, they are without a scruple, and feel conscientiously that they may venture to act as pilots to others. Some, again, there are, many more I trust in number, and I cannot but think more happy, and quite as safe, who have never enquired at all, because they have thought the controversy either unnecessary, or beyond their reach; who have been content to accept the creed in which they were brought up, and their parents before them; and striven only to walk humbly, and truly, according to its teaching. Some, again, there are, and certainly I knew some remarkable instances at the time to which I refer, persons of timorous, scrupulous, even captious natures, easily offended, and impatient of a doubt. It cannot be denied, that for such persons many stumbling-blocks were raised at this time, and to be free from the difficulties which then were pressing on them too often seemed to be the only object of such persons. They reversed Hamlet's rule,—rather than bear the ills they knew, they would fly to others that they knew not of. My quarrel with some of these was, that being hopelessly, often avowedly, incompetent as guides, they yet could not refrain from troubling those who were at peace in their own course.

Keble belonged to no one of these classes ; he thought the controversy of great importance ; he was in a general way sufficiently instructed in it, perhaps enough so to warrant him in believing, that even after more enquiry, he should be unable intellectually to find on either side the truth, the whole truth, and nothing but the truth. Then he thought, and the thought was congenial to his humble, tender nature, that the true question for himself was, Shall I be safe where I am ? this allowed him to admit all moral arguments into the enquiry. Was he to affirm that so many great and good men, whose writings had been his study, whose characters the objects of his love and admiration through life ; or that his father, his mother, his sisters, all as he believed saints in heaven ; had lived and died out of the Church of Christ ? There may be some who may smile, not one I hope who will sneer, at what he writes of those which he believed to be the parting looks and words of his wife, when her pure spirit seemed to him to be as it were in sight of Paradise. These may have no place in a strictly theological argument ; yet I shall not shrink from saying that in my opinion, considering what was the object he proposed to himself, he acted rightly, even in a judicial sense, in giving great weight to such an incident.

They were in effect the same as the dying words of her who had been for years his true and fond partner and helpmate, his counsellor in all his pastoral labours and troubles, who knew better than any one the worth of his work in the sphere in which God had placed him, and who at that trying, perhaps enlightening, moment was testifying in a very conclusive manner, that to her, at least, there was comfort and a blessed hope in the creed to which she besought him to cling. These are circumstances, which as motives to conduct may properly have their weight, which yet do not come into the category of strict proof; and I for one should not estimate as of no value the conviction which fastened on the mind, I admit in some measure through the feelings, and it may be the experiences, of such a man as John Keble.

In the course of these later pages Keble has spoken of Confession, against which the general opinion, perhaps even more the general feeling, is so strong, that I can scarcely avoid saying a few words to prevent a misimpression as to himself. It must be remembered that he was not so much propounding a system, as stating his own experience in his own parish. The parish was a country one, not over-sized, and the circumstances, at least as favourable to the effectual discharge of pastoral duty as ordinarily occur to any incumbent. He was, indeed, painfully sensitive to the existence of

sinfulness, but he was not a severe man, nor of repulsive manners; on the contrary, his singular humility and tenderness, with his great simplicity of
address, made him as well fitted as most men to
attract the confidence of the closest natures, and to
dispel the fears of the most timorous. "Yet," he
says, "after all my care I am, in fact, in darkness
as to the moral and religious condition of my people, and I am so for want of being able to use the
arm of Confession." No thoughtful opponent will
meet this merely with scorn or indignation; on
the contrary, unless Keble exaggerates the inconvenience he complains of, a modest man would be
led to doubt whether he himself was living in so
much light as to his own parish, as he had before
perhaps imagined; and he might not improbably
join, at least, in Keble's regret, however great the
countervailing evils of introducing Confession generally might be admitted to be. He might not in
the end agree with him on the whole, but he would
still have somewhat of a fellow-feeling for him in his
avowed difficulty.

I own I thought Keble did unintentionally exaggerate his difficulties. I told him so, and that I supposed a clergyman, whose cure was of the manage-
able size of Hursley, need not and would not be so
ignorant of the spiritual condition of his people, as
he professed himself to be, if he brought to his task

the requisite intelligence, industry, kindness and devotion; and that if he did not, it was clear he ought not to be trusted with the delicate and difficult duty of taking confessions. I trusted he would gradually find the light dawn on him. In a subsequent letter, written in 1847, he spoke more cheerfully :—

"The Building," says he, speaking of the church, "goes on and gives satisfaction; and what is a greater comfort, I think the Parish is altogether in a more hopeful state. We have just had a Confirmation, and the young people seemed more in earnest; and Peter Young is more and more appreciated."

He speaks here of his excellent Curate, and, as might be expected from him, seems inclined to attribute more of the improvement he is thankful for to him than to himself.

I rather think that feeling the introduction of Confession as a general, or compulsory rule, to be hopeless, he did not then enter into the consideration of the evils, which even under the wisest administration of it, seem almost inseparable from it, or of the abuse to which it is so singularly liable. Perhaps, too, he did not heed this practical objection, that it would be impossible to make every incumbent, as such, confessor of his parishioners; and that wherever a stranger took that office, as all he knew would be under the seal of secrecy, the incumbent would remain in the same ignorance in the discharge of his pastoral duty as before. If these matters had been fully considered, he would perhaps have admitted that the question was one of so great difficulty, that it might be wise to accept the present rule, which allows Confession as a voluntary act, and does not make it a part of the ordinary discipline of the Church. On this he himself acted habitually ; he found it in his own case a comfort and guide, and resorted to it ; and when he was desired, he did not refuse to use it as such to others.

I will now subjoin the poem which has led me into so long a digression. I might have omitted it, because I have good reason for expecting that it will be included in the promised publication of his poems, but it is so important, rightly considered, to a full acquaintance with his opinions, that I think it better to give it a place here also. In August, 1844, the Keble family had made what Keble calls "a rather ambitious ramble," reaching as far north as Fort William, and among other excursions, says he, "young Tom and I climbed Ben Nevis, much to the aching of my old muscles, but to the great satisfaction of my mind." It was in this tour the incident occurred, which is mentioned in the commencement of the poem. A lady, writing upon good authority, has informed me that in the course of it he was the guest of Mr. Stuart in the Highlands. Dugald, the host's son, came suddenly into the room where he was, and looking all about him, sorrowfully exclaimed, " My mother is not here." He was much touched by the incident, and wrote on the occasion that which follows : which first bore the title, " The Annunciation," S. John xix. 27.

MOTHER OUT OF SIGHT.

I.

" Saw ye the bright-eyed stately child,
With sunny locks so soft and wild,
How in a moment round the room
His keen eye glanced, then into gloom
Retired, as they who suffer wrong,
Where most assured they look and long ;
Heard ye the quick appeal, half in dim fear
In anger half, ' My mother is not here.'

2.

" Perchance some burthened heart was nigh,
To echo back that yearning cry
In deeper chords, than may be known
To the dull outward ear alone.
What if our English air be stirr'd
With sighs from saintly bosoms heard,
Or penitents to leaning angels dear,—
' Our own, our only Mother is not here.'

3.

" The murmurings of that boyish heart,
 They hush with many a fostering art:
 ' Soon o'er the islands of the West,
 The weary sun shall sink to rest ;
 The rose tints fade, that gradual now
 Are climbing Ben-y-Vear's green brow ;
Soon o'er the Loch the twilight stars will peer,
Then shalt thou feel thy soul's desire is here.'

4.

" Lightly they soothe the fair fond boy ;
 Nor is there not a hope and joy
 For spirits that half-orphan'd roam,
 Forlorn in their far island home ;
 Oft as in penance lowly bow'd,
 Prayer like a gentle evening cloud
Enfolds them, through the mists they seem to trace
By shadowy gleams a Royal Mother's face.

5.

" The Holy Church is at their side,
 Not in her robes a glorious bride ;
 As Sister named of Mercy mild,
 At midnight by a fever'd child,
 Might watch, and to the dim eye seem
 A white-robed angel in a dream ;
Such may the presence of the Spouse appear,
To tender trembling hearts, so faint, so dear.

6.

" The Babe for that sweet Vision's sake,
   Courts longer trance, afraid to wake;
   And we for love would fain lie still,
   Though in dim faith, if so He will.
   And wills He not? are not His signs
   Around us oft as day declines?
Fails He to bless or home or choral throng,
Where true hearts breathe His Mother's evensong?

7.

" Mother of God, O not in vain,
   We learn'd of old thy lowly strain;
   Fain in thy shadow would we rest,
   And kneel with thee, and call thee blest.
   With thee would magnify the Lord,
   And if thou art not here adored,
Yet seek we day by day the love and fear
Which brings thee with all saints near and more near.

8.

" What glory thou above hast won,
   By special grace of thy dear Son,
   We see not yet, nor dare espy
   Thy crowned form with open eye.
   Rather beside the manger meek,
   Thee bending with veiled brow we seek;
Or where the angel in the Thrice Great Name
Hailed thee, and Jesus to thy bosom came.

9.

" Yearly since then with bitterer cry
　Man hath assail'd the throne on high,
　And Sin and Hate more fiercely striven
　To mar the league 'twixt Earth and Heaven.
　But the dread tie that pardoning hour,
　Made fast in Mary's awful bower,
Hath mightier prov'd to bind than we to break ;
None may that work undo, that Flesh unmake.

10.

" Thenceforth, whom thousand worlds adore,
　HE calls thee Mother evermore ;
　Angel nor Saint His face may see
　Apart from what He took of thee ;
　How may we choose but name thy Name,
　Echoing below their high acclaim
In Holy Creeds ? since earthly song and prayer
Must keep faint time to the dread Anthems there.

11.

" How but in love on thine own days,
　Thou blissful One, upon thee gaze ?
　Nay every day, each suppliant hour,
　Whene'er we kneel, in aisle or bower,
　Thy glories we may greet unblam'd,
　Nor shun the lay by Seraphs framed.
Hail Mary full of grace ! O welcome sweet,
Which daily in all lands all Saints repeat ;

12.

" Fair greeting with our Matin vows,
　　Paid duly to th' Enthroned Spouse,
　　His Church and Bride, here and on high,
　　Figured in her deep purity.
　　Who born of Eve, high Mercy won,
　　To bear and nurse the Eternal Son.
O awful Station to no Seraph given,
On this side touching Sin, on th' other Heaven.

13.

" Therefore, as kneeling day by day,
　　We to Our Father duteous pray ;
　　So unforbidden we may speak,
　　An Ave to Christ's Mother meek.
　　(As children with ' good-morrow' come,
　　To Elders in some happy home,)
Inviting so the Saintly Host above,
With our unworthiness to pray in love.

14.

" To pray with us, and gently bear,
　　Our falterings in the pure bright air ;
　　But strive we pure and bright to be
　　In spirit,—else how vain of thee,
　　Our earnest dreamings, awful Bride !
　　Feel we the sword that pierc'd Thy side ;
Thy spotless lily flower, so clear of hue,
Shrinks from the breath impure, the tongue untrue."

CHAPTER XIV.

"LYRA INNOCENTIUM."—CHARLES MARRIOTT'S COLLEGE.—GLADSTONE CONTESTS.

I COMMENCED what I shall have to say respecting the *Lyra Innocentium* in the preceding chapter, but the part which Dyson and I myself took as to two or three of the poems intended to form part of it, led me to enter at once into an account of the difficulties which passed through Keble's mind on the great religious question of that day, and to their final settlement. It seemed to me better to dispose of these at once, and now return to the volume itself, which Keble begged our criticisms upon, and which we passed to the publisher. The volume appeared in April, 1846. The title, which has since been frequently used with different additions, was not common then, and probably was suggested by the *Lyra Apostolica*, to which he had contributed many poems. I may as well state here, though out of place, the little fact, that the title of his great work was taken from the fourth Sermon in John Miller's "Christian Guide;" he asked his permission for this, which was of course readily accorded. Certainly it was an excellent title for such a work.

On the present occasion he did publish his dedication at once, bearing date February in that year.
Some people think the *Lyra* has a dry and hard
character; the dedication, at least, is free from this
defect; to me it was perhaps the more touching,
because I knew how faithful a picture it presented,
at once painful and soothing, of the troubles of mind
which he had gone through, and of the humble and
devotional spirit which was vouchsafed to him to
shed its peace on him, at least on this point for
the remainder of his life.

Keble's fame, the just claim which he has to the
admiration and gratitude of his countrymen, indeed
of the inhabitants of all lands where English is
spoken, must rest upon his sacred poetry. He wrote,
indeed, many things in prose, of great value, and
which alone might have earned him reputation, yet
it would have been such only as would have classed
him among many other excellent writers. But "The
Christian Year" is generally admitted, and I think
justly, to have placed him alone, far above all our
other sacred poets; to have made him in truth the
sacred poet of the nation.

I do not expect a general agreement in opinion
with me, when I say that the *Lyra Innocentium*, if
not equal to "The Christian Year," as a whole, is
at least more than equal in some parts, and on the
whole worthy of its author. Though very successful
in comparison with the generality of such works, it

has not had a circulation at all proportionate to
that of "The Christian Year;" it has not become
a *manual* in general use, and has not consequently
been studied, and is not known in the same degree.
I may therefore be excused a few words upon it.

A dear young friend of mine, a happy young
mother, writing to me from New Zealand, calls it
a mother's book, and most justly; it has suffered,
I think, by being considered a book *for* children,
properly it is one *about* children. The title-page
says it is "on children, their ways and privileges."
It begins with their baptism, (and the Author's belief as to that sacrament gives a specific character
to the whole,) it follows them through their cradle
life, and infancy, their childhood sports, troubles,
encouragements, and warnings; it unfolds the lessons which nature, and the lessons which grace
teaches them; it dwells on their sicknesses, their
deaths. No one, perhaps, but a parent, can fully
enter into all parts of it, and yet he who wrote it
did not marry young, and was never a father. It
is matter of wonder how one so circumstanced could
ever have known enough of children from infancy
to have written such a volume, yet I am persuaded
that the more one has seen of them, the more will
the life-like truth of the painting strike one. It will
naturally be asked where and how did he acquire his
knowledge. First, and above all, I think from his intense love for children, and from his feeling about them,

in which the heartiest tenderness was mingled with
something amounting almost to reverence. A newly-
baptized child was to him an emblem of the most
spotless purity of which human nature here below
is capable. I never shall forget being present once
as godfather, when he baptized a child of Sir William Heathcote's.   The child, after he had administered the sacrament, lay in his arms so still and
sweet, one might believe it conscious of the blessing
it had received. Keble held it in his arms some
little time, looking on it with an inexpressible look
of delight and love, a tear was in his eye, and he
seemed loth to part with it again to its godmother.
In 1853 that dear child died, and I will not keep
back the letter which he wrote to Miss Baker, his
governess, who was in deep distress for the loss of
him ; it testifies so strikingly and touchingly to the
love and feeling I have been speaking of :—

                                    " Hursley,
                                " 14 *June*, 1853.

    " My dear ——,

    "I must write a line, tho' I know what poor help one
can give in such mournful trials as this ; for I have been
thinking of you almost as much as of his parents ever since
I heard of it ; and if it seems so sad to me to think of not
seeing him any more with his dear quiet little ways going
in and out with you (he alludes here, I believe, to the daily
morning service) ; how much severer must it be to your
affectionate heart.   But He who pours the love into the

heart, has ways of His own to make the sorrow that comes
with it tolerable. I make no question, dear Friend, but
that you feel this already very much. From what Sir
William told me in Saturday's note, there was a treasure
of comfortable and happy thoughts and memories which
dear little Godfrey was permitted to leave to you all, when
he was just going,—a treasure for you to make much of as
long as you live. Whatever happens you will always be
able to say in humble thankfulness, 'By God's mercy I have
been permitted to help in rearing *one* plant at least, which is
now blooming for ever in Paradise, and I am sure (if there
is remembrance, and who can doubt it) of being remembered
by one at least who is there.' My dear ——, encourage
these soothing thoughts, if they come to you ; for surely
they are the truest thoughts ; but if you cannot quite enter
into the comfort of them as yet, be not too much disheartened, bear the dreariness bravely for His sake, and for the
dear child's sake, who is now in such sweet rest. Do not
trouble to write, but

> " Believe me always,
> " Your loving friend,
> " J. K."

When in the volume he speaks to the good child
of its blessings, or to the froward one in blame,
he constantly recurs to its baptism to think upon, to
be grateful for, and to be warned by. Those who
differ with him in his doctrine may yet admire the
beautiful illustration of it in the poem entitled,
" Guardian Angels," in which he sees in a dream
infants brought by their angels to the fount :—

" There one moment lay immersed,
    Each bright form, and ere it rose,
Rose regenerate, light would burst
    From where golden morning glows,
With a sudden, silent thrill,
Over that mysterious rill ;
Ne'er so bright, so gentle, sweep
Lightnings o'er the summer deep.

" In a moment came that ray,
    Came, but went not ; every sprite
Through its veil of mortal clay,
    Now is drench'd in quickening light ;
Light, wherewith the seraphs burn,
Light, that to itself would turn,
Whatsoe'er of earth and shame
Mars e'en now the new-born frame."

                              Holy Baptism, Poem 3.

Then there were his brother's nursery, the children at the park, the large fine family of his neighbour, Dr. Moberly, his own school, where he was a very frequent teacher, his cottage visits, the numberless opportunities which presented themselves to him in his rambles from hamlet to hamlet, and all these presented to that receptive spirit, and faithful memory, inseparable from the true poetic nature. These may well be thought sometimes to have created, sometimes authenticated, sources of information, and subjects for meditation, which would escape ordinary perceptions. From internal evidence,

where direct is wanting, and there is direct evidence
in very numerous instances, I believe that had we
the means of tracing, we should find at least a foundation in fact for every one of the poems, which professes to narrate, or comment on an incident.

I have no doubt he wrote to me the simple truth,
when he spoke of the comfort he had received in
his anxieties from the composition of these poems ;
the thoughts which they suggested took him out of
himself, away from his doubts and cares ; he was engaged in what was most delightful to him when playing with children, teaching them, or warning others
by what they taught himself. And he was seldom
more picturesque in his language than when he had
one of these subjects in hand ; what pictures does
he give us for example in this stanza of " Children's
Thankfulness :"—

> " Why so stately, maiden fair,
>   Rising in thy nurse's arms,
>   With that condescending air,
>   Gathering up thy queenly charms ;
>   Like some gorgeous Indian bird,
> Which, when at eve the balmy copse is stirr'd,
>   Turns the glowing neck to chide
> Th' irreverent foot-fall, then makes haste to hide
>   Again its lustre deep,
> Under the purple wing, best home of downy sleep."

It seems to me that not a word could be altered
in this, except, if indeed it be not too minute cri-

ticism to remark, that the bird's *making haste* to
hide rather breaks the repose of the remainder of
the picture, and is in itself perhaps not quite true
to nature. Then, after following the subject through
some stanzas, he lifts it up, which he seldom failed
to do in his application, in the last stanza :—

> " Save our blessings, Master, save
>   From the blight of thankless eye ;
>   Teach us for all joys to crave
>   Benediction pure and high ;
>   Own them given, endure them gone,
> Shrink from their hardening touch, yet prize them won.
>   Prize them as rich odours, meet
> For love to lavish on His sacred feet.
>   Prize them as sparkles bright,
> Of heavenly dew from yon o'erflowing well of light."

Sometimes the poems are exquisitely pathetic ;
there are few to be met with anywhere more so
than the two entitled, " Bereavement" and " Fire,"
both founded on facts. Mr. Eddis has found in the
former subjects for two pictures, of which the en-
gravings are well known. The Poet meets two sisters in the joyous flower-time of April, the elder
leading the younger :—

> " One a bright bud, and one might seem
>   A sister flower half-blown,
>   Full joyous on their loving dream
>   The sky of April shone."

He meets them again on a chill and damp Sunday evening in autumn, but the elder is following the younger to her grave ; the motto to the poem is, " The Lord gave Job twice as much as he had before," and so he cheers the mourner with his favourite idea of communion with the departed spirit :—

> " What if henceforth by heaven's decree,
>   She leave thee not alone,
>   But in her turn prove guide to thee,
>   In ways to angels known.
>
> " O yield thee to her whisperings sweet ;
>   Away with thoughts of gloom !
>   In love the loving spirits greet,
>   Who wait to bless her tomb.
>
> " In loving hope with her *unseen*,
>   Walk as in hallowed air ;
>   When foes are strong, and trials keen,
>   Think, ' what if she be there.' "

The most delicate and ideal artist need not take it amiss to be told that this last was hardly a subject for his art.

But I forget, while I indulge myself, that I am speaking of a volume which has been in many hands for more than twenty years, and I must not pursue this farther ; at the same time I should add that in some of the poems Keble appears to me to

have struck a higher note than he ever reached in
" The Christian Year." I instance the " Lifting up to
the Cross," " Church Bells," " Easter Day," " The
Waterfall," and " The Starry Heavens." Perhaps in
some measure from Church associations he was specially fond of the music of church bells in chiming.
After a visit to us in October, 1844, he writes :—

" I wish I had a better ear, and truer memory for sounds,
that I might recall the church bells of St. Mary Ottery, the
one deep tenor at $7\frac{1}{2}$, and then the chimes at $\frac{1}{4}$ to 8."

Eight o'clock was the hour of our daily service in
the morning.

In the course of our correspondence on the subject of the poems which Dyson and I had recommended him to withhold for the present, I had
collected that he was rather in want of others to
supply their place, and I first suggested to him
a passage from St. Augustine's Confessions : " Post
et ridere cæpi, dormiens primo, deinde vigilans,"
and as he did not seem disposed to write on it, I
ventured to do so myself, and he very kindly gave
the stanzas a place among the Cradle Songs ; altering, however, my first stanza, in which he thought
I had misunderstood my text, and I dare say I
had obscurely expressed myself so as to warrant
him.

" St. Augustine," says he, " seems to me to speak not of
a smile in the first sleep, but of the first smile being in

sleep, which is a different, and a deeper, and as those who have experience tell me, a truer idea."

I afterwards suggested to him another subject from the Confessions; the passage is to be found in the 8th Book, ii. 6 and 7, in which an analogy is drawn between the lost sheep, the piece of silver, the prodigal son, and, among other things, the dear one of the house recovered from sickness. "It strikes me," I said, "that a child after sickness, in the garden, pale and feeble, yet the object of peculiar joy and attentions from brothers, sisters, mother, &c., though less bright and beautiful than any of the circle, with the same application, might suit your purpose well." This hint pleased him, and he wrote the beautiful poem of "Languor" upon it. I mention my own suggestion, for it may be worth seeing out of how scanty and rude materials he constructed so beautiful and so entirely original a poem.

And now I must leave a subject on which I have indulged my own feelings too long; but I am really desirous of obtaining for the *Lyra* the position which I think it deserves. Let me add my advice to young persons to read it at all events as I have recommended "The Christian Year" to be read. Although in the beginning Keble did not write it with reference to the course of our Prayer-book, yet even in the first edition he appropriated certain poems to certain days, and he subsequently carried that idea out through them all. It will be found, I believe, that we shall appreciate them more justly, and enjoy them more, and learn more from them, if we follow the author's guidance as our rule for reading them.

I forget how Keble had learned that I thought of preparing a review of the *Lyra*, and offering it to the "Quarterly." He wrote to me on this so characteristic a note, that it is worth inserting here :—

"As to the Review, I wish you to be entirely guided by your feelings while you are doing it. I mean if you get into a glow as you are about it, and are conscious that you are doing it well, go on with it, and don't spare me ; I shall get a deal more credit by discriminating praise, than by a mere out-pouring of friendship. I must make one bargain with you ; *pray* don't say a word about me *except as a writer.* I feel so painfully more and more the deceitfulness of the C. Y. especially, that I *must* beg this of you ; though I dare say your own discretion would tell you the same in a general way, yet a word might escape you here and there, were you not under special caution."

There are some few still living, and among them one very eminent man, who may remember the formation of something like a brotherhood, though adopting no such name, to assist the members in the regular discharge of their private religious duties. I mention it now, because it was in the latter part of this year, 1845, that Keble was applied to to draw up, or correct, I forget which, a little code of rules for its guidance. I mention the incident as an instance of the manner in which his help was

sought and rendered on many occasions, quite beyond his ordinary duties. He had lost his own copy,
and asked me for mine, which he soon returned with
this note :—

                                    "*Dec.* 1, 1845.
   "Many thanks for the papers, which I have copied. I
don't wonder at your finding great difficulty in acting on
them, placed as you are. I, who have, so to say, every
advantage, do not, I fear, realize any one of them. Still
I think it is good to have them in one's desk, and in one's
mind, as tokens of what one wishes and hopes, and as
helps towards *something* better than the present."

   This short notice may recall to the minds of some
few, times and thoughts long passed away from their
recollection ; the thoughts, I trust, will not have lost
their influence, but I hope they will remember not
merely the great simplicity and kindness with which
Keble dealt with us, but the profound reverence
which at that comparatively early period we all felt
for him.
   It was about this time that Keble's attention was
drawn to a scheme of his friend Charles Marriott
for the establishment somewhere of what was commonly called among the favourers of it a Poor
Man's College, the object being to train for Holy
Orders the sons of parents who were unable to meet
the expense of educating them at the Universities.
He was very anxious for the success of such a scheme,
and he considered attentively two preliminary ques-

tions, how to meet the expense, and where to place the institution. As to the first, it so happened that Mr. Hope's munificent intentions as to a Missionary Training College were then announced, but not carried into effect, and Keble was anxious that the two foundations should be consolidated. He pointed out how economy as to both might so be effected, and a greater breadth, and importance, and perhaps efficiency, thereby given to both. I cannot now say on what grounds this advice, which seems so reasonable, was rejected. As to the second, he felt the difficulties which might arise in placing it at Oxford, both as to its inception and its position after establishment. He had too, as may well be supposed, not a very strong confidence in the spirit with which the governing body might regard it; still he was decidedly for Oxford :—

"I stick," he wrote to me, "to my old mumpsimus, that where you can get it, 1st most independent, and 2nd worked by the best men, there it will answer best, and I am sure Oxford, *if you can get it there,* (which is surely worth trying,) has both these qualities."

This opinion prevailed, and the devoted founder actually purchased a site, not I think very wisely, at the top of Headington Hill, near to the spot well known to Oxford men, where stands, or stood at least, Joe Pullen's Tree. But in spite of his own great liberality, and that of others, Marriott's scheme

failed for want of funds. And this I cannot now
much regret, for two reasons; because it seems to
me to have been a mistake to limit it to students
for the Church only; but even more because that
failure left the ground open for a larger, and for
what promises, with God's blessing, to be a much
more liberal and useful institution, the Keble College now in progress. It was right to notice this
effort, however, because it enables me to put out of
doubt, that if any public tribute were to be made
to his memory, (of which, however, he would undoubtedly have thought himself wholly unworthy,)
the institution I speak of is one which, it may be
presumed, would have been exactly according to
his wish.

Mrs. Keble's severe illness made a change of air
and scene expedient for her more early in this
year, 1846, than usual, in order to perfect her recovery, and in the latter part of May they moved
to St. Brelade's in Jersey, and remained there until towards the end of June. He seems to have
thoroughly enjoyed this little place; I had several
letters from him while there, and he wrote of it
always with great delight. I had been obliged by
ill-health to give up my attendance in court for
a Term, and I was sent to Brighton by my friend,
Dr. Latham.

" I wish," he writes, " you could be with us instead of
Brighton, and see this gem of a little bay, filled at high

water with the bluest possible sea, and at low water half-way with the finest clear sand. On the right a most graceful ridge of pinnacled rocks, seeming to reach half-across it; and on the bank between us and it a curious though not very beautiful Church, the water in high tides washing the Churchyard-wall; with just trees enough to make a frame, both to right and left; a rock or two, and a vessel or two, in the middle; on the left a bold rocky point, and part of the sweep of a scolloped bay. This for the outside; and on the inside, Mrs. Keble writing away and professing, (after an early rising and steam voyage, a drive, and two walks,) that she is better able to draw her breath than she has been for a long time, so that by the blessing of God I hope we have found a place which will really do her good."

To be near the sea, or on it, was always restorative to her; in a few days after their arrival, they sailed to St. Helier's to meet Dyson, who paid them a visit from Southampton; the sea was to him for many years what it was to Mrs. Keble; and the meeting would make it, no doubt, more cheering and beneficial to all three.

Again, he says :—

" This coast has really a store of beauties, which it would take one a long while to tire of; I tell you this *for a secret*, for I should be very sorry to get it much belauded among the fashionable people in England; it would be so soon spoiled, if the pleasure-hunters got hold of it. How long we shall stay I don't know, but I shall be glad to wait till Charlotte has left off coughing; only one does get into such intolerable acquiescence with one's usual habits of idleness."

They made a short excursion to France while
at St. Brelade's, and saw Coutance, and soon after
returned home.   Parting from it so lovingly, one
would not have expected that they would never
revisit it ; but so I believe it was.   On St. Matthew's
Day he writes to me in thankful commemoration of
God's mercy in having spared so many of those
most dear to him in the course of the preceding
twelve months.   The day before that festival in the
preceding year, 1845, he had returned home from
his tour in Cornwall and Devon, and his wife's long
and dangerous illness had commenced ; his brother's
also — and he had besides been in much anxiety
about Dr. Pusey, Isaac Williams, and myself—all were
now in apparently comfortable health ; all are specially and affectionately enumerated in a letter to
me.   On Michaelmas Day his brother had a consecration of an additional church in his parish, which
Keble was able to be present at ; and we had that
of "the little church" in our parish ; he had been
much interested in our work, and contributed to our
funds.   We were commencing also the restoration
of our venerable Priory Church ; and pressed as he
was to provide for his own undertaking, he insisted
on *throwing back*, as he called it, a "'score of pounds,
towards your far more beautiful work ;' but I fear
there is no chance of our being able to afford more,
consistently with our plan of devoting 'all profits of
trade' to the work here."   It conduced to the cheer-

fulness with which he ended this year, that there were "symptoms now of his church work beginning." Materials were being collected on the spot; it was found that much, if not all the main walls of the old church, so far as the proportions agreed, would only require to be cased, so well and solidly had they been built; and an alarm about the foundations had turned out to be groundless.

Yet he opened the year 1847 in language of the deepest humiliation — language of the kind which I have given specimens of before, but of which I cannot withhold another. My readers will, I feel assured, not misunderstand the unintentional exaggeration of it; and it must surely be useful for many of us, going on in our easy ways, to see with what deep humility such a man regarded his own inward condition. It may serve to damp the self-applause of some, and awaken the slumbrous state of conscience in which too many of us habitually live.

"Well can I understand from what I see in others, and a great deal too well from myself, the heart-deep truth of every word you say on the matter of those sermons of Pusey's on 'Sin and Love:' they are two great depths ; too deep, by far, for our sounding. I suppose our safest prayer would be, that we may be led gradually on to the perception of where we are in respect both of one and the other, and not permitted to dwell on either exclusively. For myself, my inward history is a most shameful and miserable one—*really* quite different from what you and others imagine ; so that I am quite sure, if you knew it, you would be startled at the thought of coming to such an adviser; so long and so late has the misery been; and it ought to be a bitter penance to me to be so consulted. But I believe that I have sinned before now, in drawing back on such occasions, and I hope never to do so again; use me, therefore, dear friend, such as I am, if I can be of any use to you at any time; but pray for me, *bonâ fide*, that I may be contrite, for that is what I really need."

Early in the summer of 1847, Keble collected and published a volume of " Academical and Occasional Sermons ;" although he contributed many sermons to other collections, and printed now and then some which he had preached for special purposes, this I think, was the only volume which he ever published. Among other important and remarkable sermons, this volume contains that on Tradition, which it seems to me ought to be in every clergyman's library; which, indeed, few laymen would not find their account in reading. But Keble's special purpose in the publication was to quiet uneasy minds in regard to their position in the English Church. And for this purpose he prefixed a preface of some length, prepared with much care.

He writes to me on March 4 :—

" I have been, and am trying, to draw up a kind of view on the present position of English Churchmen, to answer, if it may be, the purpose which Dodsworth talked about that day at your house. Perhaps I may send it you when it is in some sort ended. The form of it would be a preface to some sermons."

In the Holy Week following, he says :—

" What I could, I have written on the R. C. Controversy, and the MS. is now in Moberly's hand for him to decide whether it be worth printing ; if he says yes, I think of sending it to you and a few more in proof, to be criticized, while the Sermons themselves, to which it professes to be a preface, are printing."

On April 23, he writes :—

" Moberly has said *imprimatur* to my papers for a preface, but I have not yet been able to satisfy myself about the Sermons which are to make up the volume. One after another, on which I once plumed myself, seems such stuff when I come to look over it."

Accordingly the proofs were sent to me, and I ventured to say on them what then occurred to me ; it is worth seeing in what spirit he received suggestions. He and Mrs. Keble had been with us in London in June ; on the 30th he says :—

" Perhaps you will be able to send those papers with the shoemaker's parcel ; I mean to add something to the effect that I take on purpose lower ground than might perhaps be taken. I want to shew that waiving all the special points at issue between the two Churches, a dutiful person ought to stay where he is ; whichever of the two is right on those points. I reserve the question of the Articles and Clerical Communion, about which I still think I was substantially right in my unpublished letter to you."

On October 25, when he had received my comments, he writes :—

" Now thank you at least 5 times for the 5 sheets which you have looked over for me. I have used all your suggestions, I believe, but one, that of enlarging the part of the argument, where it is maintained that the distinctive Roman tenets are none of them recommended by the same overwhelming proof as our common Christianity. It would have delayed me too long to have verified and exemplified this; and you know the whole tenour of the preface is merely to suggest arguments, not to carry them out. It is all printed that you saw in MS., and a little more; but the eye gets over it so much more quickly in reading it in type, that it seemed to you less. Of course it might be greatly enlarged; but I had not the time now, it being an object on several accounts to get it out without delay; and if I had ever so much leisure, I think I should still wish the job in the hands of somebody of more learning and dialectic skill. In *such hands* I really think it might be made a good deal of; at least, the more I think of it, the more substance there appears to me in it—but of course it will attract intense scorn from opposite parties. I believe I have qualified the 2 or 3 passages which you were most afraid of."

The volume, when published, had not perhaps all the success which it deserved; it passed, however, to a second edition, and I am informed that it is now being asked for a good deal. Both these facts may well be accounted for: the Preface was addressed to neither party in the controversy then raging; and it was natural that neither should find satisfaction in it, the Romanizers on the one hand, or the undoubting and vehement Protestants on the other.

The argument framed on the Butlerian model purposely took low ground, and this itself was of course a cause of offence, as it has been with many men in regard to the model itself. It was assumed that Keble's own convictions rested on these and none other, and the concessions made by supposition and for the sake of argument were taken for real admissions. Now that the heat of controversy is somewhat lulled (I wish it were more so), the argument may be read and fairly judged on its own hypothesis. It seems to me a very valuable contribution to our theology. Every composition is fairly liable to criticism, both in regard to its design and to its execution, but the latter must be judged with reference to the former. Keble's special design was neither to re-convert those who had already seceded, nor to defend the English Church generally against the Romanist controversialist. His object was to quiet the minds of those, (and no one knew better than he how many they were, nor how worthy of care and comfort,) who in heart desired to be true and loyal to the Church of their Fathers, but in whose minds uneasiness had been excited, either by the example or the publications of seceders, or by scruples which circumstances at the time had given occasion for, and which they were unable to satisfy for themselves. This seems to me, at least, to have been a definite, and a very sufficient object. Some may wish that he had attempted more. Keble had a just, and no more than a just opinion of the importance and difficulty of such a work: he did not think himself equal to dealing with the whole question commensurately with these; and he certainly would have shrunk with something like indignation from attempting so to deal with it in a preface or a pamphlet.

I must leave the execution of his design to the consideration of those who will now read the Preface candidly as a piece of Butlerian argument. One thing, I hope, we shall all be pleased with, his conclusion in a strain not very usual for a controversial pamphlet, but very characteristic of himself :—

"May one be permitted (though most unworthy) to offer one concluding suggestion, which will surely be taken in good part by all kind readers of whatever section of the Church? It is this; that at one time or another in our daily devotions, we should offer up Our Lord's Prayer, as a prayer in special for Church union : if so be He may graciously accept it, remembering His Own Eucharistical petition, " That they may be One as we are."

This is followed by the Lord's Prayer, broken up into its several petitions, with an application of each to the special purpose.

His letters at this time remind me that in this year, 1847, the Gladstone contests for the representation of the University in Parliament commenced. In these he took a very lively interest, perhaps this was to be expected in the beginning ; his own prin-

ciples found a more exact representative in Mr. Gladstone than in his opponent; and he had a much
higher opinion of him in his private capacity. But
the interest continued unabated to Mr. Gladstone's
only and final defeat in 1865. Compared with his
successive opponents, Keble always thought there
was no ground for hesitation ; he was always in his
opinion the best and most creditable representative
of the University. Even when, as sometimes happened, he might not have been prepared to follow
him in what he had said or done, he still thought
that there being no reason to doubt the honesty and
singleness of his intentions, it was unjust and unwise
in a private man to withdraw his support of a representative, because his judgment, probably more informed, and guided by a better appreciation of difficulties, differed from his own. All through the series
of contests his support was given heartily, I may say
affectionately and actively; in the contest of 1852,
he wrote to Sir Brook W. Bridges, who was, I believe,
Chairman of Dr. Marsham's London Committee, and
an old pupil of his own at Oriel, a letter "On the Representation of the University of Oxford," which is
probably now forgotten. Keble, however, does not
use merely occasional arguments on an occasional
subject ; this letter shews the principles on which
he thought it right then to continue his support to
Mr. Gladstone, and on which in substance he acted
to the end. His support was, I need not say, very

influential on many minds. The issue of the contest in 1865 he deeply lamented.

I have made an extract from a letter written towards the close of 1846, in which he speaks of his " church work really beginning ;" this was steadily pursued all through 1847, and until October, 1848, when the church was reconsecrated.

Writing to Cornish, he says :—

" H. V., June 30, 1847.

" As for ourselves, we jog on comfortably enough, far more so than one of us deserves : and just now the days are made very short by the pleasure of watching our new church, how it gradually gets on, encasing the old one. I don't know whether you would like it ; I do, as far as it has gone, very much."

It was found, wherever the old and new buildings coincided, that the old walls were so well built, that they would need only to be cased in stone ; wherever it was necessary to build anew, from the difference in size or design, the village masons, under proper direction, laid in the foundations. About Easter, 1847, he made his contract with Messrs. Locke and Nesham, "for £3,380, exclusive of these foundations, the seats, and other fittings, most of the flooring and windows." And he roughly estimated these at £1,200 more. Had he completed his design for the windows, and been at the sole cost, he must have provided a much larger sum than that for this last item alone. For his mind turned with the fondness of old associations to the numerous and costly windows of Fairford Church; he did not indeed desire strictly to copy them, the different sizes and characters of the two churches forbidding that; but he wished to fill all the windows at Hursley with a connected series, according to the general design of that at Fairford. His idea was to carry a kind of sacred history all round the church from the Fall to the Day of Judgment.

His design was in due time, not exactly, but in some sort, completed; and only a comparatively small portion of the expense fell on him. Mrs. Heathcote presented one large quasi-transeptal window; Sir William and Lady Heathcote the other; Lady Lothian and Lady Bath, each contributed a window; two I think were provided out of an overflowing offertory on the day of consecration; and it having occurred to some of his friends that this was a seasonable opportunity, and a right mode of testifying their love for him, and admiration of his character, a subscription was raised, and applied towards completing what should remain. The management of this fund financially devolved on me, and I regret that I long ago destroyed or lost all the accounts and papers relating to it; but among my own letters returned to me I have found one, which enables me to state that although the subscribers were numerous, and the sum raised large, it did not suffice for the whole expense; and that I applied, with his sanction, part of the monies paid to me by his publisher from time to time, to make up the deficiency. As the windows would require to be paid for one or two at a time, and sometimes at considerable intervals, I took on me to advance him portions of this fund, as money was needed for the church. It was arranged that for these advances he was to pay interest; but as he had himself to supplement the fund, that arrangement of course fell to the ground. Keble was extremely touched and gratified by this testimony from his friends. He took great pains and interest in the designs first, and in the execution afterwards; and I mention with pleasure the friendly part which artists and professional men took in the matter out of respect to him; Mr. Dyce volunteered help as to designs, and much correspondence took place between the two on the subject; a more learned and tasteful assistant he could scarcely have had; Mr. Copley Fielding was a contributor; Mr. Richmond also; but eventually he had the good fortune to secure the direction and inspection of Mr. Butterfield, a candid but severe judge, who, I remember, was not satisfied in respect of the east window, until the third essay had been made; two, which were finished and placed, were removed wholly or in part to make way for it. It is but justice to Mr. Wailes, who, I think, executed all the windows, to say that he submitted to his judgment with perfect good temper.

The first stone had been laid on May 20, 1847; the consecration, as I have stated, was on Oct. 24, 1848. I had the happiness to be present at it with my brother Patteson; and I met a large assemblage of common friends, many whom I had not seen for many years, some whom I saw then for the last time; in the retrospect of such meetings there is usually, I think, more of sober pleasure than of sorrow. The numbers who assembled at an early service in the Barn which had been used as a temporary church, and afterwards at the church itself, were large; and in my memorandum, made at the time, I perceive that I noted with pleasure the due proportion of smock-frocks among the congregation. Our only drawback, and a serious one it was, was the ill-health and suffering looks of Sir William, who, however, although unable to go through all the services and fatigues of the day, opened his house to a very large number of the guests, and entered into the feeling of the day heartily. In the memorandum to which I have already referred, I see I note "the sweet state of humble happy thankfulness" in which Keble and his wife appeared to be; it was happiness to him to see assembled at the Vicarage, which was full to overflowing, so many whom he dearly loved, and who so cordially sympathized with him; but it was, as I called it truly, "humble and happy thankfulness," with which he regarded the

completion of his long-cherished, long-laboured design—the erection of a church according to his means,
suitable for the worship of God, and in advancement
of the best interests of his parishioners. The money,
a large sum for him, nearly, if not quite, double
the amount specified in the first limited contract,
was perhaps the least part of what it had cost him ;
everything, from the first materials to the last finish
even of the minutest article in the ornamentation,
had his personal care bestowed on it. I remember
specially admiring the aptness of the several texts
with which the steps from the entrance of the church
to the altar were faced ; and the same attention to
fitness was to be observed in every part of the
church. There was no stained glass in the windows then, but, as I noticed at the time, we
scarcely missed it. It is but just to say that Mrs.
Keble participated most heartily in his care first,
and delight afterwards, and was, in heart at least,
a willing contributor to the expense incurred.

The completion of the tower, and the addition of
a beautiful spire, were subsequently accomplished
by Sir William ; and I scarcely know any parish
church where the spire is so beautiful an object
from so many points as this. Keble, at the request
of the builder, mounted to the summit, and with his
own hand placed the last stone on it, when that
finishing act was to be done, not, as he told my in-
formant, without fear of a fall.

He was happy and thankful. But it was during the progress of the work that the state of affairs in the Church weighed heavily on his spirits; he says, writing to me in May about his building :—

"Meantime I try to make up my mind to that which seems to me, considering all things, every day more and more likely, viz. that I shall not myself ever do duty in that church; at least, so it seems to be agreed by those who are at present in authority, and nobody speaks a word against it. Nevertheless, I suppose it is one's duty to go on just as if all were encouraging. I know, at least, whose fault it chiefly is, if one could but have the heart so to take it: and *that* I hope one's friends will be so good as to ask for one. But enough of that."

This was the year in which Dr. Hampden was placed as Bishop in the See of Hereford. Keble and he had been brother fellows of Oriel, and personally he had a great regard for him. It was, therefore, a painful duty to him to take part in the proceedings which were instituted to prevent his Confirmation; abortive they were; but they had the effect, at all events, of calling attention to the needless and shockingly profane mockery which the law enforces in the election and confirmation of bishops; and it may be hoped, that some day it will turn out that in this respect, at least, those proceedings were not wholly useless.

Keble's apprehensions, however, it must be admitted, were exaggerated, not only for himself, but for the Church. He was not only able to remain the Incumbent of Hursley to his death, with the good assent, I believe, even of those who differed from him most widely in opinions ; but the Church of England has maintained, I will not say the position which he thought she ought to hold, and those who think with him desire she should, but one at least as near to it, as he had seen her in possession of at any time in his life.

For himself personally, he was an object of general love and admiration, without respect to any religious differences. And this was strikingly manifested on occasion of an accident which befel him in the Close at Winchester in November, 1847. He always spoke of the exceeding kindness then shewn to him, especially I think by Canon Woodrooffe, but generally by the residents there. He was driving with Mr. Rogers, a brother of Sir F. Rogers, and, as he says, "by a very foolish piece of carelessness" of his own, the carriage was run away with, and both of them thrown out. It was owing, he says, "to a very merciful Providence," that they escaped with their lives. He was laid up for a short time, but no material injury was in the end sustained by either.

CHAPTER XV.

SHOULD KEBLE HAVE BEEN PREFERRED TO DIG-
NITY IN THE CHURCH.—TOUR IN WALES, AND
VISIT TO IRELAND, 1840.—TOUR IN SCOTLAND,
1842.—UNDERTAKES TO WRITE LIFE OF BISHOP
WILSON.—VISIT TO ISLE OF MAN, 1849.—MAR-
RIAGES WITH SISTER OF DECEASED WIFE, 1849.
—SECOND VISIT TO MAN, 1852.—TRIP TO SKYE,
1853.

I HAVE ventured to intimate an opinion at the
close of the preceding chapter that Keble sometimes allowed himself to indulge too much in what
might almost be called a querulous foreboding as
to the Church of England, and the utterances of
a severe spirit against the proceedings of the authorities both in Church and State in regard to measures affecting Her; and that in the intensity and
single-mindedness with which he pursued a principle,
he scarcely made due allowance for the difficulties
which beset those in high places. It will be understood, I hope, or injustice would be done him, that
this mode of thinking and speaking was by no means
extended to persons; if in a moment of irritation he
said or wrote anything " scornful," (as he called it,)
of any one, he would be seriously angry with him-

self, and add probably some severe term of general self-condemnation.

I have mentioned the intensity of his spirit as one cause of what I remark on, and I may add that as years passed on, the authority of his character so deepened, and the greater part of those with whom he lived, and of whom he saw most, had such a reverence for him, that his opinions were seldom canvassed with that freedom in conversation with himself which is good for the wisest of men. For myself I liked, I confess, to express my occasional oppositions to him in my correspondence, rather than in conversation; I could do so more freely, although I always felt not merely the superiority of his intellect, but of his knowledge on most of the subjects we discussed. But I remember conversing with Dyson on some matter, "Synods" I believe, on which Keble and I had differed. He happened to agree with me, "But then," said he, "when Keble is with me discussing such things, he is so earnest, and I have such a feeling, that one with so much holiness, as well as learning and ability, must be right, that I succumb at the time to arguments and assertions, which, when I think them over afterwards, do not always satisfy my reason, or my acquaintance with history." And then adverting to the subject of discussion, in reference to Keble's argument, he added, what I have recollected ever since, "In such matters we ought not to be *fet-*

tered by the forms and precedents of antiquity, but should look to the spirit and to the circumstances of respective ages; never losing sight of these latter, making them indeed our pole-star, but dealing respectfully, yet not servilely, with the forms."

No one, moreover, could be more hearty, or humble in his expressions of thankfulness for personal kindness, or of commendation, where any measure seemed to him taken wisely, or pursued in a right spirit, even by those from whom he very commonly differed in judgment.

But I should not write sincerely, if I did not say that there were some things said and done which might well wound him in the tenderest part. "The sorrow of his life," as I have called it, the loss, namely, to the Church, and to himself, of his dearest friend, he attributed in good measure, and I think with too much justice, to the conduct systematically pursued towards him; and it was but an embitterment when men with much coarseness and little wisdom of spirit pointed to the result as a justification of their course of conduct. And this was not uncommonly done by those who seemed little able to trace the complex motives which often operate to produce human actions, sometimes even without the consciousness of the doers of them. This, however, is a subject on which I can do no more than touch for obvious reasons.

Beyond this, however, which wounded him so.

deeply, it must be remembered that he thought
sincerely that vital doctrines of the Faith, and the
Catholicity of the Church were, at least, endangered
more than once by things allowed, or sanctioned
by, sometimes even directly proceeding from, those
in Her high places. No interests were dearer to
him than those involved ; he might be wrong in his
opinions, but he had, at least, a right to hold and
to express them ; for no one could impute that he
took them up hastily ; or that he had not thought
and read deeply on the subjects to which they related ; or that he had any but the purest motives
in his advocacy of them.

Dignities in the Church, I think, never entered
into his contemplation for himself. I cannot recollect in all our correspondence, or in our most
intimate conversations, a single expression which
pointed that way ; and I believe that, if they had
been offered, they would have been declined. I
have, perhaps, no right to express an opinion on
this subject, except to say in fairness that it must
have been so gratifying, and obviously so popular
a thing to exercise the power of patronage in his
promotion, that independently of all personal considerations, a strong presumption arises that the ab-
staining from it, whether wise or not, was strictly conscientious. Yet I cannot but believe that it would
have been good for Keble, good for both parties
in the Church, and what is more to the purpose,
have conduced to the holding of opinions with more

charity, if honours had been offered to and accepted
by him. A long experience confirms me in thinking that where persons oppose each other honestly,
however decidedly, in belief or opinion, the cause of
truth, which commonly lies between both, and of
charity, without which even truth itself can scarcely
be maintained truly, is greatly served by the necessities, the softening and enlightening necessities, of
personal and official communion.   Rarely, indeed,
do fallible men hold the truth without some ad-
mixture of error, and even where they hold to that
which is error in the main, commonly this is mitigated, morally at least to the individual, by some
infusion of truth in particulars.   Moreover, in the religious differences of Christians there must be much,
and of importance too, which is common ground ;
and where honest men are compelled by their position to act together in some common duty, or with
regard to some common interests, this ground be-
comes more apparent, and is estimated more justly
as to its importance.   These are general considerations ; but in regard to Keble it is not the over-
weening fondness of friendship, I feel sure, which
makes me say that there were exceptional considerations also which ought not to have been without weight; as his was a nature so humble, and
so loving, that personal influences would have specially touched and softened his heart, so were his
claims and merits so undeniable, and so remarkable,
that to pass him over was in effect not merely to

ignore them, but to imply in some measure a condemnation of him.

I have mentioned that Mr. Wilson, the first Incumbent at Ampfield, was the first Curate of Keble's appointment at Hursley. This connection was the commencement of an intimate friendship between them which ended only with Keble's life. Mr. Wilson has been kind enough to furnish me with many of Keble's letters, which, among other things, uniformly disclose the delightful footing on which the Vicar and Curate stood towards each other. The first letter in which the Curacy is offered, gives the tone to all that follow; at that time Mr. Wilson was comparatively a stranger; but nothing can be more open, or considerate, or kind; and the series shews how pleasant that relation may be made to the parties, how instructive to the younger, how beneficial to the parish. Whenever Keble was absent, he received minute accounts of everything which occurred in the parish, of importance for him to know, and especially of every sick, or offending parishioner. It is obvious from his answers that he maintained not merely the interest, which was of course with him, but such a knowledge in detail of all that required his advice, or interference, that he might almost be said to be present in directing or sanctioning whatever it might be necessary to do. I reserve some particulars as to this matter for a later stage in my

work, but I mention these letters now, because having anticipated events in order to complete at once
what I had to say respecting the new church, I
go back and shall be indebted to them for some
facts which seem worth mentioning, especially as
Keble will be himself for the most part the nar-
rator of them.

He did not willingly take leave of absence from
Hursley, but there were few years from about the
period of his life at which I am now arrived, in
which Mrs. Keble's delicate health, and indications
of lassitude or weakness, rather than absolute failure
in his own, did not make a change of air and scene
for her, with relaxation from his work for himself
desirable, if not necessary ; and so he commonly
left home for some few weeks in the summer ; and
this I think he would scarcely have consented to,
unless he had felt perfect confidence in the substitute, upon whom the care of the parish devolved in
his absence.

Perhaps I have mentioned before, that in 1840, he
was in North Wales, and stayed some days at Barmouth.   Thence he made his way by Harlech to
Tan-y-bwlch, and so by Bedd-gelert to Llanberis,
Carnarvon, and Beaumaris.   From this last place
he writes to Mr. Wilson.   He passed a Sunday at
Llanberis, and describes it thus.   So many years
have elapsed, and matters, I dare say, are now so
much mended, that I may print the account with-

out fear of giving pain to any one. The date is August 19, 1840:—

"This implies our being at home by Sunday, the 14th Sept[er], at the very farthest. It is an unconscionably long absence, but if it really sets up my wife with tolerably good health against the winter, it is perhaps one's duty to stay out even that long time. And I cannot but say it is very pleasant. I enjoy Wales and the Welch, the mountains, and shores, and waterfalls, of all things; but I am afraid I shall come home without going up either of the great mountains. And I have an unpleasant feeling that my time passes away very quick in proportion to the work I do; there is always some wonderment or other to hinder either reading, writing, or thinking, and yet one feels that such objects as Snowdon, whether far or near, ought to make one think to the best purpose. One thing I really imagine one does learn by travelling in Wales, and that is to realize in earnest the present condition of the Church in G. Britain. E.g. last Sunday we were staying at the nearest good Inn we could find to Snowdon, and we found, that in the Parish Church (of Llanberis), there was but one service, varying in time from $11\frac{1}{2}$ to $1\frac{1}{4}$, the Clergyman living 6 miles off, and no one knowing which the hour would be, the parish perhaps 15 miles long. So we went at 11, that we might have plenty of time to look about us. When we got there, we sent our car away, and wandered a little up the glen, which, as I dare say you know, is most romantic, till we heard the Church Bell. We hastened back and found that in the Church was going on, not service, but a sort of school of adult Welchmen, and some children, who seemed to be learning to read, and saying a sort of catechism to a man whom I much suspected of acting sometimes as Teacher in a different sort of place about 200 yards from the Church, it was all Welch.   However, we went in, partly for shelter, as it begun to be cold and drizzling, and the people seemed very little put out by our being there.   After a time they had finished their work, and went home, I suppose, to dinner, the man first saying a prayer in Welch, with seemingly much grave devotion.   We were left in the Church alone, and so had time to read the best part of the service together in English, during the latter part of which some children were watching us, but behaved very well.   At last, a good deal after one o'clock came the Parson, put us into a pew, and the regular service proceeded.   There were but few persons, and the singing was much inferior to what we have generally heard in Welch Churches, but all was to the ear very unaffected and solemn ; and to the eye also, except the *extreme* dirt and negligence of the old Church, and all its appointments ; it is *very* old, standing a far better chance, I imagine, of belonging to the 7th Century, than most of those whereof our friend S—— did so vaunt himself ; and it is a very handsome plan of a church, a long nave with a triple Chancel, and a large and old font at the West End ; the stone so massive, with such varied roughnesses and weather-stains, as almost to give the effect of architecture by itself.   It is a good deal the worse for Churchwardenizing ; but *that* is nothing to the dirty disrespectful condition in which the whole of it is left,—from the tottering three-legged Communion-Table, which stands so near the rails, that a man leaned his hands on it to say his prayers, when he first came into Church, to the tumbled frill of the Minister's Surplice, every thing shewed a consistent dislike of soap, and of ecclesiastical decency.   One thing only was satisfactory, the seats of the people were as dirty and uncomfortable as anything else.   And all this in the midst of the most glorious sights and sounds in nature. Well, good-bye. God mend us all. Your ever affectionate,

J. K."

From Wales they crossed to Ireland, "Went on board at 7, and woke up in Kingston Harbour in a most exquisite calm moonlight at 1¾." Their direct object was a short visit to Mr. Trench, near Athy, and they seem to have well employed their time for a few days in seeing much that was interesting. He writes again from Tan-y-bwld on the 30th of August, in his way to Bisley and home. They reached the latter safely, and much refreshed, and I think Mrs. Keble's health occasioned no movement from home for any length of time during the remainder of that or all the following year.

In the summer of 1842, he went to Scotland, and it is worth while to insert here parts of a letter to Mr. Wilson, dated from Edinburgh on the 29th of July; a great deal of it is taken up in minute directions about persons and things in Hursley, but much relates to his tour. If he had been scandalized at the outward appearance of things relating to the Church in Wales, it was to be expected he would be not less so at what he saw in Scotland; even the contrast of the past, which beautiful ruins presented to his eye, made the present more distressing to him. His language is strong, but it must be remembered that he is writing in the freedom of intimate correspondence. He calls it at the close of his letter, "a spit of toad-like venom."

"We came here," he says, "yesterday, from Melrose, by way of Abbotsford and Peebles, to which latter we turned, expecting to meet a coach, but were too late for it. I have been more struck with this place even than I expected, and only wish I could kick down their heathen Parthenon, and put a true Church in its place, a York or Lincoln of the best proportions. As yet I have scarce seen any thing but from this window, for we found so many letters and proof-sheets waiting here, that we have not yet done our necessary morning's work in answering them. But I think of calling on Mr. Ramsay, not only as you seemed to wish it, but also because I want to get into some Library to get some of the sheets corrected. The Kirks, and the manner in which they defile and insult the sacred places, e.g. Jedburgh Abbey, are even more horrid than I had expected. I would not be in one of them at service time on any consideration. They proclaim aloud, every inch of them, 'down with the altar.' The true churches, except the ruins, seem few and far between ; they told me at Melrose, there was none nearer than Kelso, or Peebles, but I suspect I saw a new one at Galashiels.

"Last Sunday we were at Carlisle, which bids fair before long to be a Kirk instead of a Church, according to appearances; a beautiful Choir, most slovenly served and attended; no one but ourselves, and one lady with 2 or 3 more strangers on St. James' Day. I was greatly disappointed there altogether. Temporally, I do not know when I have seen so thriving a country as these Lowlands; the little manufacturing towns on our road, though rather complaining, seemed still to have work ; and the tillage seemed to surpass any thing I ever saw. Between Kelso and Jedburgh they were reaping barley, and the corn crops are spoken of as excellent. But the great delight is to see the places one has read so much of in W. Scott. We went by

Kelso, that we might see Sandyknow, where, you know, he was at nurse, and I am very glad we did so; we called also at Dryburgh in our way to Melrose, and Abbotsford, and passed by Ashestiel in our way to Peebles; in short, we seem to meet him everywhere as we did Wordsworth in the Lake Country. We have missed Yarrow, which I was sorry for, but the weather was unpromising yesterday morning. As to Melrose, I like it altogether the best of any ruin I ever saw; but surely something bad must happen to the Scots for resisting so many years the witness which such places bear against them. The scrolls, and the few images which remain, are most beautiful circumstances in it. I suspect the Presbyterian Teacher there is afraid of the effect of the Abbey on people's minds, as he has built up a high wall in his garden to obstruct the view where he could. It was comfortable in the Lake Country to see so many good new churches, and to hear the people everywhere talk so kindly of the Squires and Parsons; also to hear old Wordsworth, how he kept falling back on Church Matters, whatever other subject was started. . . I conclude, sending you all good wishes, and among the rest, that we may soon meet again; although I must own the Grampian Peaks looked very tempting to-day from Mons Meg. Ever affectionately yours. J. K."

Wordsworth and Walter Scott were objects of his most affectionate admiration; how he testified this, as to the former, I have already mentioned; and as to the latter, I ought to refer my readers to a well-known article by him in the "British Critic," on Lockhart's Life of him, remarkable not only for its ability, but for the loving and ardent spirit in which it is written. In spite of the strong language in his

letter, he retained a very kindly recollection of his
tour, and of Scotland. Writing to Mr. Wilson in
1846, who was then in that country, he says :—

" You will get this at Monteviot I hope. How pleasant
it is to have such a home feeling about so many of the
places you go to. Remember us most kindly to your
hostess, and to your travelling Tutor. I wonder if you
will like Jedburgh Abbey, and Ferniehurst, (if you see it,)
as well as we did."

I ought to have mentioned before this, that Keble
had lent his aid to some friends who were associated
together for the purpose of editing a Library of
Anglo-Catholic Theology. This seemed to him a
cognate scheme to that of the Library of the Fathers,
and he joined in it heartily, served effectively on the
Committee, and personally undertook to superintend
the publication of a complete edition of Bishop Wilson's works, to be preceded by a Life of the Author,
which he promised to write. The Bishop was a special favourite of his, and he entered on the work
heartily ; but many interruptions retarded the execution of his promise, and the Life was not finished
until 1863. What there may be to say about it, I
will reserve for the present ; and I mention it now
mainly, because, in 1849, he was induced by it to
make his summer sea excursion for Mrs. Keble's
benefit a trip to the Isle of Man, that he might
procure information on the spot, and see the places
in which the Bishop lived and acted for so many
years of his life. The scheme answered very well

both for her, and his own object. He was much amused, and returned refreshed in body and mind. Writing to me on various matters on September 26, after he had reached Hursley, he says :—

"I have lots to say about Mona, and Bishop Wilson, but cannot now go on with it ; the tour was a very pleasant, and on the whole not an unsuccessful one. The Bishop *very* kind and hospitable, and as off-hand as Lloyd used to be. The clergy a nice set, but rather Wesleyanized."

I believe Lord Auckland will not be offended at this free comparison of him with Bishop Lloyd ; in Keble's mouth it meant a great compliment, for the Bishop of Oxford was one in whom he delighted ; nor I trust will the clergy of the Island, should any of them chance to see it, be scandalized at his remark on them.

It was while he was in Man that he received intelligence of the death of George Cornish's eldest daughter, and I shall be forgiven for inserting the letter which he wrote to the afflicted parents ; it has to me a special and mournful interest from the recollection that within a month from the date of it, the father to whom it was addressed, himself sunk under his many trials :—

> " Douglas, I. of Man.
> " *August* 22, 1849.

" My dearest George,

" We got your letter here only last night, and it was a sort of stunning blow to me, for somehow I had grown to be sanguine about dear Essy's recovery; and in many ways it comes very near one. God grant that when one's own turn comes, (who knows how soon?) one may leave as little cause of anxiety to those who shall survive, as she has now left; and if pain, like her's, be needful to prepare us, may He in His mercy send it, and give us grace to bear it. You know, dear friends, that our thoughts are very much with you, and those of one of us at least, to good purpose. We shall be anxious for the next account of you all, but don't trouble yourselves to write; let it come through Bisley, where we hope to be, one or both of us, in the course of the next week. It is comfortable to think of your being so many, so loving and dutiful, and of the help you will be of to one another; and I need not say to you, because you must know it full well, how desirable it is to lose no time in using yourselves to speak freely and calmly to one another of those who are out of sight, as though they were, as they are, *only* out of sight. I am more and more thankful that dear Robert is with you. Do take all care of yourselves, and let him take care of you. What a treasure to their Father, and to you, must be those little children. May they prove so more and more.

"We hope to get back to England to-morrow, and to Bisley, or Hursley, by the end of next week. Here we have been living, as it were, under the shadow of Bishop Wilson's wing; and surely it is a thing for which we ought to be the better.

" C. sends her loving remembrances to you all, especially to dear Kenie. May we all love one another the better for each one of us who is taken to the Home of Love.

" Ever your most aff^{te},
" J. K."

I have spoken already, in my notice of George Cornish, of his death in September of this year, and how Keble mourned for his loss; his feelings towards all that generation of the Cornish family were those of a very fond elder brother; and the affection towards his widow, and all that remained of another generation, continued unabated. Indeed, it was strengthened by the engagement of his brother's only son, whom he regarded as his own, to her to whom special remembrances are sent by the name of Kenie; and in 1851 he married them at Salcombe. He went to Sidmouth for the purpose, and as he had so often done before, he coupled with this the benefit of a sea-side visit, and change of air for Mrs. Keble. They re-visited Lyme Regis for a while before going on to Sidmouth, from which last place they came to us at Ottery for a few days. He and I were much together alone, and a great delight it was to have again that sort of intercourse with him. He was in good spirits, and no one, when he was in spirits, could be a more delightful companion. They returned home towards the end of September. Writing to me, when the wedding party broke up, to fix the day of his coming, he says :—

"It was a very happy wedding, as far as we can judge, and I am in good hope that it has done much good to poor dear Harriet; it was very touching to see her in her mourning, and to look round the room, and remember things and people. I will do as I am bidden about Sunday, and shall be really glad, if I can save Henry a little, for I dare say he over-works himself. But somehow or other, my sermons seem more and more disagreeable on a second preaching."

I like to dwell, and perhaps I dwell too much, on these passing expressions; they disclose so naturally the tenderness and simplicity of his character; and I note here what was observed of him repeatedly in later life, how he liked to preach when from home and he had the choice, in a small country church to the simplest congregation, rather than to a large number in a church of more display.

It was in this year, 1849, that the measure of legalizing the marriage of widowers with the sisters of their deceased wives was vigorously pressed in Parliament, and out of it. Keble felt very strongly upon this matter, and he opposed it earnestly, perseveringly, and effectually; by his personal influence, wherever he had opportunity to exert it, by framing and circulating petitions against the Bill, and by the publication of a vigorous pamphlet. He relied on the authority of the Church uniform and consistent, on Scripture, on the tendency of such unions to impair the holiness of marriage, to disturb the peace, and corrupt the purity of social life. Some Hebraists and theologians have questioned the interpretation of Scripture which he adopted. It rests, I understand, on great authorities, and seems very consonant with common sense; and he believing in it, of course could not pass it by. I confess it always seemed to me that the last grounds were abundantly clear, and in themselves quite sufficient for his argument; and because they were more easily understood and appreciated, the best on the whole for the generality to rely on. Keble also pointed out the indirect and personal motives to which the movement was owing; its onesidedness as to the sexes; and also how untruly it was urged that the alteration of the law was at all generally desired by English women. The attempts to pass the Bill failed, and I believe other attempts have been equally unsuccessful. Measures of this kind, however, once put forward, are seldom given over finally, and it is to be feared that the efforts to carry this will be renewed. Should they be, I commend the pamphlet to the notice of my readers.

It was somewhat earlier in this year of 1851, that I consulted him on a difficulty which occurred to me, in regard to a clergyman who had been my own pastor, and who had seceded to Rome. He was a pious and amiable man, and we had lived in a good deal of social intimacy. Keble answered me thus :—

"Now to the question you asked about. I suppose it has been practically answered by this time; it is a difficult one to answer for another person; but if it were my own case, I should keep up as much intercourse as I could in the way of morning visits with the rest of the family;

but I could not have him to dine. I should consider it scandalous in respect of the servants, to say no other; they know that he is a clergyman who has renounced his Orders; and it cannot be but certain thoughts must enter into their minds, if they think of such things at all.

"In one respect this Lent is much pleasanter than last, that one does not live in a perpetual fever of Church Union Meetings, &c. : how far it is the calm of despair may admit of a question, as far I mean as our cause is a *public* cause ; for as to private feelings, one seems, thank God, to be more and more sure that one was and is right in staying. Now, good night, dearest friend. From your ever loving, J. K."

It was about this time that he was consulted by a gentleman who was meditating a very unusual step. I am at liberty to mention the circumstance, and I do so chiefly for the sake of the letter in which he gave his answer. The gentleman was at the time a layman, not a young man, and engaged actively in a liberal profession ; circumstances had occurred in his family, which made it seem to him a sort of special duty to give as strong a testimony as he could personally to the Church of England ; he thought therefore of applying for Ordination, and to be allowed to fill a vacancy that had been made in a small country cure in his neighbourhood. It was obviously a matter that demanded much consideration, and, as so many others did in their difficulties, he turned to Keble for advice. His letter I have not the means of referring to, but I have the answer before me, and I am at liberty to use it. He says :—

" Concerning your scheme, one can feel nothing but joy and thankfulness that such a thought should have come into your heart. It startled me, I own, at first, but on coming to ask myself why, I really believe that this was only from its being so new and unusual a thing, though in a certain sense it may seem very old ; for who knows but it may have been put into your mind for the same kind of purpose, which made so many of our forefathers of all ages and stations enter the religious life. I do not of course compare the two, but may it not be in our day the same *kind* of thing in some measure ? This I say to myself to meet the scruple you hint at, and which a great many would feel, about being less useful so, than as a Layman trying his best. It seems to me that this would be more to the purpose, if you cut short your active professional life for the sake of doing this ; but it would not be so ; it would be something substituted for miscellaneous and not strictly professional work, and in that respect would perhaps involve a good deal of self-denial ; of course you will consider well beforehand, whether, applying yourself as you would wish to do to your new profession, you will have leisure for the many calls for time and thought which are sure to be made on you in your retirement. You will not like to put them by, and I can fancy them going on on such a large scale as to interfere seriously with your pastoral work.

" I only mention this for consideration ; there may be nothing in it, your habits being so active.

" The *testimony* both as regards religion generally, and faith in our own Church particularly, would, as it seems to me, be the stronger in such a change, than in a person's continuing a dutiful Layman.

" On the whole, (I have been just reading over your letter again,) I am much inclined to say, go on and prosper, and may a great blessing attend you."

Keble, from his own experience perhaps, seems to have had his attention principally drawn to the calls, which might probably be made on the gentleman, for advice in matters relating to his abandoned profession, and be an hindrance to him in his new one ; he seems to have overlooked that it was intended evidently to cut short the professional life ; but in itself he had no difficulty in assenting to the sacrifice. This might have been expected from him.

There was a second letter from him, from which it appears that another friend had also been consulted, whose opinion was opposed to the change. It did not alter Keble's view, for which he gives his reasons.   However, whether from the occurrence of new circumstances, or some change in the gentleman's mind, I know not, his purpose was never carried into effect.   But I have thought it fitting to mention the incident, and publish the letter; they recall the recollection of that anxious time, when the hearts of serious men were greatly searched by a flood of doubts and questionings on the controversy between the Two Churches. The secessions to Rome, though not numerous, and with a very few exceptions little note-worthy or influential as examples, yet produced in the families in which they occurred the deepest and most lasting distress. They, indeed, who then left father and mother, brother and sister, and made great temporal sacrifices, were not in truth generally those who suffered the most, or the longest. It pleased God to guard our Church from any permanent depression, or injury; and it may be hoped that we have learned to regard such events with sorrow indeed, and it may often be self-reproach, but with a more comprehensive, and I will add reasonable charity, than we could easily exercise at first. I will not undertake to say whether, as regards the individual case which has occasioned these remarks, Keble or the dissentient friend was on the whole right. The wisdom of the resolution may be questionable, but there is no reason to doubt of the gentleman's sincerity, and I cannot but agree in the opinion that as a testimony the step would have probably been impressive on many minds. However, events have shewn, and we may acknowledge it thankfully, that it was not a necessary one.

Later in the year 1851, I was threatened with a very heavy sorrow by the seemingly desperate illness of a married daughter, which I mention only to introduce a letter I received from him when matters appeared to be at the worst. It would seem to me ingratitude to withhold such a testimony at once to the tenderness of his heart, and to the religious aspect in which he contemplated all such trials :—

"H. V., 4 *Nov^r*, 1851.

"MY DEAREST COLERIDGE,

"I cannot be easy without writing one line to you at such a time as this, though I well know how impossible it is for me really to sympathise with your distress. Only I cannot help imagining that your dear child's sufferings are in kind rather like my Mary Anne's in 1826, concerning which I have always felt that it seemed a case which the Great Physician had taken most entirely into His own hands, so utterly powerless did all human means appear from the very beginning ; and the distress in kind so utterly unlike what one could have expected for one so sweet and loving. So that ever since, one has thought of her, I trust not presumptuously, as of one much nearer a martyr's estate than most even of those whom one remembers most thankfully. My dearest friend, your fatherly heart, as it will feel the rending and tearing of such a visitation in a way which such as I cannot imagine, so it will be by His mercy, I trust, opened to receive this treasure of comfort far beyond my comprehension. He who has granted you to take care of this precious jewel for Himself, will enable you to bear your temporary loss of it, I am sure of *that;* and who knows how available her presence *there*, (if He should now take her,) may be to avert some of the evils which we have been most dreading of late ? I must write one line to dear M——, God grant it may be of some small comfort to her. We have mentioned dear A——, though not by name, in our prayers and communion, since we heard of her illness. Our affectionate love is with you all. Your most loving, J. K."

Again, in 1852, Keble made his summer sea-side trip for Mrs. Keble's sake serve the purpose also of his own preparation for the Life of Bishop Wilson, on which he was now engaged. They went in August to the Isle of Man, "got a lodging in a very pretty place," enjoyed their stay much, and returned "the haler and the heartier for it." He wrote to me from Leeds, whither he had gone in his return by desire of Dr. Pusey, to compose some little differences ; he spoke with great gratitude of the kindness they had received from the Bishop and his whole family. He drops, too, a hint of that which had for years been much on his mind, and on which perhaps he thought a little too much in the composition of his Memoir :—

"If one had skill, the information gathered might be made very profitable, partly as to the good Bishop's personal character and opinions, but still more as to the discipline of the Island, as a fragment of former days, and perhaps as furnishing hints for the future."

I have mentioned one of Keble's trips to Scotland. In 1853 he made another, which he speaks of shortly in the following letter :—

"H. V., 6 *Oct^r*, 1853.

" MY VERY DEAR COLERIDGE,

" I am tired of not writing to you, though I have very little to say. But I do wish to know whether you have any objection to appropriating the proceeds of the next

Edition of the *Lyra* to Fredericton, for I very much wish to
do some little for dear Medley, and hardly know how to do
it any other way. We had a most successful flight to Skye
and back, staying out two Sundays. We escaped all the
violent weather, and had the perfection of steam travelling
in every respect, but the crowds that were with us; Sea,
Mountain, and Sky, all along performing the most exquisite
Trios for our amusement. I suppose, putting the hours together, that I was not less than seven days on board, and
I was not at all sick the whole time, a great triumph for
me; and C. I think entirely enjoyed it; and though she
came back with a cold, she is certainly able to walk farther than she could. Skye scenery beats what I expected,
and so does the whole of the Inverness and Rosshire Coast,
as we saw it from the steamer; the Coolea Hills are not so
high as some others, but their forms are, I think, the finest
I have seen. Among other people we met the Bp. of
London, and his family, who were staying at Ballachulish,
and they were very good-natured. On our way home we
stayed a night at Bisley, which was very refreshing, and
now we have been at home near a month, and have had
several visitors; R. Wilberforce especially, about whom there
is still more anxiety than one could wish; though his book
is meeting with such success as I for one could never have
dreamed of. But I really cannot imagine a person of his
truthfulness, learning, *and good temper*, putting up with the
Roman system as a Convert. [Keble is speaking of Archdeacon Wilberforce's able and learned treatise on the
Doctrine of the Holy Eucharist.] I should be glad to
hear anything you can tell me of the Lay Crusade against
the *parti prêtre*. My expectation is, (God avert it,) that
———— &c., will have their own way, and that if the world
lasts, there will be something as bad as Popery, only in

another direction, marring the Gospel as Popery did, for want of simple faith in the first Gospel as the Apostles left it. . . . . I wish I could find the *double* of Wilson for Ampfield, for I grieve to say he is obliged to go for reasons of health. It is the greatest loss. Our very kind love to all. Your ever loving J. K."

I am unable to say what answer I returned as to the *Lyra*, nor is it material ; but I would not omit the question, because it is a testimony to a dear friend, one of the most sound, and zealous, and able of our Colonial Bishops, which it will give him a pleasure, he well deserves, to see recorded.

My next letter from him, on the 16th of November, 1853, was but a note, written under his dictation by Mrs. Keble, and only signed by himself. It was merely an invitation to come down to Hursley, in respect of a charitable object which he thought I might further, and he ends it thus :—

" My worthy friend the Iodine is only just beginning to tickle me, but I dare say it will do its work in time. Many thanks for my pleasant visit to you. Affectionately yours,

" J. K."

This attack was probably a precursor, or forewarning of that with which he was visited so much more seriously not many years after ; it was more serious, however, than he seems to have regarded it as being ; for three months after, writing to me, he speaks of his " nearly recovered hand." I was about

to say it would have been well if he had learned
from it to be more prudent, and to remit in some
measure the constant strain to which he submitted
both body and mind in the discharge of the duties,
regular and irregular, which fell on him.   But I will
not say this ; it was well for him to labour as he did,
though his frame sunk under it at last ; it was happier for him so to do in this life, and who can doubt
that it is far happier for him in another.

CHAPTER XVI.

DEATH OF W. C. YONGE, 1854.—OXFORD UNIVERSITY REFORM.

EARLY in the year 1854, Keble was visited with
a great affliction in the sudden death of William Yonge, whom I have had occasion to mention
before. In any way it would have affected him much,
but in the particular circumstances it was specially
afflicting. His only son, a young soldier, was to
sail with his regiment on what turned out to be
the Crimean expedition, and the old soldier busied
himself with his usual activity in equipping him for
the service ; perhaps, it may be feared, beyond his
strength. On his return home from this exertion he
had an apoplectic seizure, and although, during what
seemed a respite, his son was able to hurry home to
see him, it was but for three hours, during the whole
of which he was asleep. No more could be allowed.
He died without seeing him just after the sailing of
the regiment, and too late for the news to reach the
son before the vessel touched at Malta. This was
a severe visitation on the mother and sister, the only
surviving members of the family ; the Kebles were
on the most intimate terms with them, and no one

would be more likely to sympathize with them in their sorrow than they; but Keble felt the loss tenderly in many ways for himself; William C. Yonge, beside his goodness and tenderness of heart, often concealed from the many, and in matters of indifference, by a somewhat stern manner, had a fondness for business and knowledge of it, a readiness of apprehension, and decision of character, which Keble was glad to lean on. "What we shall do here without W. C. Y.," he says, in communicating the event to Mr. Wilson, who was abroad, "I cannot think." He writes to me :—

"I am grieved to the heart to think that the first letter I write to you with my nearly-recovered hand should have to announce such sad news."

And after describing the particulars, and the state of the widow and daughter, he says :—

"What *they* will do without him, what we and all the neighbours will do, especially what Otterbourn will do, I am sure I cannot say. There is really no one that I know of in this Parish at all to take his place. But our loss, (we may speak it, D. V., with more absolute confidence than usual,) is his exceeding gain."

And, again, on the 31st of March he says to me :—

"But you would be surprised to see how we miss *him* at every turn, and find that it is indeed a gap which will never be filled up. But of course this is a feeling of which one must expect more and more. . . . Do you not mean to come this Circuit again some time, and let me have one of my pleasant drives, or walks with you ? I have no Wilson, nor Yonge now, and only half-a-Heathcote. [Sir William was now attending in Parliament as Member for the University.] But thank God my wife is well for her, and walked the day before yesterday $2\frac{1}{2}$ miles. With love to you all, I am affect^{ly} yours, J. K."

It will be seen that Keble in the earliest of these letters to me, from which I have made extracts, dated on the 26th of February, 1854, speaks of his "nearly recovered hand." It appears from the same letter, that it had been thought desirable for him to come to London for advice in regard to it, and that I had urged him to do so again ; he refused, saying, " It is so nearly well, that I do not think it need go a consulting any more. I only wish I was as likely to make a good use of it, as to have the use of it." Whatever the affection was, it seemed to pass away; he wrote as much as ever, and I see no marked change in the character of his handwriting for several years after this.

A subject now arose which interested him most deeply, I may say painfully ; the Oxford University Reform Bill, consequent on the report of a Royal Commission of Inquiry. It is well known that the provisions of this Bill, which occasioned much debate in Parliament, were framed so as to make great changes in the Constitution of the University, and to permit some also in the several Colleges. In respect to the former, the measures were for the most part defined at once by Parliament; to carry out the latter, an Executive Commission was appointed, and the members were named in the Bill, among these were Sir John W. Awdry, and myself. If what was then done had been final, it might have sufficed to mention generally that Keble was very much opposed to the whole measure; but much of what he wrote applies itself to questions now pending, and therefore I make some extracts from his letters.

He wrote to me on seeing the first draft of the Bill, on February 26, 1854:—

"I suppose it will be no breach of confidence now to speak to you of the University Reform Bill, the draft of which was shewn to me by permission. I was regularly scared at it, and much fear that it will make a sadder disruption of parties than ever. The Constitution it enforces will leave us (unless we are continually running up from the Country) entirely at the mercy of the Tutors and Professors, (the latter a completely new sort of folk to be as such an organic part of the Body,) and there is no reason to believe that either is not fairly represented by the present persons, who seem to me, I must confess, rather different from the Copelands and Rogers's and Aclands of former days, in respect both of temper and of reverential feelings. Then the plan is expressly Anti-Collegiate: it goes on the principle that it is actually good (*cæteris paribus*) to have a lot of Students who are not *alumni* of some old Founder, but disciples of Arnold, or Marriott, or Newman, or whoever he may be, as if this was not the immediate way to encourage Party of all sorts, and as if there were not elements of good and happiness in the Collegiate Life, which we ought to provide as far as we can for all our Students, and as if it would be possible, one might say fair, *that* system once admitted, to avoid admitting Dissenters. With the Colleges it deals *rather* less radically, but all through with a notion that *examinations* and talent are everything, and with another notion which I deprecate from my very heart, that natural preferences for homes, kindred, &c., are not to be allowed in eleemosynary endowments. I think it an indication of a certain hard priggishness, which I fear is getting to be characteristic of this generation. Well, here is grumbling enough for one time, but you must not suppose that in what I say of this Bill, I mean to be condemning the person, whom I suppose we must consider its author. I have no doubt he is designing himself to do the best he can for us. He is still to my mind ' Pusey in a blue coat.' But the die seems to me virtually to be cast ; I believe the Anglican portion of Christendom, for the sake of doing good, to be on the point of commencing a process not unlike that by which the Papacy rose and throve, in its disregard of Primitive Models, and I hope a great deal of good may be the immediate result ; but one cannot but fear the event on a large scale, looking to what has come of the Papacy. Of this great movement, the University Reform is a part, as I take it. But *ohè jam satis*, especially as I know that on this subject, if I were to write for a year, I should only make my heart and wrists ache for nothing. And so I rest, dearest friend, ever your most aff^te, J. K."

On the 31st of March, 1854, he again wrote to me in part on the same subject. After expressing his

pleasure that Sir J. Awdry and myself were among
the Commissioners, he says :—

" I trust that, if it please God, you will be enabled to do
a good deal towards drawing the sting of it,—that a sting it
has, and a many-forked sting, I wish I could doubt; and I
certainly could not myself have been a party to it, were it
only for the needless, and, (as it seems to me,) therefore
irreverent degree of interference with Founders' Wills ; but
in this, I believe, not even Pusey agrees with me. I thought
I had got over it ; but as it was my first thought, so it has
come over me stronger than ever. But I am not going now
to trouble you with my feelings and fancies ; if you think it
worth while you may see a specimen of them which I sent
yesterday to Heathcote ; but, indeed, I poured myself out
to you more than enough the last time I wrote. I wish I
may be very much mistaken, but the aspect of things op-
presses me more almost than ever. This war is to me so
horrible ; surely we ought to be most thankful for our
Lord's saying about Peace and a Sword ; else such things
would be almost too much for us."

Again, on the 24th of April, he wrote to me on
the subject of the Private Halls, which then seemed
likely to be of much importance, but from which so
little as yet has resulted ; though it may be that more
may now arise :—

" But what I wanted now to set before you was two or
three thoughts obvious enough, yet, (as I fancied,) worth
writing down, which have occurred partly to E. B. P., and
partly to myself, in considering this plan of Private Halls.

" First of all, he thought whether it might be well to

make a list beforehand of persons who are eligible to them, (as the V. Chancellor is to make a list for the first gathering of the new Congregation,) rather than give a vested interest to every M.A. to the Licence. I cannot but look on this with very great dismay ; except (which I do not think unlikely, Woodard says it will certainly be so,) it fall dead to the ground for economical reasons, and I shall be most anxious to see what rules you the Commissioners will prescribe, or accept, to guard it. Might not one be, that no one shall have a licence except he have gained such and such distinction, unless he will consent to undergo an examination for it. Might not the V. Ch. have a Council assigned him, a Committee, say, of the new Hebdomadal Board, who shall certify in some solemn form, whenever they grant a licence, the same kind of points as are required to be certified by this Act, when a man is elected to a Fellowship ? Might there be a kind of *Si quis* put forth for a certain time at the meetings of the Hebdomadal Council, for the chance of excluding persons positively discreditable ? Might it be ruled that the Licensed M.A. must be either a Priest, or provide to the satisfaction of the Licensers a sufficient Chaplain to look after his pupils ? Might not the licences, for a certain time, at least, be restricted to persons associating with them a certain number of coadjutors, such as to give security to the University, that *between them* they would give their pupils a fair chance of completing the University Course, thus forming a sort of voluntary Colleges, (but S—— says this would not do, they would quarrel so.) Might not some kind of pecuniary guarantee be insisted on ? I mean that a M.A. should shew to the satisfaction of the Licensers that he has a fair chance of success, by producing promises in writing from respectable persons guaranteeing him in all so many pupils to begin with ; or in any other way. Rules like these, it seems to me, will be requisite to guard against direct swindling, and charlataneries ; but what I most apprehend, if the plan succeed, is a succession of A's, or V's, or W's, or A's, or B. N's, or F. N's, each with his school or personal following, unsoftened by the Collegiate feeling. What will become of Peace and Reverence ? and where will you find any safeguard against this ? I must see whether I can think of anything against to-morrow morning, for it is midnight.

" Well, now it is to-morrow morning, and I have been thinking chiefly of my dreams, but a little of my being to-day 62 years old, and how little I have to shew for it, except in one way, which is not pleasant to think of.

" I hope to see May here presently, and that will be a comfort.

" As to the evil last mentioned, I suppose it must be taken as a necessary result of ' our unhappy divisions ;' however, I dread it exceedingly. I should think also it would be harder to keep up discipline ; offences will much more readily be slurred over when a man's bread depends on the number of his pupils ; and Proctors will be thought ill of, if they do not a little spare the father of ' six small children,' or ' of eight marriageable engaged daughters.' On the whole, I fear litttle Bernard has small chance of learning the old Oxford ἦθος, any more than he has of loitering with a book under a real hedge-row of the old English Fashion.

" I have just got your letter ; many thanks. In your notion of the small effect of this Bill in itself, I very much agree ; the loss of ἦθος I fear has taken place already.

" Ever your very loving, J. K."

" Surely the Private Halls *do* make a great opening for

Dissenters, at least, with those who think that the *Colleges*
are in some sense bound by the Churchmanship of their
Founders."

On the 1st of May he writes :—

" I wish I could be reassured by anything in your letter,
or in what W. E. G. said the other evening, that the direct
and necessary tendency of this Bill is not to separate Oxford
from the Church. As I understand *him*, one of the first
things after the Bill shall have passed, will be that the
University will be called on to consider how far ' the natural
and reasonable desires' of Dissenters to get into it may be
gratified ;' and one of the faults of the Hebdomadal Board
is their not having allowed that question to be mooted.

" I have very little doubt that we shall have to deal with
it every year till it is done, and how long then will it be
before the Colleges are thrown open also ; considering that
J. D. himself told me the other day, ' he did not care for
Founders and Benefactors ;' they were his very words.

" I can only see one way in which this measure can
amount even to a forlorn hope, that is, if there were such
a lot of people like Woodard and Wordsworth, &c., to occupy the Private Halls, that they should even take the place
by storm, and do their work so as to defy competition ; but
what chance is there of that ?"

On the 19th of June he wrote again to me. I was
coming on the Western Circuit, and had promised to
go to Hursley in my way :—

" MY DEAREST FRIEND,

" Indeed it is too true that you have not heard from me
for very long, and I wish I did not know too well whose
fault it is. *Pray* let us see as much as ever we can of you
when you come here. I was intending to write to ask you

this before your's came. If you *could* but give us a quiet
Sunday! Such things are more and more precious every
year as we feel how little we can reckon on them. I am
sure you will do what you can for us. We are more of
a family than usual, having three of Peter Young's children,
while he is being *watered* at Malvern; I hope successfully,
but I am far from being easy about him. But the youngsters
would not be at all in your way. Heathcote you know may
now see his fill of you in London. . . . .

"I very much like, as far as I can judge, the changes
which have been made in the Oxford Bill, only I am afraid
they will greatly increase your trouble. It is not so much
the proposed amount of change that I deprecated, as the
cool way in which Parliament was decreeing, without asking
those most concerned, that Founders' natural preferences
should go for nothing, thereby laying down the principle
which Woodgate seems to me to have unanswerably exposed, that endowments may be seized not only for doing
harm, but for not doing all the good they might. I consider that principle to be now withdrawn, and that is to me
a great gain, be the practical result what it may. Still my
quarrel with the first half of the Bill remains. I consider
myself and some 4,000 others to be unconstitutionally and
wrongfully treated in not being even consulted on so great
a thing as the whole scheme of our Corporate Government;
and that while it is expressly enacted that Convocation is
to retain its privileges. If we had been guilty of ever so
great malversation, we could not have been used worse."

Again, on July 13, he wrote :—

" MY VERY DEAR FRIEND,

" One word for fear I should miss you by-and-by, to say
that I was not quite so simple as to dream of shutting Dissenters out of Oxford. I think you had not time to read

the printed stuff I put into your hands, p. 10, else you would not have misunderstood me. What I ask for is simply that the restriction of a mile and a half from Carfax be taken away, so that people may study any where, and only come up to be examined, &c., at Oxford, and this for all denominations alike, even as all alike will be free of Oxford itself.

"I dare say this is unpractical enough, but it is not, I think, quite so unreal as what you understood me to mean."

From time to time during the sittings of the Executive Commission he wrote to me on the subject of Affiliated Halls, (which he recommended to be allowed without limitation as to distance or denomination). and the Private Halls to be established under the Bill. I will extract from one of these, written from Oxford on the 14th of June, 1855, very soon after the Statute as to Private Halls, which I believe is still in force, had been passed. This adhered to the originally proposed limitation as to the distance from Carfax, within which alone the Hall could be opened ; and modified, but not in Keble's opinion sufficiently, that which prescribed within what period before the grant of a Licence, the Head must have been resident within the University. These limitations he would have wholly done away with.

The letter is interesting on several accounts :—

" DEAREST COLERIDGE,

" I have been looking at the Statute for Private Halls, which I understood is now before you the Commissioners, and I have been a little dismayed at finding that nobody may open a Hall unless he has been lately resident at Oxford. This entirely spoils a favourite dream of mine, that such as Wilson, (e.g.) might make a lodgment in Oxford under cover of the new system, and do something to counteract the terrible secular spirit which has come over the place, naturally enough by the re-action consequent on Newman's secession, and other such things. You see the present Tutorial Body in Oxford, (I don't mean to disparage them, it was but to be expected in their position,) are just of that Academical Generation which was most likely to be influenced in that way. The old Country Stagers were too well settled beforehand, and I hope their children after them will prove to be the same; but there is no doubt, from all I can hear, that the religious tone of the Common Rooms just now is very much gone down from the level of Copeland, Rogers, Tom Morris, &c., and I cannot but think that an opening for such as I am thinking of is very desirable. The obvious way would be to strike out the limitation about time, and leave those who recommend to state what quantity of experience their protegés have, as well as how they stand in other respects. And the Candidates might be invited to bring the best testimonials they could *from any quarter*, as when Rugby or Winchester School is vacant; and the Hebdomadal Council might judge of them, or appoint a Committee to judge, provided always the Committee were *impartially* constituted, in which last clause I apprehend the difficulty would lie, but we *must* trust somebody.

"Perhaps I have no business to write to you on this matter, if so, just put me in the fire.

"I am here for two days for Bp. Wilson, but go home to-morrow."

I have brought these letters together for the general, and as to some of them the present, importance
of the subjects on which they are written. The
strong inclination of Keble's mind was obviously to
preserve Oxford so far, at least, as regarded Resident
Students, to members of the Established Church ;
though he would have conceded the Oxford Examinations at Oxford, and of course the honours, with I
presume the Bachelor's degree, to Nonconformists of
every denomination ; he would have had much more
regard paid to the intentions of founders than would
be satisfactory to the Reformers ; and he clung with
the greatest earnestness to the revival and preservation in full force of what he called the Oxford ἦθος,
which he considered to be of infinite value, and to be
dying out in the new state of feeling there.

These three points are of present and abiding importance ; on all of them Keble's opinions would be
considered perhaps by many persons as now out of
date ; but in order to judge of them fairly, we must
transport ourselves to the time when they were
given, and remember the general object which he
set before his own mind. The doctrine of the Na-
tionality of the Universities, because their property
was the gift of the nation, and their establishment
the act of the State, was at that time little heard
of ; and when stated, rather assumed than proved.
I do not mean now to controvert it ; and it is perhaps hardly a practical question how far as a whole

it could be historically proved; but conceding this, if one thought that the State was about so to exercise its right of interference as to impair the gift which it had already made, it would be neither inconsistent, nor narrow-minded, to oppose such exercise. Looking at the interests of the classes which were actually in an ancient and undisturbed possession, it seems to me even now very questionable, whether *their* place of education, and *their* education, may not suffer unnecessarily and seriously by the measures which have been adopted since the Oxford Reform commenced. The engrafting of the Collegiate system on the University teaching used to be considered a circumstance advantageously distinguishing Oxford and Cambridge from all other Universities. I am not prepared to abandon that notion, and if this distinction could have been preserved, with a due regard to the claims of Nonconformists, no Oxford man could be blamed, I think, or considered illiberal, for endeavouring to accomplish it. The scheme of Private Halls may be said to have failed; it was a concession, perhaps a necessary one, to the feeling of the day, but it had the seeds of its failure inherent in it; all the Colleges and Public Halls were not, and I believe are not even now full, and the Private Halls presented no advantage which might not have been had in greater degree in one of them. At the end of thirteen years but two appear to exist, which contain together eighteen Students in all, a number which might certainly have been conveniently provided for without their establishment. The scheme now started of simple teaching apart from the Collegiate life, I fear may result in a similar failure, although it presents the temptation of economy ; unless it be supplemented by something, which it does not and could not promise, and the happening of which, however probable, is still precarious and uncertain. I mean some such event as that which Keble desired, the devotion of themselves by some marked and gifted men to the tuition of the *Non-ascripti.* It does not seem safe in regard to this to rely on the ordinary rule of demand creating supply ; here the supply should in some sort precede the demand ; and it must be remembered that the Colleges must be expected to present commonly much greater temptations to eminent men to become Tutors, than the class of pupils we are now speaking of.

But waiving these difficulties, it seems to me that this plan, (and Keble's no less,) has been framed in forgetfulness of that which is essential to satisfy the claims both of Churchmen who require more economy, and of Nonconformists who seek admission to University education ; it may, and I hope it will, conduce to the teaching a greater number of persons the languages and science, and may give to more of our youth some of the benefits resulting from University Honours and Degrees. And I do not desire to undervalue this advantage. But we deceive ourselves, if we suppose that these gains will satisfy the reasonable desires of parents. Quite apart from these, however valuable, there is and there ought to be, even in the minds of those who neither expect nor desire for their sons Scholarships, or Fellowships, a strong desire to give them the benefit of a Collegiate education; it is the College Hall and Common Room, the College Tutor's classes, not too large to become the seed plots of friendships, the College society and associations, which they know tend to introduce their sons, free from all invidious distinctions, into full membership in the best English society. Their feeling is our own; what is it now which we look back upon with the most affectionate feeling and innocent pride? not so much the University as our College; not merely to our having been First Class men, or having won this or that University prize, but to having been fellow-pupils with such and such men of this or that Tutor at Balliol, or Corpus, or New College, or elsewhere; or perhaps, ·with some of us, even fellow-oarsmen in this or that College boat; it is the College which creates habits, which forms or cements friendships, which stamps indelible memories and associations. It may be a melancholy conclusion, and involve some serious consequences, (I hope none so serious as excellent men, and Dr. Pusey among them, foretel,) but I am convinced, that if changes are to be made with a view of satisfying those who are now without, nothing short

of a full and free admission to the College will have
that effect with the most influential of the claimants.
If they know what they seek, and I doubt not they
do, they will accept nothing short of this.

But suppose my conviction to be ill-founded, and
also that the new measure should be well accepted,
and lead to a large influx of young men of all denominations, it is surely matter of grave consideration
how far the order, and discipline, and internal harmony of the University can be securely maintained
with so large a body, consisting of young men of previous habits so different, and so prone in themselves
to give and take offence. It is mere folly to suppose
that a machinery by which, or an area in which, a
thousand or twelve hundred Students may work well
together, will have strength or space for the number
indefinitely increased ; and it is much to be feared
that irreparable injury may be done to those who
now occupy the ground, without conferring the desired benefits on the new comers. The change, it
must also be remembered, is not a mere change of
numbers ; besides many differences in themselves,
the new comers will not be under the same favourable circumstances for discipline as those under which
the Undergraduates are now placed.

One evil which Keble, it has been seen, estimated
as very grave, the loss of the old Oxford ἦθος, it
would be scarcely fair to attribute to anything done
under the Oxford Reform Statute ; for he speaks of

it as having already happened when he wrote, and
attributes it to another cause. Some of my readers
may ask what Keble meant by the quality which he
so much valued, and called by a Greek name. The
familiarity of Students of our Oxford days with
some, at least, of the treatises of Aristotle, and especially with the Ethics, and the remarkable ex-
pressiveness of his diction, occasioned the frequent
use among ourselves of his terms ; they were ever
in the mouths of Keble and Arnold in conversation or correspondence. I dare say the same remark might be true now. This was one of those
terms. It is a somewhat remarkable one. The
same it is which denotes custom, or usage generally, differing only in this, that the first letter is
then pronounced short, and is either doubled or
pronounced long when it denotes, at least in Aristotle's mouth, not a custom, or usage generally, but
one that is moral [a]. With Keble it imported certainly
no intellectual quality, scarcely even any distinct
moral one, but an habitual toning, or general colouring diffused over all a man's moral qualities, giving
the exercise of them a peculiar gentleness and grace ;
it was not that the Oxford lad was more dutiful,
more brave, more truthful, more punctual in his religious duties than any other, but that these qualities were habitually exercised by him with more of

[a] ὅθεν καὶ τοὔνομα ἔσχηκε μικρὸν παρεκκλῖνον ἀπὸ τοῦ ἔθους. Eth.
B. ii. cap. 1.

deference, and reverence towards his elders, more gentleness and loving-kindness to all.

Few will dispute that this $\mathring{\eta}\theta\sigma$, especially in youth, may be of great value. Keble certainly would have sacrificed a great deal of that which was more showy, and more likely to advance a young man in the world, to preserve it. I hope his notions about it are not entirely out of fashion in the present day, and I think it would be, and would denote, a great evil, if any constitutional or administrative reform should be found to throw a blight on this grace at Oxford.

With regard to the respect due to the wills and intentions of Founders, a question of great importance, and very general application for the future, as well as the present, I do not think the Commissioners differed so much from Keble in the principle, as in the application of it to particular cases; they no more than he, would have assented to the doctrine that *no* respect was due to them. This may be a tenable doctrine in a jurist's mouth, founded on the nature of property generally, and, in England specially, on the statutable and judicial restraints on the disposition of it; but when all that is said and allowed, it is still a doctrine which is shocking not merely to ignorance and prejudice, but to the most generous and reverential feelings of our nature. I say nothing of the impolicy of it. On the other hand, to maintain that the intentions of Founders should for all time be considered in all respects sacred and inviolable, is neither reasonable, nor in a true sense deferential to them. It was the duty, I conceive, of the Commissioners, so far as they could, to place themselves in the position of the Founders, to give them credit for wisdom, enlightenment, and justice; and, so far as they could, to ordain, as it might be believed they would have ordained under the altered circumstances; doing away absolutely what had become useless or mischievous, or impracticable, and advancing the original design in what was good in spirit, but narrow, or impeded in execution; changing nothing wantonly, but not staggering at the mere greatness of any change, if it fell within this principle. I think they acted according to this; they may have erred, they probably did err sometimes; but I do not think they were actuated by a spirit which Keble would on consideration have disapproved of.

It would be disingenuous, as well as foolish, to deny that a difficulty will probably be experienced in conducting the teaching of classes composed of pupils of different denominations; or that a danger may exist when the tutors of a college, either simultaneously, or in succession, should be themselves of different persuasions. Wholly to overcome this seems to me impossible. I remember Arnold telling me that he should fear no difficulty, if he were Regius Professor of Divinity, in lecturing, Greek Testament in hand, a class of pupils of all denominations. I will only say he was no common man; but yet he never had to make the experiment; moreover a Divinity class at the University naturally implies one of which the far greater part consists of those who are being prepared for Holy Orders, and therefore presumably members of the Church. If, however, it be part of the duty of such a Professor to expose heresies, and shew how they are to be guarded against; or to explain and confirm our Ecclesiastical Polity, ordinary men would find it difficult, I think, if not impossible, to conduct their lectures so peaceably and so effectively as my dear friend anticipated.

But what cannot be denied to exist may yet be much diminished in extent; ability and good sense, a conciliatory temper, with a spirit at once liberal and firm, that manifestly pursues the truth yet with consideration, and a large charity, will do much. The Church of England would begin with great advantages, and it is fair to presume that Heads of Houses would appoint College Tutors with a due regard to the circumstances. And after all it has with justice been asked, Have you security now against the evils you foretel? unless some Colleges are much belied, you have not. Many a thoughtful and conscientious parent, I believe, now exposes his son to the lectures and influence of tutors whose religious opinions he condemns, on account of their ability, their industry, or their moral influence for good. And so, I apprehend, would it be found with not a few Nonconformist parents; as in the National

Schools, the good master in a Church school attracts the Dissenters' children of every denomination ; so at Oxford, I apprehend, the Tutor, deservedly popular on general grounds, will draw to his College, and influence, it may be, with his special teaching, young men who have been brought up in opinions very much differing from his own ; giving them, for a time, at least, his own bias, but not always settling them into a faith different from that in which they were nursed, nor yet leading them " to care for none of these things ;" but making them more truly liberal ; by shewing them how much of goodness and truth there exists among those who hold that which they with some exaggeration as to the fact have been accustomed to regard as mere freethinking on the one hand, or as superstition or priestcraft on the other. If it be said that these are but vague and hypothetical answers to distinct denunciations of evil, it must be remembered that they are not the whole answer ; they are addressed rather to deprecate exaggeration and heat ; to suggest that in matters such as these the strictly logical deduction from the premises is not always found in practice the true one ; other unregarded considerations often intervening to qualify the conclusion ; and let me add, to warn excellent and earnest men against the embitterment which flows from unavailing opposition to the inevitable.

I hope I may be forgiven, considering my personal interest, not only for these last remarks, but for having dwelt at so much length on the Oxford Reform past, and that now impending, or on its trial. If I have expressed my fears and doubts as to the great measure recently determined on, I must not be supposed to condemn the authors, or to speak with unbecoming confidence. It would be unnatural in me not to feel the most intense interest in the future welfare of Oxford. All should agree that we must consider the Oxford *that is*, as well as the Oxford *that is to be;* for myself, I would have sought to give an access to those who have hitherto not had it, free, as nearly as possible in the spirit of the old University, Collegiate, and capable of gradually opening more widely to meet what may be expected to be a gradually increasing demand. I should have thought this might be done by Colleges founding Halls, in subordination to themselves, supplied with Principals and Tutors of their appointment from among their own Fellows, and conducted on a strictly domestic and economical principle. Keble College, I may say in a parenthesis, though necessarily in some degree exceptional, yet seems to me, speaking reverently, to have been providentially founded at this very time. What is demanded for Noncon- formists is, at least, an equally just matter of claim for Churchmen, who may desire to secure for their children not merely an economical education, but one framed strictly on Church principles. It is well at such a time that a College should exist, to which whoever resorts, (and I hope that access will be refused to none on account of difference in religious principles,) will enter with notice that there, at least, the teaching he will receive will be that of the Church of England, as Keble understood and subscribed to it.

Upon much consideration I would have everything in the Colleges, of profit as well as honour, that is now to be gained after competitive examination, open to all the Students in these Halls ; to this as a conclusion necessary, and under the over-ruling providence of God not a hurtful one, I have come by slow steps, not very willingly taken. I fear in this Keble and I should have differed ; but I would have said to him, what I say now to some of his dearest friends, (one especially of whom it would be difficult to say whether Keble more loved, or honoured him, and whom he used to characterize as the most hopeful of men,) recognize an inevitable necessity, not the less inevitable because you may struggle against it with partial success once and again ; make a virtue of the necessity ; seek to guard your concession with all such conditions as may in your opinion make it most salutary for the future ; but remember that England is no longer what she was when our colleges were founded, that her population is not more increased in numbers than in wealth, and in, at least, a certain and improveable kind of educa-

tion and refinement; in upward aspirations, to be
guided rather than checked; and that the desire for
academical training it is almost unnatural for the
Universities to oppose; that, consequently, they who
now besiege your citadel have at the very least a
plausible ground of right; that their claim, if it be
indeed rightful, should and can only be satisfied by
full and frank concession, concession worthy of yourselves; that it is a case in which you give nothing,
if you give less than all; that it is far better that
those who press on you should enter by the gates,
than through a breach, and that it is far more
Christian-like, and therefore far more politic, to admit them as brothers, than as conquerors.

> καὶ νῦν ἔασον, μηδέ σοι μελησάτω.
> πάντως γὰρ οὐ πείσεις νιν· οὐ γὰρ εὐπιθής·
> πάπταινε δ᾽ αὐτὸς, μή τι πημανθῇς ὁδῷ.
>
> *Prom. Vinct.* 332.

CHAPTER XVII.

1854, BISHOP OF NEW ZEALAND AT HURSLEY.—
FRANCIS GEORGE COLERIDGE'S DEATH.—VISIT TO
THE WEST. — THE VINEYARD AND DARTINGTON
RECTORY. — ARCHDEACON WILBERFORCE. — SER-
VICE FOR EMIGRANTS.—NORTH OF DEVON.—PRO-
FESSOR REED.—DECISION OF THE DENISON CASE.
—TOUR IN NORTH WALES.—ARGUMENT ON THE
DIVORCE BILL.—DEPARTURE OF MR. YOUNG AND
FAMILY.—1857, TOUR IN SWITZERLAND.—EUCHA-
RISTICAL ADORATION.

IT is high time that I should return to my narrative, which I have interrupted too long by remarks of my own ; although on a subject which
seems to be but a part of that which, it has been
seen, awakened the liveliest interest in Keble's mind.
As regarded his own little circle, and his parish, the
year 1854 was gliding peaceably away. The Wilsons were seeking health principally on Mrs. Wilson's
account on the Continent, and I have lying before
me a long letter from Keble to them, the greater
part of which is full of parish details. He had used
to receive such letters from Mr. Wilson when he was
himself away, and now he communicated to him

abroad the same kind of details. He could tell him everything material as to Ampfield, and he knew that Mr. Wilson continued to feel a strong interest in all that related to Hursley.

I will transcribe parts of this letter, which give a lively picture of Keble in his parochial ministrations :—

"*H. V., begun* 2ⁿᵈ *June,* 1854."

" MY MOST DEAR FRIENDS,

" You will not have wondered, but you may well be 'put out,' at not having heard from me so long after so very welcome a letter as you sent me. But you will bear it as you have so many things. The chief matter that we have been thinking of lately has been poor Holmes. You will have heard all particulars from Lady H. Very little passed between her and me that could be specified ; indeed, from the first time I saw her, she was too ill to say much ; but all was resigned, and peaceful, and warm-hearted. She asked to have the H. C. every Monday, and received it 3 times ; the first time Charlotte was there ; the last, the whole body of the Nurses, her Sister, Mrs. C., Mrs. S., and the other servant who was so much with her ; she could not then speak at all, but was entirely conscious, and particularly soothed by the Commendatory Service, which I read to her from the *Visitatio Infirmorum.* There was something she tried to say, but we could none of us make it out ; I begged her not to distress herself on that account, and from her countenance I don't think she did. She was buried at Ampfield this morning, *rather* near to the Grave we all think of, though not so near as Lady H. wished ; however, I hope it will have been all right. I love to think of her, and of Lady H., and the groupe of Park Servants waiting on her.

" Peter Young wrote very cheerfully of himself the other day, and talked of being home in three weeks, I am thankful to say. I believe he is much better, but I don't expect him to be well enough for work for a good while, and I am much afraid of his worrying himself ill again. We have the two girls and little Edward with us, and a great splotch of sunshine they make in the house, especially the boy ; and you would be amused by Jemmy's funny consequential ways, when he comes here on leave-out days. I hope and trust he is doing well in material points. I wish you could be at home at one or two things that are coming on, as the Christening of this 15th Moberly, who, some say, may perhaps be called Cyril ; the Bp. of New Zealand in our School-Room on Friday next, with Mrs. Selwyn, and, I hope, Johnny.

" This place, I am sorry to say, distresses me almost more than ever ; there is something very very bad going on among the young people, and I cannot fathom it, any more than Bessy can why people are ever naughty ; a question she asked to-day at breakfast.

" As to public matters, I will not say anything, they are got beyond me. I am sure people mean what is right, but somehow it has got strangely blended with what one has been used to think very wrong. One thing I fancy I discern, that the Puritan Party is getting on amazingly. I fully expect that before long Oxford will be thrown open to all but R. C's.

" And so with dear love to you, Maria, Mary, or Miriam, and to both the youngsters, I am always yours, J. K."

The person whose illness, death, and burial, he

speaks of in this letter, had been a faithful and favourite servant in the Trench family, and, among other services, had tenderly nursed a sister of Mrs. Wilson through her last illness. It is the grave of this lady in Ampfield Churchyard, of which Keble speaks, near to which it had been desired that the servant should be laid. In her illness, when it became serious, Lady Heathcote had brought her to Hursley Park, where she died; which explains the incidents he describes so simply and feelingly.

It was on the whole a tranquil time for Keble, or rather, I should say, no external anxieties prevented him from cheerful family meetings or parochial celebrations. The visit which he speaks of as anticipating from the Bishop of New Zealand to his school-room, took place, and Johnny, who was a great favourite of his, was of the party.

My extracts take me sometimes far back into the lives of those who are now, it may be, filling their own responsible places in their professions; but I do not like to cut out these little notices, and I trust not to give offence to the Jemmy and Johnny who find themselves here introduced as children.

It was a common practice with Keble, whenever he could, to procure for his school children, and any of the parishioners who might like to assemble, the entertainment and instruction which a Colonial Bishop, a missionary, or a traveller, might be willing to afford them by some account of what he had

seen, or done, or suffered in foreign lands, and by
a description of the people or the country.   Those
who have the honour of being acquainted with the
Bishop of New Zealand, especially those who may
have seen him with children in a school-room, and
witnessed his wonderful gifts, I may call them, of
adaptation and illustration, of rendering things unknown before easy of comprehension and interesting
to his audience, will understand what instruction and
amusement Keble probably procured on this occasion for the young and uneducated of his flock.
Nor for them only.   He himself was among those
who, perhaps, were as much delighted as the children and villagers ; and perhaps also in some matters not less instructed.   He had talk of course with
him besides on higher subjects, and, it will be seen
by a letter which I will not withhold from my readers,
he did not in all points agree with him.   Before they
read it, however, I desire that they should consider
that, in 1854, the Bishop's large plans for the con-
stituting the Church in New Zealand were scarcely
matured, and only partially tried in practice, and that
in some respects they departed from the primitive
models, to which Keble had always looked up duti-
fully and reverently ; he might, therefore, be well
allowed to doubt of their wisdom without diminution of his high esteem for the man.   I do not think
that it is to be inferred at all from anything he writes,
that were he now alive, and had seen the working of

the constitution in New Zealand, or could now see the partial adaptation of it, which the same great man is attempting in his present diocese in England, he would have found any ground for differing with him. One or two matters there are in which I fear, unless he misunderstood the Bishop, he would have still differed, and many will think, not without justification. It is no disparagement of Bishop Selwyn to say that Keble knew more of the character and dangers, in England at least, of Romanism on the one hand, and Rationalism on the other, especially that he knew more of the working of either spirit in the Universities, at least in Oxford. It was not that he thought too lightly of the former; nor did he doubt that there was ground for apprehension; but he believed with the strongest conviction that the issue of the latter in Oxford might be infidelity; and he thought, (and what unprejudiced believer can doubt that he was right?) that honest secessions to Rome were but slight evils, however great in themselves, in comparison with fallings off to infidelity. I say nothing here of what is called Ritualism; at the time I am now writing about, it was so entirely in its infancy as to attract little attention. I say the less on the subject of what Keble calls the Bishop's Protestantisms; my readers will know what Keble's convictions early and late were in regard to this matter, how uncatholic he thought Dissent, direct or indirect, and we do not know to what expressions of the Bishop he is alluding.

The following letter to Dyson, on the 7th of July, 1854, I desire to be read with reference to these remarks ; it may be thought they have been too long, but I have not the gift of expressing myself shortly, and I should be very much distressed, if for want of some such introduction, I gave pain by publishing it :—

" When is the great Bishop coming to you? for I am very desirous of having a finger in that pie ; so you must not wonder if I should happen to drop in at the time, and I shall make sure of getting a bed somewhere within reach. I have an extreme desire to hear you questioning, and him answering. I am afraid though I must confess, (will your sister forgive me?) that my courage has a little cooled as to going along with him, since he was here. Impossible as it is not to admire and love him, he makes me *shiver* now and then with his Protestantisms, crying up the Ch. Miss. Society, abusing Becket at St. Augustine's as ' a haughty Prelate,' and encouraging in his tendencies the same way. I am told his Ordination Sermon at Cuddesdon was altogether *Anti-Roman*, as if there were no other evil spirit than Popery now possessing Oxford. It is very horrid to find any fault, but I tell you all this, that you may order your logic as you think best with him. Well, this is crossness enough for one time."

I have little doubt that much passed at the meeting which would have been well worth listening to, and nothing which disturbed the kindly feeling be-

tween the two. In the following month he had the
great pleasure of family visitors at home.

"We have had a gathering," says he, writing to me on
the 25th of August, "for which we ought to be very thankful; both Bisley and Vineyard have been here, and it was
a thorough family fortnight, only too pleasant. Peter Young
is home again, much mended, but still in a delicate state.
However, we live in hopes of returning our family visits
before winter; and if we can, *won't we* come to Heath's
Court for a short visit, at least? we shall not need pressing
if we can manage it."

In this letter he expresses a hope that a dear brother of mine, of whom he was very fond, might be
recovering from an illness under which he was then
lying; but it pleased God to release him on the very
day after his letter was written, and on the 29th he
wrote to me again:—

" MY DEAREST COLERIDGE,

" I did not somehow expect the account you sent me,
and it is a sad thing to me to think of, that I lingered so
long in writing. And so he is gone without a kind word
from me, so kind and loving as he always was to me. May
it please God to soften the blow to you and all the rest, and
to make it rather medicinal than otherwise. . . . It is comforting, and yet alarming, to see so many of one's own
standing go, and all seeming so much more ready than one
feels oneself to be. Only think, it is 41 years since I first
knew your kind brother, and I wish I may not have been
going down hill rather than up. God help us to pray for

ourselves, and for one another.   With affectionate love to
you all, I am always, dearest friend, most truly yours, J. K."

I do not mention my brother's death, and cite
these passages merely because they relate to myself, but Keble's love for him was characteristic of
himself.   My brother was a man leading a perfectly
retired and quiet life, free from ambition for himself, but rejoicing in the success of those he loved ;
pursuing steadily an humble vocation, that of an
attorney ; and finding his graver pleasures in doing
acts of kindness, his lighter in his garden, his books,
and the antiquarian researches which our interesting
old Church favoured ; this was the sort of man in
whom Keble delighted ; he sought out not the man of
talents or learning, so much as the good, and gentle,
and loveable.

He began to make his summer excursion in September, 1854, and I heard from him dating from the
Vineyard, where the Champernownes resided, between
Totness and Dartington, proposing to come to us in
his way home ; but he was then anticipating an event
as near, which he had been dreading for some time,
the secession of Archdeacon Wilberforce to the Church
of Rome.   From extracts which I have made in former letters, it will have been seen how much he loved
and respected his old pupil, and what a specially bitter sorrow the loss of him was to him :—

"God grant," says he, "that those who are near and dear

to one another may keep more together than they have done of late.

" *This* Archdeacon, (he is speaking of the late Archdeacon Froude, who was still flourishing in a green old age at the Rectory at Dartington,) is very refreshing to see."

He wrote also to Mr. Wilson from the Vineyard on the 18th of September :—

" It is very pleasant being here, and seeing a newspaper only once or twice a-week, and walking among real live hedges, with no thought of grubbing, and paring, and burning, and wattle-hurdles along each side of the road. And this Archdeacon is quite as he used to be, except old age, wonderfully strong in voice ; and the memory of R. H. F. is very fragrant. We go to Ottery for a few days on Friday, and mean to make our way to Bisley, perhaps by the North of Devon, so that on the whole I expect to be 3 Sundays away from home ; but we have the comfort of hearing that Peter is improving in our absence. I hope to go to Oxford, among other things, to put the *Sacra Privata* to the press. Poor dear R. W., I own I was surprised at last ; for the last report I had heard was an improved one, and I had heard nothing for a long time. . . . I dare say your account of it is the right one ; but it disappoints and mortifies one to see one, who used to be so truthful and candid, lending himself at once to the violent contradictions of fact, and *petitiones principii*, which are quite necessary to every part almost of the Roman Theory. I wish I could compose, and write on it, it would be a sort of relief. In theory, I think, his position of Lay Communion is tenable, at least, I wish to think so ; for at the rate men are getting on, no one can say how soon he may himself be reduced to it. But I do not in the least expect that R. W. will have patience for it. I hear he is very miserable ; from himself I have only had one short and kind note. . . . .

"I am in correspondence with Rogers about a service for Emigrants on their voyage ; a very pleasant work, if one had nothing else to do. And the other day I saw Bp. Wordsworth and his really beautiful family of children. I cannot tell you how kind he was, and how I admired his quiet cheerful way of alluding to his own difficulties. Well, now I must say good bye, with our dear love to you all ; and in hope of knowing more than I do about the Simplon before long. I am always yours most lovingly, J. K."

They came to us on the 24th, and left us on the 26th ; too short a visit, but a very pleasant one ; saddened only by our talk about the secession I have just mentioned, and by his apprehension for the consequences. We went together to see Mrs. George Cornish ; it was a great pleasure to him to see her, as she was, residing in the house where he had once been so familiar, with her large family ; and bravely, yet not ostentatiously, bearing up against the sorrows that had befallen her.

They left us for the North of Devon, and intending by that route to go into Gloucestershire to Bisley. It must have been a great pleasure to him once more after the long interval to re-visit again the romantic country, which had so delighted him when young. But I did not hear from him until November, on the 6th of which month he wrote to me from Hursley :—

" DEAREST FRIEND,

" It really seems quite unnatural when I think of it, to have been so· long without thanking you for all your affectionate love and care of us. God reward you for it, and yours also, both of Heath's Court, of the Manor House, and of Feniton. I would not but have paid that visit to Ottery for a very great deal. And our Circuit was altogether prosperous. We met the girls at Exeter, shot across to Barnstaple, staid two days at Linton, and one at Stinchcombe, and over two Sundays at Bisley, paying a visit from thence to Fairford, and Coln, and Cirencester; and we also saw something of Bussage. So that on the whole it was a complete Family Tour, and very comfortable it was in every way; the 'cumulus' being 'imposed' upon it by young Tom, his wife, and Babe, coming here for three weeks; they only left us on Friday last; and I am only afraid we are too proud of them. But it is a wholesome check that my nephew makes one ashamed of oneself; however, I will not talk about that. I hope your visit from Worcestershire was a great joy, and that dear Frank's family are going on as comfortably as circumstances allow. John told me, what I was most deeply grieved at, the loss of our kind friends in the 'Arctic,' and how much you felt it. Indeed, I suppose it must be looked upon as a public calamity; for probably there are few such as Professor Reed left in the United States. But the comfort in thinking of such as he (no doubt) was, is solid and growing,—not so the thought of poor dear R. W., whose departure touches *me* almost more nearly than any one's; except, perhaps, that of Newman himself. I did not until very lately think that he would really go *there.* I thought he was too good-tempered, besides his learning and truthfulness. But he had got into an Utopian dream, and rather than give it up, he shut his eyes and made a jump, and now he must, and I suppose will, keep his eyes shut all his life long."

A word or two it seems fitting to add by way of comment on these extracts. I think it is not the first time that Keble had given utterance to his feelings about the grubbing, and paring, which he connected with high-farming ; it was really a passion with him, his love for coppices, hedge-rows, and wild-flowers ; a few years before he had expressed it in the beautiful "Round Robin," which he drew up for *Anemone Nemorosa, Primula Vulgaris,* and others of the same family, which will be found in his poems, addressed to the Lord of the Manor of Merdon. It is dated from Ladwell Hill, where he often lingered in his parish visitings, and soothed his mind under parish troubles, and other causes of distress, gazing on the poor petitioners, who were, as he feared, now doomed to give way to the plough :—

> " To himself we've heard him say,
> 'Thanks that I may hither stray ;
> Worn with age, and sin, and care,
> Here to breathe the pure glad air,
> Here Faith's lesson learn anew,
> Of this happy vernal crew ;
> Here the fragrant shrubs around,
> And the graceful shadowy ground,
> And the village tones afar,
> And the steeple with its star,
> And the clouds that gently move,
> Tune the heart to trust and love.'"

Ladwell Hill, I hope, will for many generations be sacred to the memory of John Keble; I am sure it will be so, as long as the present Lord of the Manor lives. It is a pity perhaps to disturb the feeling which the poem cannot fail to create; but in justice to the "Giant High Farming," (as I am told on the best authority,) it must be said that he had nothing to do with what was contemplated, or done in regard to the hedge-rows. Dear as they were to the Petitioners and to the Poet, they were obnoxious to another Rural Deity scarcely less powerful than the Giant, with whom also the Poet was on very good terms, by name Landscape Gardening. She desired to let into view from the Park, the meadows, across which the hedge-rows ran, and which they concealed. The irregular forms of these meadows also, when laid open to view, made picturesque breaks in what had before seemed a continuous line of wood; this surmounted the whole scene, and the breaks in it produced a much more graceful effect. So much, not too much I hope for the sake of accuracy, even in a little matter.

Keble speaks of Sir Frederic Rogers's application to him respecting a Service for Emigrants during their voyage. Sir Frederic was at that time one of the Emigration Commissioners; he appealed on behalf of a very interesting portion of our fellow-subjects, and in respect of one of their pressing wants. This was just a matter which Keble would

E e

delight to be employed in, and the result, without waiting until he had nothing else to do, was a very nicely arranged service with three really beautiful hymns. I am afraid that although the service is still printed and distributed to the emigrants, the hymns, for what reason I know not, are omitted ; they will be found, however, in the forthcoming volume of his poems.

He speaks also with true feeling, and renders no more than a just tribute to the memory of Henry Reed, Professor of Rhetoric and English Literature in the University of Pennsylvania. It has been my good fortune to know and to have received as my guests several citizens of the United States, especially from Pennsylvania ; and I have the great honour to count among my friends, only through the medium of a long and intimate correspondence, (for we have never met,) that wise and loving-hearted old man, Horace Binney, the great citizen of Philadelphia. Taken as samples, these shew me what rare and gifted men are to be found in the great Republic. Henry Reed it was impossible to know without loving him ; he came with his sister-in-law, Miss Brownson, from a great distance to bid us farewell immediately before their return to America ; and they came just at the time of my brother's death. They heard of this event only when within a few miles of my house, and though they still came on, it was only to shake hands with us ; we could not induce them to stay. I remember that we walked on my little terrace until the light failed. Miss Brownson, who was as a mother to his children, visited my grandchildren in their beds ; for both were full of his own treasures at home, and she wished to describe an English nursery to them ; and so we parted, he promising to bring his wife to visit us the next summer. He then went to Rydal to bid farewell to Mrs. Wordsworth, and in a few days wrote to me shortly from Liverpool. The next thing I heard of him was his death in the miserable collision of the "Arctic" steamer with a French vessel. He and his sister, it is said, were seen sitting together hand locked in hand, silent and tranquil, calmly awaiting their fate, but a few minutes before the ship went down with nearly all the passengers, who had been left on board, and, as it is said, left shamefully on board, by a cowardly commander and crew, escaping themselves in safety [a].

[a] My friend, Mr. Binney, writing to me in respect of this narrative, makes this comment, which I gladly insert, and must express my sincere regret for any injustice of which I may have been guilty :— "There is a single word in your reference to Capt. Luce, and the 'Arctic,' which does not precisely exhibit our version of his part in that most deplorable case. The account, you must have had in England, is not ours ; which my son informs me is in that part more accurate. Capt. Luce behaved ill in the first stage of the collision. He did not maintain his command of the crew, and resist, as he ought to have done to death if necessary, the cowardly seizure of the principal boat by the crew, and their desertion of the ship. Luce, however, said that he would not leave the ship, and would not permit his young son to get to the boat, though the crew offered to take him. He and

I trust to be forgiven this passing mention of my
friend, but the way in which Keble speaks of him
reminds me of the American feeling towards himself.   The circulation of the " Christian Year" in the
United States has fallen little short of that which
it has had here.   Again and again my American
friends, and sometimes even strangers, have sought
for an introduction from me to him.   I remember
well a gentleman, one of the former, the son indeed
to whom Mr. Binney alludes in the note below, with
whom I visited Hursley Park.   In the morning we
walked down to the Service, and when it was over,
we had a long talk with Keble.   At the close, and as
we were taking leave at the Vicarage porch, which
is covered with ivy, my friend drew me apart, and
asked me· if I thought Mr. Keble would take it
amiss, if he begged of him a branch of the ivy, cut
with his own hand.   Keble was much amused, and
cut it for him, as of course, and unsparingly.   As we
two walked away, he said, "You may smile at my
request, but I assure you I know and could name
the persons at home who would give me, (I am
afraid to mention the sum he mentioned,) for every
leaf I have in my hand."

The winter of 1854 passed away, and I see by our

his boy both went down with the ship, and when he rose to the
surface of the sea, he saw one of the ship's round tops, or a part of
a wheel-guard, or cover, and got upon it, and so I think did the son."

His bad or weak conduct at first, excluded him afterwards from
maritime service ; he left it certainly, and is no longer spoken of.

correspondence that he was busying himself a good deal with, and very anxious about, the proceedings against Archdeacon Denison, and I received many letters from him about them ; but I shall pass this matter over very shortly, not because I think the doctrine involved in it of any but the gravest importance, or that I differed from my friend in his belief in regard to it ; but that I thought as I still think, it was in that case needlessly and unsatisfactorily made the subject of litigation.

I must confess, therefore, that I was not sorry when the case went off on a bye-point, and the issue raised received no decision from the Court of Appeal. Indeed, I have never been able to see what the Church has gained in certainty of teaching, though I fear it has lost not a little, at least for a time, in charity of judgment, by the several cases carried of late years before ecclesiastical and lay tribunals in respect of assumed heresy or schism. What has Ritualism gained or lost by Westerton *v.* Liddell, or the belief in Baptismal Regeneration by Mr. Gorham's Appeal ; the Catholic doctrine in regard to the Holy Eucharist by the suit I have just mentioned above, or the hold of the fundamental verities of the Christian faith on the minds of Christians by the proceedings against the " Essays and Reviews ?" I believe little or nothing ; certainly nothing fit to be compared with the distress of mind to thousands of tender souls, and the fatal offence which some of these cases gave to over-scrupulous, and as I think mistaken persons; who, although they thought the Anglican belief, our creeds, formularies, and articles, orthodox, and the decisions erroneous, yet abandoned the former on account of the latter. Of course I am not suggesting that no such litigation should ever be instituted, and I do not forget the solemn undertaking of the Bishop on his Consecration. It would seem presumptuous in me to say a word in limitation, or explanation, of the words then used ; our Fathers in the Church will act, it must be presumed, each according to his own understanding of their obligation ; yet it seems, at least, hard to conceive that any one is bound by them to appeal to a tribunal, the constitution of which he thinks to be uncanonical, or the decisions of which he holds to proceed on unsound principles ; especially when so much may be done in the spirit of the undertaking by other means.

Keble's motive, indeed, was a different one. He was very sensitive to the imputation, which he feared he might labour under, of adhering to the Church from interested motives ; and therefore he desired in his own case on some occasions, that his belief, or his practice, if impugned, should be brought under some authoritative judicial cognizance. It was, however, always I think more wisely considered that such a reference was neither necessary nor expedient.

Mr. Wilson remained abroad and in Italy in the

spring of 1855, and appears to have interested Keble very much by his letters therefrom. On the 6th of May he wrote a long answer, from which I will make some extracts; a great deal of it is devoted to parish matters :—

"MY VERY DEAR FRIENDS,

"Here is a letter from you, Robert, which came in this morning, lying as yet unopened; because I feel as if the beginning of it would be less heart-breaking, or, however, I hope to feel less unworthy of it, if I make a decent beginning of this before I unseal it. I am really very penitent, but you would partly forgive me, if you knew how tired my hand gets by the time I have written a letter or ½ a Sermon. Else full gladly would I have accepted the exercise of writing to you in exchange for the 2 last things which have hindered me from it; a long Anti-Roman letter to a Lady, and a sketch for ——, of part of an argument against this bill for letting people marry their wives' sisters, which is now in full career again. Well, however, now I have really begun, and I *will* go on I am '*termed.*' . .

"I think it might not be a bad time to suggest to our worthy friend the Public the notion of having *a brotherhood for Education*, like the Freres Chretiens; who, as an Ecclesiastical Body, would be under control, and from their slight touch of Asceticism would work as cheaply as they could. I have long had it in my mind to suggest this to you; it would be quite in your line to undertake it, (among other things,) from your knowing so much of the Christian Brothers; pray think of it while, (as you may guess by the above,) [here a line is drawn up to some blunders in the writing,] I indulge myself in a small nap.

"Well, I have read your kind, long letter, and cannot

tell you how much I am obliged to you for it; it does but
confirm the impression which one is daily receiving from
all one can read or hear of the matter, that Rome, so far as
she is *distinctive*, builds not only upon falsehood, but upon
falsehood of which she has a certain consciousness; only
she has made up her mind that it is her duty to back up
her system, (being, she says, substantially true,) with any
amount of needful, or very profitable deception.   The Le-
gendary services in the Breviary, with that for the 15ᵗʰ August at the head, are a standing instance of this ; and so
will this new doctrine be, in whatever degree they allege
antiquity for it.   They cannot but know in their hearts,
that it has not the shadow of a Tradition ; and yet see
what their Abp. of Armagh, poor dear ——'s select patron
says of it.   Most fearful it is to me, that neither among the
more moderate Romanists, nor among our Romanizers,
(with one exception that E. B. P. told me of,) does it seem
to have produced any sort of scruple or re-action.   From
the highest to the lowest they satisfy themselves, I imagine,
with your friend's argument, ' How can we be certain that
it is not so ?'

"Your account of Rome really makes one shudder, when
one connects with it this idea of unreality, and comes nearer
than anything for years past to bring back the old Ultra-
Protestant notions that one learned as a boy out of Newton
on the Prophecies.   With it (i.e. with your account) on my
mind, I feel as if I would go miles out of my way to avoid
seeing Rome ; it seems so very shocking; and if this be
a man's feeling, I suppose there would be no special danger
in going there, and he would be free to choose as health
and convenience and other duties dictated.   But I should
be very thankful on a great many accounts, if you are able
to get work and stay here.   We really have need of all the

help we can get. Outwardly our friends from Exeter Hall
are having it all their own way; all appointments, public
meetings, &c. But underneath is, I much fear, a deep and
gradually swelling tide of Rationalism, in unison with the
revolutionary spirit, which has disclosed itself upon occasion of these mismanagements in the War. But enough
and too much of this croaking. I saw a letter the other
day from Moorsom to Upton Richards, dated, I think,
Easter Monday, in very good spirits, and altogether comfortable. Also I know you will be glad to hear that I think
your successor is making his way very nicely in the place
and neighbourhood; he puts me often in mind of George
Herbert's lines :—

> 'Be useful where thou livest, that they may
> Both want and wish thy pleasing presence still.'

I find myself continually resorting to him, as in old time to
dear W. C. Y. At this present he is superintending a negotiation for a new Clock in our Church. . . . .

"Dear Mrs. Heathcote, you know better than I, was a
great loss; it was very touching to be with her son just
afterwards. Thirty-five years ago I think it was that I saw
them first together, and I thought then I never saw a Mother and Son on such *lover-like* terms; and they have never
been apart for six months together. . . . . With dear love to
your wife and bairns, ever yours affect^ly, J. K."

It will be seen how Keble speaks of the new dogma
of the Immaculate Conception, and he felt the same
as long as he lived. The promulgation of it pained
him much; it constituted in his opinion, so long as
it remained unrevoked, an absolute bar to the unity
of Christendom. In this letter he specifies one ob-

jection to it on which in all such cases he relied
much, that not only was there no authority for it
in Holy Writ, but, as he expresses it, not a shadow
of tradition. It will be obvious, that his reliance on
this involves his denial of others of the foundations
on which Romanism rests ; as for example, the infallibility of the Pope, and his supreme power in matters of faith.

I make no apology to Sir W. Heathcote for printing the short extract relating to his mother. It will
give many pleasure to look at the picture which
Keble paints like a poet in a single word, and I
am sure it will give him no pain to have such recollections revived. Fifteen years before, I think, she
had been visited with a serious illness, a paralytic
seizure, the effects of which on her bodily frame
were never removed ; but her mind was spared to
the last, and she passed away in 1855 in her son's
house, in which she had lived during the interval,
painlessly and peacefully, from gradual and gentle
decay, rather than from illness, in the presence of
the son, who was thankful to God that he was allowed " to watch her last breath."

I think the case of Westerton and Liddell was decided in this year, 1855. Keble's opinions in regard
to Ritualism will have to be noticed more fully hereafter, but I may say in passing that this decision
vexed him a good deal, though he did not exaggerate
its importance. I had allowed him to read a very

beautiful letter to myself from my nephew, now Bishop Patteson, who had attached himself to the Bishop of New Zealand, and gone out with him in the spring of 1855 to that island. Keble wrote on the two subjects to me on the 11th of December, 1855 :—

"Thank you over and over again for the sight of that noble, tender letter; surely it is one of the most perfect things altogether that one ever met with in this worky-day world. One cannot, as the people say, think enough of it. Surely there must be in store some very good thing for the Church in those parts, that such men should be attracted towards it. It is enough to make up for —— pretending to determine how Christian People should think of and behave to the Holy Sacrament. I have something to write to you on that matter, which I shall try and put on another piece of paper, for my own mind's relief, for I don't suppose it can be of any use. No doubt, as you say, there is a tendency in all this to drive unstable minds to Rome. The souls, however, must be very unstable, indeed, less settled than the loosest possible tooth, if such a matter can cough them out from among us. For what is it to the proof or disproof of the Pope's Supremacy, or the *ruling* powers of the B. V. M., whether I may have a Cross on the Altar Table, or no? Though I must own, I do expect that when these outward signs of the Truth are suppressed, the Truth itself which they symbolize will be openly persecuted, and probably forbidden to be taught in the Established Church ; but not a bit the nearer should one be to Rome for that, as I understand the matter."

The state of Mrs. Keble's health during this year fluctuated much, but generally speaking it was such as to cause him anxiety; and though, as he said affectionately in one of his letters to me, referring to another cause of discomfort, " As for Charlotte, I know nothing can *really* hurt her;" yet there was so much doubt as to the real cause of her ailments, and they were so variously accounted for at different times, as much to increase his uneasiness. However, he tried again the remedy, which was never without some effect, and I find several letters to Mr. Wilson dated from North Wales; they were at Llandudno, and Capel Curig, and, I believe, Barmouth in August; and before they returned to Hursley, they visited the Bishop of Oxford at Lavington. The trip answered in some measure for her; but his letters shew that wherever he went, he carried his Church anxieties with him, and beyond these, his Church work also. After " tossing about the South Downs for a few days," he was busy now with the present Archdeacon Freeman, in comparing their notes about two proposed Hymnals, Sarum and Scottish.

Indeed, he never rested; and if he was anxious for his wife's health, her anxiety for him was very great; and earlier in the year it had led her, without his knowledge, to communicate with me respecting him. Her account of his ailments, and his determined exposure of himself in parochial ministrations, even at night when suffering under erysipelas, infected me with her fears. The necessity for imprudent ex-

posure often arose from his excellent Curate being
only a Deacon, and unable to obtain Priest's Orders.
This was a matter of conscience between the Bishop
and him, in which of course I could not without
difficulty interfere. At last, however, from anxiety
for one friend, and confidence in the personal kindness of the other, I made an attempt, which was
unsuccessful; and the consequence was the separation of Keble and Mr. Young; a separation peculiarly bitter, as there was the greatest intimacy and
a connection between the families; and the services
of the Curate were so dutiful, and earnest, and so
acceptable to the parishioners, that without any reflection on his successors I may in justice say, they
never were, and scarcely could be entirely replaced.
As I had no right to interfere, so I desire to be
understood as making no reflection on the decision;
there was, I am certain, nothing personal in it; the
motive was a conscientious one, and however I might
regret the judgment at the time, it is not for me to
reflect upon it.

I went on the Winter Circuit into the West this
year, and saw Keble for a very pleasant Sunday
evening at Hursley Park on the 30th of November.
I had come out from Winchester after the morning
service to the afternoon service at Hursley; there
was no party, and we had some quiet talk together;
but my work was very heavy, and distressing, and I
had no time to see him again. His mind, however,

was now at work on the Divorce Bill, which was about to be brought into Parliament. I need not say how strongly he felt against the measure, which in one of his notes he calls "a Bill for legalizing Adultery." Early in the spring of 1857 he published "An Argument for not proceeding immediately to Repeal the Laws, which treat the Nuptial Bond as Indissoluble."

It was a plea for delay at all events; and the argument on the general question was professedly left incomplete, because it was necessary he thought to enquire how far the practice of the Church from early times agreed with the construction which he gave to the passages of Scripture on which he grounded his opinion. Nor does he appear to have objected to separation under certain circumstances, as distinguished from divorce. With these qualifying remarks the argument seems to me, if I may presume to say so, sound and ingenious, and to display that intimate acquaintance with Scripture which he certainly possessed. The Bill, however, as we know, passed into a Law; in vain stoutly resisted by Mr. Gladstone clause by clause. Whether society in its morality has received the benefits which it promised may well be doubted; the old practice of divorce by special statutes was certainly very objectionable; and the new law has to the present time had the advantage of being administered by two judges in succession of rare excellency, men who may be

equalled, but will scarcely ever be surpassed in their
own province; and yet when I consider the effect
on the purity of the public mind, of the proceedings
in the Court, daily circulated among all ages and
classes; the collusion between parties, sometimes defeated, but too often no doubt successfully practised;
and above all, the fatally strong temptation which
its open doors must offer to conjugal infidelity;
I cannot think that Keble had cause to regret
anything but the ill-success of his very moderate
argument. I do not believe that the eminent judges
to whom I have referred, could we have the benefit now of their advice, would be disposed to commend the law which they have been called on to
administer. But it is one of the instances of legislation in which

" Vestigia nulla retrorsum."

The ill-success of my interference in respect of
Mr. Young, and a just consideration for him, could
lead only to his giving up the Hursley curacy. How
best to arrange this for him had been for some time
a subject of sad consideration for Keble; it was of
course no easy matter; but on the 30th of March,
1857, he wrote to me from Hursley as follows :—

"We are here just now in the agonies of parting with
dear Peter Young, and Caroline, and the 8 minor dears.
It is a great deal of sunshine to be shut out from us, from
my poor wife especially. But if they were to go, and to
a place as poor as they leave, they could not well have

more comfort in going. What do you think of our farmers here, quite and clean of their own accord, getting up a subscription, which by liberal addition from the Park, amounted to £142, collected entirely in the Parish, and with such love and good-will from all sorts. It took my breath away when I heard of it; and it was done in such a delicate and feeling manner too; £16 applied to find him a set of vessels for Private Communion, the rest for expenses of migration. Also 3 voluntary and unpaid teams start to-night at 12 o'clock to carry his goods as far as the Fisherton Station at Salisbury. It makes me love the place better than ever. You should have heard the little speech which Heathcote made to him this morning before a select audience, consisting of the Collectors, i.e. the principal tenants, and a very few wives and daughters. We are going to προπέμπ (escort) them as far as Salisbury. Two of the children are left with us at present."

It was no doubt a cause of great present distress to Keble, and of lasting sorrow, the departure of the Youngs; it was more than the mere loss of an affectionate and diligent Curate on whom he could entirely depend; he felt the loss of his companion, of the whole family, not least, perhaps, of the little children; and he felt also for the great privation which he knew it brought with it to Mrs. Keble. However it was inevitable. He had the great consolation after a while of seeing Mr. Young preferred to the living which he now holds. I need not say that I am speaking of the author of the " Daily Readings," which those who know them will not think I

overrate, when I say they are an invaluable addition
to our family libraries, and help to our family prayers.
His place as curate was well supplied for a time by
Mr. Le Geyt, but circumstances thenceforward occasioned many changes in Keble's curates, and as he
was before long compelled, sometimes by his own,
and sometimes Mrs. Keble's ill-health, to be absent
from home for long periods, he increased the number,
and had two.

In the summer of this year, 1857, Mrs. Keble and
he made a tour on the Continent, of which he gave
me a short account in the following letter, written
from Hursley the 23rd of October :—

" DEAREST COLERIDGE,

" This is, indeed, worse than ever, that I should never
yet have thanked you for your most kind letter received,
I think, at Thun, and so welcome every way.   But you
are too much used to my idle ways, and I to your for-
giving ways.   Somehow, when I was out, I had even less
inclination to write than usual.   I cannot say that I had
not time, but I accepted all manner of excuses.   Our
journey was very full of interest, and I hope has done my
wife's health good on the whole, notwithstanding one very
serious drawback, of which I dare say you have heard.
Our course was to leave the main Railway at Dijon, and
scramble over the Jura, chiefly for the sake of the grand
view, (which, however, we missed, owing to a certain M. de
Brouillard, who had a trick of waiting upon us just when
his presence was least acceptable,) and to come down upon
the Lake at Nyon, (for we agreed to cut Geneva,) and after

two nights at Vevay, to go a little way up the Valley of the
Rhone, and turn to the left according to a route which
Wilson had given us, avoiding the Mont Blanc side as too
much for Madame. We went up the Val d'Ormont, staid
three nights, including a Sunday, at Sepcy, a curious specimen of a Swiss Village ; then by Chateau d'Oex to Thun,
Interlacken, Lauter-brunnen, and Grindelwald for our third
Sunday. The next week took us from Grindelwald to Mey-
rinzen, then up the vale of the Aar to the passes of the
Grimsel and Furca, and down the Reuss to Andermatt,
and these two days were the noblest part of our doings to
my mind ; then down the Lake and up the Rigi ; then to
Lucerne for the next Sunday, (the pleasantest *town* I think
that we made acquaintance with). We lingered a little
there to nurse a cold, which she had caught, and then went
on to Basle, intending to make our way home down the
Rhine ; but at Basle she was suddenly seized with a violent attack of pleurisy, with some inflammation of the lungs.
It was in the middle of the night, but by God's good Providence a friend, (Laura Richards,) was with us, who proved
a most admirable nurse ; and we got some leeches then,
and some good advice the next day ; so that we were able
to get to Strasburgh by the end of that week, and came
home by Paris, Dover, and London, giving up the Rhine
of course, and also giving up, which I more regret, our
Devonshire visits, amongst which we had quite reckoned
on one to you. Since then she has been rather mending,
and could do in the way of moving about rather more than
before we went abroad. Just now she is suffering from
a cold, but I trust it will not come to much.

" I have been too much taken up since we came home
with a little book I have been trying to write on Eucharistical Adoration. I hope it will be out next week. The

subject I fear will be very disturbing to us again ; and I want, if I could, to quiet people, or, at least, shew those who wish to be quiet, that they are not wrong in being so. Alas, that dear Pusey should still be unable to write for us ; I fear for a long time yet."

The book of which Keble speaks in this letter appeared soon after its date, a second edition in 1859, and a third has been published since his death. Its fuller title is, " The Worship of our Lord and Saviour in the Sacrament of Holy Communion." Its object and its plan are so shortly and so fully stated in the opening paragraph, that it may be well to transcribe it ; as I could not pass over in entire silence a work by Keble on a subject on which he felt so deeply, and had thought so intently and laboriously for so many years of his life. The subject, indeed, is so important, and the treatise so able, that I regret it has not obtained a wider circulation, and I should be glad to draw to it more attention from serious people, whether for praise or condemnation :—

" The object of this Essay is to allay, and, if possible, to quiet the troublesome thoughts which may at times, and now especially, occur to men's minds on this awful subject, so as even to disturb them in the highest act of devotion. For this purpose it may be well to consider calmly, not without deep reverence of heart, First, what Natural Piety would suggest ; Secondly, what Holy Scripture may appear to sanction ; Thirdly, what the Fathers and Liturgies indicate to have been the practice of the Primitive Church ; Fourthly, what the Church of England enjoins or recommends."

The words, "now especially," refer to the decision of Archbishop Sumner in the Denison Case, which was the cause for writing the book ; and after an orderly and careful discussion of the four points above stated, a fifth and concluding chapter is added on the duties of Churchmen in respect of that decision. This is a very interesting chapter, and has an importance as applicable to other possible cases. It is of course addressed to those who might think the decision erroneous ; and it first establishes, that however gravely erroneous it might seem to a man, even if he conscientiously believed it to be heretical, it would have been, even if final, no cause for leaving the Church, or declining communion with its author ; because it would not bind the conscience ; the refusal to act in obedience to it might expose one to temporal penalty, but it could do no more ; the penalty must be submitted to meekly, and if it fall not on an individual personally, he must help with his prayers and out of his means those on whom it should. Further, there might remain protest and appeal, the former is "the course of those who feel themselves aggrieved, but know of no legal remedy," it supposes "the final authority to have spoken ;" the latter supposes some higher authority, which may be applied to and has power to reverse the decision.

For the satisfaction of conscience Keble would, and, indeed, I believe, did protest, but he relied on appeal; not to any other English tribunal, but to an Œcumenical Council when it should be assembled. Here it was that many have considered his course an unreal and chimerical one.   He was aware of this, but his opinion was not hastily taken up, nor, as he thought, without the sanction of great authorities.   He had had occasion more than once in his life to consider the matter deeply, and it had quieted his conscience, and made him easy in a loyal adherence to his Church.   Those who deride or condemn his view, should in justice read, at least, this part of his work, for it is not easy to give the full force of his argument in a short analysis.   He considered it—

" Of the very last importance that we should keep in our own minds, and before all Christendom, the fact that we stand as Orthodox Catholics upon a constant virtual appeal to the œcumenical voice of the Church, expressed by the Four Great Councils, and by general consent in all the ages during which she continued undivided."

And he asked,—

" If that voice be disputed, is there any conceivable way of bringing the dispute to an issue, except only by another true Œcumenical Council when such by God's grace may be had."

Further on he says :—

" The question may well be asked,—much more easily

asked than answered,—whether in the present divided state of Christendom, all who believe in the Holy Catholic Church must not in reality, however unconsciously, be going on under this very appeal, at least, as against other claimants. The Greek will say, 'I go by the voice of the present Church diffusive;' the Latin, 'I go by the infallible voice of the See of St. Peter;' the English, 'I go by what has been held fundamental everywhere, always, and by all;' but who is to decide between them, which of these measures is right. Yet all, one may hope, would agree to defer to the decision of such a Council as has been specified, were it attainable. It is our common position; and we in England have so much the more reason to acquiesce in it, as it does not force us to "unchurch," (as it is termed,) either of the other great sections of Christendom; as they do mutually one another and us."

It may be said there is no true analogy between the case of one branch of the Church at issue with others, and that of an individual or individuals who cannot in conscience accept an authoritative decision in their own branch, as for example, that of the Judicial Committee of the Privy Council; but certainly there is no difference in principle between the two cases in respect of that on which mainly the charge of unreality must rest, namely, the present apparent hopelessness of a really Œcumenical Council being assembled. It will not be doubted, that if so unlikely an event should occur, the Council would be the proper place in which should be considered the grievance of those individuals who, like Keble, had invincible objections to the Latin and Greek branches, who loved and adhered to their own branch, and who complained only of a judicial decision which seemed to them to taint its orthodoxy.

I do not know that any allowance need be made, or, indeed, ought to be made, in considering Keble's reasoning, for the extreme anxiety he felt for those who were troubled by the judgments to which he alludes. He was familiar with all their sorrows, and I think he felt it in some sort his mission, (though in his modesty he would have shrunk from acknowledging this,) to soothe them, and reconcile them to follow in the path in which he himself had found peace. Time has in God's good will had a healing force; many have forgotten, many never knew the anxieties of that day; but it is good to remember them, that we may learn tenderness for others, and be grateful, too, for ourselves.

I see about this very time I wrote to him expressing my anxiety about the pending judgment:—

"I have seen," I said, "how mischievously these judgments do disturb and overthrow men's minds. We have lost an excellent man here, a pious, good-hearted clergyman, a perfect blessing to his little flock, simply on the Gorham proceeding: against the scruples which it inspired he has been fighting for five years, and at last given in. He told me with tears in his eyes, that he was worn in body almost to a skeleton, and would rather die than go through again all he had suffered."

However mistaken such persons were, their agonies were real; to such persons Keble in the conclusion of his treatise addressed himself affectionately, and it seems to me conclusively :—

" Many a devout and loving heart, I well know, will rise up against this view of our case. To be on this conditional temporary footing will strike them as something so unsatisfactory, so miserably poor and meagre, so unlike the glorious vision which they have been used to gaze on, of the one Catholic Apostolic Church. And poor, indeed, and disappointing it undoubtedly is, but not otherwise than as the aspect of Christianity itself in the world is poor and disappointing compared with what we read of it in the Gospel.

" Men will not escape from this state of decay by going elsewhere, though they may shut their eyes to the reality of it. Rather, whatever be our position in the Church, since God Almighty has assigned it to us for our trial, shall we not accept it, and make the best of it, in humble confidence that according to our faith it will be to us ?

" This, please God, is the way of truth and peace, and therefore in it we may hope for a blessing, the rather if it should prove to be the way of the Cross also. But to engage oneself, by a strong act of the will, to the whole system of a body new to us, not upon the proper evidence of that system, but because some in temporary authority among ourselves have denied our holy doctrine ; this has something in it so very unreal, that it can hardly agree with truth ; and so like ill-temper, that it gives but a bad omen for peace."

CHAPTER XVIII.

1857, DEATH OF THE REV. J. D. COLERIDGE.—BUILD-
ING OF SCHOOL CHAPEL AT PITT, 1858.—DEATH
OF MRS. T. KEBLE, JUNIOR, 1858.—TROUBLES IN
THE SCOTTISH EPISCOPAL CHURCH. — STAY AT
OXFORD, 1859. — TOUR TO THE NORTH. — VISIT
TO EDINBURGH, 1860. — DEATH OF ELIZABETH
KEBLE, AUGUST, 1860.—DEATH OF C. DYSON.—
VISIT TO DEVONSHIRE. — DEATH OF J. PATTE-
SON, 1861.

IT may seem that I take advantage of my present task to obtrude impertinently my own trials
or sorrows on my readers. I hope, however, that
my motive has been seen by them, and the sort of
necessity that was laid on me, not to omit some of
the choicest out-pourings of Keble's tender heart
and religious spirit. I must crave their indulgence
when I commence this chapter in the same way.
On Christmas Eve, in the year 1857, my eldest
brother, with whom I had walked, for sixty years
and more, from the earliest childhood in love that
had never had one remembered breach, nor even
the slightest diminution, was almost suddenly taken
from me. I communicated this of course to Keble,

and on the 29th of December he wrote to me as follows :—

"DEAREST COLERIDGE,

"I am, indeed, grieved that your Christmas should have been saddened by such a loss, a loss I too, deeply feel, irreparable in this world; and you have had so much to go through in that way; but 'the time is short,' and Christmas is happier *there* than even here; and surely his being taken just at that time, and with so little comparative suffering, seem special marks of favour and blessing. He will be sadly missed. . . . Dear Heathcote feels as you know he would; he did not say he would write to you, but I dare say he will. What a gathering, dear friend, we are permitted to think of as time goes on, one after another taken out of sight to pray for us, and wait for us in peace. The last I had much to think of, was the little babe on whose account this is edged with a little black; Charlie Young, the least of our little cousins, 13 months old. He came with his mother to pay us a little visit in November, and you would not believe, yes, *you* would know better than I, how he wound himself round all our hearts, and how much my dear wife thinks of his little grave, close to the Church door at Brooking; which has made the place seem like a home to them, more I dare say than any other kind of thing could have done. To all appearance, our next parting in the family is likely to be still more trying, very much more, but who knows? and who dare choose? I wish in one respect that your kind thought for Tom could have been realized, one fancies that work would be a help and relief; but I dare say it is best as it is. The rest of our lot, thank God, are in tolerable Christmas order. . . .

"I thank you with all my heart for your encouraging

words about my little Book. I shall be very thankful, if
it does some little good, and no harm. Something of the
kind, I am sure, was very much wanted, especially just
now in Scotland. Have you heard of Bp. Forbes's troubles?
but I have not time to write more now.

God bless you, dearest friend, and dear Mary, and your
wife, and all, and give you a full share in all the good
prayers that are offered up at this time by all His people
everywhere. With kindest love from me and my two betters, ever yours, J. K."

It may be remembered that in an early part of my
memoir, I stated that after all the church arrangements made for the benefit of the two parishes which
formed Keble's incumbency, there was still a hamlet
in Hursley parish not provided for as he desired.
This was Pitt, which lies between Winchester and
Hursley, in a little green valley as you descend
from the upland downs which separate the one from
the other; it is as much as three miles from Hursley
Church. For a long time a service was performed
in it weekly in a cottage, to which Keble walked
often and often, as long as his strength was equal to
it; but in this year, 1858, a school-chapel was built
there, which was licensed on the 31st of March, and
not long after a residence was supplied for a school-
master. This last was due to the liberality of several
contributors; for the former, Keble and this portion
of his flock were indebted to my dear relative,

Charlotte Yonge, the daughter of him whom I have more than once before-mentioned, whose name is deservedly well-known in the literature of England. I may not particularize, indeed I cannot, and I believe no one but herself could particularize all her munificent acts done in the same spirit, which render her literary works the greater blessing to herself, and yet the very least of her claims to the love and respect of others. She could scarcely have gratified Keble more than by this offering, though he could scarcely love her the more for it, than he had done before. He seems, from the manner in which he always writes of her, to have regarded her almost as a daughter bequeathed to him by her departed father.

Pitt flourished. Writing in the following year to the Wilsons, he says :—

"The Pitt district seems at present to thrive under the care of Mr. Baker, (a nephew by marriage of Moberly,) who is very kindly curatizing there for me in the intervals of his work as Chaplain of the College. He brought 8 candidates to Confirmation at Otterbourne the other day, and had 17 Communicants in the little School-Chapel on Easter Day, and a congregation of 72 on Good Friday, the population of Pitt being under 100. I advise you to get a Moberly-bred Curate."

Keble alludes in his letter of the 29th of December, 1857, to the illness of the young lady, the daughter of George Cornish, whose marriage I have mentioned above, and he wrote no letter for some time without speaking of it. She, however, lingered until the end of the year; meantime he had been made very anxious by an alarming illness of Sir William Heathcote; and writing, as I now do, when that same dear friend is recovering, as I trust, from an illness at one time equally alarming, I cannot help inserting a word from one of Keble's letters at the time. My readers may remember my mention of the baptism and death of one of his children; it was in this year that he was taken, and the loss was a very trying one.

Keble, speaking of Sir William, says:—

" Indeed, I trust by God's blessing, that he is now really getting better. I saw him on Wednesday for $\frac{1}{4}$ of an hour, very sweet and cheerful, but much pulled down. It was much owing to his anguish about that dear little Godfrey."

It is for the sake of both, the living and the dead, that I set down any notice of this interview; it impressed Keble very much. I find it mentioned in three letters; in one to Mr. Wilson he says:—

" I saw him on Tuesday for $\frac{1}{4}$ of an hour, and I cannot tell you how it impressed me. Would that I were worthy but to remember it all exactly, much more to enter into it. He was so sweet, and noble, and humble, and loving."

In this year Keble and I lost our dear old Corpus friend, Noel Ellison, and at the close of it, the niece of whom I have just spoken died also. He expresses his feelings on this and other similar visitations in the letter which I now insert :—

                              "*H. V., Innocents' Day*, 1858.

"DEAREST COLERIDGE,

"You will have heard, I dare say, that the long-expected blow has at last fallen on us. Our dear Niece at Sidmouth was on Thursday gathered to her Father, and Sisters, and Brother, and her little first-born Child. She had been very much worse for several days; and a very little before had given a sort of signal of what was going to happen by saying with one of her bright looks, when she was asked to take something, 'Nothing but Holy Communion will do me good now.' So we were quite spared what I had much dreaded, that her mind might give way before her body, as I believe often happens in such extreme weakness. Poor dear Tom, he will be all the more desolate, from having been able all along to devote himself exclusively to her; but of course it is a pain, which so far he would not part with for all the world. His Father and Mother, I trust, are with him now. He and Harriet, (Kenie's Mother,) were the only persons with her at the moment, 2 P.M. At 7 that same morning dear Moberly saw the departure of his second son Arthur, a most promising youth every way. He is by this time buried in the cloisters of the College, where also Kenie's brother George is laid. And a few days before, a Coxwell, nephew of Caroline Young, 'the only son of his father, and he a widower,' died, and was buried at Hurst Pier Point. Dear Kenie is to be buried at Salcombe on Thursday next. It is, indeed, a trying, though a very soothing Christmas. This one day seems to diffuse itself, as it were, over all the twelve. You will think of us all, though I sadly feel that I never thought enough of you in your many troubles. My own dear Sister alarmed us also a good deal this day week, but I thank God that she is now apparently getting better and better.

"But, O my dear friend, what is it all in comparison, whether we and those dear to us are here a few days longer, or no. If we may but be with Him, and with one another by and by! This has been a trying year all along,—Miller, Ellison, Marriott, W. Barter,—each as he went seemed to say, 'Your Time must soon come.' Yet the comforts left are unspeakable.

"Dec 29. I could not manage to finish this yesterday, and now, lest I should be prevented again, I must go at once to business. The sum you speak of, (which in spite of your asseverations I can scarcely believe to be all mine,) may be paid to my account with D. L. and Co., Winchester, whenever it is convenient. Of course I am glad of it; but I wish people would *consider* my prose, as well as *like* my verses. Or rather, I wish that some one of real learning and ability might be raised up to *force* good people to put their minds to the truths which I believe they are instinctively acting on, though they are afraid to enunciate them in words. That is my account of this Scottish Controversy, as well as of a good deal that is going on in England. And having that view I cannot but hope that matters will be overruled, so as to spare us a Schism, though at present matters look very like it. I have not read Mr. Mansel's book, and do not at all expect I should understand it if I did. I hear people speaking very highly of it, and sadly of the need of it. . . .

"I like to hear of your visits to John, how happy they must make all parties. My love to all three generations, and especially to poor Mary, when you see her. May all go well, and may the New Year be every way happy to you, prays your loving friend, J. K."

In more than one previous letter he had spoken of the Scottish Controversy, which was much on his mind, both on account of the subject—the Holy Eucharist—and because, according to his usual mode of judging himself with severity, he fancied he had done harm by mingling in it unnecessarily and presumptuously :—

"I am paying," says he, in writing to me, "for my conceited interference, (for so I fear it must have been indeed before the All-Seeing,) with this Eucharistical question, by being made the instrument of rending (too likely) the Scottish Church. I know that in all your own cares you will find room to pray that I may be spared this."

At this time among the persons prominently engaged were two men, both of whom he had long known intimately, and both of whom he esteemed and loved very greatly — Bishop Wordsworth, and Bishop Forbes ; and he had always regarded the Scottish Episcopalian Church with deep reverence ; he had accepted with pleasure a titular canonry in the College at Cumbrae. It so happened that Dr. Pusey's ill-health had prevented Bishop Forbes from having free recourse to him, whom he ordinarily consulted in his difficulties, and so he had applied to Keble, who of course could not

shrink from answering the call made on him. He
had not obtruded himself in the matter, and I suppose no one but himself could have seen any im-
propriety, or anything like conceit or presumptuous-
ness, in his giving advice or support to one whom
he believed to be in the right, and who seemed in
danger of being overpowered.

In the May of this year, 1858, six of the bishops
of the Scottish Church had met in a special Synod,
and issued a Pastoral Letter condemnatory of a
Charge which had been delivered to his own clergy,
and published, by the seventh of their body, Bishop
Forbes. And this occasioned the publication by
Keble of " Considerations, suggested by a late Pastoral Letter on the Doctrine of the most Holy Eucharist." " Interference" by me now in a controversy
on this mysterious subject would be, indeed, to use
Keble's word, " conceited," and I shall pass it over,
except that, to prevent my leaving a wrong impression as to the spirit in which Keble interfered, I
think I ought to add an extract from one other of
his letters :—

" I have been harping on a string, which I fancy might
be pacific, if people would be so minded, between the two
Champions, Brechin and St. Andrews. My firm belief is
that they both agree in *this*, that there is in the Holy Eucharist a Presence Real in the utmost possible degree of
Reality : and that they only differ about the question, what
degree is possible, i.e. of course possible to God. And

about this, since no paramount Church Authority has expressly decided it, the right course is to allow each side to hold and teach their own opinion with express toleration of the other."

And this in truth was the spirit in which he was a controversialist. He certainly had strong opinions as to what he deemed the true faith, and they were to him matters of the holiest obligation ; he had been brought up in them, he had read deeply and largely upon them, and he thought he saw moral failures traceable to a departure from them in the belief of men. But with all this he ever made the largest allowances, and his most inward desire was for peace.

Nevertheless, I call to mind that I was uneasy at what I feared in him, the growth of a controversial spirit, and we had a little correspondence about it. I urged him to give the world some of his parochial sermons. I said :—

" I am sure you undervalue them, and the good which by God's blessing they might do. Of this I think you should let others judge. But in addition to this other and direct motive, I am also, I must confess, somewhat influenced by the effect it would have on your reputation as a Divine and Parochial Clergyman. I should be sorry that you should only be known by strangers as a controversialist. I wish they should see that the occasional short publications, which the more part never look at for fear of being ' perverted,' are as nothing to the amount of your work and teaching as Vicar of Hursley."

He answered, referring me to the neglected sermons he had published, and I replied, insisting on a volume of parochial sermons, with his name :—

"You have not tried this, and there are in my opinion two good reasons why you should, one for the good I believe they would do, the other personal, (partly so only,) that the world may be undeceived, or better informed about you, and not suppose you are merely a Controversial Divine, engaged in propping up unpopular opinions in the Church."

I went on also to urge him on to his Life of Wilson, which seemed in danger of being never finished :—

"Still another last word ; ὦ μελλήτων μελλητικώτατε, where is thy Wilson ? You are not so old as I am, and you have learned to linger by the way as much as I do. Why is it that the shorter our time, the more we loiter over our work ? Procrastination should be the thief of younger days, but she delights to gather up the lengthening shadows."

I stumbled on these letters among those returned to me, and I cannot expect others to read them with the feelings which they roused up in myself. Alas, though younger, he was not allowed so many days to loiter in and on his work, (if, indeed, I had justly accused him of loitering,) as have been allowed to me. But he did not loiter, he was continually, too continually, at work. I failed to persuade him as to the sermons, unfortunately, as I still think ; but

he undervalued his compositions; it was unpleasant
to him to undertake a selection, and a reviewal of
them for publication.   This would of course have
been necessary, but he might have bequeathed to
the Church something like the gift which Dr. Newman has left behind him, differing indeed in character in some respects, and perhaps inferior in general merit, but still a great and good gift.   In delivery he did not give his sermons the advantages
of an ordinarily eloquent preacher, but he was eminently winning; he let himself down, I do not mean
in language or argument, but in simplicity and child-
like humility, to the most uneducated of his audience; he seemed always to count himself one of
the sinners, one of the penitents, one even of the
impenitents and careless, whom he was addressing, and the very quietness, the almost tearful mo-
notony of his delivery became extremely moving,
when you recollected how learned, how able, how
moved in his own heart, and how earnest was the
preacher.

His brother, I am happy to say, is now seeking to
repair our loss in this respect by a serial issue of his
sermons, and for this we shall thank him much; but
of course he will not venture to correct them; and
it must have been desirable that Keble himself should
have had the opportunity of finally perfecting them
before publication.

I was more fortunate as to the Wilson; at least,

not long after I wrote, in the spring of 1859, he writes to me :—

"We go to Oxford a bit if we can after Whit Sunday to kill off Bp. Wilson, if possible. It would be very pleasant work if one had nothing else to do, and plenty of time to do it in. As it is, I expect it will be a good deal of a failure."

He made out this visit to Oxford, and I think Dr. Barrow, then the Principal of St. Edmund Hall, lent him his house. On his return, he wrote to me from Hursley on the 1st of August :—

"You may be quite sure that it would be a great delight to us both, if we could answer your most kind invitation in the way we desire; as one grows older, such meetings are more precious, but somehow harder to be managed ; nevertheless, I live in hope of managing it before the end of the available weather. We had a dear little two days of Dogmersfield lately. I had fancied falling in with you at this Election, but you were gone before I emerged. Somehow I am become quite a gownsman again. I like my new place as Head of a Hall very much ; how it would be if there were anything to do is another question ; and also whether it be ' tanti' as regards Bishop Wilson ; but I believe it could not be helped ; there were so many little odd points to be verified and explained. About the 15th we are to join the Wilsons at Whitby, which I hope will give Charlotte a little strength for the winter. I *may* have to go to the I. of Man again ; but if I can do without that, my dream is of the ' Sweet Shire ;' only I cannot engage."

He did not go to the Isle of Man, but he accom-

plished his scheme of a tour northward, and on the
4th of October he wrote again very cheerfully about
it, and himself :—

" One is almost ashamed to be so well and thriving oneself, when one's dear friends and betters are suffering ; but
so it is, that we have had a most enjoyable wandering ;
and my wife is thought to be looking much the better for
it.   Certainly it was a very pretty little programme of an
English Tour.   A month or 6 weeks at Oxford, revelling
in Gardens and Libraries, which we had all to ourselves ;
a fortnight's sea-whiff at Whitby, 2 days at York, and 1 at
Rivaulx Abbey ; 4 or 5 at the Wilsons at Baldersby, near
Ripon ; 1 at old Collins's at Knaresborough ; 3 at Hubert
Cornish's, near Chatsworth and the Peak ; 1 at G. Mackar-
ness's, near Isaac Walton ; and a week at Bisley, including
the Elijah, at Gloster Music ; where the two old Codger
Kebles were seen sitting side by side."

I have not thought it right to go into the details
which Keble's letters furnish me with as to the part
he took in what he called the Scottish troubles ; it
would not have accorded with the rule which it
seemed proper to lay down for myself in this Memoir ; and as I trust they are now happily composed
on charitable principles, it would be clearly wrong
on all accounts to incur the least risk of reviving the
feelings of the past ; and this I might have done, intending nothing less, even by the most accurate and
careful use of my materials ; which, however, it must
be remembered, are all from one side.   But one of

Keble's letters of February 21, 1860, from which I must make an extract, reminds me of an incident which ought not to be passed over, as shewing his heartiness and activity in rendering help to a dear friend in distress :—

" I was most glad of your letter, for I was longing for some account of you ; but I wish you could have reported more cheerily of your belongings. Why did you not say a word about your own self? We are scrambling through the cold as well as we can, but C. feels it a good deal, E. less, I think, in proportion. I am rather frightened at the returns of the C. Y., what shall I do with it all ? Of late all one's spare time has been taken up with turning over Indices of Anglo-Catholic Divines, Benedictine Fathers, &c., on behalf of our dear Lord of Brechin ; moreover, I actually ran down to Dun-Edin, and was there the week before last, from Tuesday morning till Friday afternoon, i.e. during the whole of the pleadings ; but I was in Court only on the Thursday to hear Mr. Henderson; for I lay *perdu* until I had ascertained that my presence would not provoke the Bishops. I fraternized with Moray, Argyll, and St. A. ; and whatever they mean to do as Judges, they were personally very kind."

I have been favoured with some anecdotes of his visit from members of the family with which he was a guest at the time, from which I will make extracts :—

" His first visit to Edinburgh was in the inclement month of February, 1860. It was cold snowy weather, and he arrived at 8 in the morning after travelling all night. It was the first day of the trial. He did not go to Court, but confined himself to calling upon his old friend the Bishop of St. Andrews, who returned his visit. He spent most of that day with my sisters, and was much amused by being told of an aged Aunt of ours, who had worn out many copies of the 'Christian Year,' and had it by heart. He talked of its success with great enjoyment and playfulness. He spoke of his Life of Wilson, and when found looking over the book-cases, said, 'I always look at books to see if I can find anything about Bp. Wilson.' He noticed the Portrait of our Uncle, Mr. Cumming Bruce, whom he had not seen since he was an Undergraduate at Corpus, adding 'I remember him quite well, a nice pleasant fellow he was.'

"Our friends crowded to see him. There was a very atmosphere of peace and restfulness in which he moved. He gave comfort to every one, though matters then seemed critical. That day he dined with my sisters.

"On the 8th, the second day of the trial, he was in Court, and his presence there was an object of interest to all. All in the crowd tried to catch a glimpse of his snowy head. The remembrance of those calm features, contrasting so markedly with the excited faces in the midst of all the turmoil, will never be forgotten by me. There was, however, an expression of profound distress upon his countenance. He dined that day with Mr. Forbes of Medwyn, where he was delighted with the children. One of these, at that time aged sixteen, thus recorded her impressions of him. 'He is old and short, with white hair, and rather plain features; but he has such a sweet heavenly expression. His voice is rather low; we cannot hear him, unless he is close to us. He is so kind, and takes such interest in the little ones. Aunt A. calls him her good old angel, and really he has such a sweet winning sort of manner, that it must make every one like and look up to him, giving one the idea that he must be one of those, who, our Saviour has said, are converted, and become as little children.'

"One day he did not go to Court, saying that he would rest, and would best do so by playing with the children, two boys of six and nine years of age respectively. He crept about on the floor, shewing them how to put up a new toy locomotive, which had been given them."

Keble again went to Edinburgh in March, 1860, although suffering much from rheumatism, when the Synod pronounced its judgment ; it was unfavourable to the Bishop, but very much milder in tone than had been expected, and a great relief upon the whole to his friends. It had been thought worth while through the whole proceeding to consult Patteson and myself, and we all three had considered carefully, (what Keble called the δεύτερος πλοῦς,) the course to be pursued by the Bishop in case a suspension should be awarded. Keble's opinion was that the Bishop should not stand out on what he might consider his strict right, but act charitably and submit :—

"His course," he said, "I apprehend should be to submit to his suspension, and remain in Dundee, visiting and school keeping, and doing works of mercy, but refraining from any Episcopal Act. Then his Clergy, whom he thinks very much of, might keep their places, and his witness would be borne to the truth."

I need scarcely say that in advice such as this Patteson and I heartily concurred, and it is cause of much thankfulness to me that our excellent friend has been for many years, and still is engaged in the discharge of his duties pastoral and episcopal in Dundee and Brechin, to the great comfort and profit of those over whom he is set. And I can scarcely doubt that even those who differed from him most widely and most warmly, must be thankful now that no such victory was obtained by them as might have led to a schism in their small body.

For a long time the name of Elizabeth Keble had appeared but little, and seldom in his letters; her life flowed on in an even course, and much as he consulted her, and was probably influenced by her, yet all she said or did was in so quiet a way as to be little noticeable; and her health, never strong, was yet not interrupted by violent illnesses, as was the case with Mrs. Keble's.

But from this time a change began; in truth her heavenly Father was preparing her and him too by more direct notices for the summons, which she was about to receive. I have no doubt both interpreted the indications correctly. I am sure he did, though he clung to every little apparent amendment with natural fondness. It was not very long, however, before her course was ended, and I shall extract what he wrote about her during the interval.

On the 4th of April, 1860, he says :—

" My two Companions, especially my Sister, seem to me almost always this winter more or less on the edge of illness, but have hitherto been kept from being quite ill, except Elizabeth's weakness, which is sometimes extreme, may be counted for an illness."

She had somewhat mended as the weather grew more genial, but it was the flickering lighting-up of a sinking patient :—

" She gets out," he says, on June 28, " in a sort of Bath Chair almost every day, but is *very* weak, and has a regular nurse, besides her servant. Tom staid, I think, 3 Sundays here, and it was such a comfort. My wife is about as she has been. I fear as things are, it will be hardly right for us to go a visiting this summer; if we do, I trust we shall get to you, at least for a short time. How strangely things seem to be twisting themselves both in Church and State. Ever your loving and hurried, J. K."

On July 16, he begins a very short note thus, (my dear sister's 70th birthday). " Dearest Coleridge .... Elizabeth continues much as yesterday, not *quite* so comfortable."

She died on the 7th of August, and on the same day he wrote to me thus :—

" Dearest dear Friend,

" Our sweet sister left us this morning, having been apparently on the verge of departure for ten days or more, during which time, and to some extent before it, she could be hardly said to have full consciousness at any time.....
The last 18 hours were nearly all spent in sleep, like that of a little child, till at 9.20 this morning, with the very slightest start, but with no expression, that I could see, of pain or

distress, she was gone.   I, indeed, did not see it, though I was very near her, reading now and then a verse from some Psalm, (which had all along been what she was feeling after). I fancied she still breathed, and went on for a while ; at last I doubted it, and asked the Nurse, who said 'she has been gone this quarter of an hour,' so you may judge how quiet it was, and from the nature of the illness we had greatly feared it might have been otherwise. . . . She will be buried here, D. V., next Saturday, not far from dear little Godfrey Heathcote, so that it will yet seem for the short time that remains very like going to Church with her daily ; and one ought to be very thankful that it is so, for it would be a strange world to one, dear friend, to be altogether without her ; for 20 years of health, and 50 of sickness, always at hand, or always within reach ; and never a look, nor a word, that I know of, but was wise and kind, with the true kindness and wisdom.   Only it makes an old man's heart sink to reflect what one might have been, with such helps, and many many more, and what one really is.   One comfort is, that those helps, and you among the rest, will remember one all the more earnestly.   I have never thanked you for your last loving letter, which will now be worth two to me, so entirely had you realized what has happened.   Mrs. Bliss, as you know, has been most kind and helpful ; I wish she were not going.   The Heathcotes come here the 18th ; with all's love to all, ever yours, J. K."

There is surely something very solemn and affecting in the picture which Keble has here drawn of himself kneeling by the side of this dear and saintly sister's deathbed, from time to time slowly reading a verse of a psalm, which her parting spirit was, as he expresses it, " feeling after."   And if she ceased

to breathe while he continued to read, is it presumptuous, or irreverent, or unreasonable, to believe
that she might still hear the familiar words, it may
be with a new and enlarged apprehension, and more
unmixed delight ; and, it may be, still see the loved
brother ; not hearing, nor seeing, as we hear and
see, but perceiving by a clearer and purer intuition
all the meaning of the words of inspiration which
he uttered.

The nursing, and the parting with Elizabeth, had
pressed heavily on Mrs. Keble's feeble frame, and
very soon after the funeral Keble was constrained
to take her to Dawlish, and there they remained for
some weeks, close to the sea ; but she was more helpless than usual in her illnesses, both as to breathing
and walking, and recovered but very slowly. He
was himself a good deal depressed when he wrote
to me on the 29th of August, from No. 12, Marine
Parade, there :—

" I have," says he, " a sort of awful, yet soothing impression of it all ; will you pray that it may never leave me ;
but you cannot imagine how quickly I forget. We think of
staying here a week longer, in hope that by that time C.
will be a little recruited; and then going on to Vineyard
and Brooking."

The proposed stay at Dawlish was prolonged,
owing to renewed illnesses of Mrs. Keble, nearly all
through September, and it was not until early in
October that he dated his letters from Brooking.

The loss of his sister was a heavy blow to him, but I need not enlarge on it; he has himself in his letter stated in few words all the circumstances that made it so great a trial. Nor was it the only bereavement which he had within a short time sustained. Just when his sister's illness was becoming a source of anxiety, Charles Dyson's declining state of health had terminated in his death; and this was in many ways a great affliction to Keble. Nothing could be heartier than the love he had for this friend of his youth, or more entire than the confidence he reposed in this counsellor of his maturer years. He could ill afford to lose such an elder brother now, when he had been bereaved in succession of so many whom he loved and leaned on; it seemed to leave him so nearly alone. In an early part of my memoir I have spoken of Dyson, his death, and funeral. At the gathering which then took place, the setting up a memorial had been agreed on, and Keble bestirred himself with pious assiduity in collecting the necessary contributions, and helping to determine on the manner in which it should be carried out. Finally this was effected by placing two stained-glass windows in the parish church of Dogmersfield, and in settling the designs for these he took a principal part. I may add before I leave this mention of Dyson, that it was a concurrent thought of Mrs. Keble and Mrs. Dyson, joyfully accepted by Keble that Mrs. and Miss Dyson should take shelter under his wing in the old parsonage at Hursley for the winter, while the arrangements for a new habitation for them at Church Crookham in the neighbourhood of Dogmersfield should be completed. This plan was carried into effect, to the great delight of the Kebles, and the comfort of the bereaved widow and sister.

In their way from Brooking to Bisley and their home, the Kebles came to us on the 5th of October, which was on a Friday, and left us on the following Monday. These short visits it is now very pleasant and touching to remember; and I refresh my recollection of the particulars by my memoranda made at the time. I see I noticed his peculiarly kind and loving manner; as we parted on the Monday, he turned his cheek to me to kiss it. My entry concludes with a hope " that I might be spared for another such meeting, and that I might have wisdom to seek the opportunity more frequently than I had done." Wisdom alas, which indolence and procrastination, and engagements more fancied than real, prevented me from acting upon as I might have done. He preached in our church on the 7th of October; my comment at the time was this:—

" One of those truly Christian sermons, opening out the Scripture, full of citations from it, going directly to the heart that would open to receive it; affectionate, earnest, true, and high; but very simple, very unadorned, just as I suppose St. John might have preached when an old man, and one which perhaps the mere itching ear would receive with indifference, and the mere literary intellectualist despise."

I have ventured to transcribe this, because I really think now that it is not an inaccurate account of his parochial sermons generally.

Thus characteristically he wrote of his little stay with us on his arrival at Bisley :—

" It is no use for me to pretend to thank you properly for all your love and kindness to my dear wife and myself, so I must be content with loving you more and more, and *you* in this passage means, ' te cum tuis.'   It was quite spoiling, and high time to come away."

This has been a melancholy chapter in respect of the bereavements and trials with which it pleased God to visit Keble at this time, and it must end in the same strain.   The winter of 1860-1, was passed at Hursley ; in the early part of the summer Mrs. Keble's cough drove them to Sea View in the Isle of Wight.   He knew that I was anxiously watching the close of my dear brother Patteson's long and hopeless illness ; and he entirely sympathized with me. Comparatively speaking, there had been personal intercourse between the two only at long intervals, and then only for short periods ; nor did they correspond ; but Keble had a very great regard for him, and the very highest opinion of him.

On the 2nd of June he wrote to me from Hursley :—

" Being here for a Sunday while my wife and nephew,

and three children, are at Sea View, I am going to try and write you a regular letter, for indeed I long to talk with you, and wish I could see you. Yet it seems almost profane to interrupt you with any kind of talk in your present employment, which must keep you so consciously on that edge where we all are. It does seem most soothing to think of dear Patteson from time to time, and of his child-like unconsciousness that he was anything out of the common, which must now seem more than ever like a gift from above."

On the 28th of June this great lawyer and judge, and good man, was summoned to his rest. Keble, to whom I communicated the intelligence, wrote to me thus on the 3rd of July :—

"I am shocked to think that so many posts have gone, and I have not told you any part of my thoughts about you and dear Patteson ; about yourself I think most, for it will be such a sad gap to you ; one feels that nothing in this world can make it up. As for him, he seems too high and noble for one even to try and follow in imagination. I should like always to connect him in memory with ' the righteous hath hope in his death,' hope in this world as well as *there.* Does it not seem like a sign from Heaven, that just before his going he did, as it were, receive the message that God had accepted his son, whom he ' had lent unto the Lord' for as long as he should live ? One comfort in thinking of him, at least to a man with a bad memory like mine, is that there was something so very *distinctive* in him, traits and tones to make an impression to be remembered all one's life even by one who now regrets more than ever that he had not seen more of him."

Keble here alludes to the manner in which Patteson had devoted his eldest son to God's service. With the fullest sense of his own loss, yet with the most unhesitating heartiness he had given up one who was dearer to him than life. He gave him up at a time when his presence was most cheering, and his help much needed and readily afforded, he being in charge of a small Chapelry within short walking distance from Feniton Court. No father and son could be more tenderly united, none could feel separation more sensibly, but neither wavered for an instant in their resolution. The son parted from his aged father in 1855, never to see him again on this side the grave ; and he has never re-visited England since. It was a great pleasure and gratification to his father very shortly before his own death to hear of his son's consecration as Missionary Bishop to the South Sea Islands ; in which office he has ever since laboured unceasingly, under what trials, and through what dangers, and with what success, I must not in this place attempt to describe.

CHAPTER XIX.

KEBLE'S SELF-DISSATISFACTION, AND THOUGHTS OF
RESIGNATION. — OXFORD LOCAL EXAMINATIONS.
—MRS. KEBLE'S ALARMING ILLNESS. — MOVE TO
SEA VIEW.—FIRST VISIT TO PENZANCE.—BISHOP
WILSON'S LIFE COMPLETED.—CHURCH DISCIPLINE.
—COURT OF FINAL APPEAL IN CASES OF DOC-
TRINE. — BISHOP OF WINCHESTER'S CHARGE.—
COMMENTARY ON THE BIBLE.—FIRST STAY AT
PENZANCE.—RETURN TO HURSLEY. — JUDGMENT
IN LONG *v.* BISHOP OF CAPETOWN.—FIRST VISIT
TO TORQUAY IN JANUARY, 1864.—SECOND STAY
AT PENZANCE, APRIL, 1864.

K EBLE began the year 1862 in good health, and
quiet spirits, yet somewhat anxious on one or
two subjects, and a little dispirited at heart. There
seems to have been a visible change for the worse
in Mrs. Keble's health; the state of his parish did
not satisfy him; and the accounts he received from
Oxford, especially in regard to the "Essays and
Reviews," at one time so much talked of, troubled
him. Mrs. Keble's decline, indeed, was not so marked
at the very beginning of the year, though even then
he notices that she was "a poor hand at locomotion

of any kind," and was indebted for what she had "to Jack the Donkey," whom she drove. But I will extract parts of his first letter for the year, dated on the First Sunday after the Epiphany :—

"I had rather," says he, "wish you joy of the Peace, and of the good feeling towards the Queen, and ask you when you are going to take us and Heathcote, as your duty is, in the way to or from London. Time steals on, and I am now 'in the seventy of mine age,' and I suppose it would be a wholesome thing, if one could always feel as if every visit, and every letter might be the last. But really my health is wonderful, as it has been all my life. What a talent to account for, alas ! . . .

"I cannot give a good account of my parish, people are sadly disappointing, and neither 'true religion, nor useful learning,' appear to me to flourish and abound. I often think that 'tempus abire tibi est,'—do think of it for me a little calmly,—and yet I creep on from day to day, fancying that perhaps I may do better, and quite ashamed to think of the condition in which my successor would find things, if I were to make a vacancy at present. 'Too late, too late,' are the words that haunt me from morning to night ; and sometimes I wish I had been at a public school, that I might be a man of business, and get on with things as I ought. You must not imagine though that I am low-spirited, I am only too jolly ; but this is the point of view in which I see things when I consider them calmly. O wretched Self, how durst thou take up all this paper. Well, God bless you and yours in both hemispheres, dearest friend, prays J. K."

These despondent remarks about himself, partly

perhaps attributable to transient depression of spirits, were however characteristic of him, and his abiding humility; but I reminded him in answer, of what he had said on other occasions, that it was not for us to measure ourselves by what we seem to effect in the path before us; that results are not in our hands, and that in his line this is especially true; we do not always know for certain what they are, we can neither measure the failures nor the successes; that much good may have been effected which no human eye will ever see, much which will appear only after a long interval. I wrote very strongly against his notion of retirement, and I heard no more of it; until some time after, when the necessity for long absences from Hursley was more pressing, and threatening to recur more often, and when therefore there was more ground for consideration of the question.

His letter had touched on some other points, one in particular, the Oxford Local Examinations, the results of which he appeared to contemplate uneasily. Not that he was unfavourable to advancement in the education of the middle classes, but that he thought the religious element was either neglected in this scheme, or even excluded. He did not speak from personal knowledge, and I thought his information not correct. I went, therefore, fully into the subject with him according to the knowledge which I then had. In the years that have

since passed my interest in the movement has never
flagged; it has seemed to me that the original principle was both wise and benevolent, and that in some
particulars, which were perhaps objectionable, and
which have been now much modified, the motives of
the originators, and the University, were misunderstood by their opponents. The fears which these last
entertained have, so far as I know, turned out to have
been groundless, or exaggerated, and the general results have been good. I can hardly doubt that in
one respect they have been so; the improvement
namely of schools and schoolmasters in the class
which certainly needed it. Still I think the time
has come for an enquiry as to the moral and intellectual effects of the experiment on young persons
of the middle class; are they really more or less
informed, more or less advanced in morals and religious habits? The enquiry might be difficult, but
there are materials now for conducting it effectually;
and it is surely very desirable to ascertain whether or
no this part of society has or has not been leavened
as one could wish by the system; for it cannot be
but that some considerable results for good or evil
have flowed from it. The whole matter is so important that I shall be excused, I trust, for these
observations.

My answer to Keble's letter, (to return,) was long,
and he knew I was unwell, and forbidden to write
much. I mention this only to account in some mea-

sure for the more than usual affectionateness of his reply, which I do not like to suppress, and cannot of course alter :—

"DEAREST DEAR COLERIDGE,

"I am full of thoughts about you, very sorry to hear of your trial, (only that by His blessing one feels sure how all trials will turn out for you,) and very much wishing that I could see you for at least an hour every day. But you *must* not write me long letters. It will spoil the pleasure of them to think of the result to yourself. I thank you for this one all the same, it will do me I hope much good.

"C. was, indeed, very ill for a while last Monday Night. The spasms on her chest so violent that I was quite frightened. Ether and hot steam in the room relieved her, and she is now well enough to be downstairs great part of the day, but very weak, and never sure but the gasping may return. D. G. we have I think a very nice doctor in the village, else I hardly know how we should have fared."

It seems to have been, indeed, a frightful attack. From a later letter it appears it had been described to him by his medical attendant as "spasmodic asthma literally stopping the action of the arteries;" and well might he say that it was a providential mercy that skilful relief was at hand in the village. If he had been obliged to send to Romsey, and wait for a medical man coming thence, the attack must have ended fatally, as life could not have been sustained for half an hour in the state in which at one period she appears to have been.

The attack left her in great weakness, from which

she recovered slowly, and it was not until May that she was strong enough to move for change of air, even so far as the Isle of Wight. He wrote to me on the 7th of that month from Sea View; he was then still in continual apprehension of a return of "those dreadful spasms," and he was perhaps the more sensitive in his feelings from having just met Mrs. Cornish, and seeing her greatly shaken and altered :—

" It really," says he, " makes one afraid and ashamed to think of one's own (now 70) years of uninterrupted health, along with the sufferings of so many persons so unlike one-self. It would be a charity if people would sometimes in their Litanies pray for the *very* healthy, *very* prosperous, *very* lighthearted, *very much* bepraised, &c. . . . .

" Now give our love to your wife and daughter, and such other belongings as are near you, and to dear Devonshire with its primroses, which it must be hard work for the Pixies to count this year; and believe me ever (I hope) yours, J. K."

They returned to Hursley in June, Mrs. Keble in a very precarious and uncertain state :—

" She came home," he says, writing on the 13th of June, " on Wednesday week, certainly the better for the sea, &c., but far from well ; that, indeed, we dare not look for in this world. Since then she has not fallen off, except for the last few days ; her breath was the worse for something in the weather on Tuesday, and she has hardly got back to the same point again. But she coughs very little, and writes, and reads, and plays, and keeps accounts ; she cannot teach, or visit cottages, but drives out, wind and weather permitting ; her going to Church is exceptional."

In this state of her health he was wisely advised to consult high medical authority in London, and he did so, Dr. Williams. The result he communicated to Mr. Wilson, and to me, which it is unnecessary to state in detail. But one particular was the positive forbiddance to remain at Hursley during the winter ; it was recommended to winter abroad, but Devon and Cornwall were acquiesced in ; and after some hesitation Keble determined in the first instance to try Penzance.

He wrote to me on the 8th of October from that place. They had rested in their way at Plymouth, refusing all solicitations to stop anywhere else ; and the first effects of the change to Penzance were so promising, that he sent home for his heavy luggage, and resolved to pass the winter there. He announces his resolution to me characteristically enough :—

" Her breath is relieved, and her walking powers improved ; she walked along this Esplanade, and looked over the lodgings upstairs and down without being fatigued, and then enjoyed a three hours' drive, and it was altogether summerish and delightful. On Sunday she went to the full morning Service ; and it was what my Sister would have called ' a very pleasant Church.' For these and other reasons, including the goodness of certain mackerel and apples, &c., that we have made acquaintance with, we have made up our minds to try a winter here, and have sent for our heavy luggage, which we had left on the road. . . .

"What a beautiful and comfortable circumstance it is of this great development of our Missions, that quiet people are come naturally without thinking of it, or writing *in a tone*, to pour out their hearts mutually to those whom they suppose to be like-minded, from the other side of the world ; just as the old folks did in the very old centuries. S. Cyprian, (e.g.) not to mention S. Paul. I say this apropos to the South Pacific, and South African Letters, which have been so much of our reading of late. It really does seem to help one in a very special way to realize the Communion of Saints, and to feel (D.V.) one not only with the distant living, but with the holy dead. What a comforting thought (among many more) for those who were mainly instrumental in the Colonial Episcopate at first. . . . .

"Your calling —— a 'middle rate' biographer, makes a certain friend of yours wince ; you can easily guess why. I do hope at any rate *that* will be soon off my hands. . . .

"I wish you could see the Mount as I do now every time I look up from my writing, with the tenderest of hazy light and shade upon it. We have got a kind cousin, Fanny Coxwell, to help take care of C., and a very great little comfort she is. And so with dear love to you all, I am as ever your lazy and affectionate, J. K."

Their first house was chosen with special reference to Mrs. Keble, "in the very best position," says he, "for seeing the whole of Mount's Bay, and feeling and hearing all that the wild waves had to tell us." Indeed, they soon found that the wild waves had somewhat too much to tell them, and they were obliged to move to a house higher up, and more distant from them. But he took intense and never-failing delight in that most beautiful Bay, sweeping round on his right, with a shore gently rising from the sea; and guarded as it were by St. Michael's Mount nearly in his front, crowned with the stately and picturesque castle and church on its summit. I have no doubt that the view was a never-failing delight to him; and to him, a mere Saxon, there was interest in the novelty, almost the strangeness, of the Cornish race, their language, and customs. But more than this; as they prolonged their stay, they were touched with the hearty kindness with which they were received, especially by the clergy; the impression which his first Sunday had made on him was deepened by more familiar intercourse, and so far as he could be, he got reconciled to the enforced absence from Hursley.

The allusion to his Wilson gave me great pleasure, much increased when, on the 22nd of November, he wrote:—

"What you will be glad to hear of, the last sheet of Bp. Wilson's Life is gone to the press, and only a little correction and some notes, with a small part of the Preface, remain to be done. I only wish any body may have the same pleasure in reading, that I have had in writing it; but that of course is a romantic idea. Suppose it, however, to do some of the kind of good one would wish, what will that be to having been a beginner and prime agent in the Co-

lonial Episcopate Fund ; the fruit of which, by God's great
blessing, we are allowed to see more and more."

This was his too kind way of alluding to my exceedingly small services as one of the Treasurers of
the Fund he speaks of ; but I do not pass it by in
silence, because in the beginning he had for some
reason looked rather coldly on the movement ; and
it was and is a great pleasure to me now to recall
with what a different feeling he grew to regard it.

Early in 1863 the Life of Bishop Wilson was published, and it formed in two parts the first of seven
volumes, which contain, I believe, a complete collection of the Bishop's works.   They are part of the
series of the Anglo-Catholic Library, and certainly
no English Churchman's library ought to be without
them.   It is now well known how shamefully the
Sacra Privata were treated by those who first professed to give them to the public ; treated so, I fear,
for party purposes.   Keble was very earnest in re-
storing that work to its integrity.   Much had been
already done in that way, and in presenting it in an
attractive and convenient form before his volume appeared ; but he still looked on what he had done for
it with more satisfaction than was usual with him as
to anything on which he had been employed.   He
was not given to praise his own performances ; but I
remember he said to me once that his volume might
be less attractive in appearance, and less portable,
and so less convenient for a manual, but that it

would be found, he believed, the most correct and full edition which had yet seen the light. As the Bishop's character was one which he most admired and loved, so this work was a special delight to him, and justly so. Many persons, I fear, are deterred from becoming familiar with it, because at first sight it seems to have so much to do with the writer exclusively in his character of Bishop, and they suppose, therefore, it can have little application to themselves; but let them persevere, and if I mistake not, they will not only be moved with the unconsciously-drawn picture of so much goodness, greatness, and holiness, but find also abundance of that which is practical for themselves. Indeed, there is a homely affectionate simplicity in everything which Wilson writes of this sort, that makes it specially fitting for the purposes of a Christian Manual.

It will have been seen how Keble speaks of the pleasure he had had in writing the Life; it was with him truly a labour of love; he wrote it carefully, and it is, I believe, perfectly trustworthy, telling us all that can be known of Wilson, and considerably more than was known before. Still it is thought to labour under the fault of being long-some; its very fulness may have contributed to this; in truth, it tells more than ordinary readers may care to know of its subject.

My readers will have long ago seen what were Keble's opinions respecting Church discipline; it was unfortunate, I think, for the work, that Bishop Wilson not only felt about this as strongly, and in the same way, but laboured during nearly the whole of his episcopate to enforce its practice. On these sustained efforts Keble naturally dwells with interest, and in much detail. It seems to me with great deference, that the conclusion in his mind might have been, (and I am not sure that it was not,) that however desirable, indeed however a duty of strict obligation in itself, it was hopeless to attempt a revival of it in our days, and in our country. If a bishop such as Wilson, so able, so venerated, and so loved, could not succeed in a diocese so small as that of Man, with a population so much more simple than our own, what could be hoped for in England at this time? But beyond this, I cannot say that even in the instances in which what is called success is recorded, I see very satisfactory evidence of *real* success. The power of the Church, indeed, was maintained in the particular instances ; she did punish the evil-doers, and they submitted ; but the impression left on the reader's mind is that the submission was too often made in order to escape the continuing temporal inconvenience rather than that the penance ended in real penitence.

"Non hoc tempus Censuræ" was the saying of Tiberius, when it was proposed to revive that office in vigour ; certainly an adviser whom one would not listen to without distrust ; yet to attempt the reform of manners in Imperial Rome by the Censorship, and in the Christian Church by Ecclesiastical Discipline, have this in common, that the one and the other were equally but means to an end, and that end in many respects the same. Now the fitness of means must depend very much on the circumstances under which they are to be used ; what might be available and good in the early days of Rome, and of the Church respectively, might be far otherwise in the days of Tiberius, or those on which we are fallen. I speak it with diffidence and unfeigned respect for my dear friend, with whom these subjects were a life-long study; but it even seems to me a fallacy to refer *everything* as he did to the standard of the Primitive Church ; and to be unwise, because unpractical. If I am asked what I would substitute for the ancient Discipline, I feel how utterly unfit I am to answer the question ; and with that feeling on my mind I yet venture to say that the pastoral care, and the influence under God's blessing on it, of *a really laborious, learned, self-denying, prayerful, and exemplary clergy*, may be at least more practical, and at all events it is that without which all other means must fail.

I have been led astray from my proper subject, Keble's Life of Bishop Wilson. I shall have done it injustice, if I leave my readers with an unfavourable impression of it on the whole. He might, indeed, no one more successfully, have caught his inspiration from Isaac Walton, and left us a tale to

be bound up with *his* immortal narratives. I wish
he had ; but I cannot wish he had not written *this*
Life, for it is the storehouse of facts, faithfully recorded, in which is contained all that can be known
of an Apostolic Bishop ; to which, indeed, whoever
desires to write something more popular must, and
may safely, have recourse for his materials.

Yet there was a branch of this subject on which I
could not and cannot but think there was much real
ground for Keble's uneasiness. I mean that a modern
Statute should have placed in the hands of the Judicial Committee of the Privy Council, assisted by two
or three of the bishops, not selected for personal fitness as judges, but in virtue of their sees, the final
decision of questions touching the doctrine and discipline of the Church. Even if the Committee were
necessarily composed of Churchmen, there would be
the question, whether such matters are properly to
be adjudicated on by laymen ; but it is well known,
that among its members may be those who are conscientiously, or otherwise, not only alien from the
Church, but opposed to it. And the evil has this
peculiarity in it, to which attention should be drawn.
Where *any* court has jurisdiction to determine the
point directly in issue before it, it has necessarily
for *the purpose of arriving at its determination*, jurisdiction to decide on *any* point collaterally arising, the
decision of which is necessary to the determination
of the point at issue. Thus a single judge and jury
at the Assizes have jurisdiction to try an action for

libel; suppose a beneficed clergyman should sue in such an action for the publication of a writing which imputed to him that he had taught something in derogation of one of the Articles; it might become necessary on the trial not only to decide on the fact of publication, and the meaning of the language used, but also the meaning of the Article alleged to have been derogated from. Rightly or wrongly the judge would have *in that case* to lay down the law of the Church; and if he interpreted the Article wrongly, he would *for the time*, and for the purpose of the cause, impose a new doctrine; but neither his ruling, nor the judgment consequent on it, would bind judge or court, bishop or clerk, in any other case. The Judicial Committee, on the other hand, often takes cognisance of the doctrine directly and as the point in issue; and it does so in the last resort; its decision binds every court, and even itself; so that if it should happen to determine certain propositions not to be contrary to the Articles, or *vice versa*, however manifestly wrong or dangerous the decision, those propositions might be maintained and preached by any incumbent to his flock with impunity; and to preach propositions logically contradictory of them might subject an incumbent to prosecution and its consequences. It cannot be doubted that this would practically be very much the same thing as making a new doctrine for the Church. There are some, it is said an increasing number, to whom this gives no pain, because they hold doctrine to be of little importance; but even these, if candid, would admit that it must be very grievous to those who hold, as Christians in general do, and have done from the beginning, that definiteness and truth in doctrine are essential to the Church in the discharge of her function, as keeper of the Faith, and teacher of the people.

Keble was one of these, and the matter touched his conscience. The judgment in what is known as the " Essays and Reviews" Case gave him, in all its circumstances, as well as the decision itself, great pain, and he wrote several letters to me ; for he rightly enough had no scruples in doing so merely because I was a member of the committee. He was not always accurate in his knowledge, and I think he did not see at first all the difficulties of forming an unexceptionable tribunal ; nor did I always agree with his inferences or propositions. I do not think I should do any good by printing the whole correspondence ; but I may perhaps revive the attention of those who might do good, by quoting some extracts from his letters to shew what a real grievance to men like him still exists :—

" PENZANCE,
" *Jan*^{ry} 7, 1863.

" DEAREST COLERIDGE,

" Thank you for your kind letter, and patience in explaining to me all the difficulties of the case. I have no doubt it *is* full of difficulty, but then I consider that Lawyers and Statesmen are the very people to whom one is to complain of one's difficulties, as one tells a Doctor when one is ill. I do hope that our friends in those professions will believe that we are really ill, (so to speak,) and not mere valetudinarians. I hope they will give themselves no rest till they have thoroughly looked into the matter, and *either* devised something which will not positively hinder the Church from executing its commission, as the present Law does, *or* ascertained and reported that no such course can be adopted consistently with the present relations of the Church to the State. Until one of these two things is done, there must be perpetual ' fears and jealousies,' until we waked up some morning and found ourselves without Creed or Discipline,—without Discipline we are indeed at present.

" Don't suppose that I am setting up my judgment on the legal and political view; I am really thinking, or trying to think, of the souls which, I believe, are daily and hourly perishing through disregard of our Lord's Ordinance. I would thankfully make use of qualified Laymen to any extent, consistently with the ' Discipline of Christ,' to which we are all sworn, and the grace for which is given us, if we are worthy, at our ordination, in our several degrees. These miserable Essay and Review Cases, more I think than anything which has happened, have brought out the fact, that the present Law of England absolutely quashes that Discipline, and also that other fact, that acquiescence in such a state of things is fast tending, as I said, to nullify our Creed. I should think *something* might be done; your reference to the Bishops, for instance, or what was it that Bp. Blomfield proposed? But do you really think that a Clergyman aware of all this should not complain of it, unless he can suggest the forms of a Parliamentary Remedy? Among other effects of things as they are, Dr. Wiseman, &c., are making a good deal of gain, as you doubtless know better than I."

What Keble calls my "reference to the Bishops," was a suggestion I had thrown out, and of which I still think *something might be made,* that in order to separate the fact, including the mere construction of the language charged to be heretical, from the doctrine itself, the Committee might ascertain the two former, and then refer to a Court of bishops to state the doctrine, and applying that to the finding of the Committee, certify the conclusion on the issue to the Committee, which should be binding on it.   This seemed to me a way to give to each branch of the tribunal what it was most competent to perform satisfactorily, relieve the minds of Churchmen, and, as far as could be, keep the doctrine of the Church from change.   Lawyers will know that my hint was borrowed from the practice, now obsolete, of trial by the Bishop's Certificate, of which some account will be found in Blackstone's "Commentaries," vol. iii. p. 335, and also from the practice of the House of Lords to put questions to the Judges on a statement of facts which the House deems to be *cardines causæ;* and usually though not necessarily, to decide the case according to the answers given.

But I was of opinion, (and this I ought not to withhold now,) that nothing could be hopefully devised to forward Keble's views, until the clergy were to some extent educated in law, and accustomed by some training, as hearers at least, to the practice of courts; it seemed to me that the most learned divine could not be fit to act as judge, without that training or experience which is so essential to constitute the judicial habit of mind.

Keble wrote to me subsequently on this subject thus :—

" PENZANCE,
Jan. 8, '63.

" MY DEAREST COLERIDGE,

" Suppose I was to dream such a dream as what follows, would it have any meaning or no ?

" That six or 8 men, good and true, were sitting cosily together some time before Parliament meets, and that their initials were such as J. T. C., W. H., W. E. G., R. P., R. Ph., E. B. P., S. O., &c., &c.

" That it were represented to them somehow what an unconstitutional position the Church of England is in. It is as a corporation having its own bye-laws, which to it are fundamental, and which the State professes to respect. Among those laws are,—

" 1st. All must hold a certain prescribed Faith, or be excluded from the Society.

" 2. The measure of that Faith is, ' Quod semper, quod ubique,' &c., being also scriptural.

" 3. The Judicial Power in regard of alleged offences against this Faith has been entrusted by the Founder of the Society to persons nominated by Him for the purpose.

" But our present Statute Law,—

" 1. Virtually annuls the penalty, viz. Excommunication.

" 2. Substitutes, in the case of Clerks, (the only case in which it allows the Church to take cognizance of any such offence,) another rule, a certain Statute of Q. Elizabeth.

" 3. Takes the judgment and decree out of the hands of those ordained by the Founder, and sworn by the order of the State itself, to administer in such causes.

" Then I might perhaps go on and dream that the said revered and highly-valued initials were set to a sentence allowing that there is more or less of truth and reason in the said complaints, and that the grievances are real grievances.

" And of course I could not then doubt that they would lay their heads together to consider what should be done.

" Would it be beyond the absurdity allowable even in one's sleep, if I dreamed again and fancied them considering about an experiment in mitigation of the mischief ?

" 1. Whether it is impossible to obtain a law taking away *all* temporal penalties, annexed to excommunication, and leaving the Church really free to enforce its own rubric and canons in case of notorious sin or unbelief. Might not something analogous to a trial by jury be invented in aid of the Bishops ?

" 2. Might there not be a declaratory Act to the effect that the Formularies must always be interpreted agreeably to Holy Scripture and general consent, (as in the Act of the 1st of Elizabeth the decrees of Œcumenical councils were made part of the measure of Henry ?) To which Act the assent of Convocation should be obtained, and recited as in the Act of Uniformity.

" 3. After providing in the completest way for perfect investigation and exact legality, still might not the Bishops in Provincial Council, with full publicity to all their proceedings, be made judges in the last resort ?

" I am much mistaken if the errors of such a system would not be, (as they had better be,) entirely on the side of leniency; especially considering how the Bishops are appointed.

" But it would save the point of principle, and take off the strain on our consciences.

" My dream, if it went on, and found that nothing could be done, would be a very frightful one ; for it would exhibit our Church in no long time reduced to the alternative of voluntaryism, or unbelief.

" Luckily it is *but* a dream, and as such I hope harmless.

" Pardon it from your loving friend, J. K."

Keble agreed in what I wrote respecting the present insufficient training of the clergy for this purpose, and the greater fitness at present of laymen in this respect, whose interference he would by no means have rejected :—

" But what," said he, " if those who appoint Bishops insisted on this quality of a judicial mind, and an education to prepare them in some tolerable way for that kind of work ? Would not such a demand in no long time produce a supply, as you seem to say it did in old times ?"

One point, however, it would have been out of his nature to give up :—

" I want," said he, dating from Penzance on January 15, 1863, " to explain one or two things in which I fear I seem to you and other legal friends more absurd than I need. One is, that it is not only nor chiefly for want of theological learning that one objects to Laymen as final judges in ques-

tions of doctrine and spiritual discipline, but because one
believes that such judgments are divinely entrusted to the
Apostles and their successors, even as the Powers of order;
and that they are specially endowed for the work; not so,
of course, as to exclude the duty of availing themselves of
all providential helps, of which one of the greatest will be
the advice and instruction which I quite believe nothing
but a legal education can supply.   Just as in interpreting
the language of Scripture, they are bound to avail themselves of the opinions of the best Scholars; but they cannot transfer to them the right of *authoritative* interpretation, because they cannot transfer the responsibility.   It is
a burthen laid upon them, and they must bear it."

He closes a long reply to me in this somewhat
sad way :—

"Don't trouble yourself, dear friend, to answer this long
prose.   I foresee that very few would interest themselves in
my scruples, so I shall keep them with my forebodings, as well
as I can, to myself.   If I was 20 years younger, I might in
time be fit to talk and write on such things.   As it is, I feel
I ought to be otherwise employed.   Yet I hope my fear is
not mistrust of His goodness, but I say to myself, what if
we are being punished for not keeping our deposit?
                    "Ever yours, with love to all, J. K."

So for the time ended our correspondence on this
subject, but not his thought or anxiety about it.
It is one of so much importance, as yet unsettled,
and one on which we may confidently say some settlement must be made, that I have been the fuller on
it.   It seems important, that whenever it is seriously

considered, this side of it, to which mere lawyers may be disposed to attach little importance, should at all events be brought into view.

I part with this subject, though it must be considered as one never long out of Keble's mind so long as he lived, and revived by him from time to time in his letters.

It was shortly before he wrote the last letter, that I received one from him, from which I extract the following passage :—

" I have only just got our Bishop's Charge, and it is really admirable to my mind, better even than the Newspapers led me to expect ; better, I think, as a composition. There was often a sort of strain in what he wrote and preached, which in this he seems to have quite got rid of ; and then as to the matter, it is *very* instructive ; and the tone is so firm yet so candid. I am very thankful, and hope to be the better for it, though it is rather late to mend ; but no more of that."

Almost before he was relieved from the Wilson burthen, it seems that the living Wilson had ventured to remind him of the Commentary on the Bible. I am not sure to what extent Keble had engaged himself at all in this work, nor for what part of the book. He shrunk from engaging at once in a new labour, and wisely now ; though he did not disclaim the obligation, nor ever entirely renounce all hope of fulfilling it to some extent. At an earlier period there was no task I think in which he would have worked with more pleasure to himself, none for which he was more fitted :—

"Pray don't begin," writes he to Mr. Wilson, "talking and speculating about Commentary. I have not yet written a word, and at my age, and according to the scale of other people's work, it really seems quite idle to think of such a thing.   But for honour's sake, I suppose I must try, and it will be *too* good for me if I *am* helped to do anything. *But you know I never could bear being looked at while I write.* I do so hate for any one to see how *I hold my pen.*"

He begins this letter with a sentence which I cannot withhold from my readers :—

"DEAREST FRIENDS,

"It is, indeed, high time I should write to you, and yet I am not at all sure that I should have been dutiful enough to do so, if she, who is my Conscience, and my memory, and my common sense, had been up to the work, but I am sorry to say she is not."

Care for Mrs. Keble indeed, nursing her when ill, interesting her when better, taking her out for a drive, or a downhill walk, when alleviation of her symptoms, or abatement of the cold permitted, occupied much of his time, and more of his thoughts. Her health fluctuated a good deal, and although he still maintained that Penzance was warmer perhaps than any other place in England, she suffered occasionally very much from a change of wind, or such like winter casualty.   And with the knowledge

he now had of her case, his best hope was that he
might be allowed to take her from Penzance not
worse than when he brought her there. I do not
suppose she was a hopeful patient, in the sense of
expecting a recovery; but she was more than resigned; she was a cheerful one, bearing her part so
far as she could in their little circle, interested in all
that was done to interest her, and seeing, when she
could, some of the many kind people who were delighted to visit her and him, when allowed to do so.
And people were *very* kind to them, full of neigh-
bourly attentions, sending such delicacies as grapes,
or wild fowl, or anything thought good for Mrs. Keble.
He found there a sister of his and my friend Mr.
Copeland, Mrs. Borlase, whom he specially mentions
for her kindness; one who was a prisoner to her
house, or able only to take carriage drives, yet
" making," he says, " a bright sunshine all round her."
But what of course charmed him most, was his cordial and congenial reception from the Clergy; in Mr.
Hedgeland and Mr. Tyacke he found two in whose
ministrations he could heartily join, and whose hearts
warmed towards him with a loving respect, and re-
spectful love, which could not but delight his humble and affectionate nature. This was a matter of
consequence to him, for he reluctantly bore to be
doing nothing in his vocation, while in forced exile
from his own Cure. He preached many times, as
often, indeed, as either of these had occasion for his

help. Mr. Hedgeland records of him, in a letter to
the "Guardian," that at his first visit he asked to
have some pastoral visiting assigned to him, and
characteristically wished it to be entirely among
the poor, and shrank from going among any who
would see in him the author of "The Christian
Year." On one or two occasions of public rejoicing
he supplied them with lines suitable for use as a
Hymn; and attending a meeting of the Society for
Propagating the Gospel in Foreign Parts, he spoke
shortly and touchingly at its close, addressing himself specially to some young children who had been
singing near him.

After his return home, Mr. Hedgeland had written
to him, sending him what Keble called "his fresh
kind present," and I will insert here, a little out of
its place in point of time, an extract from his acknowledgment."

"*June* 13, 1863.

" My dear Mr. Hedgeland,

" The sight of your handwriting, and fresh kind present,
was very welcome indeed, and made me feel how wanting
I had been in not doing sooner what I had been all the
while intending, to write to you a word of hearty thanks
for your and your parishioners' very great kindness to us.
Such it was as must always make the very bends and turn-
ings of the streets, let alone the Mount and the Bay, and
the lanes and flowers, and moors, and cairns, and crosses,
most pleasant to think of."

Mr. Hedgeland, in the same letter to the "Guardian," mentions an incident which I also insert here, though out of its place. He visited him after his return to Hursley, and in the course of a walk, directed his attention to a broken piece of ground, a chalk-pit, as it turned out :—

"Ah," said he, "that is a sad place, that is connected with the most painful event of my life. It was there that I first knew for certain that J. H. N. had left us. We had just made up our minds that such an event was all but inevitable, and one day I received a letter in his handwriting. I felt sure of what it contained, and I carried it about with me all through the day, afraid to open it. At last I got away to that chalk-pit, and then forcing myself to read the letter, I found that my forebodings had been too true ; it was the announcement that he was gone."

I do not know whether it was a habit of his to select retired spots like this for such purposes ; but I remember well on some occasion, when he and I had to talk over some serious matter, his taking me to an abandoned chalk-pit, one, at least, in which the growth of brambles and coppice wood indicated that it had not been worked for some time ; and there we discussed our question. Few spots, by the way, are more picturesque than these old chalk-pits sometimes are ; and this may have been to him, like Ladwell Hill, with its wild flowers, a familiar spot, in which he chewed the cud of sweet and bitter fancies.

Keble had hoped to return to Hursley for Easter, but he was obliged to give it up, and on Palm-

Sunday, March 29, he wrote to me from Penzance, commemorating a visit to them from his brother and sister-in-law, with his usual sense of great enjoyment. Mrs. Keble continued better, but—

"Everybody advised us to give up our dream of being at home at Easter; and there has been a slight flavour of March lately, even in the West Winds, which proves them right; and I am rather ashamed to own myself too lazy to feel as uncomfortable as I ought about it."

On the 19th of May, 1863, he wrote to me from Hursley, after having been at home for some little time; he was full of the kindness he had received at Penzance, the beauties of the place and neighbourhood, and perhaps, above all, "what one might call three distinct immigrations from home." Among these he reckoned one from Mr. James Young, the son of his old Curate, whom he loved, and treated as one of his own family, who looked up to and regarded him and Mrs. Keble as Uncle and Aunt, and who was destined in some sort to repay their love by being allowed to watch over, and attend on, and nurse both to the close of their last illness.

It was evident that Mrs. Keble had returned not substantially better than she went, and he intimates to me the thoughts which arose in his mind, and which not long after he propounded to me more distinctly. He writes :—

"It would be very wrong to complain, wrong also to look forward, though I cannot conceal it from myself that in all probability it will be wrong, (supposing we have the chance,) to spend another winter here, and therewith come practical questions which I need not now specify, but I suppose one ought to look on to them so far as to pray for guidance."

In accordance with these thoughts he wrote to me on the 3rd of July :—

"Although Charlotte has not been absolutely ill since we came home, and many think her improved in looks, I cannot flatter myself that she is radically reformed, and a very little makes her exceeding weak. We are rather deferring to take any medical opinion about our staying here next winter. I do not myself doubt what the Doctors will say ; but how to manage afterwards ? (This is private). Ought I not, at least, to lay the matter before the Patron and the Bishop, and place the Nomination to the Cure in their hands. In plain English, should I not offer to resign ? Do tell me your first impression, i.e. what you feel would be your first impression in my case. I have not whispered it to *her*, but it must, I should think, have come into her mind. Well, now I must leave off for the present ; with all love to all, ever yours more and more, J. K."

I told him that my first impression was that he should do as he proposed, *because* I felt sure that both Bishop and Patron would say, it was better for the living and Church that he should retain the incumbency now, even if he were sure to be absent another long winter. But I thought the question must be looked at from a different point of view ; that it was a question for himself, not one for the

Bishop and Patron to decide for him. And then with
the view I had of Mrs. Keble's health, as gently as I
could, I distinguished between the case of one who
had no prospect of renewing his winter residence
for the whole of his lifetime, and his own case. I
tried to induce him therefore to narrow his consideration only to the absence for the coming winter; and
in that point of view there seemed to be no doubt,
that he ought for the sake of his people to retain the
incumbency for the present. I believe he was satisfied. However, as late as the 8th of October, the
necessity for a determination had not arisen :—

"We live on," says he, at that date, "from day to day,
in hopes to be allowed to spend the winter here, my wife
continuing on the whole, I think, nearly as well as when
we left the West. But I consider myself as under orders
to be ready to move at a very short warning."

It was about the time of his July letter that the
Judicial Committee had decided an appeal by a
clergyman of the name of Long against the Colonial decision of an action he had brought in the Supreme Court there against the Bishop of Capetown.
The judgment of the Committee was adverse to the
Bishop. The case was not one under the Church
Discipline Act, but simply a Common Law appeal
from the court in the colony. I cite the following
extract from Keble's letter for several reasons, which
it will itself suggest :—

"As to Cape Town, I said that about legal and theological half in jest to Butterfield, but when I read the sentence, I saw that the abstract I had seen of it was erroneous, viz. 'that Synods were pronounced altogether illegal;' but its real tenor seems to me a gain to us, in discountenancing *voluntary* 'synods,' framed, for the nonce, of Laity as well as of Clergy, and throwing us back on the Common Law of the Church. And a wiser pen than mine, writing from Bisley, says unasked, 'To me it seems a wise decision, and what in the end will produce good.' Indeed, there seems but one opinion about it."

" The orders to move," which he spoke of, arrived in December. On the 4th Sunday in Advent he wrote to me :—

" We have had too plain warning that we must move. She has not had a regular attack, only her breath is very weak, and not near so fit for travelling I fear as last year. I have no time to write on other things now ; so can only say, our dear love, and 1,000 thanks for your kind letter. I had *such* a kind one from our Bishop yesterday."

Mrs. Keble feared the long journey to Penzance, and the substance of the letter was to ask me help in finding good lodgings for them at Torquay. I had advised him to try that place. His letter found me just breaking up from some weeks' stay there ; but his god-daughter, with a niece of mine resident there, soon found him a comfortable abode in a house called Endèrlie, in Croft-road, and on the 3rd of January, 1864, I had the pleasure of receiving from him a cheerful account of his patient, and an assurance that they were comfortable.

K k

They remained at Torquay for about three months, and I need scarcely say that Keble was received by the clergy generally with kindness and respect, and by some of them with more than even those words import. Enderlie is in the Tor district of that large parish, and in close neighbourhood to St. Luke's Church ; he delighted in attending the services there, and was very much drawn to the incumbent, Mr. Harris, and his father, the Incumbent of the Mother church at Tor, which is at no great distance. He was not slow to render help where it was needed, and, as at Penzance, he always preferred the smallest churches, and the simplest congregations for his own ministrations. It was not, however, from the clergy only, that he and Mrs. Keble received the kindest attentions ; people were not merely delighted to do him honour, their hearts seemed to flow out towards him with love and gratitude, as well as admiration. But he shall speak for himself on this matter. His first letter from Penzance, (for to Penzance they went from Torquay,) was dated April 18, 1864 :—

" MY DEAREST COLERIDGE,

" It is, indeed, too high time for me to write to you on 100 things, and first of all, to thank you over and over for your good and timely advice about Torquay. You heard of us from time to time through dear Mrs. Martyn, and the rest of your kind allies and clanspeople there, who seemed as if they could not do enough to befriend us. On the whole, considering to what a ripe age I have attained, I have a marvellously fragrant remembrance of Torquay on my mind, which will last me, I dare say, to the end of my brief remaining time. The Churches and the Sundays were so pleasant, and so much real sympathy, and all that is best within a few yards of us. Charlotte was not very much in visiting, or in visitable order, during a great part of the time, so that we did not make so much as we should have wished of our privileges ; but she did mend, or, at least, was kept from suffering as she would have done at home ; so as to make us very thankful that we took your good advice, and went there when we did. She was not then in a condition to go much further, had we wished it ever so much. And so when the Spring weather came, and we got on here, she was in a condition to enjoy thoroughly her dear old friend, the open sea, to the very edge of which we have crept as close as ever we could, our house being within about 12 feet of high-water at moderate Spring Tides. And we see, both from bed-rooms and sitting-room, all round the Bay from Mousehole to the Lizard. She has mended upon it, as in old days ; for a great part of her time she neither coughs, nor suffers neuralgia ; and the E. wind which has prevailed, has come to her very much mitigated by the sea. She goes often to Church, and sometimes can take a tolerable walk downhill. Altogether, I very much wish that I could invest in a decent sea-side house and garden some-where in this climate, with a good aspect, and within reach of a good Doctor ; but such a thing is more easily wished for than found. Sometimes I dream of combining such a plan with being Curate of Hursley, (if I might,) in the summer time. But I have not yet said anything of this to the Patron ; *she* keeps on saying, ' Let us try another winter.' One ought not to listen to this (?), for what a thing it would be if one made the trial once too often."

It was not a long visit which they paid to Penzance at this time, and I need not repeat the account which I have given as to Keble's course here, or the reception he met with; but I think I must not withhold part of a communication which I received from Mr. Tyacke long after, dated from St. Levan, to which he had been removed :—

" One trait in Mr. Keble's character, and one essentially Christian, was his sympathy; this I had the opportunity of personally experiencing when I have seen him in Penzance, since I came here to live. He took such real interest in the character and progress of the work I am seeking to do here ; he also expressed himself with such kindliness respecting the position of Dissenters, in this too long neglected place, as shewed the loving nature of his heart.

" His *humbling* humility, too, shewed itself here as elsewhere, when he would thank one for coming to see *him*, and put himself into the position of a learner, when in conversation he asked an opinion for information.

" I seem to feel ' The Christian Year' a different book, or rather a book of greater power now than I did before, and I am thankful to be able to do so, it makes me reverence his memory more."

I cannot help attaching importance to the inferences to be drawn from such a letter as this ; the particular circumstances are in themselves perhaps not very remarkable ; but as naturally drawn traits, which an intelligent stranger, (for such was Mr. Tyacke to Keble,) observed so strongly, they give us accurately the character to which they belonged.

Keble's next letter was dated on the 29th of April at Dartington Parsonage, where Mrs. Keble and he were resting in their way home ; they reached Hursley a few days after, and remained there for many months.

CHAPTER XX.

SUBSCRIPTION AND OATHS OF THE CLERGY.—RE-
TURN FROM PENZANCE.—PRACTICE AS TO CON-
FIRMATIONS. — PARALYTIC SEIZURE, NOVEMBER,
1864. — SECOND VISIT TO TORQUAY. — REMOVAL
TO PENZANCE.—THE COLENSO APPEAL.—PASTO-
RAL LETTER TO THE CONFIRMED AT HURSLEY.
—VISIT AT HEATH'S COURT, MAY 10.—RETURN TO
HURSLEY.—ABOLITION OF TESTS AT OXFORD.—
MRS. KEBLE'S SEVERE ILLNESS. — VISIT OF DR.
PUSEY AND DR. NEWMAN.

IT was at the close of 1863, or very early in 1864,
that a Royal Commission issued to consider the
existing laws as to oaths taken and subscriptions
made by the Clergy. The late excellent Primate
was placed at the head of it, the Archbishops of
York and Armagh, and several other Bishops, were
members; and it was certain that it was not issued
in any spirit hostile to the Church. I hardly know,
however, whether at first it was an unmixed pleasure to Keble, that Sir William Heathcote and
myself were also members. Although he did not
fear the spirit in which the Commission issued, and
by which its functions were carefully guarded, he saw

clearly, or thought he saw, that the real motive for issuing it was to satisfy men who did not in truth believe in all that the clergy swore to and subscribed; and he was apprehensive that in the desire to do this some portion of vital truth might be conceded. He doubted, too, where this small beginning would end. Before he is condemned as narrow and unreasonable in this, some of the publications of the day, and their acceptance, as well as the state of religious opinion and teaching at Oxford and elsewhere, must be borne in mind. The strange language also must be remembered, which, it was commonly said, had proceeded from a high legal authority even in judgment, as to the meaning of such a word for example as "everlasting," in reference to the punishments of the other world. Years before he had said no less beautifully than forcibly :—

" *Then* is there hope for such as die unblest,
    That angel wings may waft them to the shore,
  Nor need th' unready virgin strike her breast,
    Nor wait desponding round the bridegroom's door.

" *But where is then the stay of contrite hearts ?*
    Of old they lean'd on Thy eternal word,
  But with the sinner's fear *their* hope departs,
    Fast link'd as Thy great Name to Thee, O Lord [a]."

And now he wrote :—

" There is never a boy or girl going up and down the

---

[a] "Christian Year," Second Sunday in Lent.

street but can catch in a moment the idea of there being
no Hell, and can apply it when tempted to deadly sin;
and, in fact, who can tell how many souls may have been
already lost by the mere broaching of the idea."

He was from this and other circumstances in a
state of mind more than commonly sensitive; and
he was at all times especially alive to anything that
touched the Common Prayer-book. When we of
the Commission were considering the declaration of
"unfeigned assent and consent to all and everything
contained and prescribed in and by it," which the
Act of Uniformity required to be made upon presentation or collation to any benefice, and I consulted him on some proposed changes of these words,
he answered me thus :—

"I have nothing to say but what appears to me the
plainest common sense, as much within the reach of the
simplest labourer believing, as within my reach. It is all
comprised in two points, 1. That the Teacher should be
pledged to the Faith and Practice of the Church, and 2,
that the Taught should know them to be so pledged. With
a view to the former, supposing men to be honest, (a thing
implied in the very notion of subscription *ex animo*,) I
don't see that there is any fundamental difference between
one of the suggested forms and another. But in regard of
the latter, the right of believing Laity to be satisfied that
they and their children shall be taught according to their
belief, these two things occur to me, 1st. that the mere
cry for alteration is to such a ground of suspicion; for it
naturally occurs to them, why do people want this altered,

except because they do not quite believe it themselves? And what is more alarming, it is not denied, it is dwelt on in Parliament as a great reason for the change that good and clever men are kept out, or, being within, are made uncomfortable, through lack of some such alteration. And what other interpretation can one put on the proposal to leave out the 'assensus and consensus,' than to license in holy ministrations language which the heart inwardly disavows? This being so, one (2) must prefer that among the proposed forms which least disturbs the existing practice. And that if I understand it rightly, is ——' amendment with Mr. ——' further resolution. I wish we could retain the 'assensus and consensus' somehow; one could have done without it, perhaps, but being there, its omission will be a positive act, and is sure to have the positive consequence above-mentioned."

If my dear friend could have been present at the meetings of the Commissioners, and witnessed the spirit which was manifested in all their discussions, I think his mind would have been made more easy, and, I may venture to say, disabused of some prejudices. Unless I am mistaken, both Houses of Convocation adopted the conclusions to which we came. It is too early undoubtedly to speak of any fruit which they have borne; they have been accepted, and I believe acted on gratefully and heartily, and not less by one party in the Church than the other.

Keble went on in the same letter to say:—

" Since the assent of Convocation is recited in the preamble of the Act establishing the Prayer-book, ought not this change in the Act to be first laid before Convocation, seeing that it (the change) will relax the binding force not of this or that part, but of the whole?"

Keble was anticipating changes in kind and degree very far exceeding what were in the end recommended and became law; but I confess in the principle of this last recommendation he seems to me quite right, and that it was a jealousy of the Spiritual power, quite unworthy of the undoubted greatness of Parliament, which refused to admit in the Preamble of the Act passed, any recital expressing in any way that Convocation had concurred in the provisions. The statute would surely have been just as entirely the act of the legislature only.

They returned from Penzance in April, (1864,) and continued at Hursley till towards the end of November :—

" My wife's behaviour," (as he called it, writing in September,) " has been tolerably good, yet not without neuralgia, and shortness of breath, coming exceptionally, and generally to be accounted for, so that we are not in a way to flatter ourselves that we shall make out the winter here ; but we *do* hope, at least *she* does, to weather it until Christmas."

Many friends visited them, and they made one visit to Church Crookham, where Mrs. and Miss

M. A. Dyson were now living ; he speaks of this thus characteristically :—

" By-the-bye, what a charming arrangement that is of the Dysons at Crookham. We were never there until this summer, and then for 2 days in the very hot weather. All the time I had almost a sense of *his* presence ; everything seemed so exactly as if he had settled it for them, and then gone out on a journey."

In the meantime he was as active as ever in the discharge of his pastoral duties ; what that activity was, I shall have occasion to shew before I con-clude. A confirmation was to take place in Hursley early in 1865. There was no one of those duties in regard to which his practice was more careful and laborious than in the preparation of the candidates for this.

Mr. Young, to whom I am under many and great obligations, has furnished me with so detailed an account of his course in regard to this most im-portant pastoral duty, that I cannot do better than introduce it here :—

" He took," he says, " great pains in preparing the young people for Confirmation ; sometimes, as soon as one Con-firmation was over, making a list of those whose turn would come next, and at all times beginning the preparation several months beforehand. His usual course was to go through in order, first the Baptismal Service, then the Cate-chism, then the Confirmation Service, and, lastly, the Office for Holy Communion. He took a certain portion each time, making perhaps 20 or 30 lessons in the whole. He usually wrote down on paper 3 or 4 passages of Scripture, bearing on the subject of the next lesson, which he required to be learnt by heart, or carefully studied ; and he was always very particular in ascertaining whether the Lesson, as he called it, had been attended to. Wherever it was practicable, he led his pupils up to their first Communion immediately after Confirmation ; but in many cases he was satisfied, if they promised to continue under instruction. One class of boys came to him for more than a twelvemonth, and read through with him different parts of the Bible, according to their own choice, before he could persuade them to turn their minds distinctly to preparation for Holy Communion. I believe his rule as to refusing to recommend for Confirmation those who would not pledge themselves to communicate, became stricter as years passed on ; but I should say generally that he was always very much guided by circumstances in regard to his adherence to particular rules."

I will add one or two particulars supplied to me by a lady, who had scarcely less personal knowledge than Mr. Young :—

" One year, at the beginning of Lent, he gave notice that there would be a Confirmation at the end of Lent in the next year, and therefore desired to receive at once the names of those who would then be of ripe age for Confirmation. The Children, whom he prepared, came to him either in classes, or *singly*, every week for about a year before the administration of the Rite. He took those of different ranks and ages separately, as needing a difference in the kind of teaching to be given ; and as there were few of the Upper Class at the same time under preparation, these usually came to him each alone every week. The knowledge of the Bible possessed by the Children long before their preparation for Confirmation began, and the way in which it was interwoven in their minds with the Creeds and the Catechism, was something uncommon, indeed. If farm lads could not come to him for press of work, he went to them, one by one, however far off."

"Latterly," writes to me another Lady, "he used to bring the first class of boys to the Vicarage on Sunday Mornings, and teach them in his Study, the door, as usual, standing wide open all the time. He said he did it in hopes it might make the big boys like coming, who might think it beneath them to go to the School. He used to say, 'I like them very much, if they would only like me ; but they always do much better as long as they are under my wife.'

"If a servant came to him who was ignorant, or who had not become a Communicant, he always taught her himself. I have known him take the most ignorant girl day after day alone, carefully instructing her ; and although she had been confirmed, deferring her first Communion from week to week, until he had reason to hope she was prepared for it."

I could multiply statements of this kind, as to this part of his pastoral duty, but I will only add now the impression which I myself received, when in his house. It seemed to me that he and Mrs. Keble were substantially the servants of the parishioners. To attend to their wants, to help them in sickness, trouble, or difficulty, at *their* convenience, not his or her's, or that of the guests in the house, was evidently the understood rule and practice.

What wonder, then, if under such a course of labour for years, such constant anxiety on her account, and such frequent distress in regard to Church matters, his constitution at last broke down. My narrative left him half hoping that Mrs. Keble's health would enable them to stay over Christmas at Hursley; and he expressed no uneasiness whatever about his own. But on the night of St. Andrew's Day, the 30th of November, while he was sitting alone after Mrs. Keble had retired, writing a letter for publication on a matter deeply interesting to him, he was struck with palsy on the left side and right arm; the latter part of his writing was afterwards found to be illegible; but he did not lose his consciousness, or his presence of mind. He went up to her room, and they knelt down as usual, and said their prayers together; his voice was observably indistinct; and at the end, asking her if she had remarked anything, he held out his hand, which was losing its power. Medical aid was sent for at once, but during the night the symptoms became worse; from the morning, however, they were alleviated.

His medical attendants who knew his constitution well, the anxieties he had long been under, and his habits of labour, advised his removal westward without any delay as soon as his strength should be equal to the journey to Torquay; above all things they were urgent for his taking rest. They attributed the attack to over-exercise of the thinking powers.

If he would rest, there was every reason to hope for
nearly, if not a complete, restoration of his health;
and none without it. Before this illness, they had
settled to go to Penzance immediately after Christmas, and their lodgings had been secured there from
the 28th of December. So long a delay would not
have been proper, and the distance to Torquay was
more convenient to the strength of both, and accordingly to Torquay they came. The medical
opinions there entirely concurred with that given
at Hursley. Keble said he was not aware of having
over-worked himself recently; and the reply was obvious, he had not been aware of it, because he had
for so many years been in the habit.

He promised obedience, and as far as he could
he kept his promise, that is, he read less and lightly,
and wrote little; indeed, writing was now more than
ever a wearisome process; its character was much
altered for the worse; but how could he prevent
thoughts? Medical advice of this kind is often
given; but it seems to me, the weaker the body,
and the organs of the brain, the less control does
the will exercise over them. Habitual trains of
thought can in such a state be almost as little put
aside as distressing dreams in illness. And as such
dreams in such a state of the frame are sometimes
more than ordinarily distinct and vivid, so it seems
probable that our waking meditations may be perfectly clear and correct in the state in which Keble

was, only that we cannot exercise the control of the will over them, nor bid the mind be still. "Indeed," wrote Mrs. Keble to me, "he does quite mean to be prudent, but he can scarcely help *thinking*." And it seems as natural that he should be thinking on the subjects which painfully and habitually occupied his mind when in health, as that our dreams by night should borrow much of their train and colouring from what may have much occupied or disturbed our thoughts by day.

It was speedily found that they could not move on to Penzance so soon as they had intended. They were, however, well placed at Torquay. All that could be done to cheer them they received; he was not allowed to see many persons, but they had the great comfort of Miss Coxwell's and Mr. James Young's attendance; these two formed part of their family, as it were, and could never be in the way; they lightened the nursing and attendance, which would have been too much for Mrs. Keble unassisted, though providentially she as yet bore up well. I was forbidden by my own medical friend to leave home, and I could render no help, except by answering for him some questions as to Church matters, which he had not been able to attend to.

Early in the year he took up his pen again to write to me, and he dated from Penzance; he wrote shortly, and in a sadly altered character, but with his usual overflowing affection. I give it entire :—

"*P.*, 31 *Jan.*, 1865.

" Dearest Friend,

" You will be sorry to hear that my dear wife had one of her very bad attacks on Saturday Morning. It soon subsided, D. G., but left her of course very weak ; however, she was down stairs yesterday evening, and is again this morning. But the attack coming *here* was a disappointment. At home, indeed, it might have been much worse. The weather has been very sharp here.

" I am very comfortable, and were it not for my wrist and voice, should hardly know that there was anything the matter with me. Thinking, so far as it has come to me, has not seemed to hurt me. I do not seek it.

" God reward and bless you for all your great love, and all yours with you. Your most affec^te, J. K."

" C. is most thankful for your letter, and very sorry she could not answer it."

However loyally he might endeavour to obey the injunctions of his medical advisers, there was one cause of anxiety over which he had no control, and which almost continually pressed on him for the remainder of his life, I mean Mrs. Keble's illnesses, which henceforward were scarcely intermittent. And now as she was recovering from her severe attack, she had the misfortune of a very severe scald in one foot, which in her then state, and with her delicate constitution, produced so much injury, and became so serious, as to compel recourse to a second medical adviser. The danger apprehended was from a failure of strength, and the difficulty how to keep it up without irritating the chest. " But," wrote he, as he summed it up, " they are good fellows, and seem to know what they are about. The rest is in His hands."

This is an extract from a note dated on the 6th of February. He wrote short notes to me about her progress from time to time all through that month. On the 10th of March he writes still from Penzance, and gives this account of himself and her :—

" All thanks for your much love. I wish I could answer it as I ought ; but my *writing* powers do not sensibly improve, and I am told not to try them much. Ditto with *speaking;* but I can read and think (D. G.) without finding any inconvenience. In other respects I seem to myself well, only not up to my ordinary amount of walking. Charlotte is regularly down in our drawing-room from after breakfast till after tea, and the wound on her foot, (now after 5 weeks reduced to about the size of a shilling,) is not I hope much of a trouble to her. She is in other respects pretty well for her, and always cheerful. The weather has mostly been very pleasant ; your snow, if it came at all to us, came in the shape of coldish rain. I wish Torquay had not proved such a failure to you."

The Oxford contest of this year was already in preparation, and he was sensitive about Sir William Heathcote, whose seat no one wished to disturb, but as to whose course in regard of what could be no more than a mere understanding between the other two candidates there was some little delicacy :—

" Can there," wrote Keble, " be possibly any doubt about H.'s position on the Oxford Poll. I should think that *all* the Hardys and the majority of the others would surely support him."

It is well known that this expectation was fully justified.

After some words about his brother and nephew, he ends thus cheerily :—

" My wife has the most charming weekly letters from Ch. Yonge, and she keeps her supplied with the most charming French Books. Moreover, we solace ourselves with a nightly *rubber* or two, a great step in old folks' education. With all love from us both, I am most affect¹ʸ yours, J. K."

I believe this nightly rubber was, indeed, as he calls it, "a step in old folks' education," with him ; at least, I never remember seeing him have recourse to the innocent pastime in earlier life.

I do not remember what book I had sent him, which he so kindly acknowledges on the 24th of March :—

" DEAREST FRIEND,

" First thank you again and again for that beautiful book, beautiful in every sense. It is so refreshing to open a collection *entirely* of old and tried gems ; tho' far the greater part of them, I must confess, are new to me. We are both of us, D. G., reasonably well, though I cannot boast much of getting on, as you see. Nor is Ch. able to get out at all ; nor has her foot even as yet quite healed. I think the E. Wind, which is here as everywhere else, though mitigated, is against both of us."

The handwriting of this letter was, indeed, very feeble, but it was much longer than any he had

written before since his illness ; for this was the time,
I think, when the issue between the Bishop of Cape
Town and Bishop Colenso was submitted to the
Judicial Committee ; and he looked on that submission, in the first instance, on the part of the Government, and the question being entertained by the
Committee at all, as grievances.   It is well known
that the appeal was finally entertained, and decided
in favour of the appellant ; the lamentable and perhaps unavoidable consequences are also well known ;
but this is not the place to enlarge on them.   I mention the matter, because in some sort it is part of
Keble's biography, and because there is no doubt
that the general subject formed to the end of his
life one of the sources of distress, which helped to
break down his strength, and accelerated its close.

The decision of the Appeal, it is right to add,
satisfied him, as he understood it.   In a letter written by Mrs. Keble under his dictation, on the 31st of
March, he says :—

" I see most thankfully that the decision annuls Colenso's
Episcopate, (meaning of course his territorial jurisdiction,)
and if I understand it rightly, almost all the Colonial Sees
as much as it does the Metropolitan's claim, and therefore
virtually leaves the matter to be settled by the Churchmen
of the two dioceses.   And what I pray and hope may be
done is,—

" 1. That this may be thoroughly and openly recognised
by the authorities in England.

" 2. That the will of Natal may be fairly and fully ascertained, (that of Capetown is ascertained without a doubt).

" 3. That so much of Natal as may wish to continue, (what it has supposed itself hitherto,) a See in the province of Capetown, may be allowed to elect its own Bishop, and Capetown to consecrate him.

" 4. That the Metropolitan with his Suffragans may freely exercise the prerogative inherent in them, of censuring, and if need be, excommunicating any heretic, Bishop or other, who may be molesting the faithful within the Province.

" 5. All, of course, subject to the correction of the Courts temporal, in respect of any temporal wrong sustained."

Such were Keble's not unreasonable wishes; we know how far they seem even now from being accomplished; nay, how disturbing even to the Church at home have been the miserable distractions of the English Church in Southern Africa. It is a very painful subject to think on. Lawyers, who considered the matter, had long suspected that the Colonial Episcopate in many of the colonies stood upon a very sandy foundation as to jurisdiction and discipline. There was a hope, which people were but too glad to indulge in, that by God's blessing on Christian holiness, discretion, and temper, years might elapse before the solidity of the foundation in these respects might be tried. If this had been granted time might have consolidated it; acts

would in all probability have been done, and acquiesced in, and the result have amounted to acceptance and consent; so presumptions would have
arisen, to which Courts of Law would have properly allowed great weight.   Unfortunately such
events occurred as made it necessary to examine
the foundation too soon, and the original defect
was laid open.   It is very convenient to lay the
blame now, in the particular instance, on the Metropolitan Bishop, but it may surely be said, without
vindicating his conduct in every step, that this is
most unjust.   The Law Officers at home, whoever
they were, on whose authority the Patent issued,
ought to be answerable for its worthlessness.   The
Bishop may have committed errors of conduct in the
course of the long warfare in which he has been
engaged ; naturally enough in the commencement
he assumed the authority of the Crown, and the
validity of the Patents which it had issued.   But
the inherent defect depended on circumstances on
the one hand, and on legal principles on the other,
which ought to have been well known and appreciated by the legal advisers of the Queen.   To state
this may give offence, but at the hazard of that,
what it is just to state ought to be stated.

I turn with pleasure from these remarks to a subject far more agreeable to think on.   On the 28th of
March, 1865, the Confirmation took place at Hursley,
in the preparation for which Keble had been inter-

rupted by his illness. It should seem to have been the first time that he had been absent on such an occasion, and now, when the day arrived, his heart was with the young ones of his flock. He sent to them from Penzance in proof of this an address, which seems to me so valuable in itself, and so characteristic of him, so worthy to be preserved, and yet so likely to be lost, that I feel it right to insert it here at length, and in its place in point of time :—

" To the Newly-Confirmed at Hursley.
" *March* 28, 1865.

" It is a real grief to me that I am not able to be with you on this, as on former Confirmation Days. But I may be able, by God's help, to say a word to you now which shall remain with you and do you good in time of temptation.

" What shall the word be, my Children?

" Our Lord Himself seems to have given it to us in the second Lesson for this morning,—St. John xv., 'abide ;'— over and over He says it,—'Abide in Me, and I in you.'

" You are now His, and He is yours. Doubt it not, but earnestly believe it.

" If you have come here to-day with a good and true mind towards Him, the Holy Spirit has come to you in the laying on of hands, and has sealed you afresh, as He had before sealed you in Baptism.

" All henceforth will depend on your keeping this Seal unbroken ; and that can be only in one way, by watching.

" Watch yourselves, then, dear Children, in all your ways. Whenever Christ's Spirit in your heart says to you, ' Do not this thing,—draw back your hand, look another way, think of something else,—for this thing I hate,'—take care to attend to Him, and obey the gracious warning at once. And when the good Spirit whispers, 'Do this,' do it at once for His sake. For instance, I know that He is now putting you in mind of Holy Communion.

"Let nothing tempt you to lose time about It, but go directly to your Minister, and tell him you wish to be prepared for It, if you have not done so already; for depend upon it, that Bread is as necessary for your Soul's Life, as your daily bread is for the life of your body.

"Thus you will be WATCHING your ways; and that you may have Grace and Power to do this, you must WATCH your Prayers too. You must try always to mean what you say, when you ask God to keep you from sin, and give you more Grace.

"So doing you will Abide in Christ, and be sure He will abide in you. There may be sorrow on the road, but all will go right in the end, for you will see His Face with joy. And, oh! how gladly will you then remember this day, if for your dear Lord's sake you shall have made it a day of such good beginnings.

"Do not then delay, but be found WATCHING, the very first time you are tried.

"God grant that it may be so with each one of you. This is the earnest prayer of

"Your loving Father and Servant in Christ,
"JOHN KEBLE."

On the 18th of April he wrote a cheering account of Mrs. Keble; they were planning their return home, and promised us a visit on their way. Of himself, he says :—

"I have not for a good time found much change in

myself, but I think I can walk farther, and perhaps read and write better ; still I don't feel as if I could do my duty at home, or a fair share of it, but *nous verrons.*"

On the 19th he wrote again, having made some mistake as to the dates of their intended movements, and says of himself, " I fear that it will be a very small fraction of my duty that I shall be able to do myself."

They left Penzance after all not until the first week of May, and he wrote on the 9th as to some particulars in regard to his visit to us, and thus he sums up as to this his last visit to Penzance :—

" I am very thankful to have so good a chance of a few hours with you ; the news from Stinchcombe makes every hour seem more precious, and every surviving friend, and indeed every departed one, dearer. My wife is less of a walker than I had hoped she might have been by this time. Penzance, though it was indeed a shelter from the extreme cold, was very trying from the spasmodic attack and scalded foot, which came together, and from the Bronchitis which followed, and she has not got herself up quite properly. But we cannot think enough of His goodness in sparing us as He has done. Heathcote is waiting to see us before starting for Malvern, so I fear we must not think of another night with you, even if it could be otherwise."

They came to us on the 10th of May, and left us on the following afternoon for home ; a short visit, and the last ; but one for which I never can be too

thankful. He seemed to me much recovered, looking
better ; and he was stronger, and far more helpful than
I had ventured to hope for ; and his " mind," I say
in my memorandum at the time, " seems perfect."
We were much alone, and conversed much, sometimes on subjects which might have taxed his powers
and his memory a good deal. I remember among
other things in speaking of one of Dr. Colenso's objections, as to the descent into Egypt of Jacob, with
his sons, and descendants, and the return from it,
his stating an explanation of his own, which involved
the repetition of many names, and some calculations ;
his memory was matter of surprise to me, though he
had a difficulty sometimes of utterance ; which impeded only, but did not prevent the statement of all
particulars. He had less command of himself when
his tender affections were stirred. We talked of old
and departed friends ; in speaking of Cornish, he
suddenly turned away, covered his face with both
hands, and shed a torrent of tears ; but he soon recovered his calmness. It is impossible adequately
to describe his sweetness and affectionate manner ;
it seemed to me then as now, that the thought of
his departed friends, and the consideration of his own
state, about which I am sure he never deceived himself, made him cling only the more closely to the
very few who remained. And so, I trust, that as
we advance in age, and strive as in reason we ought
to do to make our attachments less and less strong

to the *things* which are merely of this earth and for this life, we may yet blamelessly, even commendably, cling with warmer and closer love to the *persons*, the friends, whom loving through life we humbly hope to love through all eternity. Keble and I parted at this time not to meet again in this world; but I was spared, and I believe he was spared from anticipating this at the time.

It was not until the 5th of June, Whitsun-Monday, that he wrote to me from the old date, H. V., and I make some extracts from his letter :—

" MY DEAREST COLERIDGE,

" I am a thankless wretch for not having long ago told you how much I like to think of the day we spent with you, our pleasant talk, and everybody's kindness.

" We are, I think, D. G., as well, at least, as when we parted; I, if any difference, rather better. I read a lesson or two in Church most days, now and then visit in one or two of the nearest houses, drive out very often; but for the most part I lead a sort of semi-vegetable life, and have no very definite prospect of promotion in that respect. But, indeed, dear friend, I ought to be very thankful that it is no worse; and I am really ashamed of the love and kindness that is shewn me. Dear H. is, I really hope, materially better, and more cheerful about himself.

" Now I have one or two little questions to ask." [I pass over what immediately follows as immaterial; he then goes on,] " 3. I can't get it out of my head, that it would be both justice and good statesmanship to state in the Preamble of the new Church Subscription Act, that the change had been

approved by the Convocations of both Provinces, as in the
present Act of Uniformity. This might be very valuable to
us, if the Parliament should take to altering the P. B. If
you think this notion worth anything, you will know whom
to apply to about it better than I. . . .

" I am reading up some of dear Isaac Williams's works,
which to my shame I had neglected ; and I find them *so*
beautiful. Ever your most affectionate, J. K."

Through the remainder of this month, and to the
middle of July, he was at Hursley, with no decline
apparently, nor any material improvement of his
bodily health. He took much interest in the Oxford Election, for which we were now preparing ;
and whatever exertion he thought it useful to make
on behalf of Mr. Gladstone, for whom he felt as
warmly and as unreservedly as ever, he made as
heartily as of old. This does not mean that he
agreed with him in every opinion, or measure, which
he was understood to favour ; as to some he would
say, that though as he understood them, he did not
wholly approve them, yet he thought it became persons not conversant with State affairs to have confidence in one, whose knowledge and ability were
superior to their own, and whose integrity of principle
they did not doubt. The Irish Church question, however, was not one of these ; as to this, I believe he
agreed with Mr. Gladstone in the principle, and I
shall have occasion to shew hereafter, there is good
ground for so believing. Beyond the principle I am

not aware of any direct evidence ; conclusions can only be drawn from the general character of his sayings and writings ; and considerate persons will, I think, pause before they pronounce confidently either way.

At the Poll, as is well known, we were defeated, to his great regret ; he thought the decision of the University a misfortune. And I fear he would with many others have thought her humiliated by her rejection of Sir Roundell Palmer in 1868.

The issue of the election, however, did not abate his interest in the University. Writing to me on the 25th of July, very shortly after my son's election by the city of Exeter, he says :—

" I should very much like to know whether John includes in his Abolition of Tests the Collegiate Foundations, as well as the Universities. If he does, I am totally at issue with him, on what seem to me legal and constitutional, as well as ·moral and religious grounds. Of course he does not mean it ; but might not what he says about the Irish Church have somewhat of the effect of a fire brand, addressed to such a very popular audience. I should have thought it fitter for a Cabinet Council or a grave book. I should also have thought it discreet not to put the matter forward so prominently, unless a man saw his way to the mending of it ; which perhaps John does.

" But I cannot say how much I am obliged to the said John for what he has done for us in the matter of Confession."

This last remark refers, I believe, to a legal opinion given in a matter which arose out of the extraordinary case of Constance Kent, and to services in it as her legal adviser. On the former part of the extract I have already said all that it is needful for me to say. Although the measure to which Keble refers was in the commencement carefully confined to the University, (and in some material circumstances the cases of the two are clearly distinguishable in argument,) it always seemed to me that in the progress of the measure it would be found impossible to preserve the distinction entire ; though it might be possible, and would certainly be just, to make modifications as to the Colleges.

On the next day, (July 26,) he wrote again a short note with some information respecting a matter we were then both interested in, an Oxford testimonial to Mr. Gladstone on the close of our Parliamentary relations with him. I extract a sentence or two in a more cheerful tone :—

" H. is just returned from spending two very pleasant days with Lord Derby at Highclere. Lord D. was full of fun, but H. is regretting that he omitted to ask him why he renders βοῶπις ' stag-eyed.' However, you see we have two strings to our bow. Homer and good wit are in fashion, whether we are Whigs or Tories."

He adds at the end :—

" My wife is very feeble, and her breath troublesome. The weather is sultry, and I fear we have too many visitors. Your most loving, J. K."

He very gently, as it was in his nature, alludes to
what had become a great and I fear a hurtful burthen to both himself and his wife in their feeble state,
the number of visitors who came to them; especially
as a considerable portion of them were strangers,
whose object was to see and converse with the
Author of "The Christian Year," a thing he particularly disliked. Some would have little in themselves to lighten the burthen of entertaining them;
and though some interested him much, yet even for
that very reason they fatigued him too; and he was
always anxious for Mrs. Keble. Yet he could not
refuse these visits, nor decline to exert himself to
please those whose motive he felt to be kind and
reverential.

A visit from Bisley, or from an old friend, was
a different thing, and with different results. August
19, he says :—

"We keep about the same, I not much better, nor yet,
D. G., any worse; *she* too often with her breath out of
order, and the other symptoms of (I suppose) a disordered
spine, but rallying again, and taking her drives. Just now
we have Tom Sen[r], and his wife staying with us, a great
delight; too great to last long." [And noticing all my scattered family, he concludes,] "Kind love to all, Swiss and
English, on the Moor or by the River."

It was clear, as the year advanced, that Mrs. Keble
must move from Hursley; the attacks on her breath
now recurred two or three times a-week, and their

good Doctor Sainsbury, of Romsey, pressed them to try the effect of change of air. Keble, who never deceived himself as to the seriousness of her ailments, felt how important it would be to diminish as much as he could the distance between her and her sister. They went, therefore, with his brother and sister to Bournemouth on trial, and the result was so promising, that they made a sort of conditional engagement to return in October for the winter. They had hoped for a month of fine weather at home ; but only three days after their return, she had one of her worst attacks ; indeed, the account he gave me of it was frightful ; feeling its approach, she began to go up-stairs to her room, but "about half-way up she was obliged to sink down on the staircase, and it was full $2\frac{1}{2}$ hours before we could move her up to her bed. By God's mercy she was relieved after a time." And up to October 9, when he wrote to me, she had had no return, though left in such a state that "to talk earnestly, even to listen with great interest," put her in danger of one. Yet strange to say she was afterwards able to take her drives as usual, and even to go to London to consult Dr. Gull, and return on the following day.

I mention these incidents of her attack with this particularity on account of the remarkable visit to Hursley, which he himself thus shortly mentions at the end of a rather long letter, written to me on the 9th of October from Hursley :—

" Ought we not to thank God more than ever for E. B. P. ?
how he *has* come out in print and in Congress. He
and J. H. N. met *here* the very day after my wife's attack.
P., indeed, was present when the attack began. Trying as
it all was, I was very glad to have them here, and to sit by
them and listen ; but I cannot write more of it now."

I was very anxious to have an account of a visit
so remarkable in itself, and about which so much
interest was felt, more detailed than Keble had
given me in the extract I have made above ; and
yet as calm, and as free from exaggeration as he
would have furnished himself, or desired to have
preserved. And I therefore took the liberty of applying to one of the survivors. Dr. Newman was
good enough to furnish me with all that I desired ;
and, further, in answer to a second request, to allow
me to publish his letter, for which I thank him sincerely, and I am sure my readers will thank him as
heartily and sincerely :—

" REDNALL,
" *Sept.* 17, 1868.

" DEAR SIR JOHN COLERIDGE,

" I must begin by apologizing for my delay in acknowledging your letter of the 10th. Owing to accidental circumstances, my time has not been my own ; and now,
when at length I write, I fear I shall disappoint you in the
answer which alone I can give to your question. It almost
seems to me as if you were so kind as to wish me to write
such an account of my visit to Mr. Keble as might appear

M m

in your Memoir, but, as I think you will see, my memory is too weak to allow of my putting on paper any particulars of it which are worth preserving. It was remarkable, certainly, that three friends, he, Dr. Pusey, and myself, who had been so intimately united for so many years, and then for so many years had been separated, at least one of them from the other two, should meet together just once again ; and for the first and last time dine together simply by themselves. And the more remarkable, because not only by chance they met all three together, but there were positive chances against their meeting.

" Keble had wished me to come to him, but the illness of his wife, which took them to Bournemouth, obliged him to put me off. On their return to Hursley, I wrote to him on the subject of my visit, and fixed a day for it. Afterwards, hearing from Pusey that he too was going to Hursley on the very day I had named, I wrote to Keble to put off my visit. I told him, as I think, my reason. I had not seen either of them for twenty years, and to see both of them at once, would be more, I feared, than I could bear. Accordingly, I told him I should go from Birmingham to friends in the Isle of Wight, in the first place, and thence some day go over to Hursley. This was in September, 1865. But when, on the 12th, I had got into the Birmingham train for Reading, I felt it was like cowardice to shrink from the meeting, and I changed my mind again. In spite of my having put off my visit to him, I slept at Southampton, and made my appearance at Hursley next morning without being expected. Keble was at his door speaking to a friend. He did not know me, and asked my name. What was more wonderful, since I had purposely come to his house, I did not know him, and I feared to ask who it was. I gave him my card without speaking. When at length we found out each other, he said, with that tender flurry of manner which I recollected so well, that his wife had been seized with an attack of her complaint that morning, and that he could not receive me as he should have wished to do; nor, indeed, had he expected me; for 'Pusey,' he whispered, 'is in the house, as you are aware.'

"Then he brought me into his study, and embraced me most affectionately, and said he would go and prepare Pusey, and send him to me.

"I think I got there in the forenoon, and remained with him four or five hours, dining at one or two. He was in and out of the room all the time I was with him, attending on his wife, and I was left with Pusey. I recollect very little of the conversation that passed at dinner. Pusey was full of the question of the inspiration of Holy Scripture, and Keble expressed his joy that it was a common cause, in which I could not substantially differ from them; and he caught at such words of mine as seemed to shew agreement. Mr. Gladstone's rejection at Oxford was talked of, and I said that I really thought that had I been still a member of the University, I must have voted against him, because he was giving up the Irish Establishment. On this Keble gave me one of his remarkable looks, so earnest and so sweet, came close to me, and whispered in my ear, (I cannot recollect the exact words, but I took them to be,) 'And is not that just?' It left the impression on my mind that he had no great sympathy with the Establishment in Ireland as an Establishment, and was favourable to the Church of the Irish.

"Just before my time for going, Pusey went to read the Evening Service in Church, and I was left in the open air with Keble by himself. He said he would write to me in the Isle of Wight, as soon as his wife got better, and then

I should come over and have a day with him.   We walked
a little way, and stood looking in silence at the Church
and Churchyard, so beautiful and calm.   Then he began
to converse with me in more than his old tone of intimacy, as if we had never been parted, and soon I was
obliged to go.

"I remained in the Island till I had his promised letter.
It was to the effect that his wife's illness had increased, and
he must give up the hopes of my coming to him.   Thus,
unless I had gone on that day, when I was so very near not
going, I should not have seen him at all.

"He wrote me many notes about this time ; in one of
them he made a reference to the lines in Macbeth :—

> "'When shall we three meet again ?
> When the hurley-burley's done,
> When the battle's lost and won.'

"This is all I can recollect of a visit, of which almost
the sole vivid memory which remains with me is the image
of Keble himself.

"I am, dear Sir John Coleridge,
"Yours faithfully,
"JOHN H. NEWMAN."

"*Sir John Coleridge, &c., &c.*"

I must not venture to add a word of comment on
this letter ; and I must be careful not to suffer my
feelings to exaggerate the interest of this meeting,
so remarkable in every way.   It is difficult, indeed,
to restrain one's emotion in thinking of what must
have been in the hearts of these three friends, once
so bound together in the prosecution of the highest

objects ; separated in the body, but not in heart, for so many years ; and now meeting under such trying circumstances, for a brief while, and for the last time in this world ; what must one of them, at least, have felt as he stood with Keble, "looking in silence on that Church and Churchyard, so beautiful and calm."

They parted, and Keble wrote the well-known lines from Macbeth.   I hope we may not irreverently look forward for them to another more blessed meeting,—

> " When before the Judgment-seat,
> Though changed, and glorified each face,
> Not unremembered ye may meet
> For endless ages to embrace."

CHAPTER XXI.

OCTOBER 11, 1865, LEAVE HURSLEY AND GO TO
BOURNEMOUTH.—LETTER ON THE RITUAL QUES-
TION.—HIS LIFE AT BOURNEMOUTH.—ILLNESS.—
DEATH, MARCH 29, 1866.—BURIAL AT HURSLEY.
—REMARKS ON PERSON AND CHARACTER.—MRS.
KEBLE'S DEATH, BURIAL, CHARACTER.

BUT little remains to be told. The illness of
Mrs. Keble, of which there had been so alarming an attack at the very time of the meeting of the
three friends, continued to manifest itself in gradually-
increasing weakness and suffering, from which there
was no effectual rallying, and never any complete
relief. She was, indeed, sometimes more easy, and
must have had considerable strength of constitution.
She was supported, too, by a cheerful heart, and entire resignation to God's dispensations. To these
last Keble bears most affecting testimony in the letters I am about to transcribe.

They were advised to lose no time in settling
themselves for the winter at Bournemouth, but they
were naturally desirous to keep the anniversary of

their wedding-day, the thirtieth, at home. This was on the 10th of October, and on the eleventh they left it, never to return alive. Domestic as he was by nature, and always prone to attach himself to places as well as persons ; and loving his parishioners, his church, his parish, and his parsonage, as he did, we may well imagine with what feelings he commenced his journey to Bournemouth. I am not sure that he had at all realized to himself that he should never return. This, indeed, was of less consequence to him who always carried his life in his hand, and whose heart was stayed elsewhere ; but I feel sure that he had realized this to himself, that if he did return, it would be to follow his wife to her grave, and linger at God's pleasure a widower on earth.

Mr. Moor tells us that on the Sunday before he went, the 8th of October, Keble took some part in the Services, reading the Lessons, and celebrating the Holy Communion ; and not only this, but zealous to the last in the work he loved most, walked with him to visit some of his poor people at a distance ; and also entertained at dinner some friends who had come unexpectedly to see him.

The journey was well accomplished on the 11th of October. I am drawing near to the end of my store of letters, and it will be seen that for what remains to be told, I make use of his own pen wherever I can ; I believe my readers will with reason thank me for this.

On the 13th of October he wrote thus :—

> " SOUTH CLIFF VILLA, BOURNEMOUTH,
> " *Oct.* 13, 1865.

" DEAREST COLERIDGE,

" We accomplished our journey here the day before yesterday, with as much comfort as we could expect, and are
well satisfied with our lodgings, which are as thoroughly
within breath of the sea as any in this place, and seem so
far very comfortable.   My niece Charlotte, and Fanny Coxwell, are with us.   But as yet I see no rallying, even to such
strength as before that last attack. . . . . I do not mean that
I am without hope that, by God's blessing on constant care
and prayer, we may hope to have her with us for an indefinite time, but she has had more frequent attacks, with less
of rallying in the intervals.

> " I am ever, my dearest Friend,
> " Most affec^ly yours, J. K."

Of course I was writing to him frequently, and I
did not scruple to consult him on any difficulties
which I might have in my reading as at other times.
Among my own letters returned to me, I find in
one, written on the 18th of October, a passage
which I transcribe for the sake of the answer :—

" Now I want an answer from you, if you can give it
without book, and without trouble.   Reading S. Bernard's
Sermons on the Advent, I am puzzled with this phrase
twice occurring.   He is speaking of our Lord's two advents ;
he urges his Monks to ponder how much He has performed
in the one, how much He has promised in the other, and
then says, ' Utinam certè dormiatis *inter medios cleros*.   Hæc

sunt enim duo brachia Sponsi, inter quæ Sponsa dormiens aiebat. Læva ejus sub capite meo, et dextera ejus amplexabitur me,' and goes on quoting Cantic. ii. 6. And, again, 'Sint ergo, si dormire volumus *inter medios cleros*, id est duos adventus, pennæ nostræ deargentatæ.' The words, ' medios cleros,' are in my edition printed in italics as a quotation. Don't trouble yourself about this, if it does not come into your head at once."

I thought the question might interest him, and from his great familiarity with the Fathers, I did not anticipate that I should put him to much trouble. I was right in the first supposition, but it will be seen what a diligent enquiry he made for me.

On the 26th of October he answered me ; and, first, he gave an account of his wife's state, and said that they were about to change their lodgings, "not being able to get a bedroom here on the same floor as this, which is quite necessary, for though we do get her carried upstairs, the walking down, and the colder air of the passages, is apt to affect her breath ;" he then proceeds thus :—

" .... I have borrowed a S. Bernard from the Vicar here, and have thought over your question as well as I could, with the help of the Bible, the Septuagint, and Gesenius. I dare say you have long ago found out that the clause is from the Vulgate Version of Ps. 68, (67,) v. 13, (14,) and that *inter medios cleros*, is what our Bible version renders, 'among the pots,' the Vulgate apparently adopting the word κλήρους from the LXX. ἀνάμεσον τῶν κλήρων. So the question is how the LXX. came to translate the Hebrew word which

we render 'pots' by 'lots,' or 'portions;' and the phrase
'between the portions' somehow led my mind back to the
rite of *dividing* victims offered to sanction a covenant, as in
Gen. xv., and Jerem. xxxiv., and a passing between the *portions* of the victims. Also the Hebrew of 'pots' is nearly the
same as that rendered 'hooks' in Ezek. xl. 43, where plainly
something is meant on which, or by means of which, the
flesh of the offerings for sacrifice was deposited on *each side*
of certain entrances to the Temple, so that the offerer or
votary going in would pass 'between the hooks,' i.e. 'between the portions' of the sacrifice, (our Translation in the
margin there says, 'or endirons, or the two hearth-stones.')
The mystical meaning, then, of being *between* these portions
would be 'being under a covenant by Sacrifice, (see Ps. l.
5,) and *sleeping* between them as Abram seems to have
done, would be, *being at rest* in that Covenant,' for which
purpose we must be sanctified as Christians, there must be
the 'wings of the dove,' &c. . . . . . I wish this may be intelligible, and have something in it; at any rate, it interested
me greatly.

* * * * * *

"I am disgusted much at finding the Colenso (public)
fund is more than £2,000, the Cape-Town hardly £200.
Hard lines for what is at worst a fault of temper. I cannot
write more just now. Ever yours, J. K."

I could not help observing to Keble, when I
thanked him for his answer, how much the Fathers
took for granted as to Biblical knowledge in those
whom they addressed. If they could do so properly, it would seem to indicate a much greater
general diffusion of that knowledge than prevails

now. Certainly, considering where the Fathers themselves studied, a kind of learning seems necessary which is now, I fear, not common even among the Clergy; it may be that a different kind is substituted; whether more or less valuable I will not venture to say. But those among them, at least, who yield to the sceptical spirit of the age, and delight rather to find difficulties and suggest doubts, than to accept old beliefs, are surely bound in conscience to acquire a deep and thorough knowledge not merely of Hebrew, but of the best and earliest commentators, of the history, usages, and ritual of the Hebrews, before they communicate their doubts or their theories to the public; considering how often they are found to trouble men's minds needlessly by doubts, which more of this knowledge shews to be groundless, or by theories which rest mainly on unwarranted assumptions.

I am not competent to pronounce any opinion whether Keble, whose answer is, at least, ingenious and learned, had correctly solved my difficulty; and I print the extract in great part to shew how entirely he still preserved his activity and clearness of intellect. But he gave a more remarkable proof of this in a letter which he wrote and published in this same month in the "Literary Churchman," on the "Ritual of the Church of England." I hope this is more known and considered, especially at this time, than I fear it is. It is written in such an admirable spirit, and with so much clearness and cogency, that one might hope it might furnish a useful guide to the clergy, and allay somewhat of the bitterness which is so much to be lamented in the manner of waging the present controversy. It is too long to be inserted here entire, but I cannot forbear enriching my pages with the concluding paragraph. The occasion recalls to my mind a wish which has been expressed by one of Keble's dearest and wisest friends, that all the occasional contributions which he made to the public journals, as well as all his fugitive pieces, should be collected, arranged, and published. I entirely concur in this ; if it be not soon done, they will surely be lost ; and as he never wrote anything for publication without care and thought, the loss of them would be much to be regretted :—

" It would seem to follow upon these statements—and I understand that there is high legal authority for the opinion —that the *onus probandi* lies in this matter upon the many who practically ignore or slight the usages (of which number I must confess myself to be one) rather than upon the few who have regularly maintained or recently adopted them. I do indeed regret the disregard of that rubric as a real blemish in our ecclesiastical practice—a contradiction to our theory, less momentous, but quite as real as our almost entire disuse of the discipline of Jesus Christ, our obligation to which, nevertheless, we formally acknowledge. But as in the latter case, so in this, the time and manner of regaining the old paths must, under our circumstances, be a question of equity and charity, not of strict law alone. I,

for one, rejoice whenever and wherever I see that kind of
revival successfully and tranquilly accomplished. But the
success will be more complete, and the satisfaction more
perfect, when those who have the work at heart shall have
ceased to indulge themselves in invidious comparisons and
scornful criticisms on such among their brethren as do not
yet see their way to it; and when, on certain kindred subjects, they have learned to make candid allowance for the
difference between our circumstances and those with a view
to which the primitive canons were framed. I allude particularly to the disparaging tone sometimes used in speaking of mid-day Communions, with small consideration, as it
seems to me, for the aged and infirm, and others who cannot come early. Again, I cannot but doubt the wisdom of
urging all men indiscriminately to be present at the Holy
Mysteries—a matter left open, as far as I can see, by the
Prayer-book, and in ordering of which it may seem most
natural to abide by the spirit of the ancient Constitutions,
which did not willingly permit even the presence of any but
communicants, or those of whom the clergy had reason to
believe that they were in a way to become such : the rather,
in that there appears to be some danger of the idea gaining
ground, which meets one so often in Roman Catholic books
of devotion, of some special, quasi-sacramental grace connected with simply assisting devoutly at Mass, over and
above that promised to all earnest and faithful prayer.

" On these and all like matters we may do well, perhaps,
to accept the counsel of our Church, in her first Reformed
Liturgy, concerning another main point of Christian discipline [a]—such as are satisfied with the more modern and
plainer ritual not to be offended with them that adopt the

[a] See the first Liturgy of King Edward the VIth. on Auricular
Confession.

more ornate and symbolical requirements of the rubric ; those, on the other hand, who find comfort and edification in the ceremonies to bear with their brethren who, for various reasons, think best to dispense with them for the present. And so, too, in regard of Communion after a meal, and of encouraging the presence of non-communicants, and the like, ' to follow and keep the rule of charity, and every man to be satisfied with his own conscience, not judging other men's minds or consciences, whereas he hath no warrant of God's Word to the same.'

" Believe me, dear——, with great respect,

" Very sincerely yours,

" JOHN KEBLE."

Thus wisely and thus gently did he express himself in print on this subject ; but he yet felt very warmly, and expressed himself warmly in conversation, and by way of advice to a young friend, on the suicidal folly of our hot contentions respecting ritual, when we had to contend against such deadly enemies as looseness of morals, and growing infidelity, sapping the very foundations of religion. He sadly sighed for unity ; he did not agree with those who thought that our only, or even our most powerful enemy, was Papal Rome. But he feared that our acrimonious disputes on matters which do not touch the foundations of our Faith, might give her a power not her own ; as the devices and engines of Imperial Rome were helped in breaching the walls of the Holy City, by the internecine contentions of the garrison within.

The passage to which Keble makes reference in this extract, it may be convenient to print here, as the first Liturgy of Edward VI. is not in the hands of all people. It stands at the end of what in our present Liturgy is the first exhortation in the Communion Service ; and it is conceived in a spirit so charitable in itself, and so applicable to all parts of the present controversy, that it is much to be regretted that it was ever struck out :—

" Requiring such as shall be satisfied with a general confession, not to be offended with them that do use to their further satisfying the auricular and secret confession to the Priest ; nor those also which think needful or convenient, for the quietness of their own consciences, particularly to open their sins to the Priest, to be offended with them that are satisfied with their humble confession to God, and the general confession of the Church ; but *in all things to follow and keep the rule of Charity ; and every man to be satisfied with his own conscience, not judging other men's minds or consciences; whereas he hath no warrant of God's word to the same.*"

He wrote to me again on the 30th and 31st of December, and I give the whole letter :—

" BOURNEMOUTH,
" *Dec.* 30, 1865.

" DEAREST DEAR FRIEND,

" It is sad work, my trick of putting off my replies to your loving letters. I can only say, as in so many former years, Forgive me. I dare say I was a little the more tardy from having no very good news to tell ; good news, I mean, according to our natural way of thinking about our dearest Charlotte's health. I cannot hide it from myself, that she is gradually growing weaker, and that one thing after another has to be given up ; walking more than a step or two, writing, chess, animated conversation, &c., &c., make her dear heart beat too freely, and she suffers sadly from night perspiration and faintness. The climate has not, as far as I can see, been against her ; it has been exceptionally mild, and for this place, I hear, exceptionally moist, and if she had been a little stronger, she might have gone out a little some days in almost every week ; indeed, she has done rather more than I expected in that way ; but I do not find that it revives her as it used to do ; and all the brandy and turtle soup they give her by day and by night only just serves to enable her to go on from day to day. The doctors said some time since that we must not expect a cure, but might hope for improvement ; now they hardly say that, but express surprise that we are yet spared other symptoms which I fear we must look for. But it all brings out moment by moment the goodness and sweetness with which He is continually endowing her ; at least, so it seems to a poor creature looking on it from below.

" 31st. I cannot report any improvement ; she has not got up at all to-day ; and by the doctor's direction we have telegraphed to Bisley. We had deferred doing so perhaps too long on account of old Tom, who is rather in a critical state of health ; nevertheless, I do hope we may see them to-morrow. Pray for us, dearest Friend, that she may be gently visited, and that I may be not found unfit to be with her, at whatever distance, hereafter. I cannot write more about myself ; of her, if I had time, and my hand was strong, I could go on for hours. With dear love for the Christmas and New Year, I am ever yours, J. K."

He wrote again on the 7th of January a short note respecting an offer he had received of translating the *Prælectiones* for publication. Mrs. Keble's symptoms had been somewhat alleviated, and the presence of the brother and sister, with the tender attentions of the latter as nurse, had cheered them all. Before he could have any answer from me to this letter, he wrote again on the 9th as follows :—

" BOURNEMOUTH,
"*Jan.* 9, 1866.

" MY DEAREST COLERIDGE,

" Thank you, and thank you again, though too tardily for your too loving letter. It is a great comfort, as your letters always are. I have not read it exactly to her, but you may be sure she loves you with a true sisterly love, and has done so all along. She has mended a little, our Doctor says, during the last week. The long nightly faintings have subsided, and if she had not caught a cold, which disorders her breath, I fancy we should have had her in our sitting-room to-day or to-morrow. I think the Doctor expects her departure to be very gradual ; I fear, with dropsical symptoms. But we try to look on as little as may be ; having been already brought farther on our way together than we could reasonably have expected. We do not at all repent of having come here, the climate has been unusually moist and mild, and we have comforts we could not have had at Penzance. God reward you, dearest Coleridge, and your dear wife and children, for all your love to her and me.

" Ever your most affec^te, J. K."

He wrote to me again on the 31st of January,

N n

and early in March; his friends, and I amongst
them, had been misinformed as to Mrs. Keble, or
the partial amendment of which he speaks in the
preceding letter had been represented too favour-
ably, and it is touching to see what he says on it.
But it is remarkable also how amid his distress at
the prospect of his approaching loss, he retained his
interest in what regarded Oxford, and Christian
Education.   In order fully to understand some parts
of what he writes, it may be well for me to state
that I had written to him among other things on
the prospects of the new Parliament just about to
open.   It seemed to me that every move, in what
is called the path of Liberal Progress, would *in the
end* be made good, and I thought that those who,
without reference to party, wished to preserve foundations, and all of good built on them, should shape
their course with this conviction on their minds.
And I deprecated the old spirit which not seldom defended that which was really objectionable in itself,
merely because it might be considered an out-work,
and because the surrender of it would probably not
appease the spirit of the invaders.   I also wrote in regard to the probable course of one in whom I was specially interested, how he desired to pass the coming
Session, his first in Parliament, and of the difficulty
cast on him by the expectations and instances of
his friends.   I also gave my opinion of the remarkable, and I may add, somewhat enigmatical book,

which he speaks of. In his mind all other Oxford interests were as nothing in comparison with the preservation of the faith there, to which he justly thought sound teaching an indispensable mean. He had an honest conviction that there was a great deal of unsound teaching at present, and that it was bearing a plentiful harvest. I wish I could believe that there was no foundation for his fears. Most reluctantly I yield to evidence which forces them upon me. It seems to me as if considerable cleverness, great respectability of conduct, popular even amiable manners, and an apparent candour, extending to every subject and system but one, are waging such a fight against Christianity as ought to make the parents of Oxford students anxious ; while, I must add, the insane and excessive passion for athletics, as they are called, (indulged in our great schools as well,) damps industry, and diverts from that severe mental labour which is among the guards to preserve the mind from yielding to sophistry.

Fears, however, I have none as to the ultimate result ; a battle is being fought, which has been fought more than once before, and victory has always been on one side ; victory not always turned to the best account ; but, alas, it must be expected that there will be many, and those not seldom the flower of the host, wounded sorely, a few, it is to be feared, slain in the combat.

I now give the letters which have occasioned these remarks :—

" BOURNEMOUTH,
"*Jan.* 31, 1866.

" DEAREST COLERIDGE,

" I wish you could have from me as long and hearty a letter as your too great kindness deserves. As it is, I can but thank you, 1, for your advice and information about Mr. ——, to whom I will soon write accordingly ; 2. for the very interesting report of dear John and his proceedings ; which seem so amiable and dutiful that I cannot but think he will have a blessing on his work, and perhaps with others like-minded, on his cause also ; such as may in good measure neutralize the harm you and I might expect from it. For myself, I am a little sanguine about the Reform ; *if it leaves the Colleges alone,* and *if the present leaven of N⁰. 90, so marvellously reviving, go on and prosper.* If the latter be not so, it matters little about other things.

" But my dearest wife,—your kind words go to my heart, so certain am I that it is far other than you say. Where Heathcote got his information I cannot guess, but I have heard more or less from friends far and near in the same tone. She, dear soul, though there may be sometimes a slight rally for half a day, grows on the whole gradually weaker ; and now I fear her power of taking nourishment is lessening. Her long faintings are very distressing. You must not flatter me about that, or anything else.

" I suppose it is the same with many more, but I for one am certain that whatever bows me down most, is best for me.

" Best love to you all,

" Your most affec^te J. K."

" Dear Bessie, our head nurse, is of the same opinion as

I am, so must every one be that watches her; and the Doctor's encouragement amounts to this, that the worst symptoms do not come on so fast as he expected."

> " BOURNEMOUTH,
> " 3rd *Sunday in Lent,*
> "(*March* 4,) 1866.

" DEAREST COLERIDGE,

" I cannot write worthily in any sense to answer your kind letters, but they always interest me, and so they would my dear wife, if she were always able to attend to them, which for a great part of her time, I grieve to say, she is not. We ought to be very thankful that she is so sweetly and gently let down, at least, to all appearances, though of course we cannot tell how much she suffers; and she is, I fancy, very dextrous in concealing such things. However, she has certainly better nights of late; and the dropsy, though it does not diminish, does not increase so fast as it did; moreover, though she likes nothing, she submits to a good deal of nourishment; so I do not know, (for I never ask that question,) but I hardly feel as if she were going quite immediately. Thank you for suggesting books, though it is little she can bear now, she gets sleepy so soon. We read Mackenzie's Life long ago; Robertson's I have not met with, and I doubt whether I should, (or she would,) like it; 'honest doubts,' as one calls them, are not very pleasant on a sick bed. For the same reason I don't care to read *Ecce Homo,* but it will be a very agreeable disappointment if the writer turns out a Christian at last; and I will pull off my hat to him, and beg his pardon. I hope you will read Miss Mackenzie's Life of Mrs. Robertson in Zululand. She and her husband appear to me the Queen and King of Missionaries, at least, among the second order, for I don't talk of Bishops. . . . .

" J. H. N. sent me his book ; it seems to me, logically, a complete failure, though of course in parts extremely good and beautiful. (I mean a failure as to the Doctrine of the B. Virgin's ' supremacy ;') the only thing that *cants* me is the fact about the Eastern Church, which one knew otherwise. I am very well, thank you ; ashamed to be so well. I have no nursing, my sister takes it off my hands ; I wish she may stand it. With kind love to all, your most affectionate J. K."

I have but one more letter to add, the last of the long series :—

" BOURNEMOUTH,
" *March* 19, 1866.

" MY DEAREST COLERIDGE,

" I am too long as usual, but you will understand and excuse it.

"Since I wrote she has been gradually getting weaker, suffering more and more from sickness, palpitation, and sometimes acute pain in the heart ; and now for several days her pulse, and power to take nourishment, have given way. The doctor was here four times yesterday, and we watch her now not from day to day, but from hour to hour. D. G. her sister keeps up pretty well, and as for myself, I eat, drink, and sleep heartily ; so you need be in no care about me, so far. I do not know well just now how to go on writing about anything else, so I will just give you all our dear love, and sign myself your most affectionate, J. K."

It may be supposed that I do not close without some emotion my extracts from a correspondence, beginning in 1811, and continued without interruption to the 19th of March, 1866. Few things I am more grateful for, (perhaps I may own I am a little proud of it,) than my having preserved from the beginning Keble's letters, and those of another dear friend, Arnold. The letters, like their writers, differ in many respects; and I will not pronounce on their interest as compositions; neither of the two when writing to me ever thought of composing what should be read by others than myself; but the letters of both are, as they themselves were, one in goodness and honesty of heart, one in overflowing affectionateness of feeling and expression.

During these last weeks Keble was, of course, in correspondence with many persons, intimate friends and anxious inquirers; sometimes from Mrs. Keble's inability to write, he answered letters addressed to her. I have copies before me of three which he wrote to Miss Mackenzie, the sister of the Bishop. He was deeply interested in the Missionary work in which her sister with her husband had been engaged; we have seen that he calls them the King and Queen of Missionaries. One of these letters I will venture to insert here, although I know I may be thought to have printed too many of the same character; for beside the circumstances under which it was written, this seems to me to have a special beauty and force, which make it wrong to omit it:—

"BOURNEMOUTH,
Jan^v 23, 1866.

" MY DEAR KIND FRIEND,

"Just one line to say how both our hearts, my dearest
wife's and my own, were smitten down this morning by the
sad news from C. Yonge, of your sad and, to us, unexpected
loss. I dread to think of the wound it must be to you:
only He who put into your heart such deep affections and
sustains them there, has the power and the love also to
mitigate the wounds, which His wise and good Providence
sees fit to make.

" You must think, dear Friend, of the mysterious moment
when He, who is Love, condescended to endure the bitterness of His Mother's grief as an addition (so to speak) to
His Own; and thereby sanctified the agonies we have
to bear in watching the sufferings of our beloved ones.
Like other pains they will be sweet, if we can be helped
so to join them to His Cross.

" But how vain of me to say all this to one who has had
your experience! God grant that I may be saying it not
in vain to myself! For indeed I have much need, and am
likely to have more. Dearest Charlotte continues in most
respects, much as when I wrote to you last; the doctor
comes every day and pronounces the pulse much as it was,
and allows her to be brought for an hour or two into our
sitting-room. But I am sure there is a gradual decay of
strength; one by one things become too hard for her, and
it is a greater effort for her to keep up; yet she does keep
up in spirit most comfortably. Your kind heart would
rejoice if you could see what refreshment she finds in
your most seasonable present of the sheets of Mrs. Robertson's ' Life ;' she took to it the moment it came, and

from hour to hour, day after day, she enjoys it being read to her. I never saw any book more successful apparently in beguiling hour after hour of weariness and breathlessness. I now really hope, that both it and the 'Net' will be a great success.

"God comfort and reward you for all your trials and all your love.

"Ever yours very affectionately,
"J. KEBLE."

It will be seen how down to the very last of these letters from Bournemouth all Keble's thoughts were for his dear wife, and how unconscious he seems to have been of any falling off in his own health. Mr. Moor informs us, that when he came there, he had, as was his custom, proffered to Mr. Bennett assistance, if needed ; which he with a wise consideration declined to accept from him. But he was regular, until his very last illness, in his attendance on the daily services in the church. His favourite help in his private prayer was the *Paradisus Animæ*, and he had so familiarized himself to it, that he not uncommonly prayed in Latin. On Sundays and Thursdays, when he regularly attended the mid-day Communion, it was in his hand all the morning before he went to church. On those mornings it was with difficulty he could be persuaded to take any breakfast ; for many years it had been his custom, whenever he was to celebrate in the course of the day, to eat nothing before. At church he usually

sat in one place, and the window over that place
has now been filled with stained glass out of respect
for his memory.   He was, I may mention here, a
strong advocate for the system of free and unap-
propriated seats, which he urged strongly on Mr.
Bennett.   It may be that circumstances prevented
its adoption at Bournemouth.   He therefore took
a seat, but never used it, and told the clerk to use
it as free.   It is right to add that the seats in Hursley Church were still in his time appropriated, which
he desired much to change.   It seems to me that
a wide distinction in principle exists between payment and simple appropriation, and that if this last
be fairly extended to the poor as well as the rich,
with a limitation to secure punctuality in attendance,
there is much to be said for it.   Payment has been,
is, and ever will be, simply mischievous.   He read a
good deal ; for himself especially St. Chrysostom on
St. John, (for he had not even now abandoned the
thought of his promised Commentary).   He read
to Mrs. Keble the Services daily ; and from time to
time, frequently it would seem, he administered to
her the Holy Communion.   In the evenings the little
party would meet in her bedroom, (which, indeed,
was his also for a large part of the illness,) and the
lessons were read usually by Mr. James Young, of
whom I have spoken before.   Sometimes he would
read to himself the first Lessons in the original.

No one can doubt that he prayed much for her ;

more than was commonly observed ; he had a life-
long faith in the efficacy of intercessory prayer, but
he shrunk from observation when he prayed alone ;
more than once, on occasions of special distress, or interest, he was observed kneeling in the act of prayer
behind a door, where it was not likely he should
be seen.

With all his sorrow, and his own weakness, which
no doubt was great, he still bore up ; and down to
little more than a week before his death he took
his walks, seemed refreshed by them, and retained
his old interest in the objects of nature around him ;
especially, it was noted by his young and loving
companion, the ever-varying sea, the ships, the cliffs,
the clouds, the sky.

Down to this time, so far as I can perceive, no
new or special anxiety was felt for his own health.
Even the sufferer, about whom all were anxious,
seemed to have but one real trouble, how he would
bear her departure, how he would be taken care of
after she was gone.   She told her maid one day,
that she should not mind dying, if it were not for
him ; that she was much afraid for him, he seemed
to bear up too well.   She was told in answer, that
his heart had seemed as if it would burst but a night
or two before.   He had had through life one remarkable blessing, that no trouble by day affected
his sleep ; he mentioned this once to a friend, and
in his usual way of self-disparagement, attributed it

to want of feeling. She put the truer and better construction on it; she would often say, "He lays aside his anxieties with his prayers; he does what he can, the issue is with God, with Whom he is content to leave it; therefore he is still, and sleeps like a child."

But he was "drawing daily nearer home," and his Master now saw fit to call His servant to Himself. The illness, under which he sunk, lasted just a week, and seemed to be occasioned at first by his rising on the 22nd of March as early as six o'clock by mistake, by his then using a cold instead of warm bath, by his praying for some time by his wife's bed-side, and then standing to read the Lessons to her, all without any food; in the act of reading he is said to have fainted; whether that was paralytic, I do not know, but he was never able to use his lower limbs again. Once when he had been helped into Mrs. Keble's room, he managed to stand by himself, to cheer her; and drew himself up, a gesture his friends will well remember as familiar with him, and playfully said, "Richard's himself again."

The severity of the symptoms, however, increased. In about two days after, he was unwillingly wheeled out of her room; and they who for so many years had had but one heart, and one mind, parted for life, with one silent look at each other. I do not pursue the details of the remaining two or three days; he was sometimes wandering, sometimes conscious, sometimes clear-minded ; whether wandering, or clear-minded, he was constantly intent on holy things, or in actual prayer ; he uttered fragments, or ejaculations in the former case, which shewed the habitual prayerfulness of his heart ; he repeated, or he composed, as it seemed, prayers ; the Lord's Prayer he uttered most commonly.

He fell asleep on the 29th of March, about one in the morning.

I have been treated with so much kindness and confidence by those who were on the spot, or had full means of knowing with certainty everything that passed, that I could have multiplied these notices of my dear friend's last illness, and dying hours ; but the sick room, and the chamber of death, are sacred ; and my only fear is, that I may have trespassed already on their sanctity. This I felt, that I was in no danger of revealing anything that was unworthy of him. One anecdote I must add, for it is the highest testimonial direct and indirect from the best of witnesses, his dying wife.

The mournful family repaired from his death-bed to her room, and knelt round her bed, and prayed ; she besought them to return thanks for her to God, that he had been taken first, that she, not he, had to bear the trial of surviving ; but she expressed a hope that she might be released so soon as to admit of both being buried at the same time in one grave.

Then she requested her maid to fetch her " Christian Year," and turning to the two last stanzas of the verses on Good Friday, " I know," said she, " these were in his dying thoughts :"—

> " Lord of my heart, by Thy last cry,
>   Let not Thy blood on earth be spent—
>   Lo, at Thy feet I fainting lie,
>   Mine eyes upon Thy wounds are bent,
> Upon Thy streaming wounds my weary eyes
> Wait like the parched earth on April skies.
>
> " Wash me, and dry these bitter tears,
>   O let my heart no further roam,
>   'Tis Thine by vows, and hopes, and fears,
>   Long since—O call Thy wanderer home ;
> To that dear home, safe in Thy wounded side,
> Where only broken hearts their sin and shame
>   may hide."

There is no exaggeration in saying that the heart of England was deeply stirred by the news of his death.   There was a grief as real and as widely spread through different classes of society, and I may say with confidence, through all denominations of Christians, as any death has occasioned in my recollection.   We felt that we had lost a true Saint, a true Poet ; a Saint whose holiness and purity no verse he ever composed could blemish ; a Poet, whose genius was elevated and sanctified by the perpetual heavenward inspiration under which he wrote.   We had lost a guide, a counsellor, a friend, so humble, so loving, so tender, that no one, not the very school-boy in his little difficulties, nor even the young woman in the troubles of her heart, (I speak from knowledge,) shrunk from addressing him for help, or advice.

He was buried on the 6th of April, 1866, in his own churchyard, close to the grave of Elizabeth Keble, as that was near to the grave where the remains of my little God-child, Godfrey Heathcote, whom he had baptized, and was so tenderly interested in, are laid. As might be expected, the high and low, the rich and poor, the old and young, crowded to the funeral; it was no common ceremonial ; Mr. Moor speaks of the day truly as never to be forgotten by those who were present.

As yet no cross or monument has been erected at his grave ; (he himself had placed a stone cross, modelled from a beautiful Irish one, at the grave of his sister). But in the floor of the chancel, on the spot where his body rested during the service, the parishioners have placed a very beautiful brass cross designed by Mr. Butterfield, which records his name, the period of his incumbency, the day when he fell asleep in the Lord, and his age, seventy-four years. This cross is let into a stone, round the edge of which on a strip of brass is inscribed a memorable portion of our Litany, which he so loved :

" BY THINE AGONY AND BLOODY SWEAT ; BY THY
CROSS AND PASSION ; BY THY PRECIOUS DEATH
AND BURIAL ; BY THY GLORIOUS RESURRECTION
AND ASCENSION ; AND BY THE COMING OF THE
HOLY GHOST, GOOD LORD, DELIVER US."

It will be to be regretted, if the graves of Keble
and his loving wife should be longer left, I will not
say neglected, (at present there is no reason to fear
that,) but without some permanent mark and protection. There may be differences of opinion how
that may best be effected ; but it is dangerous to
rely too much on a continuance of the same warmth
of pious feeling with which these graves are now regarded ; and the green-sod grave, which is so pleasing
to the eye and to the imagination, with its flowers renewed from time to time by pious hands, is yet from
its very nature mouldering and perishable. According to the proverb, what is everybody's business is
no one's ; and after the lapse of a few years, the
pilgrim who comes to bend over the grave, may find
it difficult, if not impossible, to distinguish it from its
neighbours. On the other hand, I agree that there is
something almost repulsive to the feelings with which
we regard the resting-place of such remains as these,
in pressing them down with a heavy mass of stone.
Is it impossible to devise something which may
permanently mark the spot, and fence it from viola-
tion, and yet leave the grave to be seen by those

who visit it, and open to be piously decked from time to time with the flowers, and specially the wild flowers, of the season.

I am not competent to suggest how this may best be done, but let us not lay ourselves open to the imputation of negligent delay now, nor trust too much to the continuing piety of our posterity. Who, (says the Lover at the Grave of his Mistress, in terms not inappropriate to Keble's) :—

" Who, when I am turn'd to clay,
    Shall duly to her grave repair,
  And pluck the ragged moss away
    And weeds that have ' no business there ?'

" And who with pious hands shall bring
    The flowers she cherish'd, snowdrops cold,
  And violets that unheeded spring,
    To scatter o'er her hallow'd mould ? "

It will not be necessary, I think, for me to enlarge in any detail on Keble's character ; however imperfectly I have constructed this narrative, a tolerably accurate notion of that will have been collected from the numerous letters I have printed. These letters do not give, indeed, a full measure of his ability, or of his acquirements ; he wrote them rapidly, often when over-fatigued, on the spur of the moment, as the occasion called for them, with no care for the writing, no notion of their being preserved ; and

O o

yet I must not shrink from saying that I think they are of high value merely as epistolary compositions; but at all events, they paint him truly as he was.

A biographer is usually expected to try to convey some impression of the person and countenance of his subject ; and this is often a most difficult part of his office. It will have been seen that a young lady, to whom I am very much obliged, writes of him in Scotland as " a plain man ;" if she intended that he was ugly, or even commonplace, I should venture to differ from her entirely ; if she intended that his face was one easily understood, I should also disagree. I look on the opinion of the practised portrait painter as of the highest authority on such a subject ; it is his business to study the countenance, and it is part of his art to render its true character. When Mr. Richmond drew the portrait of him in the prime of his manhood, which was afterwards engraved by Mr. S. Cousins, he told me that out of so many as he had drawn, he never found one so difficult to comprehend. Curiously enough, when Mr. Cousins had studied the successful picture, and had brought his engraving to an unsuccessful first proof, he told me he had never met with a more unintelligible portrait, and begged to see the original. Keble and he accordingly breakfasted with me, and afterwards he also gave him a sitting ; " Now," said he, " I understand the picture," and he certainly succeeded admirably in his rendering of it. Mr. Richmond, it is well known, drew Keble's head again in old age, and he pronounced it then most beautiful, and beautiful is the drawing, and, though I venture to think a little wanting in strength, also true on the whole. For that is not the true portrait which gives the face as it strikes careless and commonplace beholders, but that which gives to congenial observers in the most agreeable way, I do not say an exceptional gleam of light or beauty, but the look that tells most vividly the characteristic workings of the mind and heart in their best moments.

To me both the portraits are full of deep interest, the earlier and the later both—each brings him back to me as he was ; in the earlier, he has some of the merry defiance he could assume in argument ; in the latter, I see the sad tenderness of his advanced years. Keble had not regular features ; he could not be called a handsome man, but he was one to be noticed anywhere, and remembered long ; his forehead and hair beautiful in all ages ; his eyes, full of play, intelligence, and emotion, followed you while you spoke ; and they lighted up, especially with pleasure, or indignation, as it might be, when he answered you. The most pleasing photograph is one in which he is standing by Mrs. Keble's side ; she is sitting with a book in her hand. The later photographs are to me very unpleasant. I will attempt no more particular description, for I feel how little definite I can convey in writing.

But there is a much more important and effectual portrait painting than such as I can give of the countenance, and before I lay down my pen, I must yet crave the indulgence of my readers to an account, as short as I can make it, of him in his ministrations as a Parish Priest. I speak thus guardedly, for I have been helped in this matter so copiously, and authentically, that it is difficult to be very short.

The characteristic of his ministrations in church, or elsewhere, was, as might have been expected, that which was the animating and pervading spirit of all his life, a perfectly simple and sincere sense of his own unworthiness, combined with a hearty conviction that every talent he had received, all his strength, all his time, all his energies, were consecrated to God's service; and that service so high and holy, that it was never to be thought of even but with the most reverential feeling of which he was capable. This last was never more marked than when he was engaged in the administration of the Sacraments. He was not what is commonly called an eloquent reader or preacher; his voice was not powerful, nor his ear perfect for harmony of sound; nor had he in the popular sense great gifts of delivery; but in spite of all this, you could not but be impressed deeply both by his reading and his preaching. When he read, you saw that he felt, and he made you feel, that he was the ordained servant of God ; delivering His words, or leading you, but as one of like infirmities and sins with your own, in your prayers. When he preached, it was with an affectionate almost plaintive earnestness, which was very moving. His sermons were at all times full of that scriptural knowledge which was a remarkable quality in him as a divine. Like one of the old Fathers, he seemed to have caught, by continual and devout study, somewhat of the idiom and manner of Scripture. In passing, let me press on my readers to profit by the sermons now in course of publication by his brother. Several of them were preached almost immediately after his Ordination, when he was not much over twenty-three. I think they will be found remarkable, among other things, for their soundness and moderation, as well as for more popular qualities.

His reverential feelings manifested themselves not merely in church, but in many almost involuntary habits of voice or gesture, in his family prayers, or in conversation, or reading. His hand would in prayer be raised so as to overshadow his eyes, or his voice would sink. Once a friend was about to read to him the daily prayers used by a poor Italian woman ; he raised his hand to his forehead in the way I speak of, caught a low chair, and knelt on it, as if that were the only proper position for him while the prayers were read.

It was but a part of this disposition which ap-

peared on many occasions in regard to his deceased
father ; he clung to *his* old ways ; among other things,
he always used Bishop Wilson's daily prayers ; in
the first instance, I believe, because he had used
them ; and when he meant to accord strongly with
some statement of doctrine, he would say, "That
seems to me just what my father taught me." Any
one who had known his father, or mother, or his
sister Sarah, who had died young, was always a welcome visitor at the vicarage.

He spent a considerable portion of his time in
the school. I will now give Mr. Young's account
n his own words, for I cannot mend them :—

"He was most scrupulous in going to the Sunday School
from 9.15 to 10.30, in the morning, and from 2 to 3 in the
afternoon. I think it might be truly said, that unless he
was hindered by illness, (which happily occurred very rarely,)
or by some special call of parochial duty, he never missed
during the 30 years he was at Hursley. Besides this, it
was his habit for several years to go to the Boys' School
every morning soon after 9, and teach the first class until
service time at 10, taking them through one part of the
Bible after another. On Friday there was an examination
in writing in the work which had been done during the
week. This he did, whoever might be staying with him,
and whatever letters, interesting or perplexing, he might
have received. School time often came on him before he
was ready, but as soon as he became aware that the clock
had struck, away he went. Many of his friends must remember to have seen him hurrying across the Lawn, and

down the Long Walk which led to the School, when he
fancied that he was late.   But he was never in a hurry in
his teaching; he was always patient, both with his Scholars,
and with his subject; dealing with it very simply and minutely, yet very deeply and practically.   He invariably
stood when he was teaching, and that not so much because he thought it gave him more command over the
boys' attention, but as it would seem because he fancied it
helped to keep him up to the mark, and hindered him from
becoming listless.   Indeed, in everything he took in hand,
if I may venture to say it, he always did his best.   He
never spared himself any labour of body or mind; but
whatever he undertook, a small matter or a great, he did
it with all his might, often with much misgiving and complaint, but always with an honest patient endeavour to give
his whole mind to it."

In connection with this subject I will insert here
an extract from a letter, in which Archdeacon Allen
gives me some account of an examination by himself of Keble's school.   It occurred a good many
years ago, when he was an Inspector of Schools,
and it was made at the request of the Bishop :—

"Sir W. Heathcote was present.   Mr. Keble watched the
examination closely, but did not, so far as I recollect, make
a single observation.   The children, as I thought, passed
an excellent examination, but I did not quite feel at home
with them.   Perhaps I felt awed by Mr. Keble's silent
presence.   The examination lasted from two till after five.
It was a beautiful summer evening, and Mr. Keble then
proposed to walk to a part of the parish, where, if I re-

collect right, he said, the green sand joined the chalk.
We mounted a hill without a word. At last Mr. Keble
broke silence and said, ' I find that you teach children on
a different principle from what I do.' ' Oh,' I said, ' I hope
not, please explain ; I am sure I must be wrong, and I wish
to mend.' ' No, I am not sure that you are wrong; but
you teach them analytically, and I teach them syntheti-
cally.' I said, ' Your words were perplexing to me, and
now I am in still greater perplexity ; what can you mean ?'
' For example, you asked them what parable teaches us to
persevere in prayer under every seeming discouragement;
I should have read with them St. Luke xviii. 1—7, and
then asked them what lesson do you learn from this ?"

I think we must all agree that Keble's mode was
the most helpful to children ; and this was the spirit
of his ordinary dealing with them.

He was always anxious to win their love ; and his
simplicity and playfulness, as well as his special fondness for the young, made this easy for him ; but he
was not afraid of sharp rebuke, or discipline, where
he thought the circumstances made them proper.
The principle which directed his general ministrations, prevailed also in this particular :—

" He never forgot," I am using Mr. Young's words, " that
he was a Steward intrusted with the souls of men whom he
had to deal with for their good, tenderly, or severely, as
there might be occasion, and with the holy things of God,
which he was to guard from dishonour."

Lying before me is a letter dated September 9,

1839, to Mr. Wilson, in which, after much about a new and higher school in contemplation, he writes thus characteristically about the parish school :—

" I am more in doubt on that score about the other School, the people here are so utterly averse to discipline. Just think of me last Sunday in humble imitation of you, inflicting a little wholesome Stick Liquorice on Ja. B. and Dick H. ; and then on my desiring old R. to repeat the dose on some small culprits yesterday, fancy his flatly refusing, in presence of the whole school, and saying he might be turned off, but he would not do any such thing ; although those before punished had shewn themselves, as I told him they would, specially attached to me in consequence. Of course I had nothing to do but to send away the boys and expostulate a little quietly with him ; but he was resolved, after his manner, having no doubt been instructed behind the curtain by Mrs. R. So I must get him to resign, and make an amicable retreat, for I shall not at all like to part with him otherwise than friends."

I do not know what became of Dick H., but Ja. B. sometime after was recommended by Keble to a situation, as the best boy in his parish ; and he has remained ever since in the same employ, maintaining the highest character, and bearing the best testimony to this wholesome castigation.

Keble's mode of catechizing was, I believe, not a usual one. He did not confine himself to the Church Catechism. He thought any opportunity of display by the children was much to be avoided ; he therefore prepared them carefully beforehand in the questions he meant to ask; if one could not answer a question, he did not put it to another, but helped the one who failed; he always repeated the answers aloud, that the parents might follow the subject intelligently. He usually took a short portion, whether of the Catechism or Scripture; and when the catechizing ended, lectured from the pulpit on what had been the subject of his questioning. He generally took boys and girls on alternate Sundays.

Mr. Young has been so kind as to furnish me with the heads of one or two specimens; it is worth while to give one. He was catechizing girls on Easter Monday, and his object was to shew how little girls might take pattern from St. Mary Magdalene :—

" He first drew from them with some minuteness the several particulars of her history in connection with the Resurrection, and then dwelt on the lessons they should derive from it, e.g. that they should prepare over-night for the work of the next day; that they should rise early; that in their difficulties they should go to those who were set over them; that they should stay by their Lord at all times, or as near Him as possible; if they were unhappy, they should still look after Him, then they would find that He would shew Himself to them in ways they least thought of; as He was with St. Mary Magdalene as a gardener; only they would not be allowed to touch Him all at once. He would train them gradually, and draw them up to Himself; and they must not think it hard, for it was His .way with His own Apostles."

This was followed the next day by catechizing the boys on the visit of St. Peter and St. John to the Sepulchre, dealt with in the same way. It may well be understood how practically and how generally useful such a system might be in hands like Keble's. He made a point at all times of the children having their Bibles in church, and following the Lessons; and for some years it was his *daily* custom to call up some of them after the service, and question them for a few minutes in the two chapters which had been read. No wonder the Hursley children had more than the usual knowledge of the Scriptures.

I have already in a former chapter spoken of him in regard to Confirmation; after it, he was always anxious that the young people should not lose sight of him, as he never did of them. His letters when from home are full of enquiries about doubtful young men, or women; and of messages, anxious, yet very considerate :—

"Why was he perfidious with me in not coming to H. C., or, at least, not coming to me to say why he kept away? If you think it more likely to answer, you need only say that I depend on having a call from him as soon as ever I get home."

With regard to the visitation of the sick and poor, and those who were in any trouble, his principle and the spirit of his practice may be summed up with exact truth in the words of St. Paul, "Ourselves your servants for Jesus' sake." He used habitually to speak of it as waiting on them, and, as I have said before, you could not be any time in the Vicarage as a guest without becoming aware how, without the least ostentation, this principle was acted on as a matter of course; equally, I must add, by husband and wife. In his practice as regarded the distribution of relief, and all perhaps that may be separated from teaching and direct ministering to spiritual wants, he was very glad to commit much to his wife and other assistants; in them he placed the most generous confidence, and gave them a wide discretion. This arose in part from his self-distrust; when consulted by them, he would say, "You will do it better than I can direct;" or, "I am sure to say the wrong thing;" but then they made the fullest communications to him; and his knowledge of persons and circumstances was remarkable. One lady, (and at the expense of giving her perhaps a moment's pain, I am bound in justice to mention her name, Miss Baker,) with many other important calls on her time, yet worked under him in this way for seventeen years; he would suggest to her cases, but he left her to work under the most general instructions; suggestions they might rather be called; she reported to him what she did, and he listened with the deepest interest, sometimes with tears in his eyes. When he was absent, she wrote to him; and if she were absent, he communicated with her on the subject of the poor :—

"Many thanks," writes he on one occasion from Penzance, "for your account of the people. Poor dear W. H. I was sorry to lose him out of the place, and I feel this more of a loss : he is one of those who have twined themselves round one's Hursley's memories. I am glad his wife did a good part by him at last. I am glad also about J. S., in whom I have always thought there was much good. My heart aches a little about the poor S—'s, especially since I feel that I have neglected them. It is also but one instance out of many. Our kind Christmas love to you, all and each, from top to toe."

Writing to her when he was at home, and she absent, he says :—

"We have had two deaths since I saw you. T. G., Mrs. F.'s servant, about the most exemplary young man in the place, was cut off last Sunday by something like diptheria, after two days' illness; and poor dear W. B. died the day before yesterday, and is to be buried on Sunday. It is very pleasant to see his family, wife and all the sons and daughters, in what a Christian way they have waited on and spoken of him all along, and I am much comforted about him."

These extracts, taken by themselves, may be said to shew nothing remarkable, but it is to be remembered they are but specimens of what was his ordinary course. And it continued to the end ; in the last month of his life, when he might have seemed borne down by incessant care for his suf-

fering wife, and his own unheeded increase of dis-
orderment, Miss Baker visited Bournemouth; he saw
her every day during her stay, talked over individual
cases with her, and grudged no time so spent.

Working by others, however, did not prevent him
from occupying himself much in personal visitation;
in this he was unwearied, in all weathers, at all hours;
and sometimes to the injury of his own health. His
was truly a ministry of consolation, and of cheering; he had consideration for all the special circumstances of each person under his charge. There
was, for example, a poor cripple, deaf and dumb,
whom he constantly found time to visit, because the
man thought he could understand the motion of his
lips; and he would hold conversations with him besides, by writing on a slate; then to amuse him in
his solitary life, he would set him sums on the slate
when he went away, and look them over at his next
visit, and correct them.

He "made friends," as one may say, with the inmates of the Workhouse, especially the old men, and
was frequent in his visits there. He got them to the
Daily Services, and, seating them on the front benches,
addressed himself specially to them, as he read the
second Lesson, reading slowly, and with pauses, almost as if he were alone with them, and were speaking to them. He was rewarded not seldom by
finding how much they learned of the Gospels in
this way.

Indeed his manner of reading the Scriptures was remarkable: so simple, that your first impression of it was that it was the reading of a very intelligent and reverent child, yet so good, that he made you understand them more, I think, than any one else. At the same time he conveyed to you in some measure his own feeling of reverence. He always paused before he began, and would often raise his hand to his forehead in the manner I have described before ; and so again at the close, he paused before he said, "Here endeth," &c.

He had made a little service by way of help and suggestion to himself, for the visitation of the sick :—

"He commonly began," here again I use Mr. Young's own words, "with the first Prayer for Good Friday, 'this Thy servant' being substituted for 'this Thy family ;' then there would be always some kind of Confession, very frequently the 51st Psalm, (indeed I believe he very seldom, if ever, said prayers with any sick person without introducing some verses at least of that Psalm) ; then came the prayers in the Visitation Service, and often Collects, special petitions being introduced here and there to suit the particular case, sometimes in his own words, sometimes in the words of the Psalms, or of the Prayer-book. When death was imminent, over and above the Commendatory Prayer, I have known him repeat at intervals verses or passages of Scripture, interspersed with short suffrages and ejaculations, extending over a considerable space of time.

"In cases of prolonged sickness he tried to pay his visit

on particular days, that it might be expected and prepared for; and if the sick person were near at hand, he would visit as nearly as possible at the same hour every day, his wish being in this as in every thing else, to adapt himself to what he thought would be most acceptable to those for whom he ministered. One case I specially remember of an old woman, whom he went to visit in this way every evening regularly, just before she settled for the night."

The Daily Services he prized much for others; for himself they were refreshment and delight, never palling; he never failed to attend when at home unless absolutely prevented, and if he could only be at part of the service he went to that.

His population was scattered over a considerable area, and after Morning Service he would commonly arrange with his curates what cases each were to visit in the course of the day; not that he entirely gave up any districts to them; for he made a point, so long as he was able, of visiting each himself in the course of every week, walking while he was strong enough, and latterly driving.

In all these ministrations great simplicity and paternal loving-kindness were the characteristics, especially in the administration of the Holy Eucharist to the sick; he would shake hands with all present, and if any neighbours attended, he always thanked them for so doing :—

"The lack of a regular system of discipline he tried to

supply in such ways as he could, making a point of finding some opportunity of reproving notorious offenders, and setting some mark upon them in the hope (to use his own frequent quotation) 'that by making their faces ashamed, they might be led to seek the Lord.' On some occasions, in the case of disgraceful marriages, he has substituted for the exhortation or sermon in the Marriage Service a short address, in which he remonstrated earnestly and plainly with the young people. Little were they whom he then, or at other times reproved, aware of the intense anxiety with which he watched their look and bearing under reproof."

I am afraid I have been long on this part of my subject, but if my readers could see the interesting store which lies before me, and from which perhaps I have not made the best selection after all, they would, I believe, forgive me. But I must not any longer abuse their indulgence, and enough has been done I trust upon the whole, to satisfy them that if Keble was a scholar, a divine, a remarkably gifted poet, if he were exemplary as a friend, a brother, son, and husband, so he was admirable in the discharge of his duties as a parish priest. These last, without unwisely weighing one obligation against another, he did esteem most pressing ; he thought his calling beyond all others holy, his mission in our Church from supreme authority, his task such as he never could believe he performed, or could perform, except imperfectly and unworthily. But as he adored the greatness and majesty, so he lovingly trusted in the mercy of his Master, Redeemer, and Comforter.

WHAT I could do in writing the story of this dear friend I have now done, and I can truly say that the severest judgment which can be passed on my workmanship will hardly be more severe than I am conscious of its deserving. But I will say no more of this. I must not finally lay down my pen before I have reverted to the sick room at Bournemouth. There, for about six weeks, to the surprise of all, Mrs. Keble still lingered, waiting in suffering and great weakness, yet without impatience, the summons which she earnestly desired. It was vouchsafed to her on the 11th of May, and on the 18th she was laid by her husband's side; a double grave had been prepared in the first instance. The order of her funeral was arranged according to that of his, except that her own female friends bore her pall.

At the time of her death I inserted a short notice of her in the "Guardian;" no one I believe questioned that what I said of her was true; but more than one well-qualified judge pronounced it insufficient, and as doing her scant justice on the whole. Two of them were ladies, who spoke upon a knowledge of her much more intimate than my own; they had known her in the parish, in society, in her own house, in health, such as she was ever granted, and in sickness; they were certainly right. I unavoidably wrote in haste, and did not recall to my mind all that even I myself had been witness to.

She was indeed, as I then said, a genuinely kind, humble-hearted, affectionate, and pious woman ; and she adapted herself with zeal to the special calls made on her as Keble's wife : with him she identified herself as much as she could ; his friends were her friends ; in his duties she took her proper part, cheerfully making exertions that were almost beyond her strength ; his principles she took for her own ; and with the truest sense of what an interval existed between him and herself, she yet laboured in all things to be his helpmate.

The schools, the poor, the sick of Hursley, must long remember her with affectionate gratitude ; the neighbours, the friends, the surviving relatives of both must long cherish the memory of her, who contributed with such grace and lively cheerfulness to adorn and render completely delightful the Vicarage of Hursley ; and so filled up the measure of the happiness of John Keble's life.

All this is true ; but it fails to convey an adequate notion with how sound an intellect and firm purpose she contributed not seldom to support her husband in doubts and difficulties ; and how she cheered and gave him confidence when he too much distrusted himself, or looked despondingly on efforts he might be making to accomplish great objects.

Nor does it by any means do justice to the wonderful piety and cheerful resignation with which she bore for so many years the trial laid on her by disease, always wearing and weakening her, often acute to the last degree. Truly might be said of her what I once ventured to say of another dear sufferer :—

> " — Her smiles at daily greeting cheer
>   The hearts whence hope hath well-nigh flown ;
>   Her smiles ; and yet she had a tear
>   For every sorrow but her own."

𝕽equiescant in pace.

POSTSCRIPT.

I HAD requested my son, the present Solicitor-General, to furnish me with his recollections of his last interview with J. Keble. Too late, however, to enable him to comply with my wish in time to insert the answer in its proper place in the text : I add it therefore as a Postscript :—

> " 1, SUSSEX SQUARE,
> *St. Stephen*, 1868.

" You ask me, my dear father, to do the most difficult thing in the world, to put down simply upon paper what I recollect of my last sight of Mr. Keble. The impression of it is indelible, but I have not the power of conveying to others that which made it so. So much depends in such a matter on looks, on silence, on manner, on the reverence which education had implanted, and which knowledge ripened and strengthened ; on a thousand things which words cannot convey, and can hardly even suggest ; that I am afraid I can be of little service to you. But this is what I can remember.

" Being on the Circuit at Winchester, and my work being over, I went on the 17th or 18th July, 1865, to Hursley, to see Mr. Keble. The Oxford University contest was just over, and Mr. Hardy had been elected ; a result which Mr. Keble had done his best to prevent, and which, with all his respect for (and every one must respect) Mr. Hardy's character and ability, he regarded as disastrous to the University and to the Church.

" I found Mr. Keble, in spite of his late illness, as bright in manner, and as clear in judgment, as ever I had seen him. His faculties were quite unclouded, and all his con-

versation, though full of grief at the result of the Oxford
contest, yet full also of hope for the future, and with much
of his old playful humour in it. He was weak in body, as
I could see, and after a little while spent with him, I was
afraid of tiring him, and said that I should go to call on
Sir William Heathcote at the Park, and that I would come
back and bid him Good-bye. In spite of all I could say, he
would go with me, and we walked through his own little
wicket into the Park, and thence across the grass under
the walnut-trees to the House, he enjoying the sunshine
and the air, and I the kindness, perhaps I may presume to
say the affection, which he shewed me then as always, and
which I recall always with gratitude, yet with a sense of
self-reproach. He talked on various, but chiefly on domestic subjects ; of my wife and children ; of my own
prospects ; of you ; of the Dysons ; of Sir William Heathcote ; and, lastly, with great warmth of regard and admiration, of Mr. Gladstone. I have no note of what he
said, and though the whole impression is distinct, I do not
pretend to be able to recall the details. We stood for some
time talking at the door of Sir William's house, and then he
walked back alone. I called at the Vicarage on my way
from the Park to the village, and saw him for the last time.
The short walk had tired him, and he was lying down to
rest on the sofa, (a thing most unusual with him,) but he got
up, walked with me down to the village ; and so we parted.
There was, I am sure, no trace of failing then to be discerned
in his apprehension, or judgment, or discourse. He was an
old man who had been very ill, who was still physically
weak, and who needed care ; but he was the same Mr.
Keble I had always known, and whom, for aught that appeared, I might hope still to know for many years to come.
Little bits of his tenderness, flashes of his fun, glimpses of
his austerer side, I seem to recall, but I cannot put them

upon paper; any words at my command would coarsen the impression, and blur the image. Of this last meeting, little as this is, I can say no more.

" Perhaps, however, it may be worth while putting down two little bits of his character, which I do remember freshly, though they belong to earlier dates. Once I remember walking with him just the same short walk from his house to Sir William's, and our conversation fell upon Charles I., with regard to whose truth and honour I had used some expressions in a review which had, as I heard, displeased him. I referred to this, and he said it was true. I replied that I was very sorry to displease him by anything I said or thought; but that if the Naseby Letters were genuine, (to go no further into argument,) I could not think that what I said was at all too strong, and that a man could but do his best to form an honest opinion upon historical evidence, and if he had to speak, to express that opinion. On this he said, I remember with a tenderness and humility not only most touching, but to me most embarrassing, that ' It might be so; what was he to judge of other men; he was old, and things were now looked at very differently; that he knew he had many things to unlearn, and to learn afresh; and that I must not mind what he had said, for that in truth belief in the heroes of his youth had become part of him.' I am afraid these are my words, and not his, and I cannot give his way of speaking, which to any one with a heart, I think, would have been as overcoming as it was to me.

" The other matter was this, and I mention it not only because it struck me very much at the time, but because it is an instance of that severer part of Mr. Keble's character, which appeared indeed but rarely, but which was there, and which all who knew him well, knew to be there. We were walking together in London in the year 1851, and I was telling him how much I had been impressed with the difficulties as to the inspiration of Holy Scripture, which were growing stronger, and spreading more widely day by day ; and that it seemed to me this would shortly become the great religious question of the time. I added that there was not, as far as I knew, any theory or statement on the subject which even attempted to be philosophical, except Coleridge's, in his 'Confessions of an Inquiring Spirit ;' and that I wished Mr. Keble, or some one as competent as he, would take up the subject and deal with it intellectually and thoroughly. He shewed great dislike to the discussion, and put it aside several times, and on my pressing it upon him, he answered shortly, that most of the men who had difficulties on this subject were too wicked to be reasoned with. Most likely he thought that a young man's forwardness and conceit needed rebuke, and he administered it accordingly ; but besides this, it was an instance of that in him which would be called severity or intolerance. I do not pretend to say that it would be wrongly called so, but it is certain that there are distinct indications of this spirit in the writings of St. Paul and St. John ; and I suppose that the more absolute and the more certain the faith a man has in religious doctrine, the more probable it is that he will be intolerant of doubt in others.

" Such, (without breaking the sacred seal of personal and tender memories,) is all I can find to send you of my recollections of Mr. Keble. It is not worth sending, but I send it in the hope of contributing in the very smallest degree to a memoir by my father of one, whom his son was taught as a child to revere, and whom he revered when he grew up, both because he was taught and because he saw the wisdom of the teaching. J. D. C."

APPENDIX.

" My dear Sir,

". . . . . I have endeavoured to make some memoranda on
the several points you mentioned to me. But when I come
to look at them, I am grieved and ashamed at their meagre-
ness, and I fear they will be useless. Perhaps, however,
if you could send them to Wilson, they might suggest something to him, and he would confirm, or correct, or supplement what I have said. I know he has several letters on
parochial matters. He has been abroad, as perhaps you
know, all the winter; but he is now in London, and hopes
to be at home next week.

" I do not know enough of our dearest friend's actual
ministrations to the sick to enable me to say what his uniform practice was. But, putting together directions which
he has given to me from time to time, and allusions he has
made to what he has himself said or done on particular
occasions, I may say that, besides the passages of Scripture which he used to read or repeat, and which he made
the foundation of whatever remark, in the way of encouragement, instruction, or warning, he wished to make, his prayers
by the bedside were in each case a little office, made for
the occasion out of the prayers and collects and Psalms of
the Prayer-book. His father, he once told me, never used
any other prayers than those of the Visitation Service, but
it was his own habit to range freely over the whole Prayer-
book. His service, so to call it, commonly began with the
first prayer for Good Friday, ' this Thy servant' being sub-

stituted for ' this Thy family :' then there would be always
some kind of confession, very frequently the fifty-first Psalm,
(indeed, I believe he very seldom, if ever, said prayers with
any sick person without introducing some verses at least of
that Psalm) ; then came the prayers in the Visitation Service and other collects, special petitions being introduced
here and there to suit the particular case, sometimes in his
own words, sometimes in the words of the Psalms or of the
Prayer-book. When death was imminent, over and above
the Commendatory Prayer prescribed in the Visitation Service, I have known him repeat at intervals verses or passages of Scripture, interspersed with short suffrages and
ejaculations, extending over a considerable space of time.
In later years I believe he has made more use of books
of devotion, and not uncommonly he has read passages
from Bishop Wilson, Jeremy Taylor (Holy Living and
Dying), and Challoner. This last was always a great
favourite with him.

"In his pastoral work generally, while he had, as every
one knows, a strong sense of the dignity of the Priesthood,
his chief personal feeling, if I may venture to say so, was
that which S. Paul expresses, when he says, ' Ourselves your
servants for Jesus' sake.' A very common form of expression with him, with regard to sick persons, was that of
waiting on them. He held himself at the service of any
of his parishioners, at any time, and almost for any purpose.
He accounted himself their ' minister,' whose duty (and
delight) it was to help them in any way. In cases of prolonged sickness he tried to pay his visit on particular days,
that it might be expected and prepared for : and if the sick
person were near at hand, he would visit him as nearly as
possible at the same hour every day, his wish being, in this
as in everything else, to adapt himself to what he thought
would be most acceptable to those for whom he ministered.

One case I specially remember of an old woman, whom he used to visit in this way every evening regularly for some time, just before she settled for the night.

"At the same time he never forgot that he was a steward, entrusted both with the souls of men, whom he had to deal with for their good, tenderly or severely, as there might be occasion, and with the holy things of God, which he was to guard from dishonour. Hence he was very plain-spoken, sometimes stern, in his treatment of sinners, where there were no signs of humility ; though, as you may suppose, no one could be more tender to those whose consciences were seriously alarmed. The lack of a regular system of discipline he tried to supply in such ways as he could, making a point of finding some opportunity of reproving notorious offenders and setting some mark upon them, in the hope (to use his own frequent quotation) that "by making their faces ashamed, they might be led to seek the Lord." On some occasions, in the case of disgraceful marriages, he has substituted for the exhortation or sermon in the Marriage Service a short address, in which he remonstrated earnestly and plainly with the young people. Little were they whom he then, or at other times, reproved aware of the intense anxiety with which he watched their look and bearing under reproof.

"Every member of his flock was a charge to him ; but his main anxiety, it may perhaps be said, was for the young men and women, and the very old. It is remarkable what a large number of aged persons could be reckoned up whom he visited regularly for periods of varying length, but in several cases for many years, and for whom he entertained the deepest respect and affection. Their death was to him the loss of personal friends, and he loved to recall their sayings or anything characteristic in their dress or manner. The thought of the simple goodness of many of them was one of his chief joys. I shall never forget the delight and thankful reverence with which he told me of one of them, an old man of a singularly thoughtful and religious tone of mind, who said to him on one occasion, when he went to see him, 'I have just been at the foot of the Cross, looking up and praying for pardon.' A short extract from one of his letters will illustrate his thoughts and feelings about the old people : 'The chief Hursley news is the death of dear old Dame H., with whom at the last, and for a good time before, all seemed more peaceful than I expected. You know how low and disturbed she used to be at times about her spiritual condition. I always dreaded this getting worse : but it pleased God to remove it entirely for a long while, months, before she died, and nothing could be more peaceful, and as it seemed more full of humble quiet devotion, till she sank away, by F. A.'s account, "like a baby from the breast."' 'It is startling about Mrs. C. ; but somehow I can fancy that (please God) it was not so startling to her. Would that it may not pass away as in a dream from the rest of them.'

"The following refer to young persons : 'Give my love to J. C., poor fellow : I trust I shall see him again ; but I should not wonder if his decay were now very rapid.' 'I am very sorry indeed about L., seeing I had utterly neglected her, or nearly so. Please to tell me anything you can hear about her, and say something kind to her mother for me. I have always been looking forward to instructing her for Confirmation, and this has come quite suddenly upon me.' 'I hope you will manage to see M. A. B. now and then, and give her a few verses of a Psalm to learn, and talk to her. This nursing work may do her the greatest good.' 'J. D. is getting *very ill indeed* with a complaint of the lungs, and will soon, I expect, take to his bed. I hope he is "answering to the scourge."'

" Here is another extract which will shew his interest in everything that concerned his people : ' At present I have scarce time for more than a message to Mrs. B. Pray tell her, with my very kind regards, that I very much advise her to be content with C.'s remaining in the army. It seems as if Providence had led him there for his good, since he has improved so much ; and if he got his discharge and came back among his old companions, I should very much fear he might fall again into his old bad ways, and then Mrs. B. would be blaming herself for it. It is far better to let well alone, and instead of being unhappy, to thank God for the chance of his being " a devout soldier," instead of a dissolute young tradesman. I do hope that she will be led to view the matter in this light, for I am sure it would be far better. Perhaps it would be a good plan to point out to her how much there is in the Bible about soldiers serving God,—Cornelius, the good Centurion, and others, David, Joshua, Jonathan, &c.'

" The two following extracts also may be interesting :—

" ' I am very much concerned about poor W., and sorry to be away ; yet perhaps it may be the better chance for him, as one temptation to be irritable is removed by my absence. And it is a great comfort that he listens patiently, and is subdued in his temper, more or less. I do not see that you can do better with him than read the commandments as Wilson suggests, and I think it likely that you will be able to draw from him the sort of confession one has heard from M. and others, that he has broken them all but the sixth, and perhaps the eighth. He ought to be pressed about the sixth, for I am afraid his unkindness to his wife broke her spirits, and led her to that course which ruined her health, and ended in her death. The matter of her funeral was, that I doubted whether to read the service, she being so notorious for drinking and neglect of the church ; only as

she permitted me to be sent for, and expressed some sort
of penitence, I did not think myself justified in treating her
as an excommunicated person. But I wrote a note to
her brother, explaining exactly how I felt, and hoping they
would consider the event as a warning. I left it to their
discretion, whether they would read it to W. or no; they
did, and he was very angry, and threatened to write to the
bishop. However we got to be on speaking terms again.
I have since seen him once (if not oftener) very drunk, and
swearing wretchedly. I would read to him, I think, such
places as Rev. xx. 11—15, our Lord's parables and prophecies about the day of judgment, and St. Paul's catalogue of
deadly sins; and then, if he is clearly alarmed and softened,
you might refer to the Prodigal Son, the penitent woman,
&c. I am afraid you will hardly bring him to much of
a special confession, but you will be quite able to judge
from time to time; and if he wishes for the H. C., perhaps
Wilson had better see him too, at least if you are doubtful.'
'I got your letter to-day, and was very glad of it; the report of poor W. was on the whole better than I expected.
I think it very likely that my absence may be a good thing.
If you have an opportunity, will you give him a kind message from me, and say how thankful I shall be if he prove
truly penitent. I suppose the great point will be to con-
vince him that it must be very doubtful whether his penitence would prove true, if he recovered, and therefore he
must go on in fear and trembling to the end. He should
clearly understand, I suppose, that any wish for the Communion must come entirely from him; that we cannot,
under the circumstances, take on us to press it.' (July 8
and 14, 1842.)

"When he first heard that one of his parishioners had
become a Mormonite, he wrote, 'I am vexed about those
unhappy Mormonites, more especially as I never yet did

anything of a shepherd's part by the —— family. Do tell me anything that passes with regard to them. From what you say I am afraid it is likely to be a very troublesome set, almost as diabolically suited to our Anglo-Saxon cravings now, as the Koran in its time to those of the Eastern Christians.' (July, 1851.)

"He took great pains in preparing the young people for confirmation; sometimes, as soon as one confirmation was over, making a list of those whose turn would come next, and at all times beginning the preparation several months beforehand. His usual course was to go through in order, first, the Baptismal Service, then the Catechism, then the Confirmation Service, and lastly, the office for Holy Communion; he took a certain portion each time, making perhaps twenty or thirty lessons on the whole. He usually wrote down on a paper three or four passages of Scripture bearing on the subject of the next lesson, which he required to be learnt by heart, or carefully studied, and he was always very particular in ascertaining whether the lesson, as he called it, had been attended to. Wherever it was practicable, he led his pupils up to their first communion immediately after confirmation, but in many cases he was satisfied if they promised to continue under instruction. One class of boys came to him for more than a twelvemonth, and read through with him different parts of the Bible, according to their own choice, before he could persuade them to turn their minds distinctly to preparation for Holy Communion. I believe his rule as to refusing to recommend for confirmation those who would not pledge themselves to communicate became stricter as years passed on; but I should say generally, that he was always very much guided by circumstances in regard to his adherence to particular rules. At one confirmation (October, 1853) he required the candidates to put their names to the following paper: 'In the presence of

Almighty God, I, A. B., seriously declare, that I am turning
my mind towards Holy Communion ; that I hope, before
very long, by God's mercy, to be fit for it ; that I will pray
to God to make me fit ; and that I will come to Mr. Keble
or Mr. Young from time to time, if they wish me to do so,
to have their advice about coming or staying away.' He
was most anxious to retain his hold on the young persons
who had been under his instruction, and never lost an
opportunity of intercourse with them. I find two short
references to one young fellow, whom he would fain keep
with him : ' If you see anything of the ——, will you enquire
after T., and say I was much disappointed at not seeing or
hearing from him before we came away.' 'There are two
things I have been forgetting to mention to you ; one is
T. S., whom I neglected to see before we came out. If
you have a good opportunity, will you find out how he is
going on, and why he was perfidious with me in not coming
to H. C., or at least not coming to me to say why he has
kept away. If you think it more likely to answer, you need
only say that I depend on having a call from him as soon
as ever I get home.' (July, 1856.)

" I enclose the address which he sent from Penzance to
the newly-confirmed at the last confirmation in 1865 ; it was
delivered to them on the day of confirmation. I send also
a copy of a short form of prayer, which he drew up for the
use of persons preparing for their first communion, and
which at one time he used regularly with his pupils. He
was particularly happy, as you know, in his catechizing,
the chief characteristics of which, as it seems to me, were
the reverent honesty with which he kept close to the passage
of Scripture with which he was dealing, and the simple
manner in which he drew out its meaning. I remember
one Easter Monday catechizing, in which his object was
to shew how little girls might take pattern by St. Mary

Magdalene. He first drew from them with some minuteness the several particulars of her history in connexion with the resurrection, and then dwelt on the lessons to be derived from it ; e.g. that they should prepare over-night for the work of the next day, that they should rise early, that in their difficulties they should go to those who were set over them, that they should stay by our Lord at all times, or as near Him as possible : if they were unhappy, they should still look after Him ; then they would find that He would shew Himself to them in ways they least thought of, as He was with St. Mary Magdalene as a gardener, and with the Nazarenes as a carpenter; only they would not be allowed to touch Him all at once. He would train them gradually, and draw them up to Himself. And they must not think it hard, for it was His way with His own Apostles. The next day he catechized the boys, and the subject was thė visit of St. Peter and St. John to the sepulchre. Boys usually (he said) hear of the Resurrection and other great Christian truths first from women ; if they are good boys, they make haste to mind what they are told. The innocent come first to the apprehension of those truths ; but the penitent, feeling their need, seek to enter more deeply into it. Then, because they seek relief for themselves, they are disappointed at finding Christ's clothes, and not Himself ; and they wonder, and sometimes doubt. The others believe and are satisfied, being made up of simple love. Both go home, that is, to their own duties, to wait and see what He will do next with them. The women on the contrary stay near the grave, to satisfy their feelings. Both are right, and both blessed, because both are in Him and for Him. He generally took boys and girls alternately, preparing them, for the most part, beforehand for the questions he was about to ask in church. He rather made a point of this previous preparation, as tending to check any disposition to self-conceit or forwardness. I may mention that he was very particular about the children having their Bibles in church and following the Lessons, and for some years it was his daily custom to call up a few of them after the service was over, and question them for a few minutes in the two chapters which had been read.

"A considerable portion of his time was spent in the School. He was most scrupulous in going to the Sunday School from 9.15 to 10.30 in the morning, and from 2 to 3 in the afternoon. I think it might be truly said, that unless he was hindered by illness (which happily occurred very rarely), or by some special call of parochial duty, he never missed, during the thirty years he was at Hursley. Besides this, it was his habit for several years to go to the boys' school every morning soon after 9 and teach the first class until service-time at 10, taking them through one part of the Bible after another. On Friday there was an examination in writing in the work which had been done during the week. This he did, whoever might be staying with him, and whatever letters, interesting or perplexing, he might have received. School-time often came on him before he was ready, but as soon as he became aware that the clock had struck, away he went. Many of his friends must remember to have seen him hurrying across the lawn and down the Long Walk which led to the school, when he fancied that he was late. But he was never in a hurry in his teaching; he was always patient, both with his scholars and with his subject, dealing with it very simply and minutely, yet very deeply and practically. He invariably stood when he was teaching, and that, not so much because he thought it gave him more command over the boys' attention, but, as it would seem, because he fancied it helped to keep him up to the mark, and hindered him from

becoming listless. Indeed, in everything he took in hand, if I may venture to say it, he always did his best. He never spared himself any labour of body or of mind, but whatever he undertook, a small matter or a great, he did it with his might, often with much misgiving and complaint, but always with an honest, patient endeavour to give his whole mind to it. Thus his dread of any kind of self-indulgence was a balance to that profound humility, which was perhaps his chief characteristic. He was always busy, though without the pretence, or even the appearance of business. Indeed, so various were his occupations and so willing was he to be interrupted, that a stranger might almost think him desultory in his habits ; but every one acquainted with him knows how *very* scrupulous he was never to lose any time. He was always engaged, he always had something to do, and he set to it at once without delay. Continuous application to one thing was scarcely possible under his circumstances, and he never looked for it ; but whenever he had anything special in hand, either in the way of reading or writing, he stuck to it closely till it was done. If he were reading a book that interested him, he would carry it about with him and read it at odds and ends of time, so that it was astonishing how quickly he got through it, though perhaps he had not been able to attend to it at any one time for an hour together. In this way he read almost everything that came into the house. If he were engaged in writing, his mind became thoroughly engrossed with his subject ; it was always in his thoughts ; and though he seldom, if ever, suspended his ordinary work, but paid his pastoral visits and taught his classes at home as at other times, these things did not seem to distract him ; he returned at once to his work, just as if it had not been discontinued, and he would sit down to write, when he had only a few minutes to spare, as readily as he would take up a book. He usually wrote on the backs of letters or stray pieces of paper, numbering each slip, and securing the loose papers in a clasp ; and then he, or more frequently perhaps Mrs. Keble, made a fair copy for the printer. He very rarely made use of his study, except for private interviews ; he greatly preferred to bring his books and papers into the drawing-room, and there he used to write, seemingly undisturbed by any reading or conversation that was going on. Nothing, however, escaped him ; he knew all that was said, and was as much interested or provoked by the book that was being read, as if he had had nothing else to attend to ; at the same time that his own special work went on as effectually and as rapidly as if there had been nothing to distract him. Once, and once only, I remember his shutting himself up in his study, to avoid interruption. It was the day before the consecration of the church (in 1848), his sermon for the evening of the next day was scarcely begun, and there were so many things to be attended to, that he was in despair, and felt that the only chance of the sermon being ready was to lock himself up for two or three hours, and give strict orders that no one was to go to him on any pretence whatever. In this way he was able (to use a common expression of his) to 'break the back' of his sermon, and to give his mind without discomfort to other matters.

"There was a small Workhouse at Hursley, which was a special object of care and interest to him. The inmates were chiefly old and infirm. At one time they were allowed to go to the Daily Service, and he often remarked with pleasure on the large acquaintance which some of them shewed with the Gospel history from hearing it continually in church. It was a great grief to him, when, in consequence of some misbehaviour, the permission was withdrawn. I send you a form of Morning Prayer, which he drew up for use in the House, and which is still used. The Evening Prayer was prepared, but I doubt whether it was ever printed ; certainly it is not used.

" I can scarcely venture to hope that these recollections will be of much service to you. For your and others' sake, I could almost wish that some one else had had the opportunities which I had. But I suppose it would be impossible for any one, by a mere statement of general facts or of single incidents, to give any true notion of that wonderful humility, which however was ever bold,—at times even forward,—in defence of truth and duty, of that consideration and reverence for others which never became softness or blind partiality, and that exquisite keenness of feeling, whether of love or indignation, which was always tempered by wisdom and good sense. Still it is a real sorrow to me to find that I am of so much less use to you than I ought to be in drawing a picture which, if drawn to the life, might have so much influence for good. . . . .

" Believe me, with very sincere respect and gratitude,
            " Yours faithfully,
                    " PETER YOUNG."

"MR. KEBLE had so little method in directing any lay-helpers who worked under him in his parish, that it is difficult to give an idea of his way of employing them. He gave no accurate directions; partly from his great humility; he used to say, 'I am always sure to say the wrong thing.' He would not even divide the work regularly amongst two or three who wished to engage in it, or assign certain portions of it to each; and in the end it fell almost entirely to one person, who worked under him for seventeen years. But he did not give her any rules or directions, except by occasionally recommending to her particular cases, if he thought it likely that she would be of use to them; and even then anything he said was in the way of a hint, which she might take or leave. To all her reports of the poor under her care, and to every minute particular concerning them, he used to listen with the deepest interest, often with tears in his eyes; and when absent, it was his habit to write carefully about each case brought before him."

Here I omit the extracts from two letters which I have already printed in my text.

"During the last months of Mr. Keble's life, the friend to whom they were written visited Bournemouth; he sent for her every day, and talked to her for a long time, enquiring carefully for individual cases. Especially (indeed this might be said of him always) you could never weary him, when talking of what concerned the sick; he never seemed to grudge time spent in any way which might comfort or even amuse them. To one deaf cripple in his parish he was a constant visitor, because the man thought he could understand the motion of his lips; he used also to hold conversations with him by writing on a slate, and to set him sums to amuse him, looking over and correcting them himself at his next visit.

" Although he did not apportion work for his lay-helpers, he was careful to do so for himself and his Curates; generally arranging with them after Morning Service where each should go to in the course of the day; not that he gave up any districts to them, for all were visited in turn by himself. There are seven hamlets in the parish (besides outlying cottages), the nearest one mile, the farthest three miles distant; these were generally all gone through in the course of each week, so that everything was brought under his eye. If anything escaped him which he thought he ought to have known, he was much distressed, and blamed himself for it. He often read when he walked alone about the parish; when accompanied in these walks by any young person his talk was almost always of the sights and sounds around them; of the clouds and the pictures in them, the birds and their notes, the sweet odours in the air; or if the bells were ringing he used to make up sentences which he fancied they were saying. In a letter from Penzance, Mrs. Keble writes, 'the cloudland here is a great pleasure to my husband.' The 'low sweet tones of nature's lyre,' always soothed and comforted him; and the rest and refreshment which he found in the visible creation greatly contributed to preserve his health amidst the deep anxieties of his later years, caused by those sorrows of the Church, which were always *his* sorrows. Sometimes indeed his friends, when eager to discuss some Church matter with him, have been disappointed to find that his mind was too full just then of some harmony of nature, or else that he was too much engrossed by some child who happened to be in the room, to give them full attention. Once when this was apparent, and he had not seemed interested in an important subject about which a friend was very eager, he answered, 'I am afraid I have been thinking of nothing, but how very beautiful the situation of that monastery which you described must be !'

"He generally made his parochial visits on foot until the last two years; after his illness, Mrs. Keble did not like him to be alone, and she drove him about in a little donkey carriage. He seemed to realize so vividly that each of his parishioners was his own special charge, that no duties elsewhere, or public affairs, were allowed to interfere with a watchful and anxious care for them, only to be compared to that which a father feels for his children. To them first, as to all in order who ever in earnest sought his counsel, his thought seemed always to be 'ourselves your servants for Jesus' sake.' Those to whom such service was at any time rendered, will remember all their lives the loving gentleness with which it was done, especially his kindness and tenderness to those in trouble, and his penitence if he thought he had neglected or wounded any one, asking pardon for it, with tears in his eyes; so that his friends learned more from the example of his humility and love than even from his direct teaching. He thought much of helping others by praying for them, and a few—very few—may have some idea how much time he spent thus for any in sickness or trouble; he made some rule about dividing those for whom he made intercession, praying for them at different times in the day. He said of one who was ill in his parish, but of whom he could not for various reasons see much, 'I am afraid he thinks I neglect him, but indeed I don't; every day I think of him and pray for him, and *for a good while.*' Especially he set much store on the common intercession of the people in church, asking it for many things, as, once, when a guest was leaving him, ' For one about to leave this place;' and always, before every Litany, ' For the Church of England in her very great and continued distress, by reason of unhappy divisions among us; for those in any doubt, trouble, or perplexity of mind; for the Churches of South Africa and New Zealand; and among sick people, especially for ——.' He always carefully considered the people in his parish, especially the old and poor, before making any change in the arrangement of the service. In 1864 a Bishop had talked to him of the advisableness of omitting the reading of the Commandments, &c., at the Morning Service, when there had already been an early Communion: in talking the subject over afterwards, though much wishing never to use the beginning of that office without celebrating, he said, ' I am afraid if I were to adopt the Bishop's plan here, that old Mrs. ——, who cannot come to early Communion, would miss the Commandments and Epistle and Gospel on the Sundays when there is not a late celebration.' He was very cautious and gentle in his dealings with any in his parish who were quarrelsome or hard to manage, waiting until he found some opportunity of doing them good. There were some in the village who were rude and rough to him, but he went patiently away, and came again after a time.

" Some speeches, however, not of rudeness to himself but such as he thought shewed a hard and unloving mind, especially towards relations, occasionally grated upon and aggravated him more than he could bear: he never seemed able to forget them, and might almost be said to be a little hard on two or three of whom he once formed a bad opinion.

" He was a very frequent visitor to the inmates of the

workhouse, who were chiefly old men. One of those to whom he had been kind was asked after he had left Hursley whether he had been happy there ; his answer was, ' Happy ? that's no word for it; I seemed to myself to be saying all day long, " Holy, Holy, Holy, Lord God of Sabaoth." ' Mr. Keble was pleased to find that these old men learned much of the Gospels by coming to church on week-days ; they sat on the front benches, and in reading the Second Lesson he addressed himself, as it were, especially to them, turning towards them and reading slowly and with pauses, almost as if he were alone with them and were speaking to them. His manner of reading Holy Scripture was very remarkable : in its extreme simplicity it was like that of a reverent child, and yet probably all who were in the habit of hearing him have felt the wonderful charm of it, and that he made them understand the Lessons better than any one else ; conveying to them also, in some small measure, his own intense feeling of the sacredness of every inspired word. He always paused before reading the Bible, often putting his hand to his forehead for a moment (as was often his way), and after the Lesson was ended he made the same pause before saying ' Here endeth,' &c. In some sermon of his he takes it for granted that the custom of pious people would be to pray inwardly before and after reading any portion of Holy Scripture. He never could bear to hear Scripture language used in general conversation, and even a half-playful allusion to any expression in the Bible, such as ' You have come at the eleventh hour,' seemed to make him shudder; he always reproved it if he could.

" He thought that much knowledge of the Bible was acquired by attendance at Daily Service, and once when it was proposed to keep the school-children from church on week-days in order that they might have more time for preparation before an examination, he said that their time in church might be made a great mean of preparing them for examination in Holy Scripture. For a long time he used each morning, after the congregation had left the church, to question the first class on the Lessons they had just heard, standing at the entrance to the chancel, the children round him, and generally ending by giving them the Blessing. For many years he hardly ever missed catechising in church on Sunday afternoons, taking the first class of boys and of girls alternately. He prepared them for it in school, just before the service, asking the same questions as afterwards in church, and was always most careful that the shy or backward ones should have full time for consideration, reproving almost sharply if one answered when not specially asked. In church he always repeated the children's answers, so that all might hear.

" For himself the Daily Services were among his greatest delights and refreshments ; if by some rare chance he was not in his place, he still came in, if possible, for some part of the Service ; if he were to dine out and the hour interfered with church, he used to dress early, come in and kneel down near the door, and stay till the last moment, often till reminded by Mrs. Keble that he must go.

" He tried having an early Litany on Wednesdays and Fridays, in the hope that labourers would attend ; also, as many believe, from the longing to be himself more instant in penitential prayer the more the gathering troubles of the Church, and the doubts and perplexities of many souls, weighed upon his spirit. It was begun in 1850, at 5 o'clock in summer and $5\frac{1}{2}$ in winter, and continued for three years. When he came into his stall on week-days he used to turn round for a few moments, and look to see who was there, and as he passed up the aisle to the vestry, he had a way of noticing without looking, and giving a slight, half smile of welcome and blessing to any child or young person whom he passed.

"His evening lectures during Advent and Lent and on Saints' Days were different in their kind from his ordinary sermons; they seemed more especially spoken to those who he thought would best understand him, and in the dimness of the church on summer evenings his words used to sound like an evening meditation. He liked Mrs. Keble to play to him while he was writing his sermons, he said it helped him; he was very fond of bits from 'Acis and Galatea,' and other works of Handel; also of the Irish melodies. He hardly ever used his study for writing of any sort, but carried his papers and books into the drawing-room, settling himself between the window and the door, which in summer were usually both open; there he seemed to hear everything that went on without being disturbed by it; even reading aloud he liked while he was writing, occasionally taking the book from the reader and going on himself for a little while, making quaint remarks as he read, and then returning to his work. The last piece which he read in this way with us was 'Honor Neale,' in which, as in the other poems of its author, he took much delight.

"His book on 'Eucharistical Adoration' was entirely written on scraps of paper and backs of envelopes, and was afterwards fairly copied out from these by Mrs. Keble; he seemed unable to write about what he felt most deeply except in this way, and at odd times; he could not always on being referred to decipher these scraps himself, they had been so frequently altered and written over. His notes for sermons or week-day lectures, which were all but extempore, were generally written in this way, on any scrap of paper which came to hand; these notes, though carefully prepared beforehand, were hardly ever referred to when he was actually preaching. He was continually gathering up matter

for his sermons and food for instruction from the common
circumstances of every-day life; no one could be much
with him without perceiving from his sermons how he had
marked and pondered over little sayings or incidents which
scarcely struck others, bringing out of them precious mean-
ings and valuable teaching, and so 'hallowing all he found.'
He writes, in 1860, to a young person as to ways of meditating on Holy Scripture: 'You might settle the evening
before, one of the last things, what text of Scripture, or
what sacred subject, should be your theme for the next
day, and during the day you would be gleaning up more
or less in reference to it, which it would be interesting to
set down, or recapitulate in memory, at night; *something in
the way in which we construct our sermons from day to day.*
You should take hints as well as you can from passing
circumstances, sayings wch you hear casually, or meet with
in reading, and wch you can connect with the subject of
the day: e.g. I observed one of our little singers to-day,
both morning and evening, with his eyes so simply fixed on
his Prayer-book, that I was quite ashamed of my own in-
attention; he did not know I was looking at him, but afterwards I told him to go on doing so: my own share in this
might, or ought to be, a lesson in the way of contrition;
and his, in the way of hope of the heavenly Watcher's approbation [a].'

[a] As early as 1813 or 14, a friend had given me Boyle's "Occasional
Reflections," which Mr. Weyland had republished in part. I lent the
book to Keble, who was much delighted with it; and I think he
adopted the practice of the pious philosopher. The book is so interesting, and the practice so useful, that I regret that it is not
more read. The practice may be summed up thus,—make every appearance, or circumstance, which you observe, or which happens to
you, however seemingly common or trifling, a ground of moral or
religious reflection. The book shews how the smallest incidents may
teach the most important lessons.—J. T. C.

" Mr. Keble was never tired of waiting on the sick in Holy Communion; he generally went to them on foot, carrying his own little black bag; and if they were poor he used to take some dainty morsel in a basket besides. He never *proposed* to give the H. C. privately, he said the request ought to come from the sick person; but he was always ready to take the slightest hint, and if he thought that shyness prevented the desire for it being expressed, he used to get some one else to speak to the sick person, and find out his wishes. One poor woman asked him to come to her every week, he thought she meant for Holy Communion, and during her illness celebrated every Monday morning by her bedside. At such times he never talked at all to the sick person by way of instruction or preparation; there was nothing but the service. He did not say anything aloud on coming into the house, but first greeted the sick person, asking about his health, and then immediately began to prepare the simple altar, which he was careful to place so that the sick person could easily see everything. He said the service very slowly and quietly, making pauses that he might the more easily be followed. After giving the Bread, he used to become so absorbed in prayer for the sick person, that more than once, when no one was present who would remind him, he entirely forgot to give the Chalice, and after long prayer went on with the rest of the service. When it was over, he used to fold up his little black stole carefully, and to lay it, with a few words of private prayer, on the foot of the sick person's bed; then, when he had put all by, he shook hands with those who had assisted, thanking them for doing so. He said once, after a private Communion, that he should like the old custom of the kiss of peace to be restored at such times; and when he came to young persons he used to kiss them on the forehead or hand. Except in extreme cases he never would celebrate more than once in the day, and before 12 o'clock, and he always wished to have at least two to communicate besides the sick person.

" The preparation of his candidates for Confirmation was extended over a long time : one year, at the beginning of Lent, he gave notice that there would be a Confirmation at the end of Lent *in the next year*, and therefore desired to receive at once the names of those who would then be confirmed. The children, whom he prepared, came to him either in classes or singly every week for about a year before their Confirmation ; he took those of different ranks of life separately, as needing a difference in the kind of teaching given, and as there were few of the upper class in his parish, these mostly came to him each alone every week. He usually went through the Baptismal, Confirmation, and Communion Services, taking a little bit each time, and illustrating it largely, especially from Holy Scripture. The knowledge of the Bible possessed by his village children long before their preparation for Confirmation began, and the way in which it was interwoven in their minds with the Creeds and the Catechism, was something very uncommon indeed.

"To some, before Confirmation, he gave only oral teaching, to others questions in writing, directing them as to the books they were to consult ; and he caused those who were capable of profiting by it to study the Ancient Latin and Greek Liturgies, helping them with the language if necessary, and pointing out where our service joined on to older and more perfect offices. If farm lads could not come to him for press of work, he went to them, one by one, however far off. As to still more close and personal teaching and guidance of conscience, whether with his parishioners or others who sought his counsel, he was always ready, though not using any kind of method, to see any one at whatever inconvenience to himself; often in his later years, when he had fallen asleep after the Sunday services, rousing himself to receive such visits. Perhaps he might be said sometimes to seem, at least, to discourage strangers, partly from wishing them, where possible, to apply to those set over them in the order of God's Providence, and a shrinking from being thought 'of more than any 'other earnest country clergyman, especially if he perceived any unreality in those who came to him—partly from his excessive humility. He used to say he was a very bad adviser, incapable of guiding any one well, and bade those whom he did advise to pray that he might be able to help them. In all such matters he was more than ever careful to observe the closest obedience to the directions in the Prayer-book : sometimes when applied to he would for answer read that part of the Exhortation at the time of giving notice of Holy Communion which refers to such cases : and he did not use the special Absolution without asking 'if it were humbly and heartily desired ;' continually exhorting those whom he taught to take all from our Lord as Personally present. ' Christ is all and in all,' would best sum up his teaching both in public and in private. He often paused if asked a question about any spiritual matter, looked down and seemed to apply to God before answering. One who knew him well said, ' I believe he was always praying, continually making ejaculatory supplications ;' and so being himself watered with the continual dew of God's blessing, his very presence brought refreshment and help to others. Though shy of teaching directly, he was always letting drop little sayings by the way, full of suggestion and instruction. Of those who differed from him, if he thought them child-like and devout, he always spoke in the gentlest way, giving them credit for being better Churchmen than they thought themselves. Of one old parishioner, long since dead, he said to a friend, 'I am afraid he did not like me nearly so well as I liked him; he thought himself a very Low Churchman, but you know he really was an excellent Churchman, he came to church almost every day.' And Mr. Keble used to tell with great glee of this old friend's delight with a sermon preached by a strange clergyman, not knowing that the preacher was Dr. Pusey.

"He writes in 1863: 'Trouble yourself as little as you can about the unbelief of others, except to pray for them: the rather as you know, at least of many, that in their unconscious hearts they really believe a great deal more than they seem to do, or are distinctly aware of themselves. Where should we be, if we let our devotions be interrupted here because people are imperfect in the doctrine of the Sacraments, and there, because they pray, as they do, to the B.V.M. ?' Very seldom, indeed, are such strong convictions as he possessed, such zeal and earnestness in contending for the Faith, tempered by humility and love like his. His own words, 'Self-distrust is a temper so suitable to us and our condition, that whatever course implies most of it, has so far a presumption in its favour,' express well the tone of his mind, the feeling which shewed itself in every daily action, and which was undisturbed by any heat of controversy. Yet the idea of the meek hermit poet which seems generally to prevail, is not altogether a true one. It is hard to describe the eager youthful energy, the strong indignation and resentment at wrong, especially at anything which threatened to touch the sacred deposit of truth, that mingled with his gentleness and humility. If anything of the sort was said before him, his whole countenance changed, and he looked for a moment as if he would annihilate the speaker. Once when speaking eagerly of something of the sort which had angered him, his eyes sparkling and flashing as they used at such times, he suddenly turned to a young girl who stood near him, his whole manner changing to a tender playfulness, as he just said, 'I hope I shan't bite *you*,' then returned to the subject which occupied him. It was remarkable that *badness* always seemed to him *stupidity*, he never seemed to be able to perceive the cleverness of wickedness; of even able things written in a bad spirit he constantly remarked, 'I cannot think how people can be so stupid.'

"Mr. Keble's power of fasting was very great, and for many years his own habit was to take no food on Fridays until evening; even after he was past seventy he scarcely took more on fast-days than a slight meal in the evening. But to others, especially in cases of delicate health, he was very lenient in this matter. He writes to one (in 1860), 'If those whom His Providence has made judges over you in such matters say, This is more than you are able to bear; I conceive you are to conclude that He has not laid this upon you. I remember the place in Mr. Bonnell [b], but you will observe he does not there (unless I mistake) disregard the direction of the Doctor, but his own feelings: "God says, 'Fast,' and I will fast, though it seems to interfere with my prayers: but O! that it may not so interfere." Is not this his meaning? But this is not your case, I believe. No doubt we often read in books of holy men purposely spending themselves contrary to medical directions: but I imagine that in most cases either it was for some definite work, as when a man devotes himself in battle; or the wisdom of it might be questionable.'

"He always received the Holy Communion fasting, although teaching every Sunday morning at the school, and generally preaching; but this also he was careful not to advise others to do unless in strong health. In a letter

[b] "Meditations of James Bonnell, Esq.," on the List of the Christian Knowledge Society.

in 1863 he writes, 'I will not say positively, but I almost think that it may be better to make up your mind to evening communion occasionally than to remain so very long absent. You may perhaps be able to order matters so as not to break the Church's rule about abstinence further than so many are obliged to do for health, e.g. you may eat some breakfast and shirk the dinner. Mr. —— told me once that he was obliged to do something of the kind in regard of mid-day (which were really afternoon) communions.'

" For himself, until his illness in 1864, there were weeks now and then when between fast-days and public and private celebrations there was not more than one day on which he took any food until the middle of the day.

" Old age brought no relaxation of work to him. Mrs. Keble's letters, after he was past seventy, continually mention his engrossing occupations, generally with thankfulness that he was still able for work. She writes in March, 1863, of his having been 'particularly well this winter, scarcely having had his usual amount of hoarseness, so that he has been able to work on at home and out, through rain and sunshine, without let or hindrance, and people have been fain to remark upon his good looks. If it should please God that I should weather this attack, I shall rejoice that I have not been the cause of his leaving his work here this winter. It has been a busy time preparing for a Confirmation, which is to be on Sunday next ; and besides this the Wilson work has kept him fully occupied in his *leisure* hours, so that a sentence of exile would have been a terrible one in that aspect, however beneficial in the lower one. I don't believe the dear husband would ever enjoy being abroad thoroughly : he could never be content without plenty of work.' In December, 1863, Mrs. Keble writes, 'I gave Lady —— a little specimen of his day's work yesterday, and I am not sure that it did not make her almost wish I were ailing enough to oblige him to go away, but (D.G.) he is well and up to his work, and most evenings, from 9 to 10 (now we are alone) we get a little quiet reading, which is a great treat, only sometimes he is so honestly sleepy that it is cruel to let him go on. Again in that year: 'Our commemoration was kept on St. Simon and St. Jude : fifteen years now we have had the blessing of this dear church in its present aspect. I have been amusing myself lately with doing little pen and ink sketches of it from the drawing-room window, which puts me in mind to tell you that my husband was so good as to victimise himself in the summer for me, and give Richmond three sittings, the result of which was a crayon head, of which Miss Richmond told me afterwards that her father considered it one of his best. He certainly did seem charmed to have that head once more before him.'

"This was his last year of health. In February, 1864, his wife writes of 'how much he has on his hands, and far, far more on his mind;' but the grief and anxiety caused by the decision of the Privy Council in that spring only seemed to make him work harder than ever. During that summer he used often to fall asleep for a few moments in the middle of the day with his pen in his hand ; the over-strain ended in the stroke (on St. Andrew's Day, 1864) which was the beginning of the end. Still, all through that summer, the happy home-life went on, though overclouded by Mrs. Keble's increasing weakness. A friend who was staying there in August wrote, ' I wish I could give you an idea of the loveliness of everything when we came out of church at 8 o'clock this moning, the sun lighting up the flower-beds, which are each a jewel in that garden, the birds feeding amongst them, the clematis hanging over the ter-race-wall, all the natural beauty of that most lovely and poetical spot glowing besides in the light which associations always throw around it. We went in through the garden window to Mrs. Keble, who had not been well enough to go to church, and just then the Vicar and the Bishop passed, the former looking like what one can imagine of George Herbert, in his cassock, trencher-cap, and white hair. Ah! even as I write comes the thought, Will the days ever be when we shall look back on such times as these, and long for all which can never come again? when the place, the flowers, the sunshine shall be the same, and we shall hardly bear to look upon them?' Those who were much at Hursley during that summer will remember Mr. Keble's interest in the *Apologia*, and also his exceeding distress and even anger when the last number (I think) reached him. He writes, June 15, 1864, 'We shall see you soon, I dare say; and in the meantime I will just thank you for the little mention of my dear friend's book, w^ch (mention) was a comfort to me in some respects: for I thought the book so very engaging, I did not know what might come of it. In *argument* it seems to me to leave things on the whole where they were, or rather (of the two) to damage the cause of Modern Rome,—I mean especially as concerns the dogma of 1854. The very title (putting a date to an Article of the Faith) seems to me to disallow it.' Mrs. Keble writes in October of their having had ' a large and engrossing party the last few weeks, now we are reduced to ourselves and servants, and, alas! this evening I shall be reduced to less than half, for in spite of its being our wedding-day, he has to go to Bristol to be ready for the discussion about Synods to-morrow at the Congress.' And in her last note a few days before his attack she says, ' My husband talked of writing to thank ——, but when will he have time? I fear he will have to go to London again next week,—I ought not to say *fear*, for he *must* work while he can, and people don't seem too eager to contend for the Faith.' Even after his illness, restoration in order that he might work seemed always to be in the minds of both husband and wife. She writes from Penzance in January, 1865 : 'We have had much stormy weather, but it has no otherwise interfered with my husband's progress than hindering his walks by the sea. He has improved greatly in his looks since we have been here ; indeed, I think you would not observe much difference, except that seven weeks of such quiescent life have made his movements less active ; he still lives by rule as to diet, and not using his head, though he dips into books rather more. The Doctors cannot relax their rule yet ; if they did, I believe he would be obliged to enforce it on himself, as he would do too much in the first day ; still we have the hope that if there is work for him to do, he may be restored to do it.' At Easter she writes : ' We were both at the whole morning service. One could not but *think* that there must have been a sharp trial in taking no part in the ministering, for the first time on that day since he has been in Orders.'

"Then came the last return, in that spring of 1865, to Hursley, and the summer months, so mournful, yet so precious, to his parishioners and friends. He had almost entirely recovered his looks, so that those who saw him during that summer for the first time since his illness, scarcely perceived any change in his face, and tried to hope against hope that years might yet be added to his precious life. Yet watching him they knew that he could not long bear the strain of anxiety and grief on Mrs. Keble's account ; and that each of the terrible attacks from which she suffered, told on him almost as much as on her. He never preached again, but often took some small part in the services, and occasionally celebrated and catechised. His last public pastoral teaching was on the seventeenth Sunday after Trinity (October 8), 1865, when he catechised his school children at the Afternoon Service on the Lord's Prayer, and 'thou art not able to do these things of thyself;' he taught them by the simile of a little child carried in its mother's arms, and continued, 'even after it is set down to walk, can it do so by itself?' 'must it not be held by the hand and helped?' 'Is there anything in to-day's Collect that teaches the same doctrine?' 'Then if His grace must go before us, could we have put ourselves in a state of salvation, or can we save ourselves?' 'But what is there that we *can* do to ourselves which is very fearful to think of?' 'Yes, destroy ourselves; and therefore St. Paul, writing to those whom he seems to have specially loved, bid them work out their own salvation, not only with hope and cheerfulness, but also with fear and trembling; for the very reason that it is God who worketh in us, and that, where He is, there should be a trembling awe and fear lest we should use the power of free-will which He has given us to destroy His work, and ourselves [c].'

" He had celebrated, for the last time in church, at 7 o'clock that morning. A friend dined and spent the evening there; he always liked, if he could, to have some one to dine with him on Sundays. He left Hursley on the following Wednesday before the hour for morning service, but he had been in his accustomed place in church for the last time on the previous day, October 10 (his wedding-day), and read the Second Lesson in the morning, the last words of which were these: 'For the Son of Man is as a man

[c] Written at the time.

taking a far journey, who left his house, and gave authority to his servants, and to every man his work, and commanded the porter to watch. Watch ye therefore : for ye know not when the master of the house cometh, at even, or at midnight, or at the cock-crowing, or in the morning. Lest coming suddenly he find you sleeping. And what I say unto you I say unto all, Watch.' "

M. T.

INDEX.

ABSOLUTION, when to use the special form, 606.

Acland, Arthur, 128.

Æschylus, Prom. Vinct., 332 ; cited, 401.

Agrarian Riots, a fruit of 43rd Eliz., 191.

Allen, Archd., letter on J. Keble, 565.

Ampfield Church, and Well, 281-3.

Andrewes, Bp., his Devotions referred to, 294.

Arnold, Matthew, Poetry Professor at Oxford, 211, 265.

Arnold, Thomas, Scholar of Corpus Christi, 18 ; letter to Sir J. T. Coleridge,42, 264 ; visits Keble from Laleham, 132 ; Head-master at Rugby, edits Thucydides, 183 ; and J. Keble, 263—267.

Ashburton, Lord, *see* Baring.

Augustine, St., the "Confessions" referred to, 328.

Awdry, Sir John, at Hursley, 133.

Bagot, Bp., Keble dedicates his version of the *Psalter* to him, 255.

Baker, Mr., Curate of Pitt, 442.

Baring, Mr., a pupil of J. Keble, 75, 79.

Barrington, Bp., 14.

Barrow, Dr., Principal of St. Edm. Hall, Oxford, 451.

Barter, Rev. R. S., Warden of Winchester College, 125.

Bartholomew, John, of Corpus Christi, 18.

Basil, St., on Tradition, 247.

Benson, Mr., author of the term "Tractarian," 274 ; Sermon at the Temple Church, *ib.*

Bernard, St., reference to his Sermons on the Advent, 534.

Bernard, Sir Thomas, " Comforts of old age," 99.

Bible, Commentary on part of, undertaken by J. Keble, 487, 552.

Binney, Horace, 416.

Bliss, Rev. W., letter to, on Sidmouth, 50 ; on authorship of the *Christian Year*, 166.

Bonnell, Mr., reference to the life of, 141.

Bournemouth, Keble's visit to, 526 ; return to, 532.

Boyes, Rev. B., Rector of East Leach, 64.

Bridges, Sir Brooke W., letter to, 342.

Brotherhood, religious, rules submitted to J. Keble, 330.

Brydges, T., mathematical tutor to Keble, 47.

Burthorpe, Keble curate of, 61.

Butterfield, Wm., gives design for a Keble memorial window at Ampfield, 283 ; designs a memorial to Mr. Keble, 557.

Capetown, Bp. of, case of Long *versus*, 494.

Cardwell, E., examining master, 1814, 55.

Carey, Bp., 30.

Carter, Mr., architect at Winchester, 281.

Catechizing, a specimen of J. Keble's method, 568, 590.

Child, a, letters on the death of, 82, 322.

Children, how to examine them, 566.

Christian Year, progress and publication of, 61, 102, 117, 122, 151, 152.

—— second edition of, 175 ; summary of the publisher's account, 155 ; remarks on its success, 159 *sqq.* ; the dedication, 122, 165 ; verses for Good Friday cited, 556.

Church and State, the limits of their alliance examined by Keble, 151.
—— authority, where to be found, 435.
—— of England, a layman's testimony to it, 369.
—— discipline and doctrine, 481.
—— in Wales, Scotland, and Carlisle, 357, 359, 360.
—— of Rome, J. Keble's views on, 367, 422.
—— the, supposed by the *Christian Year* to be in a state of decay, 167.
Churcher, J., a servant of J. Keble, 243.
Churton, Mr., his illness, 1828, 183.
Clarke, Charlotte, 184 ; J. Keble's future wife, 236.
Clarke, Mrs., at Lyme, 184.
Colenso, J. W., Bp. of Natal, J. Keble's letter on the "Colenso Judgment," 514, 536.
Coleridge, Rev. J. D., his death, 440.
Coleridge, Sir J. D., and the Abolition of Tests Bill, 523 ; letter on J. Keble, 579.
Coleridge, Sir J. T., letter to Keble, 46.
—— W. Hart, Bp. of Barbados, 113.
Coln, St. Aldwin's, the benefice of J. Keble's father, 7, 108.
Confession in the Church of England, 300, 310, 541.
Confirmation at Hursley, J. Keble's preparation of Candidates, 506, 517, 589, 605.
Cooke, George Leigh, tutor of Corpus Christi College, Oxford, 16 ; tutor to Keble, 47.
Copleston, Edw., Provost of Oriel, 9, 54, 77, 176.
Cornish, G. J., Scholar of C.C.C., 18 ; sketch of his life, 29, 30 ; author of poem to the Redbreast in the *Christian Year*, 31 ; extracts from poems of, 32, 33 ; his marriage, 88 ; his death, 365 ; death of his married daughter, 444.
Cornish, Mrs. George, visited by Keble, 412.
Corpus Christi College, Oxford, 9, 10.
Creweian Oration, by J. Keble, 1839, translation of the peroration, 258.

Darnell, Mr., tutor of C. C. C., afterwards Rector of Stanhope, 13, 14.
Davison, John, 54 ; leaves Oriel, 74 ; at Washington, 98 ; revises the *Christian Year*, 120, 153 ; publication of his " Remains," 265.
Denison, Archdeacon, proceedings against him, 419, 434.
Divorce, J. Keble on the Divorce Bill of 1857, 428.
Dogmersfield, C. Dyson Rector of, 40.
Dyce, Mr., R.A., gives a design for stained glass windows at Hursley, 345.
Dyson, C., friend of Keble at C. C. C., 18, 74 ; sketch of his life, 35—46 ; at Nun Burnholme, 99 ; letters to Sir J T. Coleridge, 146, 245 ; his death, 460.
Dyson, Jeremiah, satirized by H. Walpole, 36.
Dyson, Mrs., 505.

Ecce Homo, J. Keble's remarks on that book, 547.
Ellison, Nathaniel, 41.
Ellison, Noel T., friend of Keble at C. C. C., 18, 41 ; at Whalton, 98 ; his death, 443.
Emigrants, J. Keble employed on a service for their voyage, 412, 415.
" Essays and Reviews" case, 481.
Eucharistical Adoration, publication of pamphlet on, 433.
Euripides, translation of *Alcestis*, 231.
Eveleigh, Dr., Provost of Oriel, 1806, 13.

Faber, F. A., introduces J. Keble to W. Wordsworth, 257.
Fairford, Keble's birthplace, 5 ; he returns to it from Hursley, 145.
Fasting, letter on, by J. Keble, 149 ; some rules for, 608.
Fathers, Library of the, 260.
Fielding, Mr., gives a design for stained-glass windows at Hursley, 345.
FitzWalter, Lord, *see* Bridges.
Forbes, Bishop, and the Scottish Controversy, 446, 453.
Forbes, Mr., of Medwyn, Mr. Keble visits, 454.
Freeman, Archdeacon, 426.

Fremantle, Mr., pupil of J. Keble, 75, 79.

Froude, Hurrell, residence with Keble at Southrop, 110; sketch of his character, 111; his "Remains," 248; sketch of his life, 252; Keble's share in editing the "Remains," 253.

Gaussen, Mr., a pupil of J. Keble, 54.

Grenville, Lord, Chancellor of the University of Oxford, founder of the Latin Essay prize, his presentation of books to Keble, 49.

Hallam, Henry, on the three disputed books of Hooker, 196, 198.

Hampden, Dr., letter on his appointment at Oxford, 242; Bishop of Hereford, 348.

Harrison, Mr., Architect of Hursley Church, 286.

Hatsell, Mr., 36.

Hawkins, Dr., Provost of Oriel, 178—180.

Heathcote, Archdeacon, Incumbent of Otterbourne and Hursley, 123; his death, 187.

Heathcote, Gilbert Wall, Vicar of Hursley, 188.

Heathcote, Sir W., introduced to J. Keble, 79; recommends Keble to the curacy of Hursley, 123; at Hursley, 1825, 131; gives vicarage-house at Hursley, 123; at Ampfield, 283; completes tower and spire of Hursley Church, 347.

Heber, Bishop, Keble introduced to him at Oxford, 94.

Hedgeland, Mr., of Penzance, 489; his letter to the "Guardian," 491.

Herbert, George, the "Temple" referred to, 173.

Hooker, Richard, Keble edits his works, 192—204.

Howley, Abp., criticism on the *Oxford Psalter*, 255.

Hursley, Keble curate of, 123, 130; the Vicarage offered to and declined by Keble, 187; G. W. Heathcote, Vicar, 188; Keble, Vicar of, 239; Church at, 285; stained-glass windows at, 345.

India House Examinations, Keble appointed examiner, 188.

Irenæus, St., translated by J. Keble, 263.

Isle of Man, visited by Keble, 362.

Jackson, Bishop, ordains Keble, 59.

Jersey, Mr. and Mrs. Keble visit Brelade, 333.

Jews, their example as a nation, 151, 219, 225.

KEBLE, JOHN, birth of, 5; verses on leaving C.C.C., 20; passed his Final Examination, 1810, 47; elected Probationary Fellow of Oriel, 1811, 48; prizes won by, 49; verses on Sidmouth, 52, 53; Examining Master, 1814, 55; 1835, 230; Deacon, 1815, 59; Priest, 1816, *ib.*; Examiner in Final Schools, 70, 102; Examiner in Responsions, 1817, 70; appointed tutor at Oriel, 1817, 72; verses on a monument in Lichfield Cathedral, 98; resigns tutorship at Oriel, 1823, 103; verses on a deceased sister, 105, 143; a present of plate given to him, 109; offered Archdeaconry of Barbados, 113; study of the Fathers, 150; consideration of questions of Church and State, 151; finishes the *Christian Year*, 152; Examiner at the India House, 188; refuses living of Paignton, 205; Poetry Professor, 206—217; Sermon on National Apostasy, 218; contributes to the "Tracts for the Times," 220, 224; estimate of the Fathers, 222, 227; publishes the *Oxford Psalter*, 254; delivers Creweian Oration, 257; the "Library of the Fathers," 260; part taken with regard to "Tract 90," 269; religious difficulties, 294 *sqq.*; verses on the Annunciation, 314; publishes the *Lyra Innocentium*, 1846, 319; verses on guardian angels, 323, 324; publishes *Academical and Occasional Sermons*, 337; *Letter on Representation of the University*, 342; visit to North Wales, 356; Tour in Scotland, 313, 359; the "Library of Anglo-Catholic Theology," 362; visits Sidmouth, Lyme Regis, and Heath's Court, 365; verses on hedge-flowers, 414; *Argument on Divorce Bill*, 428; Work on *Eucharis-*

618 INDEX.

tical Adoration, 433; *Considerations suggested by a late Pastoral Letter*, 447; thinks of resigning Hursley, 466, 493; Commentary on the Bible, 487; *On the Subscription and Oaths of the Clergy*, 501; illness, 508, 553; the Oxford Election, 512; the Colenso Judgment, 514; *Address to the Newly-confirmed at Hursley*, 517; *Letter on Ritual*, 537; death, 555; burial, 557; memorial to him, *ib.*; character of as a Parish Priest, 563.

Keble, John, letter to Miss Baker, 322.
———— Letters to Mrs. Billamore, 91.
———— Letters to W. Bliss, 50, 160.
———— Letters to Sir J. T. Coleridge, 26, 56—59, 62, 65, 70—72, 80, 82, 85, 88, 89, 93, 103, 114, 117, 131, 134, 137, 153, 164, 176, 180, 199, 220, 235, 237, 246, 247, 250, 270, 288, 290, 297, 305, 332, 372, 409, 413, 431, 444, 469, 511, 521, 534, 541, 543-8.
———— Letters to G. Cornish, 6, 24, 60, 101, 119, 149, 237, 246, 263, 363.
———— Letters to C. Dyson, 28, 31, 39, 85, 94, 99, 104, 115, 118, 147, 164, 177, 193, 200, 219, 238, 306, 408.
———— Letters to H. Froude, 121, 139, 178, 187, 201.
———— Letters to Sir W. Heathcote, 125, 127.
———— Letter to Mr. Hedgeland, 490.
———— Letter to Elis. Keble, 13.
———— Letter to T. Keble, 234.
———— Letter to Miss Mackenzie, 550.
———— Letter to Mr. Pruen, 122.
———— Letters to Mr. Richards, 220, 229.
———— Letters to S. Walker, 172.
———— Letters to R. F. Wilson, 403, 421.
———— Letters on his approaching marriage and settlement at Hursley, 237, 240, 241.
Keble, John, sen., Vicar of Coln St. Aldwin, 7; death of, 229.
Keble, Joseph and Richard, ancestors of J. Keble, 4.
Keble, Mary Anne, John Keble's sister, 103, 104; her death, 137.

Keble, Sarah, mother of John Keble, her death, 103.
Keble, Sarah, John Keble's sister, her death, 56.
Keble, Charlotte, letter to Elis. Keble, 242; wife of John Keble, her illness, 469, 525, 542 sqq.; her death, 576; her character, 577.
Keble, Elisabeth, eldest sister of John Keble, 13; her illness, 55, 62, 136; letter on her father's last illness, 229; her death, 457.
Keble, Thomas, his illness, 85; curate of Burthorp and Southrop, 130.
Keble, Thomas, jun., 189; his marriage, 365.
Keble College, Oxford, xv. *see* Oxford.
Knox, Alex., letter on his "Remains," 250.

Leach, East, Keble curate of, 61, 109.
Le Geyt, Mr., assistant curate of Hursley, 431.
Lichfield, Keble's visit to, and verses on a monument in the Cathedral, 98.
Lincoln, Keble visits it, 100.
Lloyd, Bp., Keble's respect for him, 152.
"Long *v.* Capetown," Keble's opinion of the decision, 494.
Lymington and Lyndhurst, Keble visits them, 6.
Lyra Innocentium, its publication, 288—319.

Mackenzie, Bishop, 547, 550.
Magdalen College, Oxford, gives a site for Otterbourne new church, 280.
Malthus, Keble's opinion of him, 191.
Malvern, visited by Keble, 101.
Markland, J. H., 265.
Marriage with deceased wife's sister, 367, 421.
Marriott, C., Fellow of Oriel College, his share in editing the "Library of the Fathers," 262; his scheme for a Poor Men's College, 331.
Matrimony, Holy, tract on, 226.
Maule, Sarah, mother of John Keble, 7.
Meditation, a method of, 603.

Medley, John, Bishop of Fredericton, 374.

Miller, John, friend of J. Keble, 23; his death, 25; works, 25, 26; at Brockleton, 101; volume of sermons, 190; suggests the Tract on the Sunday Lessons, 225; his "Christian Guide" referred to, 319.

Milman, H. H., Dean of St. Paul's, University prizes won by, 49.

Milton, John, Keble's judgment of, 67-9.

Moberly, Dr., Head Master of St. Mary Winton College, 125.

Mormonites, the, 588.

Nazing, C. Dyson's benefice, 38.

Newman, Dr., visits Keble at Hursley, 248; edition of the "Library of the Fathers," 260; and "Tract 90," 269—278; letter on his meeting Dr. Pusey at Hursley Vicarage, 1865, 527; the *Apologia*, 611.

Norris, Mr., of Hackney, 244.

Nun Burnholme, C. Dyson's benefice, 38; visited by J. Keble, 99.

Ordination, thoughts on, 57, 60.

Oriel College in 1818, 77; letters from Keble on the Provostship, 1827, 8, 176—181; Statutes examined by Newman, 248; testimonial presented to J. Keble, 109; Provostship election, 176.

Otterbourne Rectory, building of new church and parsonage, 279 *sqq.*

Oxford University ἦθος, 393.

—— Poetry Professorship, 206; Assize Sermon preached by Keble, 1833, 218; University Reform Bill, 379; Local examinations, 467.

———— Reform Bill, 379 *sqq.*

———— Private Halls, 382.

—— Keble College at, 399.

—— Local examinations, 467.

—— University, contemplated changes at, 545.

———— election contest, 1865, 513, 523.

Oxford Psalter, the, 254 *sqq.*

Paignton, presentation to the living declined by J. Keble, 205.

Patteson, Sir John, 82; death of his wife, 84; his death, 463.

—— John Coleridge, Bishop of Melanesia, 453.

Peel, Sir Robert, resigns his seat for Oxford, 185.

Pennington, Mr., 75.

Penrose, T., 18, 103.

Penzance, J. Keble winters at, 471; his ministrations at, 489, 495.

Pitt, a hamlet of Hursley, 284; school chapel built there, 441.

Plumer, Charles, at Hursley, 133.

Poetry, J. Keble's theory of, 121.

Prælectiones Academicæ, 206—217; an offer of translating them received by J. Keble, 543.

Privy Council, Judicial Committee of, 479.

Pruen, Mr., Curate of Fladbury, 89.

Puritanism, its growth in England, 1828, 185.

Pusey, Dr., one of the editors of the "Library of the Fathers," 260.

Quakers, note on the literary Remains of a deceased convert, 149.

Reed, Professor, 413, 416.

Richmond, George, R.A., gives design for stained-glass windows at Hursley, 345.

Ritual, J. Keble's letter on, 538.

Robertson, F. W., remarks on his biography, 547.

Robertson, Mrs., 547, 550.

Rogers, Sir F., requests J. Keble to compose Services for Emigrants, 415.

Rolleston, Mr., English Verse Prize gained by, 1808, 14.

Sainsbury, Dr., of Romsey, 526.

Scotland, Keble's tour in, 359.

Scriptures, J. Keble's manner of reading the, 573, 600.

Selwyn, Bishop, at Hursley, 405.

Sermons, parochial, by J. Keble, 449, 461.

Shairp, Professor, note on his Essay on Mr. Keble, 156.

Sidmouth, Keble receives pupils there, 49; description of the scenery, 50, 51.

Smith, Stafford, Rector of Fladbury, Keble's godfather, 8, 90.

Southey, Robert, his opinion of J. Miller's Sermon, 26; Keble introduced to him, 93; letter to Nevill White, 97; "Colloquies" suggest a form for a new edition of Keble's *Prælectiones*, 215.

Southey, Dr., 304.

Southrop, Keble curate at, 108.

Stanley, A. P., Dean of Westminster, extract from his Life of Thos. Arnold, 10.

Subscription and Oaths of the Clergy, 503.

Sumner, Charles, Bishop of Winchester, applied to to license the *Oxford Psalter* in his diocese, 254.

Sunday Lessons, on the Principle of Selection, 225.

Switzerland, visited by Keble, 431.

Taylor, Jeremy, Keble's judgment of, 67-9.

Torquay, Keble's stay at, 495.

"Tracts for the Times," their publication and effect, 220, 228; "Tract 90," 268 —278.

"Tractarians," when first so named, 274.

Tradition, Sermon on, 247.

Troyte, A., at Hursley, 129; *see* Acland, A.

Tucker, J., a friend of J. Keble at C.C.C., 18; at Lenham, 121; at Hursley, 133.

Turner, W. H., a friend of J. Keble at C.C.C., 18.

Tyacke, Mr., of Penzance, 498.

Tyler, Mr., of Oriel, 88.

Vows, letter on, by J. Keble, 150.

Wailes, Mr., memorial window to J. Keble designed by Wm. Butterfield, Esq., 283; executes the Hursley windows, 345.

Wales, J. Keble's tour in, 357.

Walker, Rev. Samuel, letter to, from J. Keble, 172.

Washington, J. Davison, incumbent of, 98.

Westerton and Liddell case decided, 424.

Whalton, Keble's visit to Ellison at, 98.

Whitby, visited by Keble, 452.

White, Mr., of Ampfield, 283.

Wilberforce, R. W., residence with Keble at Southrop, 110; his treatise on the Holy Eucharist, 374; his secession to the Church of Rome, 410.

Williams, Isaac, residence with J. Keble at Southrop, 110; the Poetry Professorship, 272.

Wilson, R. F., J. Keble's first assistant curate, 283; first incumbent of Ampfield, 355, 359.

Wilson, Thomas, Bishop of Sodor and Man, his Life by Keble, 362, 463, 478.

Winchester, Sermon at the Archdeacon's visitation preached by J. Keble, 246.

Wordsworth, W., J. Keble's acquaintance with his poems, 17; his admiration of the *Christian Year*, reception in the Theatre at Oxford, 18, 257; Keble dedicates his *Prælectiones* to him, 18, 259; interview with J. Keble, 361.

Yonge, Wm. C., gives the design for the Otterbourne and Ampfield churches, 280; his death, 377.

York, city of, visited by J. Keble, 452.

Young, Peter, assistant curate at Hursley, 312; leaves Hursley, 427 *sqq.*; his account of Mr. Keble's pastoral work, 505, 583.